S0-AHI-097

DOCUMENTS OF
American Catholic History

DOCUMENTS OF
American Catholic History

EDITED BY
John Tracy Ellis

VOLUME 1
1493 to 1865

MICHAEL GLAZIER
Wilmington Delaware

About the Editor

John Tracy Ellis is Professorial Lecturer in Church History in the Catholic University of America. He is a member of the American Catholic Historical Association and the American Society of Church History. Throughout his career he has received many honors. In 1978 he was honored with the Laetare Medal of the University of Notre Dame—an award presented to the outstanding contributor to the life of the Church in the United States. Monsignor Ellis has written seventeen books over the course of his career and he is best known for *The Life of James Cardinal Gibbons, Archbishop of Baltimore, 1834-1921* (2 volumes); and *American Catholicism.*

Published in 1987 by Michael Glazier, Inc., 1935 West Fourth Street, Wilmington, Delaware 19805 •

Library of Congress Cataloging-in-Publication Data

Documents of American Catholic History
Volumes 1-2 are reprints Originally published:
Chicago : H. Regnery Co., 1967. Vol. 3 is a new work.

Includes bibliographies and index.
Contents: v.1. 1493-1865 — v. 2. 1866-1966 —
v. 3. 1966-1986.
1. Catholic Church—United States—History—
Sources.
2. United States—Church history—Sources I. Ellis,
John Tracy, 1905-
BX1405.D63 1987 282'.73 86-80801
ISBN 0-89453-611-7 (vol. 1)
0-89453-612-5 (vol. 2)
0-89453-588-9 (vol. 3)

Printed in the United States of America.

In Loving Memory of My Brother

NORBERT E. ELLIS

October 10, 1913–October 3, 1953

Contents

Preface to the Fourth Edition xv
Preface xvii

THE SPANISH COLONIES

1. The Bull *Inter caetera* of Pope Alexander VI, May 4, 1493 1
2. The Treaty of Tordesillas, June 7, 1494 . . 3
3. The Bull *Universalis ecclesiae* of Pope Julius II, July 28, 1508 4
4. The Bull *Sublimis Deus* of Pope Paul III, June 2, 1537 7
5. Juan de Padilla, the Protomartyr of the United States, Is Murdered by the Plains Indians, c. 1542 . . 9
6. Assignment of the Florida Missions to the Dominicans; Don Luís de Velasco to King Philip II, September 30, 1558 11
7. Agreement Between Philip II and Pedro Menéndez de Avilés for the Conquest of Florida and the Assignment of Jesuit Missionaries, March 20, 1565 . 12
8. St. Francis Borgia Withdraws the Jesuits From the Florida Missions, March 20, 1571 . . . 14
9. Alonso de Benavides' Description of the New Mexico Missions, February 12, 1634 15
10. Report of Bishop Calderón of Santiago to Queen Mother Marie Anne on the Florida Missions, August 14, 1674 18
11. Fernando del Bosque's Account of the First High Mass in Texas, May 16, 1675 23
12. Report of Eusebio Francisco Kino on the Missions of Pimería Alta (Arizona) in 1710 . . . 24

13. Junípero Serra's Farewell to the Old World, August 20, 1749 27
14. Concordat Between the Franciscans and Dominicans Dividing the California Missions, April 7, 1772 . 31
15. Junípero Serra Makes His Final Report on the Mission of San Carlos de Monterey, July 1, 1784 . 34

THE FRENCH COLONIES

16. "Instructions for the Fathers of Our Society Who Shall be Sent to the Hurons," by Jean de Brébeuf, S.J., 1637 49
17. "How Father Jogues was Taken by the Hiroquois, and What He Suffered on his First Entrance into Their Country," by Jerome Lalemant, S.J., 1647 . 52
18. France's Representatives Take Formal Possession of the Western Country, June 4, 1671 . . 60
19. The Conversion and Holy Death of Catherine Tegahkouita, 1676–1680 63
20. The French Récollets in the Illinois Country, 1680 72
21. Louis Hennepin's Description of the Difficulties Encountered in Trying to Convert the Indians, 1697 75
22. The Quebec Seminary Priests in the Mississippi Valley, 1700, and the Installation of the First Pastor at Mobile, September 28, 1704 81
23. The Government's Provision for Capuchin Missionaries in French Louisiana, May 16, 1722 . . 84
24. The Banishment of the Jesuits From Louisiana and the Illinois Country According to François Philibert Watrin, S.J., September 3, 1764 86

THE ENGLISH COLONIES

25. The Charter of Maryland, June 20, 1632 . . 95
26. Baron Baltimore's Instructions to His Colonists, November 13, 1633 98

27. The English Jesuits Establish the Mission of Maryland, March–April, 1634 100
28. The State of Catholicism in Maryland, 1638 . . 108
29. Virginia's Act Against Catholics and Priests, March, 1642 110
30. Massachusetts Bay Passes an Anti-Priest Law, May 26, 1647 111
31. Maryland's Act of Religious Toleration, April 21, 1649 112
32. Disfranchisement of Catholics in Maryland, October 20, 1654 114
33. Persecution of the Maryland Catholics, 1656 . . 115
34. New York's Grant of Religious Toleration, October 31, 1683 116
35. An Act Against Jesuits and Popish Priests in Massachusetts, June 17, 1700 118
36. The Coming of the Acadians to Massachusetts, November, 1755–August, 1756 120
37. Bishop Challoner on Ecclesiastical Jurisdiction in the British Colonies, September 14, 1756 . . 124
38. The Missionaries' Reasons for Not Wanting a Bishop, April 22, 1773 125
39. Charles Carroll's Defense of His Religious Beliefs, 1773 128
40. The Quebec Act Grants Religious Freedom to the Catholics of Canada, June 22, 1774 . . . 130
41. John Adams' Impressions of a Catholic Service, October 9, 1774 132
42. Reactions of the Continental Congress to the Quebec Act, September 17–October 26, 1774 . . . 133
43. George Washington Bans Guy Fawkes Day in the Army, November 5, 1775 136
44. The Dawn of Religious Freedom for American Catholics, 1776–1791 137
45. Father Gibault Lends Assistance to the American Cause, 1778–1780 141
46. John Carroll Is Appointed Superior of the American Missions, June 9, 1784 142

47. Carroll Answers an Attack Upon the Catholic Faith, 1784 145
48. The First American Report to Propaganda on Catholicism in the United States, March 1, 1785 . 147
49. Lay Trusteeism in New York, January 25, 1786 . 150
50. Thomas FitzSimons Urges Pennsylvania's Early Ratification of the Constitution, September 29, 1787 . 154
51. Daniel Carroll Argues for Marylanders to Ratify the Constitution, October 16, 1787 157
52. The Foreshadowing of Trusteeism in the First National Parish of the United States, 1787 . . 160

THE NATIONAL PERIOD

53. The Brief *Ex hac apostolicae* of Pope Pius VI Erecting the Diocese of Baltimore and Appointing John Carroll as the First Bishop, November 6, 1789 . 163
54. The Beginnings of the First Catholic College in the United States, 1789 167
55. The Catholics' Congratulations to President Washington, 1789, and His Reply, March 12, 1790 . . 169
56. Bishop Carroll's Sermon on Taking Possession of His See, St. Peter's Pro-Cathedral, Baltimore, December, 12, 1790 172
57. John Carroll's Prayer for the Civil Authorities, November 10, 1791 174
58. The French Sulpicians and St. Mary's Seminary, Baltimore, April 23, 1792 175
59. Religious Conditions in Louisiana, November 1, 1795 177
60. Father Badin's Description of the Church on the Kentucky Frontier, April 11, 1796 179
61. President Jefferson Reassures the Louisiana Ursulines About Their Future Under the American Government, May 15, 1804 184
62. The United States Government Declines to Commit Itself on a Bishop for Louisiana, November 17–20, 1806 185

63. Mother Seton's Plans for Her Religious Community, February 9, 1809 188
64. Robert Walsh's Prospectus for His *American Review of History and Politics,* January 1, 1811 . . . 190
65. The First Bishop of the Middle West Arrives in His See, June, 1811 197
66. A Detroit Visitor Records His Impressions of Gabriel Richard, S.S., June, 1816 200
67. Archbishop Maréchal's Report to Propaganda, October 16, 1818 202
68. The Abuse of Lay Trusteeism at Norfolk, Virginia, June–September, 1819 220
69. The Inauguration of the *United States Catholic Miscellany* of Charleston, June 5, 1822 227
70. Bishop England's Account of His Address Before Congress, January 29, 1826 228
71. The Cholera Epidemic in the Diocese of Mobile, November 10, 1832 231
72. De Tocqueville on American Catholics in Relation to Democracy, 1835 233
73. Mathew Carey Explains How He Came to Write the *Olive Branch,* March 13, 1835 236
74. William Gaston Pleads for Complete Religious Freedom in North Carolina, June 30, 1835 242
75. The Aid of the Society for the Propagation of the Faith to the Archdiocese of Baltimore, January 31, 1838 246
76. The Papacy's Relation to Temporal Affairs Explained by Bishop Kenrick, 1838 251
77. The Church in the Republic of Texas, April 11, 1841 253
78. Father De Smet's Promotion of the Indian Missions of the Far West, May 1, 1841 259
79. Canon Salzbacher's Observations on American Catholic Colleges for Men, 1842 261
80. The Launching of the American Protestant Association Against the Catholic Church, November 22, 1842 263

81. A Rural Colonization Project for German Catholic Immigrants, October 12, 1843 265
82. Bishop Spalding's Impressions of Protestant Revivalism on the Frontier, 1844 269
83. Samuel Mazzuchelli, O.P., on the Catholic Temperance Societies, 1844 272
84. A Report to the Ludwig-Missionsverein on Catholicism in Wisconsin, April 23, 1845 274
85. Consecration of the Cathedral of St. Peter in Chains, Cincinnati, November 2, 1845 278
86. Boniface Wimmer Outlines the Future of the Benedictine Order in the United States, November 8, 1845 279
87. The Inauguration of the First Conference of the Society of St. Vincent de Paul in the United States, November 20, 1845 288
88. A Broadside on the Infant University of Notre Dame, January 1, 1847 291
89. The Act of Foundation for the First Permanent Trappist Monastery in the United States, October, 23, 1848 294
90. The Catholic Missions in the Far Northwest, January 12, 1849 296
91. Conditions in the Diocese of Chicago, December 13, 1849 300
92. The Advent of Bishop Lamy to the Southwest, June 29, 1851 301
93. A Missionary Bishop on the Edge of the Great Plains, August 6, 1852 303
94. The Church in San Francisco in the Days of the Gold Rush, June 15, 1853 304
95. The Conversion to Catholicism of Eliza Allen Starr, February–December, 1854 306
96. Asiatic Cholera in the Diocese of Savannah, August 29, 1854 310
97. A Plan for the Western Colonization of Catholic Immigrants, March 15, 1856 311
98. Father Kindekens Appeals for an American College at Louvain, November 5, 1856 315

99. Archbishop Hughes' Opposition to Western Colonization for Catholic Immigrants, March 26, 1857 . 317
100. Chief Justice Taney's Reflections on Slavery, August 19, 1857 322
101. Bishop Elder on the Apostolate to the Negro Slaves in Mississippi, 1858 325
102. Archbishop Hughes Interprets American Liberty and Its Abuses to the Holy See, March 23, 1858 . 329
103. An Appeal for the North American College at Rome, November 13, 1858 335
104. Father Hecker Sketches His Plans and Hopes for the Paulists, July 24, 1859 339
105. James A. McMaster's Criticism of the Lincoln Administration, June 8, 1861 342
106. Bishop Lynch Presents the South's Case for Secession, August 4, 1861 347
107. Wisconsin Catholicism at the Outbreak of the Civil War, August 30, 1861 357
108. The Nursing Sisters in the Military Hospitals of Virginia, January,. 1862–April, 1865 368
109. The Efforts of Archbishop Hughes to Keep France Neutral During the Civil War, January 29, 1862 370
110. American Diplomatic Relations With the Papal States, September 27, 1862 374
111. A Catholic Chaplain With the Union Armies, October 2, 1862 376
112. Father Purcell's Stand in Behalf of Emancipation of the Slaves, April 8, 1863 378
113. Brownson Defines the World Mission of the American Republic, 1865 383

Index

Preface to the Fourth Edition

The preface to the original edition of this work was dated August 15, 1955. Since it explained the method and procedure used in assemblying the documents, it has been thought advisable to let that statement stand as written, adding only an expression of regret for the deaths of so many who helped in compiling the original collection. Meanwhile the work passed through two other editions that brought the documents down to 1966.

As the American Catholic community has matured in the twenty years since the close of Vatican Council II, the documentation on every aspect of that development has increased enormously. On the official level that fact was illustrated by the publication of the four volumes edited by Hugh J. Nolan, *Pastoral Letters of the United States Bishops, 1792-1983* (Washington: National Conference of Catholic Bishops, 1984), Volume IV alone running to over 500 pages for the brief period, 1975-1983. Numerous other documents of every variety touching Catholic affairs in the United States have supplemented the Nolan collection, none more amply and significantly than the weekly issues of *Origins* now in its fifteenth volume, a publication that contains in addition to official episcopal statements important pronouncements from the clergy, religious communities, and the laity, as well as Catholic organizations of a national, diocesan, and parochial level. The sixteen new documents in this new edition have been drawn in the main from the Nolan volumes and from *Origins*. An effort has been made to select items that have had a notable influence during the last two decades, such as that of nuclear warfare, racial and ethnic trends, and issues of public policy that have a direct bearing on moral values.

While reiterating my thanks to all who helped in the earlier editions of this work, I wish to mention especially David Gibson, editor of *Origins*, and his staff who were more than generous with their time in furnishing texts; likewise Michael Glazier, the publisher, who gave me wholehearted co-operation in every detail. A final note of thanks to Judith Jablonski for making the index to Volume 3.

John Tracy Ellis

The Catholic University of America

Preface

During the past generation an increasing amount of literature has been published on the history of the Catholic Church in the United States, a fact which indicates a growing interest in the part that the Church has played in American history. But nowhere in the literature on the American Church has any attempt been made to draw together in one volume a sampling from the original sources from which its history has been written. The need for such a book has long been felt by those who wished to integrate the story of Catholicism with courses and seminars in American history, and this has been especially true in recent years due to the constantly increasing emphasis on the study of the history of the United States directly from the sources. The lack of such a collection has likewise proved a handicap to the relatively few who offer courses in the history of the Church in this country in Catholic seminaries, colleges, and universities. It was with a view to supplying this need in part, as also to making some of the principal documents of American Catholicism readily available for interested readers outside the classroom, that the present work was undertaken.

In the choice of the contents of this volume the editor was guided by no precise rules of selection, except that the term "document" was broadly interpreted to include any written record that would illustrate an event from a contemporary point of view. Thus one will find here official documents, such as papal bulls and encyclicals and state laws and charters, as well as a wide variety of writings of a purely private and personal nature gathered from archival records, printed letters, newspaper editorials, biographies, memoirs, and even a few selections from the poetry and prose compositions of prominent Catholic literary figures. A conscious effort was made to have the principal churchmen and laymen of the American Catholic past represented, and to include sample material that would give some idea of the chief organizations and institutions of the Church. Yet in spite of the care that was taken in this regard, it was not possible to embrace all the persons, religious orders, institutions, and organizations that might, with some justice, be thought proper subjects for a collection of this kind. Doubtless some will look here in vain for a document on a favorite missionary, on a Catholic society at whose birth an ancestor stood sponsor, or for the mention of a local or sectional celebrity whose life reflected high credit upon the Church. With such readers the editor can only plead that he did not feel he should impose upon his publisher's generosity beyond the size which this volume has assumed. Moreover, he is of the conviction that the vast extent and complexity of the American Catholic body at the present time make it virtually impossible to represent within the covers of a single book all their manifold activities and historic backgrounds.

A word should be said about the method used in collecting and editing the documents. First, with the exception of those from the colonial period, the arrangement is chronological. Since the Catholic missions of the three European powers that sent out colonies from the sixteenth through the eighteenth centuries are usually treated as separate units, it seemed best to break the chronology in this earlier section and list the entries under the headings of Spain, France, and England. It was also thought preferable to put two or more items on a single person together under the date of the first document rather than to separate them. Most of the material was naturally taken from sources in English, but for that written in foreign languages standard translations were used whenever they were available. In a few cases, however, translations were made either by the editor himself or were supplied to him through the kindness of friends. In the main the documents are printed just as they appear in the original source, although in some instances minor changes have been made either to improve the translations from foreign sources or to insert punctuation in certain English documents in order to clarify the meaning. For each item a single source has been cited in the introductory note, although in some instances the same document may be found in several collections. The translations of papal bulls and encyclicals generally give the student a reference to the official collections of the Holy See where the original may be read in Latin. While reference has frequently been made in the introductory notes to pertinent books and periodicals, no effort has been made to add a formal bibliography with each document. Most of the better books in American Catholic history contain bibliographies, and for all the essential works published up to three years ago the editor's *A Guide to American Catholic History* (Milwaukee: 1959) will serve the purpose.

The editor is conscious of the fact that some readers may feel the need for more of a commentary than they will find in the introductory notes. An effort was made to supply the necessary background for a proper understanding of each document; nonetheless, a few over-all comments may help to clarify certain matters that recur in a number of the entries. This is especially true where the material touches on ecclesiastical points of a somewhat technical nature that are often not familiar to the lay reader. One of these points relates to the question of financial support for the clergy of the American Church in different areas and periods of its history. In the Europe of the sixteenth to eighteenth centuries, from which the missionaries came, the methods of support varied widely. In Spain and France where Church and State were united the clergy received a stipend or salary from the government, or lived off of the income from a benefice which had been assigned to them. This was also true of the missionaries in the areas of the future United States that were ruled by Spain and France during the whole of the colonial period. Their income was either direct, in the form of a yearly stipend that not infrequently was in arrears, or indirect such as the revenues from the Pious Fund (No. 116). In the English colonies, on the contrary, the missionaries were compelled to support themselves by taking up farm lands like any other colonist and living off their income. Needless to say, Protestant England furnished them no assistance at a time when the clergy in the mother country were reduced by the penal laws to living off the charity of the wealthy Catholic noble families. The subject of financial support thus frequently became the source of friction between the civil officials and the missionaries in the American dominions of Spain and France, and, at times, too, between the missionaries and the proprietary government of Maryland. One can easily imagine, for example, how the successful enterprises of a missionary like Father Kino (No. 12) might arouse the cupidity of greedy officials, and how the loss of all their temporal goods in Maryland (No. 33) and in Louisiana (No. 24) would seriously affect the Jesuit missions in those regions.

A second point involves the question of ecclesiastical jurisdiction. From the beginning of the colonial settlements down to 1790 the entire area of what later became the United States — whether it was ruled by Spain, France, or England — was regarded by the Holy See as missionary territory. In other words, America was then, in the familiar phrase, *in partibus infidelium.* The normal government of the Church, therefore, with its resident bishops and diocesan priests serving under them, was for the most part lacking, for one could scarcely regard the somewhat spasmodic efforts in behalf of the Catholic colonists by bishops in distant Havana, Durango, Quebec, or London as in any sense a regular form of episcopal rule. The missionaries got their faculties, or the authority to administer the sacraments, through various channels: the Spaniards from the crown which alone had the authority, given to it by the Holy See, to appoint the clergy to posts in the colonial empire; the French from the Congregation de Propaganda Fide, the superiors-general of their respective orders, or the Bishop of Quebec. In the English colonies the missionaries, practically all of whom were Jesuits, at first had their faculties from the Propaganda through their general or the English provincial, and at a later date from the Vicar Apostolic of the London District. But one can get some notion of how unsatisfactory this system was by the ignorance of American conditions revealed in the London vicar's report of 1756 (No. 37).

Because there were no resident bishops on the scene to implement normal ecclesiastical government and because of the awkward methods of jurisdiction employed, lengthy disputes over jurisdictional questions were not uncommon betweeen different religious orders, diocesan priests and religious, religious and distant bishops who claimed jurisdiction, and, of course, between missionaries and civil officials. It was small wonder, then, that neither the priests nor the people should have had any clear concept of the methods by which the Church was customarily ruled in old and settled places. Lack of experience of episcopal authority would in part explain the reluctance shown by the American priests when the Holy See raised the question of appointing a bishop (No. 38), and the abuses to which lay trusteeism gave rise in the rule of some Catholic congregations in the new Republic (Nos. 49, 52), to say nothing of the disorderly state of ecclesiastical affairs as pictured by the first resident bishop in Louisiana (No. 59).

There were real and deep differences among the clergy on these matters in colonial America, as well as differences of another kind in a later age. One encounters them, for example, in the conduct of certain unruly priests who threw in their lot with rebellious trustees (Nos. 67–68), in the school controversy which divided the hierarchy in the 1890's (No. 132), and in the agitation over Americanism at the turn of the century (No. 143). But these controversies were usually the outgrowth of factors like the loosely disciplined Church of the early national period (Nos. 38, 49), of conflicting national backgrounds and experience on the part of churchmen (No. 133), or of the natural division between prelates and priests of a conservative versus liberal turn of mind (Nos. 126–127). It would be easy to magnify these disputes out of their true context and to see in them grave violations of charity, or even doctrinal divergences. Actually more often than not they were but the legitimate differences of opinion of forceful and conscientious churchmen who availed themselves of the free American atmosphere to declare their minds. This is a phenomenon as old as the Church itself, for at the historic meeting between St. Peter and St. Paul in Antioch nineteen centuries ago they differed on the question of the Jews' relations to the Gentiles, and as St. Paul said, "I withstood him to his face, because he was deserving of blame."[1] When properly understood, therefore, the disputes of ecclesiastics need give no ground for scandal, for as Pope Leo XIII said in speaking of falsehoods circulated by the Church's enemies, "nothing is more proper, nothing more efficacious, than to bring them face to face with the truth itself as revealed in the irrefragable testimony of texts and documents."[2]

The idea for this edition of source materials on American Catholicism was first suggested to the editor six years ago by his former student and friend, the Reverend Colman J. Barry, O.S.B., assistant professor of history in St. John's University, Collegeville, Minnesota. Father Barry not only took a leading part in the work of the seminar which for two years was engaged in the task of collecting and editing, but after the completion of his graduate study he continued to follow the project with the closest interest and to furnish several lengthy documents which he had translated and edited from foreign sources. A special expression of gratitude is, therefore, owed to Father Barry. The editor wishes also to thank the following priests who were members of his seminar and who were most helpful in hunting out documents and editing them for the collection: the Reverends Francis T. Hueller, S.C.A., Vincent de Paul McMurray, S.S., Peter J. Rahill, David F. Sweeney, O.F.M., and R. Felix White, M.M. He is under obligation, too, to the students of the Catholic University of America who worked on various documents as a part of course assignments during the summer sessions of 1950–1952. For kindly supplying material from archives and manuscript collections, in several cases in their own translations, or for direction to the editor on questions of selection in the field of their specialization, he desires to thank the following: the Most Reverend Richard O. Gerow, the Right Reverend M. James Fox, O.C.S.O., the Right Reverend George G. Higgins, and the Reverends Patrick H. Ahern, Benjamin J. Blied, John J. Considine, M.M., Vincent F. Holden, C.S.P., Richard C. Madden, Paul Marx, O.S.B., Thomas T. McAvoy, C.S.C., Robert F. McNamara, William C. Repetti, S.J., and Antonine Tibesar, O.F.M. For similar assistance he is grateful to Professor Francis E. Litz, Mr. Ward Steimer, Mother Anselm McCann, S.B.S., Sisters Mary Virgina

[1] Gal. 2:11.

[2] E. Soutif, C.S.C., "Leo XIII and Historical Research — Recent Work in the Vatican Library," *American Catholic Quarterly Review*, XX (October, 1895), 756.

Geiger, S.S.N.D., Marie Carolyn Klinkhamer, O.P., and Isabel Toohey, D.C., Dr. Annabelle M. Melville, and Miss Betty Barbara Sipe.

It is a pleasant duty to record the numerous courtesies extended by the staff of the Library of Congress, and especially those of Mr. Raphael Brown. The editor is under the deepest obligation as well to Mr. Eugene P. Willging, director of the Mullen Library of the Catholic University of America, and to the staff whose patience he tried on more than one occasion, but who bore his incessant calls for assistance with real fortitude and met every demand with the most kindly and friendly treatment. To Miss Rosabelle A. Kelp he is likewise under obligation for her expert work in making the index. Finally a debt quite beyond the ordinary was incurred to two good friends who read through the entire work: the Right Reverend John K. Cartwright, rector of St. Matthew's Cathedral, Washington, whose sharp eye caught many a clumsy construction or doubtful translation, and the Reverend Henry J. Browne, former archivist of the Catholic University of America, who not only improved the manuscript by his critical reading, but also suggested items and handed over a number of documents to the editor's custody for inclusion in the collection.

JOHN TRACY ELLIS

Washington, D. C.
August 15, 1955

THE SPANISH COLONIES

1. The Bull *Inter caetera* of Pope Alexander VI, May 4, 1493

WHEN the news of the success of Columbus' first voyage reached Europe it was rumored that the energetic King John II of Portugal was preparing to dispute the Spanish claims to the new territories. Ferdinand and Isabella, therefore, sent a hurried appeal to Pope Alexander VI (1492–1503), asking that he confirm their possession of the lands discovered by Columbus. As a consequence, the pontiff issued several documents in the year 1493, the best known being that which drew the imaginary "line of demarcation" which assigned to Spain all lands west of a meridian 100 leagues west of the Azores and Cape Verde Islands. Although the line was later changed to Portugal's advantage, the bull *Inter caetera* — known from the first words of the original Latin text — is included here to illustrate, among other things, the prestige which the Holy See enjoyed at the time for settling disputes between nations. Source: Frances Gardiner Davenport (Ed.), *European Treaties bearing on the History of the United States and Its Dependencies to 1648* (Washington: Carnegie Institution of Washington, 1917), I, 75–78.

Alexander, bishop, servant of the servants of God, to the illustrious sovereigns, our very dear son in Christ, Ferdinand, king, and our very dear daughter in Christ, Isabella, queen of Castile, health and benediction. We have indeed learned that you, who for a long time had intended to seek out and discover certain islands and mainlands remote and unknown and not hitherto discovered by others, to the end that you might bring to the worship of our Redeemer and the profession of the Catholic faith their residents and inhabitants, having been up to the present time greatly engaged in the siege and recovery of the kingdom itself of Granada were unable to accomplish this holy and praiseworthy purpose; but the said kingdom having at length been regained, as was pleasing to the Lord, with a wish to fulfill your desire, chose our beloved son, Christopher Columbus, a man assuredly worthy and of the highest recommendations and fitted for so great an undertaking, whom you furnished with ships and men equipped for like designs, not without the greatest hardships, dangers, and expenses, to make diligent quest for these remote and unknown mainlands and islands through the sea, where hitherto no one had sailed; and they at length with divine aid and with the utmost diligence sailing in the ocean sea, discovered certain very remote islands and even mainlands that hitherto had not been discovered by others; wherein dwell very many peoples living in peace, and, as reported, going unclothed, and not eating flesh. . . . wherefore, as becomes Catholic kings and princes . . . you have purposed . . . to bring under your sway the said mainlands and islands. . . . And, in order that you may enter upon so great an undertaking with greater readiness and heartiness endowed with the benefit of our apostolic favor, we, of our own accord, not at your instance nor the request of anyone else in your regard, but out of our own sole largess and certain knowledge and out of the fullness of our apostolic power, by the authority of Almighty God conferred upon us in blessed Peter and of the vicarship of Jesus Christ, which we hold on earth, do by tenor of these presents, should any of said islands have been found by your envoys and captains, give, grant, and assign to you and your heirs and successors, kings of Castile and León, forever, together with all their dominions, cities, camps, places, and villages, and all rights, jurisdictions, and appurtenances, all islands and mainlands found and to be found, discovered and to be discovered towards the west and the south, by drawing and establishing a line from the Arctic pole, namely the north, to the Antarctic pole, namely the south, no matter whether the said mainlands and islands are found and to be found in the direction of India or towards any other quarter, the said line to be distant one hundred leagues[1] towards the west and south from any of the islands commonly known as the Azores and Cape Verde. With this proviso, however, that none of the islands and mainlands, found and to be found, discovered and to be discovered, beyond that said line towards the west and south, be in the actual possession of any Christian king or prince up to the birthday of our Lord Jesus Christ just past from which the present year 1493 begins. . . . Furthermore, under penalty of excommunication *latae sententiae* to be incurred *ipso facto,* should anyone thus contravene, we strictly forbid all persons of whatsoever rank, even imperial and royal, or of whatsoever estate, degree, order, or condition, to dare without your special permit or that of your aforesaid heirs and successors, to go for the purpose of trade or any other reason to the islands or mainlands . . . apostolic constitutions and ordinances and other decrees whatsoever to the contrary notwithstanding. . . . Let

[1] The old Spanish *legua,* frequently mentioned in the documents that follow, was the equivalent of about 2.63 miles, although the Spaniards used another standard in California the exact equivalent of which was never determined.

no one therefore, infringe, or with rash boldness contravene, this our recommendation, exhortation, requisition, gift, grant, assignment, constitution, deputation, decree, mandate, prohibition, and will. Should anyone presume to attempt this, be it known to him that he will incur the wrath of Almighty God and of the blessed apostles Peter and Paul. Given at Rome, at St. Peter's, in the year of the incarnation of our Lord one thousand four hundred and ninety-three, the fourth of May, and the first year of our pontificate.

2. The Treaty of Tordesillas, June 7, 1494

THE provisions of the bull *Inter caetera* did not satisfy John II of Portugal, and the Spanish sovereigns agreed, therefore, to move the line of demarcation 370 leagues west from the Cape Verde Islands. The rectification was embodied in the document which follows and was approved by Alexander VI. Spain and Portugal have long since lost all their American possessions, but one of the enduring cultural effects of the alteration of the original division of the pope is the Portuguese language spoken in Brazil in contradistinction to the Spanish language which is spoken throughout the remainder of South ,and Central America and Mexico. Source: Frances Gardiner Davenport (Ed.), *European Treaties bearing on the History of the United States and Its Dependencies to 1648* (Washington: Carnegie Institution of Washington, 1917), I, 93–100.

. . . Whereas a certain controversy exists between the said lords, their constituents, as to what lands, of all those discovered in the ocean sea up to the present day, the date of this treaty, pertain to each one of the said parts respectively; therefore, for the sake of peace and concord, and for the preservation of the relationship and love of the said King of Portugal for the said King and Queen of Castile, Aragon, etc., it being the pleasure of their Highnesses, they . . . covenanted and agreed that a boundary or straight line be determined and drawn north and south, from pole to pole, on the said ocean sea, from the Arctic to the Antarctic pole. This boundary or line shall be drawn straight, as aforesaid, at a distant of three hundred and seventy leagues west of the Cape Verde Islands, being calculated by degrees. . . . And all lands both islands and mainlands, found and discovered already, or to be found and discovered hereafter, by the said King of Portugal and by his vessels on this side of the said line and bound determined as above, toward the east, in either north or south latitude, on the eastern side of the said bound, provided the said bound is not crossed, shall belong to and remain in the possession of, and pertain forever to, the said King of Portugal and his successors. And all other lands, both islands and mainlands, found or to be found hereafter . . . by the said King and Queen of Castile, Aragon, etc., and by their vessels, on the western side of the said bound, determined as above, after having passed the said bound toward the west, in either its north or south latitude, shall belong to . . . the said King and Queen of Castile, León, etc., and to their successors.

Item, the said representatives promise and affirm . . . that from this date no ships shall be dispatched — namely as follows: the said King and Queen of Castile, León, Aragon, etc., for this part of the bound . . . which pertains to the said King of Portugal . . . nor the said King of Portugal to the other side of the said bound which pertains to the said King and Queen of Castile, Aragon, etc. — for the purpose of discovering and seeking any mainlands or islands, or for the purpose of trade, barter, or conquest of any kind. But should it come to pass that the said ships of the said King and Queen of Castile . . . on sailing thus on this side of the said bound, should discover any mainlands or islands in the region pertaining, as abovesaid, to the said King of Portugal, such mainlands or islands shall belong forever to the said King of Portugal and his heirs, and their Highnesses shall order them to be surrendered to him immediately. And if the said ships of the said King of Portugal discover any islands or mainlands in the regions of the said King and Queen of Castile . . . all such lands shall belong to and remain forever in the possession of the said King and Queen of Castile . . . and their heirs, and the said King of Portugal shall cause such lands to be surrendered immediately. . . .

And by this present agreement, they . . . entreat our most Holy Father that his Holiness be pleased to confirm and approve this said agreement, according to what is set forth therein; and that he order his bulls in regard to it to be issued to the parties or to whichever of the parties may solicit them, with the tenor of this agreement incorporated therein, and that he lay his censures upon those who shall violate or oppose it at any time whatsoever. . . .

3. The Bull *Universalis ecclesiae* of Pope Julius II, July 28, 1508

BY THE bull *Universalis ecclesiae* of July 28, 1508, Pope Julius II (1503–1513) conceded to the Spanish crown universal patronage over all ecclesi-

astical benefices in its New World possessions. Whether or not this bull granted for the first time the *real patronato,* or whether it merely reconfirmed rights already bestowed by the Holy See, it continued to be regarded as the principal documentary evidence of the legal right of the Spanish sovereigns to exercise jurisdiction over the Catholic Church in the New World down to the nineteenth century. Source: J. Lloyd Mecham, *Church and State in Latin America* (Chapel Hill: University of North Carolina Press, 1934), pp. 18–20.

Julius, bishop, servant of the servants of God. We, presiding by divine choice, although unworthily, over the government of the Universal Church, do concede voluntarily to the Catholic kings principally those things that augment their honor and glory, and contribute effectively to the benefit and security of their dominions. Since our beloved son in Christ, Ferdinand, illustrious king of Aragon, and also of Sicily, and Isabella, of cherished memory, Queen of Castile and León, after having expelled the Moors from Spain, crossed the ocean and planted the Cross in unknown lands, and subjugated many islands and places, and among these being one very rich and extremely populous named New Spain, thereby fulfilling to the extent of their ability the saying *in omnem terram exivit sonus eorum* — Therefore, we, in order that it (New Spain) might be purged of false and pernicious rites, and the true religion be planted there, have acceded to the most urgent requests of the king and queen, and do hereby erect for the greater glory of the name of Christ, a metropolitan church in Ayguacen, and two cathedrals in Maguen and Bayunen,[1] and if the converts imbued by the new faith should attempt to found any church or pious place, they should do so in such a way as not to injure the new religion or the temporal dominions of the king.

In view of the fact that the said Ferdinand, who is also at present governor-general of the kingdoms of Castile and León, and our most cherished daughter in Christ, Juana, queen of the same kingdoms and daughter of the aforementioned Ferdinand, wish that no church, monastery, or pious place be erected or founded either in the islands and lands already possessed, or in those subsequently acquired, with-

---

[1] The Archdiocese of Ayguacen (Hyaguata) and the suffragan Sees of Maguen (Magua) and Bayunen (Bayuna) never existed except on paper. After the impracticality of their sites had become known, and after Ferdinand of Aragon had objected strenuously to assigning to the bishops a part of the tithes on gold, silver, and precious stones, Julius II issued a brief on August 8, 1511, that suppressed these jurisdictions and in their place erected three new dioceses at San Domingo and Conception de la Vega in Española (Haiti) and at San Juan in Puerto Rico, all made suffragans of the Archdiocese of Seville.

out their express consent and that of their successors; and considering that since it is convenient to those kings that the persons who preside over churches and monasteries be faithful and acceptable to them, they desire that they be conceded the right of patronage and of the cathedral churches already erected, or to be erected in the future, and for all the other ecclesiastical benefices inside of a year of their vacancy, and also for inferior benefices; and in case the ordinary should refuse without legitimate cause to grant the one presented with canonical institution inside of ten days, any other bishop, at the request of the king should grant it. We, appreciating that these privileges increase the honor, beauty and security of those islands, and also of the said kingdoms, whose kings are always devout and faithful to the Apostolic See, and heeding the reiterated demands made on us by King Ferdinand and Queen Juana, after mature deliberation with our brothers the cardinals of the Holy Roman Church, and with their advice, by these presents we concede with apostolic authority, other constitutions, ordinances, and laws to the contrary notwithstanding, to the said Ferdinand and Juana, and to the future kings of Castile and León, that nobody without their consent can construct or build in the above mentioned islands, now possessed or to be possessed, large churches; and we concede the right of patronage and of presenting qualified persons to cathedral churches, monasteries, *dignities,* collegiates, and other ecclesiastical benefices and pious places in this manner: respecting benefices that are instituted in the consistory, the presentation is to be made to Us, or Our successors, within one year after the vacancy occurs; and respecting the other benefices, presentation will be made to the respective ordinaries, and if these refuse without cause to give institution inside of ten days, any bishop in those lands, on the petition of King Ferdinand or of Queen Juana, or the king ruling at that time, can bestow, under those conditions, free and legal canonical institution on the person presented. Nobody should deign to infringe on or act contrary to this concession, and if any one attempts to do so, let him know that he will incur the indignation of God Almighty and of the blessed apostles Peter and Paul. Given in Rome, etc., July 28, 1508.

4. The Bull *Sublimis Deus* of Pope Paul III, June 2, 1537

TO COMBAT the charge that the Indians were not capable of receiving the Catholic faith, Paul III (1534–1549), following representations by the Dominicans, Bernardino de Minaya and Julian Garcés, Bishop of Tlaxcala in New Spain, issued on June 2, 1537, the bull *Sublimis Deus*. By this action the pope reaffirmed the traditional teaching of the Catholic Church concerning the spiritual equality and brotherhood of all men. This is a key document in the lengthy controversy over the intellectual capacities of the American Indians. Although it is impossible to say how many of the Spanish *conquistadores* really believed the Indians to be animals [*bruta animalia*], there is no doubt that some held this view. If it had prevailed without challenge it would have enabled the Spaniards to use the lives and properties of the defenseless natives unchecked by the protecting hand of the Church, and thus the task of the missionaries would have been rendered much more difficult than it actually was.

Emperor Charles V became so concerned over the effect of the *Sublimis Deus* in the Spanish dominions that he brought pressure to bear on Paul III to revoke it. As a consequence, the pope issued another bull on June 19, 1538, which revoked all previous papal briefs and bulls that might prejudice the power of Charles V in his colonial empire. In the latter document the pope did not take back what he had said in the *Sublimis Deus* concerning the Indians' capacity for conversion, but he did declare all ecclesiastical censures and penalties imposed by the missionaries on the *conquistadores* to be null and void. This action seriously hampered the missionaries' efforts to check the rapacity of the Spaniards, but as one scholar has stated, "the bull Sublimis Deus lived on as a force to be reckoned with in the endless disputes over the true nature of the American Indians because the nullification was not widely known." Lewis Hanke, "Pope Paul III and the American Indians," *Harvard Theological Review*, XXX (April, 1937), 97. Source: Francis Augustus MacNutt, *Bartholomew de Las Casas* (New York: G. P. Putnam's Sons, 1909), pp. 427–431.

Paul III Pope. To all faithful Christians to whom this writing may come, health in Christ our Lord and the apostolic benediction.

The sublime God so loved the human race that He created man in such wise that he might participate, not only in the good that other creatures enjoy, but endowed him with capacity to attain to the inaccessible and invisible Supreme Good and behold it face to face; and since man, according to the testimony of the sacred scriptures, has been created to enjoy eternal life and happiness, which none may obtain save through faith in our Lord Jesus Christ, it is necessary that he should possess the nature and faculties enabling him to receive that faith; and that whoever is thus endowed should be capable of receiving that same faith. Nor is it credible that any one should possess so little understanding as to desire the faith and yet be destitute of the most necessary faculty to enable him to receive it. Hence Christ, who is the Truth itself, that has never failed and can never fail, said to the preachers of the faith whom He chose for that office 'Go ye and teach all nations.' He said all, without exception, for all are capable of receiving the doctrines of the faith.

The enemy of the human race, who opposes all good deeds in order to bring men to destruction, beholding and envying this, invented a means never before heard of, by which he might hinder the preaching of God's word of Salvation to the people: he inspired his satellites who, to please him, have not hesitated to publish abroad that the Indians of the West and the South, and other people of whom We have recent knowledge should be treated as dumb brutes created for our service, pretending that they are incapable of receiving the Catholic Faith.

We, who, though unworthy, exercise on earth the power of our Lord and seek with all our might to bring those sheep of His flock who are outside into the fold committed to our charge, consider, however, that the Indians are truly men and that they are not only capable of understanding the Catholic Faith but, according to our information, they desire exceedingly to receive it. Desiring to provide ample remedy for these evils, We define and declare by these Our letters, or by any translation thereof signed by any notary public and sealed with the seal of any ecclesiastical dignitary, to which the same credit shall be given as to the originals, that, notwithstanding whatever may have been or may be said to the contrary, the said Indians and all other people who may later be discovered by Christians, are by no means to be deprived of their liberty or the possession of their property, even though they be outside the faith of Jesus Christ; and that they may and should, freely and legitimately, enjoy their liberty and the possession of their property; nor should they be in any way enslaved; should the contrary happen, it shall be null and of no effect.

By virtue of Our apostolic authority We define and declare by these present letters, or by any translation thereof signed by any notary public and sealed with the seal of any ecclesiastical dignitary, which shall thus command the same obedience as the originals, that the said Indians and other peoples should be converted to the faith of Jesus Christ by preaching the word of God and by the example of good and holy living.

5. Juan de Padilla, the Protomartyr of the United States, Is Murdered by the Plains Indians, c. 1542

IN THE three centuries between the entrance of the first priests into Florida in the early 1520's and the founding of the last of the California missions at San Francisco Solano in July, 1823, hundreds of Catholic missionaries labored in every section of what was to become the United States in an effort to convert the native Indians to Christianity. In the attempt many of these men met death at the hands of the savages. On the epochal exploring expedition of Coronado which started north from old Mexico in February, 1540, and during the next two years traversed so large a part of the American Southwest, there were three Franciscan friars, Fathers Juan de Padilla and Juan de la Cruz, and Brother Luís de Ubeda (DeEscalona). When Coronado turned back in disappointment in the spring of 1542 the friars remained behind in the hope of evangelizing the Indians. Soon thereafter Padilla was murdered by the red men and thus became the proto-martyr of the future United States; the other two were never heard from again. In the account which follows, written by one of Coronado's soldiers, Pedro de Castañeda, he described the little that is known about the fate of the friar. The exact date and location of Padilla's death are uncertain, although most authorities think it took place shortly after Coronado's departure southward and probably occurred somewhere in southern Kansas. Source: "The Narrative of the Expedition of Coronado by Castañeda," Frederick W. Hodge and Theodore H. Lewis (Eds.), *Spanish Explorers in the Southern United States, 1528–1543* (New York: Charles Scribner's Sons, 1907), pp. 372–374; now included in *Original Narratives of Early American History,* copyright Barnes & Noble, Inc., New York.

When the general, Francisco Vásquez,[1] saw that everything was now quiet, and that his schemes had gone as he wished, he ordered that everything should be ready to start on the return to New Spain by the beginning of the month of April, in the year 1543 [1542].

Seeing this, Friar Juan de Padilla, a regular brother of the lesser order, and another, Friar Luis [Descalona], a lay brother, told the general that they wanted to remain in that country — Friar Juan de Padilla in Quivira, because his teachings seemed to promise fruit there, and Friar Luis at Cicuye.[2] On this account, as it was Lent at the time, the father made this the subject of his sermon to the companies

---

[1] Francisco Vásquez Coronado (1510–1554) was Governor of Nueva Galicia and leader of the expedition.

[2] Cicuye was synonymous with Pecos in New Mexico.

one Sunday, establishing his proposition on the authority of the Holy Scriptures. He declared his zeal for the conversion of these peoples and his desire to draw them to the faith, and stated that he had received permission to do it, although this was not necessary. The general sent a company to escort them as far as Cicuye, where Friar Luis stopped, while Friar Juan went on back to Quivira with the guides who had conducted the general, taking with him the Portuguese, as we related, and the half-blood, and the Indians from New Spain. He was martyred a short time after he arrived there, as we related in the second part, Chapter 8.[3] Thus we may be sure that he died a martyr, because his zeal was holy and earnest.

Friar Luis remained at Cicuye. Nothing more has been heard about him since, but before the army left Tiguex[4] some men who went to take him a number of sheep that were left for him to keep, met him as he was on his way to visit some other villages, which were fifteen or twenty leagues from Cicuye, accompanied by some followers. He felt very hopeful that he was liked at the village and that his teaching would bear fruit, although he complained that the old men were falling away from him. I, for my part, believe that they finally killed him. He was a man of good and holy life, and may Our Lord protect him and grant that he may convert many of those peoples, and end his days in guiding them in the faith. We do not need to believe otherwise, for the people in those parts are pious and not at all cruel. They are friends, or rather, enemies of cruelty, and they remained faithful and loyal friends.

After the friars had gone, the general, fearing that they might be injured if people were carried away from that country to New Spain, ordered the soldiers to let any of the natives who were held as servants go free to their villages whenever they might wish. In my opinion, though I am not sure, it would have been better if they had been kept and taught among Christians. . . .

---

[3] At the point referred to Castañeda stated: "A friar named Juan de Padilla remained in this province, together with a Spanish-Portuguese and a negro and a half-blood and some Indians from the province of Capothan in New Spain. They killed the friar because he wanted to go to the province of the Guas [possibly the Kaw or Kansa Indians], who were their enemies. . . . The Indians from New Spain who accompanied the friar were allowed by the murderers to bury him . . ." (pp. 364–365).

[4] Tiguex was situated at the site of Bernalillo on the Rio Grande River in what is today New Mexico.

6. Assignment of the Florida Missions to the Dominicans; Don Luís de Velasco to King Philip II, September 30, 1558

ONCE the Spaniards had established themselves in Mexico they thought of settling the Florida coast which lay along the Atlantic route to the homeland, as well as on the route of the vessels coming northward from the mines of South America. A primary consideration of all colonization by the crown was the conversion of the native peoples to the Catholic faith. Hence it was not surprising that the Viceroy of New Spain should outline to Philip II his decision to entrust the mission of Florida to a single group of religious, in this instance to the Dominicans. Due to a series of disasters, however, the expedition failed and the Dominicans withdrew in 1561 with the Spanish military. Source: Herbert Ingram Priestley (Ed.), *The Luna Papers. Documents Relating to the Expedition of Don Tristán de Luna y Arellano for the Conquest of La Florida in 1559–1561* (Deland: Florida State Historical Society, 1928), II, 257–261.

The ships and people which are to colonize on the coast of the land of La Florida and the Punta de Santa Elena are being prepared; I think they will be ready to set sail sometime in May of 1559. Five hundred Spaniards will go; four hundred of them, soldiers, two hundred being mounted, and two hundred on foot armed with arquebuses and crossbows for the defense of the religious and ecclesiastics who are to go to preach our holy faith to the natives, and one hundred artisans to engage in building the towns and the fort which your Majesty commands to be built. Also the instructions are being drawn up which are to be given to the governor, religious, and officials of the royal treasury, and other persons who have positions of authority. . . .

I gathered together the provincials of the orders of St. Dominic, St. Francis, and St. Augustine, in the presence of this royal audiencia, and asked their opinion as to whether it would be fitting at the beginning for the religious of all three orders to go or only one, and if they agreed that only one should be represented, which it should be. They all were agreed that religious of but one order should go, and that they should be those of St. Dominic, as your Majesty will order herewith. Six religious have been named, men of chosen life, letters, doctrine, and of age to be able to work among the Indians and learn their languages. It seems that for the present these will suffice. They will have to be provided with ornaments, crosses, chalices, bells, and other things necessary for the service of the divine cult, with clothing and shoes for the religious, and these cost four times as much in this country as in Spain. . . .

In the meantime I am sending out three religious to the new mines of San Martín, which are between the mines of Los Zacatecas and Copala, thirty leagues from the mines [of Los Zacatecas] and as many more, according to what the Indians of that country say, from Copala. They are to assist a good cleric who has baptized a number of Indians between the country of San Martín and Copala, to attract the rest of the people of the district, and to make sure what the province of Copala is, so that when convenient it may be entered, pacified, and colonized. . .

. . . Mexico, the last day of September, 1558.

Your Catholic Royal Majesty's
faithful servant who kisses your Majesty's royal feet,
Don Luis de Velasco

7. Agreement Between Philip II and Pedro Menéndez de Avilés for the Conquest of Florida and the Assignment of Jesuit Missionaries, March 20, 1565

ON FIVE different occasions within a half century Spain had tried and failed to conquer and settle Florida. To the earlier insurmountable opposition of savage natives there was later added the armed hostility of European intruders. Among the first to foresee the dangers to the Spanish Empire and its commerce in the New World from a permanent loss of Florida was Pedro Menéndez. It was at his urgent appeal that the Velasco-Luna expedition was organized to construct defensive settlements on the Florida coast. Finally in 1565 Menéndez was authorized to organize another expedition, and while the *asiento,* or royal patent, granted to him and his heirs many titles and the revenues from the lands he should conquer, it likewise laid the expense and burden of the entire undertaking on the shoulders of the new Governor and Captain-General of La Florida. Source: Jeannette Thurber Connor (Ed.), *Pedro Menéndez de Avilés. . . . Memorial by Gonzalo Solís de Merás* (Deland: Florida State Historical Society, 1923), pp. 259–270.

The King: — Whereas we have given *asientos* at various times for the discovery and settlement of the provinces of Florida, and likewise charged Don Luís de Velasco, who was our Viceroy of New Spain, to send a certain number of people and religious to settle that country, and an *asiento* was last made concerning this with Lucas Vasquez de Ayllón; and efforts have been made by the persons to whom we gave the said *asientos,* as well as by the Viceroy aforesaid; never up to now has that land been colonized; nor has what we desired, which was the aforesaid settlement, been accomplished; nor the teaching and conversion of the natives of those provinces, and the bringing them into our Holy Catholic Faith; and as we have in mind the good and the salvation of those souls, we have decided to give the order to send religious persons to instruct the said Indians, and those other people who are good Christians and our subjects, so that they may live among and talk to the natives there may be in those lands and provinces of Florida, and that [the Indians] by intercourse and conversation with them may more easily be taught our Holy Catholic Faith and be brought to good usages and customs, and perfect polity. And to you, Pedro Menéndez de Avilés, Knight of the Order of Santiago, have I offered and do offer, because of the desire you have for the service of God Our Lord, and for the increase to the Royal Crown of these kingdoms, that during the coming month of May of this present year, you shall hold ready and prepared to sail, in San Lucar de Barrameda, in the port of Santa Maria or in the Bay of Cádiz, in order to depart with the first opportunity, six shallops of fifty *toneles* each, more or less; and four swift *zabras,* with their oars, arms and munitions, laden with supplies and fully prepared for war; and that you shall take five hundred men, one hundred of them farmers and one hundred sailors, and the rest of them naval and military men and officials, others professional stonecutters, carpenters, sawyers, smiths, barbers, locksmiths; all of them with their arms, arquebuses and crossbows, and helmets and bucklers, and other offensive and defensive weapons which you may see fit and which may be suitable for the said voyage; and two priests; and that you shall do other things declared above, all of this at your cost and under your commission, without Our being obligated, or the Kings who may come after Us, to pay or indemnify you anything thereof other than what may be conceded to you by this Agreement, as you have entreated me to make it with you and to grant you certain favors. . . .

Furthermore; You offer and pledge yourself that within the said time, and among the number of the said people whom you bind yourself to take, you will include at least ten or twelve religious, of the Order which may appear best to you: persons who are of a good life and example; likewise four others of the Society of Jesus, so that there may be religious instruction in the said land, and the Indians can be converted to our Holy Catholic Faith and to our obedience. . . .

Therefore by these presents, if you, the said Pedro Menéndez, do carry out the aforesaid at your cost, according to what is contained in the aforesaid, in the manner thereof; and if you fulfil all that is included in this agreement, in the instructions which shall be given you, and in those which shall be given you later on; likewise the provisions and ordinances We shall make, and order to be observed, for the said country and settlements, and for the good treatment and conversion to our Holy Catholic Faith of the natives there, and of the settlers who may go there; I say and promise, by my faith and my Royal word, that this Agreement shall be observed, in your favor, and everything therein contained, wholly and absolutely, according as it is therein contained, without your meeting any opposition thereto; but that if you should not so fulfil and accomplish that to which you obligate yourself, we shall not be compelled to keep with you and carry out the aforesaid [agreement], nor any part thereof; rather shall we order that you be punished, and we shall proceed against you as a person who does not observe and fulfil, but trespasses against, the commands of his King and natural Master.

And we order that these presents be given to that effect, signed by our hand, and by the members of our Council of the Indies, and countersigned by Francisco de Erasso, our Secretary.

I the King.
By order of his Majesty,
Francisco de Erasso.

Done in Madrid, on the
20th day of March, 1565.

8. St. Francis Borgia Withdraws the Jesuits From the Florida Missions, March 20, 1571

During the six years, 1566–1572, that the Jesuits spent in the missions of Florida they moved up the coast from St. Augustine into what are now the states of Georgia and South Carolina, with a brief and fatal effort in 1571 as far as Virginia. They met with little or no success and the deaths of a number of the missionaries at the hands of treacherous Indians convinced the Jesuit General that he could not retain so expensive a mission field in which there was so little prospect of permanent results, while the missions of New Spain were clamoring for more priests. In the following letter from Rome St. Francis Borgia (1510–1572), General of the Jesuits, explained to Pedro Menéndez the reasons for withdrawing his men from Florida. Source: Felix Zubillaga, S.J. (Ed.), *Monumenta antiquae Floridae*

(*1566–1572*) (Rome: Apud "Monumenta Historica Soc. Ieus," 1946), pp. 489–490.

. . . Since you know our Institute and the purpose of this small Company, it will be superfluous to speak of the desire which God, our Lord, gives to those who belong to the Company of going to help those people who are in greater need and in the danger of being lost, for this is our vocation; and according to this vocation may the infinite and divine goodness inspire us with such desires and the will to act in accord with them. This is the reason why the members of our Company so promptly go throughout the world, and why they went to Florida — the few that are there. They have worked and suffered in Florida with a constancy that has been manifest and yet they have seen little or no fruit of their labors, which is the greatest suffering of all for those who seek only the good of souls for the greater glory of God. Since, therefore, those pagans are so badly disposed that they are said to prefer the devil and to go to hell with him rather than to our God, and say that he who talks against their god, cannot be good; and since it is evident, in our long experience in Florida, that we could count, so to say, with the fingers of our hand those who during this long period have been converted, and even they have turned back to darkness, and since, moreover, there is in this Company, as I wrote to your Excellency, and it is truly so, such a small personnel for the many enterprises which the Company has assumed; it is evident that for a time until God our Lord, little by little, stirs those pagans in the capacity of their souls, that not only is it not fitting to keep the Company in that land, but it must not be done; for even if there were many missionaries, we are always obliged by the Christian religion and our own Institute to seek the greater glory of God and the greater good of our neighbor, for as our Lord says: 'If they do not receive the sacred Gospel in one place, we should go from that land to another, shaking the dust from our feet. . . .'

9. Alonso de Benavides' Description of the New Mexico Missions, February 12, 1634

DREAMS of the conquest and settlement of New Mexico had stirred up a great deal of enthusiasm in the sixteenth century and many competitors vied for the position of *adelantado* or Governor of New Mexico. In 1595 the contract for the conquest of New Mexico was awarded to Don Juan de

Oñate. Spiritual charge of the enterprise was assigned to the Franciscans and a custody of that order was established in 1616. In 1630 Fray Alonso de Benavides (d. 1636), commissary of the custody until 1629, returned to Spain to report to the king and to the Minister General of the Franciscan Order, Fray Bernardino de Siena, on the more notable happenings in the custody of New Mexico. In 1634 this same friar presented a revised report to Pope Urban VIII which was designed to promote missionary activity in New Mexico and to urge the establishment of a bishopric in that mission field. The following extract is indicative of the work of the friars for Church and State in colonial New Mexico. Source: Frederick Webb Hodge, George P. Hammond, and Agapito Rey (Eds.), *Fray Alonso de Benavides' Revised Memorial of 1634. . . .* (Albuquerque: University of New Mexico Press, 1945), pp. 100–103.

Since the land is very remote and isolated and the difficulties of the long journeys require more than a year of travel, the friars, although there are many who wish to dedicate themselves to those conversions, find themselves unable to do so because of their poverty. Hence only those go there who are sent by the Catholic king at his own expense, for the cost is so excessive that only his royal zeal can afford it. This is the reason that there are so few friars over there and that most of the convents have only one religious each, and he ministers to four, six, or more neighboring pueblos, in the midst of which he stands as a lighted torch to guide them in spiritual as well as temporal affairs. More than twenty Indians devoted to the service of the church, live with him in the convent. They take turns in relieving one another as porters, sextons, cooks, bell-ringers, gardeners, refectioners, and in other tasks. They perform their duties with as much circumspection and care as if they were friars. At eventide they say their prayers together, with much devotion in front of some image.

In every pueblo where a friar resides, he has schools for the teaching of praying, singing, playing musical instruments and other interesting things. Promptly at dawn, one of the Indian singers, whose turn it is that week, goes to ring the bell for Prime, at the sound of which those who go to school assemble and sweep the rooms thoroughly. The singers chant Prime in the choir. The friar must be present at all of this and takes notes of those who have failed to perform this duty, in order to reprimand them later. When everything is neat and clean, they again ring the bell and each one goes to learn his particular specialty; the friar oversees it all. . . . After they have been occupied in this manner for an hour and a half, the bell is rung for mass. All go into the church, and the friar says mass and administers the sacraments. . . . Mass over. . . . all kneel down by the church door and sing the *Salve* in their own tongue. . . .

At mealtime, the poor people in the pueblo who are not ill come to the porter's lodge, where the cooks of the convent have sufficient food ready which is served to them by the friar; food for the sick is sent to their homes. After mealtime, it always happens that the friar has to go to some neighboring pueblo to hear a confession or to see if they are careless in the boys' school, where they learn to pray and assist at mass, for this is the responsibility of the sextons and it is their duty always to have a dozen boys for the service of the sanctuary and to teach them how to help at mass and how to pray.

In the evening they toll the bell for vespers, which are chanted by the singers who are on duty for the week, and according to the importance of the feast they celebrate it with organ chants as they do for mass. . . .

One of the weekdays which is not so busy is devoted to baptism, and all those who are to be baptized come to the church on that day, unless some urgent matter should interfere; in that case, it is performed at any time. With great care, their names are inscribed in a book; in another, those who are married; and in another, the dead.

One of the greatest tasks of the friars is to adjust the disputes of the Indians among themselves, for, since they look upon him as a father, they come to him with all their troubles, and he has to take pains to harmonize them. If it is a question of land and property, he must go with them and mark their boundaries, and thus pacify them.

For the support of all the poor of the pueblo, the friar makes them sow some grain and raise some cattle, because if he left it to their discretion, they would not do anything. Therefore the friar requires them to do so and trains them so well, that, with the meat, he feeds all the poor and pays the various workmen who come to build the churches. With the wool he clothes all the poor, and the friar himself also gets his clothing and food from this source. All the wheels of this clock must be kept in good order by the friar, without neglecting any detail, otherwise all would be totally lost. . . .

This, Most Holy Father, is the state of that new and primitive church which the seraphic sons of Saint Francis, its only workers, have founded and watered with the blood and lives of ten of their brethren. . . .

10. Report of Bishop Calderón of Santiago to Queen Mother Marie Anne on the Florida Missions, August 14, 1674

WHEN Don Gabriel Diaz Vara Calderón (d. 1676) became Bishop of Santiago de Cuba in 1671, no bishop had visited Florida in more than sixty years, although it was a part of the Diocese of Santiago de Cuba. Having first made an episcopal visitation of the island of Cuba, Calderón set sail from Havana on August 18, 1674, convoyed by a fleet which entered the harbor of St. Augustine on August 23. While the record of his visitation of the missions in Florida is far from complete, there is sufficient evidence, as seen in his letter to the Queen Mother of Spain, to know that the episcopal visitation was no mere form. Source: Lucy L. Wenhold (Ed.), "A 17th Century Letter of Gabriel Diaz Vara Caldéron, Bishop of Cuba, Describing the Indians and Indian Missions of Florida," *Smithsonian Miscellaneous Collections* (Washington: Smithsonian Institution, 1936), Vol. 95, No. 16, pp. 2, 7–9, 12–14.

Señora:

Your Majesty is pleased to command me, in the two royal cédulas of the 4th of March of the year 73, to visit at this time the provinces of Florida and apply the proper remedy in the matter presented to Your Majesty by the Bishop of the city, Rodrigo, my predecessor here. No bishop has gone there [to Florida] in more than 60 years, and the presence of one is needed, not only to celebrate confirmations and correct the faults and abuses that have come in during so long a time in the case of [a] people so recently converted, and to investigate the state in which the priests of San Francisco have the work of converting the Indians and the instructions of the converts under their care, but also to lend encouragement to the converting of the Indians of the province of Apalachocoli who have for years been asking that missionaries be sent to teach and baptize them; a request never yet granted for lack [of missionaries]. In this field the Bishop believes the Dominican priests of this city would accomplish much.

Señora, this my predecessor said to me in the city of San Lucar where I was by order, awaiting the first opportunity of passage to this incumbency. I replied to him that I wished first to come to the city of Cuba, seat of this bishopric, visiting it, and to go then to the mission. Accordingly, as soon as I entered this city, obeying your Majesty I began to plan for the carrying out of that purpose. Having now completed the visitation of this entire island, I have it in such good condition that within 8 days under the favor of God I shall set forth.

And because [although I recognize the great zeal of the Dominican priests, who have offered themselves to me willingly], to take them now would be to introduce great discord with the Franciscans and jeopardize the conversion of those miserable heathen, it has seemed to me wiser to make use of the latter, both because they are well versed in that language and because they are in control of the entire province of Apalache which borders upon that of Apalachocoli. [I go] to investigate first the condition of that land, and then to enter upon the work of conversion for which I am taking chalices and all the necessary vestments of the Divine Cult. May it please Our Lord that the holy zeal of Your Majesty attain its end for the greater glory of the Divine One and the salvation of those souls.

May Our Lord keep the Catholic Royal Person of Your Majesty in His Holy grace with health and complete felicity to the greatest good of Your vassals.

Your Majesty's humble servant and chaplain,
Gabriel, Bishop of Cuba.

Havana,
August 14, 1674.

Florida and the Florida Missions

Señora:

What has been discovered, up to today, concerning the entire district of Florida, both along the seacoast and inland, is as follows:

On the coast of the northern border, 30 leagues from Cape Canaveral, [where] the canal of Bahama disembogues, is located, on the 30th parallel of latitude, the city of Saint Augustine which was founded about 1559 [1565] by the Adelantado Pedro Menéndes Avíles. It is the capital of the provinces of Florida and has more than 300 Spanish inhabitants, soldiers and married people. Its harbor is very secure by reason of a very dangerous sand bar which it has at its entrance, which shifts its position in storms and at high tide has 20 spans of water. The city is built lengthwise from north to south. It is almost cut off by an arm of the sea which surrounds it and buffets it, leaving it half submerged from hurricanes as it lies at sea level. Its climate is somewhat unhealthful, being very cold in winter, with freezes, and excessively hot in summer, both of which extremes are felt the more as there is no protection nor defense in the houses, they being of wood with board walls. The soil is sand and therefore unproductive;

no wheat grows, and corn only sparsely and at the cost of much labor. Thus the inhabitants are compelled regularly to depend for their sustenance upon the products of the province of Apalache. The section does not produce any sort of raw material which could attract trade, and has no resources other than the government allowance which it awaits each year from the city of Mexico, and by which the infantry is fed and clothed.

As regards its spiritual welfare, it has a parish church dedicated to Saint Augustine, served by a priest, a sacristan and acolytes, and a Franciscan convent, headquarters for the province, called Saint Helena, with three monks [*sic*], a superior, a preacher, a lay brother, and with authority by a royal decree of Your Majesty to have three curates for the three principal languages of these provinces, Guale, Timuqua and Apalache, for the teaching of Christian doctrine and the administering of the sacraments to the Indians who usually attend to the cultivating of the lands of the residents of the Post [Saint Augustine]. Of the four hermitages which formerly existed, only two remain: San Patricio and Our Lady of Solitude, and a hospital contiguous to the latter with six beds. For defense there is a fortress with 20 guns and a good garrison, a governor resident in the city, a sergeant-major, 2 captains, 300 enlisted men, and 2 royal officials.

Going out of the city, at half a league to the north there is a small village of scarcely more than 30 Indian inhabitants, called Nombre de Dios, the mission which is served by the convent. Following the road from east to west, within an extent of 98 leagues there are 24 settlements and missions of Christian Indians, 11 belonging to the province of Timuqua and 13 to that of Apalache. . . .

Nine leagues from Encarnación, on the northern frontier, is another [village] named San Nicolás, of about 30 inhabitants, and 3 leagues further on is another, San Carlos, of something like 100 inhabitants. Both these are of the Chacatos nation, which 14 years ago requested baptism and had not their desire fulfilled until the 21st of June of last year, 1674. In that section, living in encampments without any permanent dwellings, are more than 4,000 heathen called Chiscas, who sustain themselves with game, nuts and roots of trees. . . .

Characteristics of the Christianized Indians

In the four provinces of Guale, Timuqua, Apalache and Apalachocoli there are 13,152 Christianized Indians to whom I administered the holy sacrament of confirmation. They are fleshy, and rarely is there a small one, but they are weak and phlegmatic as regards work, though clever and quick to learn any art they see done, and great carpenters as is evidenced in the construction of their wooden churches which are large and painstakingly wrought. The arms they employ are bow and arrows and a hatchet they call *macâna*. They go naked, with only the skin [of some animal] from the waist down, and, if anything more, a coat of serge without a lining, or a blanket. The women wear only a sort of tunic that wraps them from the neck to the feet, and which they make of the pearl-colored foliage of trees, which they call *guano* and which costs them nothing except to gather it. Four thousand and eighty-one women, whom I found in the villages naked from the waist up and from the knees down, I caused to be clothed in this grass like the others.

Their ordinary diet consists of porridge which they make of corn with ashes, pumpkins, beans which they call *frijoles,* with game and fish from the rivers and lakes which the well-to-do ones can afford. Their only drink is water, and they do not touch wine or rum. Their greatest luxury is [a drink] which they make from a weed that grows on the seacoast, which they cook and drink hot and which they call *cazina*. It becomes very bitter and is worse than beer, although it does not intoxicate them and is beneficial. They sleep on the ground, and in their houses only on a frame made of reed bars, which they call *barbacôa,* with a bear skin laid upon it and without any cover, the fire they build in the center of the house serving in place of a blanket. They call the house *bujío*. It is a hut made in round form, of straw, without a window and with a door a *vara* high and half a *vara* wide. On one side is a granary supported by 12 beams, which they call a *garita,* where they store the wheat, corn and other things they harvest.

During January they burn the grass and weeds from the fields preparatory to cultivation, surrounding them all at one time with fire so that the deer, wild ducks and rabbits, fleeing from it fall into their hands. This sort of hunting they call *hurimelas*. Then they enter the forests in pursuit of bears, bison and lions which they kill with bows and arrows, and this they call *ojêo*. Whatever they secure in either way they bring to the principal cacique, in order that he shall divide it, he keeping the skins which fall to his share. Offering is made to the church of the best parts, and this serves for the support of the missionary priest, to whom they are in such subjection that they obey his orders without question.

In April they commence to sow, and as the man goes along opening the trench, the woman follows sowing. All in common cultivate and sow the lands of the caciques. As alms for the missionaries and the needy widows, they sow wheat in October and harvest it in June. This is a crop of excellent quality in the province of Apalache, and so abundant that it produces seventy *fanegas* [a *fanega* is about a bushel and a half], from one *fanega* sown.

Each village has a council house called the great *bujío,* constructed of wood and covered with straw, round, and with a very large opening in the top. Most of them can accommodate from 2,000 to 3,000 persons. They are furnished all around the interior with niches called *barbacôas,* which serve as beds and as seats for the caciques and chiefs, and as lodgings for soldiers and transients. Dances and festivals are held in them around a great fire in the center. The missionary priest attends these festivities in order to prevent indecent and lewd conduct, and they last until the bell strikes the hour of *las ánimas* [the *de profundis* bell].

These Indians do not covet riches, nor do they esteem silver or gold, coins of which do not circulate among them, and their only barter is the exchange of one commodity for another, which exchange they call *rescate.* The most common articles of trade are knives, scissors, axes, hoes, hatchets, large bronze rattles, glass beads, blankets, which they call *congas,* pieces of rough cloth, garments and other trifles.

As to their religion, they are not idolaters, and they embrace with devotion the mysteries of our holy faith. They attend mass with regularity at 11 o'clock on the holy days they observe, namely, Sunday, and the festivals of Christmas, the Circumcision, Epiphany, the Purification of Our Lady, and the days of Saint Peter, Saint Paul and All Saints Day, and before entering the church each one brings to the house of the priest as a contribution a log of wood. They do not talk in the church, and the women are separated from the men; the former on the side of the Epistle, the latter on the side of the Evangel [Gospel]. They are very devoted to the Virgin, and on Saturdays they attend when her mass is sung. On Sundays they attend the *Rosario* and the *Salve* in the afternoon. They celebrate with rejoicing and devotion the Birth of Our Lord, all attending the midnight mass with offerings of loaves, eggs and other food. They subject themselves to extraordinary penances during Holy Week, and during the 24 hours of Holy Thursday and Friday, while our Lord is in the Urn of the Monument, they attend standing, praying the rosary in complete silence, 24 men and 24 women and the same number of children of both sexes, with hourly changes. The children, both male and female, go to the church on work days, to a religious school where they are taught by a teacher whom they call *Athequi* of the church; [a person] whom the priests have for this service; as they have also a person deputized to report to them concerning all parishioners who live in evil.

Your Majesty's most humble servant and chaplain.
Gab'l Bishop of Cuba.

11. Fernando del Bosque's Account of the First High Mass in Texas, May 16, 1675

THE first authentic report of the celebration of Mass on the soil of Texas is found in the diary of Fernando del Bosque (d. c. 1700). Repeated requests for missionaries from the native tribes who lived beyond the Rio Grande and the insistence of Fray Juan Larios, O.F.M., were the incentives for a formal expedition. While the Bosque-Larios undertaking across the Rio Grande was not large in size, it was, nonetheless, important. It was the earliest well-authenticated expedition on record to cross that river from the south. On May 16, 1675, the party was at a place which they called San Ysidro and which must have been on one of the branches of the Nueces River. Concerning this episode Carlos E. Castañeda has said: "In the above statement about this being the first High Mass, the reason why it was not mentioned before, was, perhaps, the fact that they did not consider it extraordinary to hold regular low Mass. It is to be noted particularly in the description . . . concerning the administration of the Sacrament of Baptism, that contrary to the grossly inaccurate assertion that the missionaries, in their zeal and fervor, often baptized thousands of Indians without giving them adequate instruction to prepare them for the sacrament, Father Larios refused to baptize them 'until they knew their prayers.'" *Our Catholic Heritage in Texas, 1519–1936* (Austin, 1936), I, 240. Source: Herbert Eugene Bolton (Ed.), "Diary of Fernando del Bosque, 1675," *Spanish Exploration in the Southwest, 1542–1706* (New York: Charles Scribner's Sons, 1916), p. 301; now included in *Original Narratives of Early American History,* copyright Barnes & Noble, Inc., New York.

In said post and river of San Ysidro . . . on the 16th day of said month and year I, said lieutenant *alcalde mayor,* certify that this day there was erected in said post a portable altar, and that it was prepared to say mass; and at a signal made with a small bell the people came to hear it. It was chanted by the father commissary missionary, Fray Juan Larios, and was attended by all the people. After it was concluded they asked the said father to baptize them; and when they were given to understand by him through an interpreter that he could not baptize them until they knew their prayers, to console them he baptized fifty-five infants, the Spaniards acting as their godfathers.

They were instructed in the doctrine, and counted, and the people of the four chiefs [Xoman, Terrodan, Teaname, and Teimamar] were found to comprise four hundred and twenty-five warriors and seven hundred and forty-seven women, boys, and girls, of all ages, making in all eleven hundred and seventy-two persons.

In said post of San Ysidro, on said day, month, and year, I, said lieutenant *alcalde mayor,* put the father commissary, Fray Juan Larios, in possession of his office and of the administration in said post, in virtue of a royal provision and of licenses. . . . Of this legal record was made in his despatches, following the rest of the ecclesiastical despatches regarding this settlement.

12. Report of Eusebio Francisco Kino on the Missions of Pimería Alta (Arizona) in 1710

FATHER EUSEBIO KINO, S.J. (1644–1711), and his companions entered Pimería Alta in 1687. Pimería Alta, the home of the Upper Pimas, extended from the valley of the Alta River to that of the Gila and thus included that part of southern Arizona which was later contained in the Gadsden Purchase. In 1687 Kino established the mission of Nuestra Señora de los Dolores more than 100 miles south of Tucson. This mission became his headquarters for twenty-four years of exploration, missionary activity, and writing. Operating from this base, Kino crossed the line into Arizona and founded the Missions of San Xavier del Bac. Guévavi, and Tumacácori. The "Favores celestiales," a manuscript history by Kino of the work of himself and his associates in Pimería Alta, was discovered in 1915 by Bolton and edited by him. In the following selection from an account written in 1710, Kino summarized his efforts with a statement of possibilities for future development. Source: Herbert Eugene Bolton (Ed.), *Kino's Historical Memoir of Pimería Alta. A Contemporary Account of the Beginnings of California, Sonora, and Arizona by Father Eusebio Francisco Kino, S.J. . . . 1683–1711* (Cleveland: Arthur H. Clark Co., 1919), II, 234–253.

Beginnings and Progress of the New Conquests and New Conversions of the Heathendoms of This Extensive Pimería and the Other Neighboring New Nations

It is well known that during almost two whole centuries the royal Catholic crown of Spain has spent more than two millions and a half for new conquests and new conversions and for the extension of the Holy Evangel [Gospel], and for the eternal salvation of the souls of the Californias; but it appears that, thanks be to His Divine Majesty, the blessed time is now coming when not only the conquest and conversion of the Californias is being accomplished, but also at the same time that of these other neighboring extensive lands and nations of this North America, most of which has hitherto been unknown, and when the Lord is adding to the rather poor lands of the Californias the necessary succor of these very extensive and rich lands, abundant champaigns, and fertile rivers and valleys. . . .

As soon as I knew that the conversion of coveted California was suspended, I asked and obtained from my superiors and his Excellency permission to come meanwhile to these heathen coasts nearest to and most in sight of California, to the Guaimas and Seris; and I having arrived at the end of February, 1687, in this province of Sonora, and gone to Opossura to see the Father Visitor, Manuel Gonzales, his Reverence came with me to this post of heathen Pimas, as the father of Cucurpe, near by, Joseph de Aguilar, was asking of him a father for them. We named the place Nuestra Señora de los Dolores. It is in thirty-two degrees and a half of latitude. We entered March 12, 1687, accompanied by Father Joseph de Aguilar and his servants; and the father visitor returning the following day to observe Holy Week in his pueblos, I went inland two hours after his departure and with said Father Joseph de Aguilar and some guides, going ten leagues beyond Nuestra Señora de los Dolores, toward the west, to the good post and valley which we named de San Ygnacio, where we found even more people, although they were somewhat scattered. We returned by the north through the ranchería of Himeres, which we named San Joseph, and through that of Doagibubig, which we named Nuestra Señora de los Remedios, which rancherías immediately, thanks be to the Lord, we began reducing to new good pueblos, making a beginning of teaching them the Christian Doctrine and prayers, by means of a good interpreter and a good native helper, whom I procured from the old Pima mission of Los Ures, and of the building of the churches and houses, of crops, etc.

Afterward I made other missions, or expeditions, to the north and farther to the west, and despatched friendly messages inviting all the heathen of these environs to receive our holy Catholic faith for their eternal salvation, in imitation of these Pimas, their relatives and countrymen. Soon many came from various parts to see me for this purpose, and we arranged for the beginning of other new missions and pueblos. There came to see and to visit us, with great comfort on our part and his Father Manuel Gonzáles. He asked and obtained, through the Señor alcalde mayor, four additional alms from the royal chest, for four other new missions for this extensive Pimería; and four other missionary fathers came to it at the time when I dedicated this my first and capacious church of Nuestra Señora de los Dolores. . . .

In general, in these twenty-one years, up to the present time, I have made from the first pueblo of Nuestra Señora de los Dolores more than forty expeditions to the north, west, northwest, and southwest, of fifty, eighty, one hundred, two hundred, and more leagues, sometimes accompanied by other fathers, but most of the time with only my servants and with the governors, captains, and caciques of different rancherías or incipient pueblos from here and from the interior. . . .

With all these expeditions or missions which have been made to a distance of two hundred leagues in these new heathendoms in these twenty-one years, there have been brought to our friendship and to the desire of receiving our holy Catholic faith, between Pimas, Cocomaricopas, Yumas, Quiquimas, etc., more than thirty thousand souls, there being sixteen thousand of Pimas alone. I have solemnized more than four thousand baptisms, and I could have baptized ten or twelve thousand Indians more if the lack of father laborers had not rendered it impossible for us to catechise them and instruct them in advance. But if our Lord sends, by means of his royal Majesty and of the superiors, the necessary fathers for so great and so ripe a harvest of souls, it will not be difficult, God willing, to achieve the holy baptism of all these souls and of very many others, on the very populous Colorado River, as well as in California Alta, and at thirty-five degrees latitude and thereabouts, for this very great Colorado River has its origin at fifty-two degrees latitude.

And here I answer the question asked of me in the letter of the Father Rector Juan Hurtasum, as to whether some rivers run into the North Sea or all empty into the Sea of California, by saying that as this Colorado River, which is the Rio del Norte of the ancients, carries so much water, it must be that it comes from a high and remote land, as is the case with the other large volumed rivers of all the world and terraqueous globe; therefore the other rivers of the land of fifty-two degrees latitude probably have their slope toward the Sea of the North, where Husson wintered. Some more information can be drawn from the maps which I add to this report; and in order not to violate the brevity which I promised herein, I will add only that in regard to the fourteen journeys for two hundred leagues to the northwest, I have written a little treatise of about twenty-five sheets which is entitled "Cosmographical Proof that California is not an Island but a Peninsula," etc.; and that of these new discoveries and new conversions in general, by order of our Father-General, Thirso Gonzales, I am writing another and more extensive treatise, with maps, of which more than one hundred sheets are already written. By suggestion of his Reverence it is entitled "Celestial Favors of Jesus Our Lord, and of Mary Most Holy, and of the Most Glorious Apostle of the Indies, San Francisco Xavier, experienced in the New Conversions of these New Nations of these New Heathendoms of this North America."

13. Junípero Serra's Farewell to the Old World, August 20, 1749

ON THE eve of his departure for the new world Fray Junípero Serra (1713–1784) wrote a letter from Cádiz to his confrere though no relation in which he spoke his farewells to his parents, friends, and all his acquaintances. Leaving behind a promising career as a preacher and a professor of theology in his native island of Mallorca, Serra took literally the words of our Lord and lived them: "No man putting his hand to the plough, and looking back, is fit for the kingdom of God" (Lk. 9:62). The principal cities of California, founded as missions by Father Serra, stand today as monuments to his faith and zeal. Source: Antonine Tibesar, O.F.M. (Ed.), *The Writings of Junípero Serra* (Washington: Academy of American Franciscan History, 1955), I, 3–9.

Jesus, Mary, Joseph!

Very dear Friend in Jesus Christ, Father Francesch Serra:

I am writing this letter in farewell, while we are getting ready to leave the city of Cádiz and embark for Mexico. The day fixed upon is unknown to me, but the trunks containing our baggage are locked and strapped and they say that after two, three, or possibly four days, the ship called *Villasota,* in which we are to embark, will sail. We had thought it would be sooner, as I wrote; it was to be about Saint Bonaventure's day, but it has been put off till now.

Friend of my heart, on this occasion of my departure, words cannot express the feelings of affection that overwhelm me. I want to ask you again to do me the favor of consoling my parents who, I know, are going through a great sorrow.

I wish I could give them some of the happiness that is mine; and I feel that they would urge me to go ahead and never to turn back.

Tell them that the dignity of Apostolic Preacher, especially when united with the actual duty, is the highest vocation they could have wished me to follow.

After all, considering their old age, their life is far spent. Beyond any doubt, the remainder is short, and should they compare it with eternity, they will see that it is no more than an instant. If this be so, it is very important, and according to God's Will, that they lay no store by the little help I might be to them. And so they will merit from God, our Lord, that if we are no more to see each other in this world, we will be united forever in eternal glory.

Tell them how badly I feel at not being able to stay longer and make them happy as I used to do. Anyhow they know quite well that first things come first; and our first duty, undoubtedly, is to do the Will of God. Nothing else but the love of God has led me to leave them. And if I, for love of God and with the help of His grace, can muster courage to leave them, might I not suggest that they also, for the love of God, be content to forego the happiness of my presence?

Let them listen attentively to the advice they will receive on this matter from their Father Confessor; and they will see, in fact, that now God has truly entered their home. By practicing holy patience and resignation to the Divine Will, they will possess their souls, and attain eternal life.

They should hold nobody but Our Lord God alone responsible for the separation. They will find how sweet His yoke can be; that what they now consider and endure as a great sorrow will be turned into a lasting joy. Nothing in this life should cause us sadness. Our clear duty is to conform ourselves in all things to the Will of God, and to prepare to die well. That is what counts: nothing else matters. If this is secured, it matters little if we lose all the rest; without this all else is useless.

Happy they to have a son a priest — however bad and sinful — who, every day, in the holy Sacrifice of the Mass, prays for them, as best he can; and very often offers for them exclusively his Mass so that the Lord send them help, that they be not without the necessities of life; that He grant them the grace of patience in their trials, of resignation to His holy Will, peace and union with their neighbors, courage to resist the temptations of the devil, and finally, at the proper time, a happy death, in His holy grace.

If, by the help of God's grace from above, I succeed in being a good religious, these prayers of mine will be all the more powerful and my parents will be the first to profit from them. And the same is to be said as regards my younger sister in Christ, my Juana, and my brother-in-law Miquel; therefore they should remember me for the sole purpose of recommending me to God that I be a good priest, and a good minister of God. That is what counts, and in that they should all be interested.

I well remember that, while assisting my father (I was already a religious at the time) when he had taken so severely ill that Extreme Unction became advisable — convinced he was to die and the two of us being alone, he said to me:

"Son, what I am most anxious about is that you be a good religious of our Father Saint Francis."

Well, father, rest assured that I keep your words always before me, just as if I hear them from your mouth, at this very moment. But bear well in mind that it is to become a good religious that I have undertaken this voyage.

You must not feel bad, then, that I am doing your will, which is, at the same time, the Will of God. As regards my mother, I know well that she has never missed offering up her prayers for me to God for the same purpose — that I be a good religious. No wonder, then, my dear mother, that God, granting your prayers, directed me in this way. Rest satisfied then with the way in which God has disposed matters. In all your troubles say always: "Blessed be God, and His Holy Will be done!"

And Juana, my sister, knows that, a short time ago, she was at the door of death, and that the Lord, by the merits and the intercession of His most blessed Mother Mary, granted her a complete recovery of health. Had she died at that time, she would not now be worrying whether I be in Mallorca or not. Anyway, she should give thanks to the Lord for whatever He does. Now, whatever He wills is always for our good; and in all probability the Lord gave her complete recovery of health so that she might be a consolation for the old folk, against the time I had to leave them.

Let us bless God who loves and cares for us all. Of Miquel, my brother-in-law, and of Juana, my sister, I have a great favor to ask — they know what it is. May they ever continue to live together in perfect peace and love and, at the same time, by showing great reverence and patience, be the consolation of the old folk; and take good care of the education of their children. In a word, foster within yourselves a love of going to church, of receiving frequently the Sacraments of Confession and Communion, of making the Way of the Cross; in short, be zealous Christians.

I know quite well that just as they have always asked God's help for me — so they will continue to do the same in the future. Thus it will come about that by praying for one another — I for them, they for me — the selfsame Lord will protect us all, and grant all of us His holy grace in this life, and, at the end of it, eternal glory.

Good-by, my father! Good-by, my mother! Good-by, Juana, my sister; Good-by, brother Miquel! Take good care of Miquelet; may he be a good Christian and a good pupil at school; likewise the two little girls, may they be good Christians. And have confidence in God from now on their Senor uncle will be there to help them. Good-by, Good-by!

My very dear brother, Father Serra, good-by to you. My letters, from now on, will be less frequent. In fact, to cheer them up and encourage the old folk, my sister and her husband, I relied first of all on our good friendship existing also between them and you; and then Father Vicar, Father Guardian and Father Master also. You all must act in place of a letter from me. If the Father Vicar and Father Master could be present when this letter is read, my parents would be so happy. But don't let anybody else be present, only these four: I mean father, mother, sister, and brother-in-law.

But if one more is to be admitted to hear this letter, let it be Cousin Juana, our neighbor, and give her from me my kindest greetings. Also to Cousin Roig, her husband; to Aunt Apolonia; Boronada, Xurxa, and all my other relatives.

My greetings to each one of the members of the Community of Petra, without any exception whatever, especially to Fray Antonio Vivés.

My Greetings to Doctor Fiol and his Brother Señor Antonio, his father and his family.

My very special greetings to Amón Raphael Moragués Casta, and his wife. To Doctor Moragués, his brother and Señora Moragués, likewise the same to Doctor Serralta. To Señor Vicari Perello, Señor Alzamora, Señor Juan Nicoláu and to the Regidor Bartolomé, his brother and the whole family. In short: to all my friends.

Please tell Father Vicar that I think the book will be returned to Señor Negra, if it has not yet arrived from Madrid when I leave; I asked the Fornaris, when they return to Mallorca, to bring it with them. Ask him, too, to promote devotion to my Saint Francisco Solano.

I am enclosing also a letter from Medo Maxica, a neighbor of the monastery. It comes from her son, Sebastián, who came back from the Indies, and he seems to me to be in the best of health.

To conclude: May the Lord bring us all together in eternal glory, and, for the time being, keep Your Reverence for many more years: that is my prayer in this House of the Holy Mission, in the city of Cádiz, August 20, 1749.

Professor Palóu sends to Your Reverence many greetings; you will be so kind as to forward the same, from both of us, to Señor Guillerm Roca and to his family.

Your cordial friend in Christ,
Fray Junípero Serra,
a most unworthy priest.

14. Concordat Between the Franciscans and Dominicans Dividing the California Missions, April 7, 1772

ALTHOUGH Don José de Gálvez, the visitor general of the King of Spain, had contended that there was no need in California for the Dominican friars, the latter secured a decree from the king that missions should be assigned to their order without prejudice to the Franciscans of the College of San Fernando. In the concordat, the text of which follows, the Dominicans agreed to take charge of the missions of southern [Lower] California while the Franciscans were to retain those in the area of what is the present United States from San Diego to San Francisco and beyond. Source: Herbert Eugene Bolton (Ed.), *Historical Memoirs of New California by Fray Francisco Palóu, O.F.M. . . .* (Berkeley: University of California Press, 1926), I, 236–240.

Most Excellent Sir:

Fray Rafael Verger, present guardian of the College *de propaganda fide* of San Fernando in Mexico, and Fray Juan Pedro de Iriarte, minister of the Holy Order of Preachers and commissary of the mission which, by order of his Majesty (God save him) be conducted to this kingdom for the Peninsula of California, in obedience to the superior decree of your Excellency of the 1st of April of the present year of 1772, in which you order them to divide between themselves, and for their respective missionaries, the missions of the Peninsula of California, in accordance with the royal decree done at Madrid on April 8, 1770, desire to say: that they have come to the conclusion, after repeated conferences upon the subject, that it is the earnest will of our sovereign and Catholic monarch that the Dominican fathers shall enter the said Peninsula of California, with their commissary, the above-mentioned master Fray Juan Pedro de Iriarte, since he so commanded in his royal decree of November 4, 1768, and lately in the one mentioned of April 8, 1770, in which, after having ordered and commanded the division spoken of, he concludes by repeating the same order. This he does notwithstanding the adverse reports of His Excellency the Marquis de Croix, predecessor of your Excellency, and of the visitor-general, Don José de Gálvez, for he thinks it not best for his royal service that one Order, and much less one monastery or college, should occupy a peninsula so extensive as the one under discussion.

At the same time it is taken into consideration that this one college has to-day in its charge not only the entire Peninsula, but also all the country that has been discovered from the port of San Diego to that of San Francisco, making about two hundred leagues of *terra firma.* And it is also borne in mind that this division ought to be, according to the royal decree, with distinct frontiers for each Order, and with such separateness and difference of field that they shall not encroach upon each other, in order to avoid in this way dissensions that might arise from the opposite arrangement. It is likewise considered that the main body of the Peninsula, on account of the nature of its territory, does not permit a variety of fields, for, indeed, it has only one frontier, that of San Fernando Vellicatá, since the place called San Juan de Diós, which was thought to be suitable for another frontier, is not (according to Captain Don Fernando Rivera y Moncada, who has examined it all repeatedly) sufficient for even a ranch, in which several fathers of this College agree. We explain this to your Excellency with all humility, so that you may not uselessly spend time and the funds of the pious donations.

In view of all the aforesaid, and desiring to faithfully carry out the sovereign will of our Catholic monarch, we have agreed upon the following division: The Dominican fathers shall take in their charge the old missions which this College has in California and the above-mentioned frontier of San Fernando Vellicatá, extending their new conversions in this direction until they reach the confines of the mission of San Diego on the harbor of that name; and, placing their last mission on the arroyo of San Juan Bautista, this mission shall terminate five leagues farther on, at a point which projects from the Sierra Madre and ends before reaching the beach. Once arrived there, they can turn to the east, slightly to the northeast, and in this way they ought to come out at the head of the Gulf of California and the Colorado River, following afterwards the direction pointed out to them by your Excellency in the royal council. And if in the country between the Colorado and San Diego a suitable road to the north or northeast should appear, they can also take it without prejudice to the other Order. It is agreed that the fathers of the College of San Fernando shall retain the missions that they now have, from the port of San Diego, following the road which they have opened to Monterey, the port of San Francisco, and farther on.

In this way, most Excellent Sir, it will be arranged so that the long coast of Southern California and the *terra firma* that follows it shall not be in charge of one Order alone, which appears to be the principal purpose of our sovereign, and at the same time that the two Orders of Dominican and Franciscan fathers shall have in it their separate spheres. We do not hold it improper that the College of San Fernando shall resign these missions, for by no other way can the principal end of his Majesty be fulfilled. For this reason the father guardian gives them up, hoping that with the vigorous measures which your Excellency has taken, the new conversions from the port of San Diego to Monterey may succeed, and that you will also take care that a sufficient number of cattle and sheep for a start shall be sent to each of the new missions, as I [Father Verger] beg your Excellency in the memorial which I presented on October 26, 1771.

Since this conquest is of such great importance and consequence as his Majesty states in the royal decree cited, he will not lift his powerful hand without bringing it to a perfect conclusion, even in case (which God forbid) that some misfortune has happened in the port of San Diego, or in one of the other missions. For the reasons expressed they humbly beg your Excellency to give your approbation to the agreement, and that you will at the same time order that it be duly put into effect, giving to each one a certified copy, with the decision of your Excellency, by which they will be favored.

Mexico, April 7, 1772.

Fray Rafael Verger,
Guardian,
Fray Juan Pedro de Iriarte,
Vicar-General.

15. Junípero Serra Makes His Final Report on the Mission of San Carlos de Monterey, July 1, 1784

WE PREVIOUSLY met Junípero Serra as a young man of thirty-six on the eve of his departure for the New World in August, 1749 (No. 13). In the document that follows we find him signing his final missionary report. In the thirty-five years that had intervened this intrepid missionary had traveled thousands of miles on foot, founded nine of California's twenty-one missions, and brought hundreds of pagan Indians into the Catholic Church. This report on San Carlos de Monterey is one of the best factual surveys we possess of his efforts, illustrating as it does, the number of Indians who were made Christians with a description of the religious practices of the neophytes, the daily life as lived by the friars and Indians at the missions, and the hardships endured from the elements and from enemies. Eight weeks after the document was signed the great missionary, worn out by his unremitting and exhaustive labor in behalf of the Indians of Mexico and of Lower and Upper California, died on August 28, 1784, at his beloved San Carlos de Monterey where his remains lie buried beneath the sanctuary floor of the mission church. Source: Manuscript in the possession of the Academy of American Franciscan History.

Hail Jesus, Mary, Joseph!

On the most solemn feast of the Holy Spirit, Pentecost Sunday, June 3, 1770, this mission of San Carlos de Monterey was founded to the joy of the sea and land expeditions. In a short time the rejoicing was shared by the entire kingdom and eagerly celebrated in both Spains.

On that day, after imploring the assistance of the Holy Spirit, the sacred standard of the cross was blessed, raised, and adored by all. The ground was blessed, an altar set up, and a sort of chapel formed with naval flags. The holy sacrifice of the Mass was sung, a sermon was preached, and, at the end, the *Te Deum* was intoned. With these (ceremonies), possession was duly taken of Monterey for (our) holy Church and the crown of Spain. A legal document covering all was drawn up and will be found where it belongs. All this occurred on the beach at the landing place of the said port, the same spot on which one hundred sixty-seven years before, as it is written, the expedition of Don Sebastián Vizcaino had celebrated Mass.[1]

The following day, after choosing the most likely spot on that plain,

---

[1] Don Sebastián Vizcaino (1550?–1615) and his exploring party entered Monterey Bay on December 16, 1602.

the construction of the presidio was enthusiastically begun by the men of both sea and land forces. By the fourteenth of the same month, the most solemn feast of Corpus (Christi), a chapel had been built, as well as it could be, at the spot in the presidio which it still occupies, and a high Mass was sung with the Blessed Sacrament exposed in its monstrance. After the Mass there was a procession, in which His Sacramental Majesty passed over the ground that till then had been so heathen and miserable. It was a day of great consolation for all of us who were Christians.

So the presidio was begun but the troop was too small to be divided into two bodies. Thus we, the religious, were forced to establish ourselves in and remain incorporated with this presidio until further arrangements [could be made], even though we knew that there we could do no sowing or any other kind of work.

We remained like this for one year, spending the time putting in order our residence and the most necessary storerooms for our supplies and in making friends with the Indians who were coming to see us; and we tried to win some children. In fact, within a short time, we baptized three and when the boat returned at the end of the year [1771], we had already twenty new Christians at Monterey. As ten religious came on this vessel, we were then twelve. We all dressed in rich chasubles and had a most solemn procession for Corpus (Christi). We had here the vestments for future missions, the men from the ship, and those of the land force, etc. Thanks be to God!

In August, 1771, with the express consent of His Excellency, Marquis de Croix,[2] at that time viceroy of New Spain, and of the Illustrious Inspector General, Don José de Gálvez,[3] both of whom officially informed me about this, San Carlos Mission was begun at the site it now occupies on the banks of Carmel River and in view of the sea at the distance of about a cannon shot where it forms the little bay south of Point Pinos. [The mission is] a little more than a league from the royal presidio, which is to the north in latitude 36°44″. The next place to the south is San Antonio [Mission], about twenty-five leagues away. Santa Clara [Mission] is in the opposite direction and a little farther away.

On the twenty-fourth of the said month, the feast of St. Bartholomew, the apostle, the holy cross was set up at the site and the first

[2] Marquis Carlos Francisco de Croix served as Viceroy of New Spain during the years 1765–1771.

[3] Don José de Gálvez (1720–1787), an energetic explorer and administrator, was very helpful to Serra and the missionaries in his office of Inspector General of New Spain.

Mass celebrated under a temporary arbor. For four months only one father stayed here with the personnel doing the building. The other priest with the two missionaries destined for the future San Luis [Obispo] Mission remained at the presidio until Christmas Eve that same year. After previously transferring everything belonging to the mission, we left the presidio on foot and arrived here with an escort of eight men: four soldiers, one muleteer, and three servants [who had been] sailors. When we received our share of the stock, after the division, there were great and small eighteen head of cattle; namely, nine cows, one bull, two heifers, and six small calves. That is all the cattle of that which the mission has and all which the mission has spent. I will write further on about the rest.

The eight remaining days of the year were spent in fiestas and in putting things in order.

1772

This mission's baptisms numbered twenty-three. In the last half of the past year, we added only three and in the whole of this year only eight, because the scarcity of provisions which had been severe during the two preceding, this year became even more critical for no boat reached [Monterey]. Neither of the two which came were able to proceed here and ported at San Diego.

We passed the time erecting around [the buildings] a stockade of stout, closely set palings, with ravelins in the corners of the square. We also finished the buildings, added some [new ones], and started a garden to help with its vegetables. No sowing at all was done in this whole year.

Before definitely establishing [the mission] here, the first concern was to have men familiar with farming see and state whether it would be easy or difficult to take water from the river for irrigating these lands. All agreed that it would be [easy]. Now when we tried to carry it out, they all reversed themselves and declared it impossible. This was the chief, if not the only, reason why there was a delay about the sowing for which we longed. Finally, in the next year, and thereafter, we determined to dry farm, which was both wise and fruitful as shall be seen from the harvests of the following years.

This year we got news of the arrival of both vessels at San Diego, at a time when scarcity had brought the greatest distress to the presidio and the two missions, this one and San Antonio, which had been founded one year earlier. Father President Fray Junípero Serra decided to accompany Commander Don Pedro Fages[4] on the trip to San

[4] Don Pedro Fages, commandant at Monterey, was later Governor of California.

Diego in order to use his influence also in procuring aid for the religious and missions.

He left this mission for that trip on St. Bartholomew's day, August 24, the first anniversary of the first Mass at this site, as was stated above. On his way he founded, September 1, Mission San Luis Obispo, in the same place where it is today, under such circumstances of want of the necessary supplies that it should have been considered rashness had it not been justified by charity and trust in God, who in fact, did not abandon the agents of such a holy enterprise as He had promised everyone: "He who trusts in Him shall not be confounded."

When the commander and the father president arrived at San Diego, they sent by land what small aid the fewness of mules permitted and it was decided that one of the boats would return to San Blas, while the other would attempt to go on to Monterey. In fact, it reached there at the end of the same year.

The father president, considering that the state of things demanded better provision for the maintenance and advancement of these new establishments, sacrificed himself to the advice of the religious present, to go to Mexico to seek aid from His Excellency, the new viceroy.[5] He sent from there a religious, who would take his place here, and gave him strict orders to trust in the Lord and proceed with the work of God in things both spiritual and temporal, etc. The father [president] embarked in the middle of October and the other came up to take his place. The vessel arrived at the end of the year with the regular provisions.

1773

In this year, there were one hundred thirty-four baptisms, which with the thirty-one preceding total one hundred sixty-five. Twenty-six marriages of new Christians were celebrated. With the two that they had before, these made twenty-eight neophyte families belonging to this mission.

Towards the end of last year, three pecks and one quart of wheat had been sowed with great difficulty and on ground only half cultivated, because as yet there was no way to plow. Despite the entire absence of irrigation they harvested five bushels, four pecks, and three quarts of good wheat. From half a quart of barley, they gathered three pecks, and from two pecks of Indian corn, four and one-half bushels.[6]

[5] Don Antonio Maria Bucareli y Ursúa was Viceroy of New Spain from September, 1771, to his death in Mexico City on April 9, 1779.

[6] The original uses the Spanish terms: *fanega, almud,* and *quartillo,* for which there is no exact English equivalent. Each Spanish measure, however, was several times larger than the English measure given here.

Horse beans, chick peas, and beans, a little of each were also sowed, but all [this] was lost. Such was the first sowing and harvest of this mission.

In this whole year, no boat at all came, even though His Excellency, the viceroy, had ordered one to set out from San Blas with the usual provisions, while better arrangements were being made. This was not carried out and since the number of religious was increased by those who had come from Lower California after they had turned their missions over to the Reverend Dominican Fathers, the privations which they suffered were most severe. Even so, the ministers of this mission kept intact the above-mentioned harvest in order to sow it all the following year, which they did.

While in this and the rest of the missions they were suffering such want, in Mexico provisions were being ordered with the greatest enthusiasm and being sent to San Blas for the prosperity of these new establishments. By December, the Father President, Fray Junípero, was again in San Blas for his return trip in the new frigate, *Santiago,* which was loaded with every good thing as no other boat that ever came to this land before or since.

1774

The frigate, *Santiago,* sailed from San Blas, January 25, 1774, and, having favorable stern winds for several days, it arrived at the port of San Diego, March 13, or in less than a month and a half. These circumstances could have brought the boat to Monterey, but it was better this way, for this place was thus succored en route as was the expedition of Don Juan de Anza,[7] which had just arrived, hungry and in great need at San Gabriel Mission.

The father president disembarked and made the rest of the trip by land, so that he could see the missions and his religious brethren. The frigate and his reverence arrived at Monterey at almost the same time to the great consolation of the entire land, for then the famine, privations, and shortages were ended. In fact, they have not returned since.

It would not be out of place to specify the provisions which, out of pure charity and without charge, His Excellency, the viceroy, sent on this occasion for these missions: corn, beans, flour, hams, clothing for the Indians, beads, etc., but suffice it to say that [the missions] were abundantly supplied and equipped to begin and to continue their

---

[7] Don Juan Bautista de Anza (1735–1788), born in Sonora, led several expeditions from Mexico to California and was later Governor of New Mexico.

spiritual and temporal labors as they did with great success. Thanks be to God!

In this mission they had one hundred two baptisms, which added to the preceding made a total of two hundred sixty-seven. There were six marriages for a total of thirty-four. Work on the land consisted in sowing the above-mentioned wheat harvest. From it, without irrigation, one hundred twenty-five bushels were gathered this year. From three short pecks of barley, twenty bushels were reaped; from six pecks of beans, five bushels, seven pecks; from eight pecks of corn, one hundred fifty bushels, three pecks; and from one peck of horse beans, one bushel; total three hundred one bushels.

This year we began to profit by the help of the six servants granted to us by His Excellency, the viceroy. We got some capable farm hands from the boat, and oxen were broken; hence, more land was prepared for the year

1775

The baptisms this year were one hundred one, which added to the preceding made a total of three hundred sixty-eight. The marriages were thirty-five, which also added to the preceding made a total of sixty-nine families.

The grain harvest this year reached a total of seven hundred nine bushels, six and one-half pecks. From one bushel of barley, one hundred seven bushels, ten pecks, and one quart were gathered and measured; from one bushel of fine wheat, sixty-three bushels, twenty and one-half pecks; from six bushels of [ordinary] wheat, three hundred fifty-three bushels, four and one-half pecks; from ten pecks of corn, after very severe damage, one hundred fourteen bushels; and the rest was garden vegetables: beans, lentils, horse beans, chick peas, and a few peas. The entire harvest came without any irrigation.

During this whole year, like last, this mission maintained seven religious and quite a few [Lower] California Indians destined for future missions. Though the king had assigned a double ration for each religious, during a five year period, to date this mission has not received this ration for even one day, nor for any religious. Though I suppose the gentlemen who have administered the royal property will have notified their superiors of the merit of this saving in their accounts, nevertheless, it is but fair that we also speak up that their honors may be increased! They also have other merits in this line. Now that the missions are on their feet we can give thanks to the gentlemen!

At the end of this year the destruction of San Diego Mission took place, a tragedy in which we all shared.[8] Blessed be God!

1776

There were seventy-one baptisms during this year, which added to the preceding made four hundred thirty-nine Christians. The marriages were twenty-two and with the preceding they made ninety. In this way, Christianity was gradually progressing in proportion to the means available in the following years, 1777, 78, 79, and 80. At the end of this last [year] we reached six hundred thirty-eight baptisms and one hundred sixty-two marriages.

During all this time we failed to get water for irrigation, even though we took extreme steps. On this account, the harvests were diverse since they depended on the rain. There were two years in which we had scarcely harvested four hundred bushels of all grains, from which we had to take the seed which was to be sown in the following year. This left very little for so many people and in one year we had recourse to Mission San Luis [Obisp] to which this [mission] paid one hundred thirty pesos in cash.

In the other years the harvest was sufficient because even though the Indian corn was never abundant, since it was sowed too late for the rains, its place was taken by barley of which we regularly gathered from two hundred to four hundred and more bushels.

In the earlier years of this period, this mission had to transport and supply [grain] as best it could, for the fathers who founded the mission of our father, St. Francis, in the year 1776.

In the middle of this year, the father president embarked for the restoration of San Diego Mission and the reestablishment of San Juan Capistrano. Both were set up successfully because of the favorable provisions made by the Knight Commander, His Excellency Viceroy Bucareli may he be with God.

The following year, Mission Santa Clara was founded and its father ministers, too, quitted San Carlos where they had resided for more than two years. This mission did well while consuming the abundant supplies which the father president had brought for it from Mexico. But they served the purpose for which they came which was the propagation of our Catholic faith.

Meanwhile, noting the little security and the lack of protection afforded by the dwellings and other buildings no matter how much these were plastered with mud, we started to make buildings of adobes

---

[8] San Diego was destroyed by fire by the Indians in November, 1775.

and gradually those were erected which are now in use and which are listed at the end of this report.

In 1778, the father president made another voyage to San Diego to administer confirmation there and, on his return trip, at the rest of the missions. The apostolic faculty to confirm had come to him this year on the same boat.

He started the voyage on St. Bartholomew's day, August 24, and he returned by land, after he had accomplished his task, December 23, the same year. During this and other similar trips, this mission had always had at least two religious.

The year after the destruction of San Diego, this mission also was menaced with several rumors that a similar misfortune was being prepared for it by the pagans known as Sanjones, old and powerful enemies of the natives of this territory. On one occasion the indications appeared so certain that on his own initiative the sergeant, who commanded the presidio in the absence of the captain at San Diego, came with quite a force and begged us religious to sleep in one place so that we could be more easily protected. They locked the seven of us in the adobe blacksmith shop, the safest place, and there, packed together, we spent the night while the soldiers passed it in the saddle, patrolling the vicinity, but no enemy showed up, nor did any later evidence appear to prove that any such danger had existed. Those who were then painted to us as such enemies are almost all Christians today. So, we pass on to the year

1781

The supplies from the preceding harvest, that were used in the beginning of this year, were sufficient and the planting of barley, wheat, and some garden vegetables promised a harvest in accordance with the amount of water. Nevertheless, the hope [persisted] of bringing water with all the possibilities of irrigation, especially for the corn which for lack of water was valueless as a crop. Father Juan Crespí,[9] now deceased, decided to try to get water. He realized through his surveys that at least for irrigating the land so far cultivated, he could get water from a point closer than the one he had until then considered. The enterprise was started with such confidence of success that corn was sown where it was thought it could be irrigated.

When there were but a few days left [of Father Crespí's work], the famous steward of San Luis Obispo came to our house offering

[9] Juan Crespí, O.F.M. (1721–1782), had been a student of Serra's; he was a favorite of the founder of the missions and had acted as assistant to him at Monterey and Carmel.

to take the same job at this mission. He started May 1, at a salary of two hundred pesos in cash, etc. He saw and approved the work that the two fathers were doing toward extracting water and, after stating that within three days we would see the corn irrigated, he went out one morning and without saying anything to us, he took the people from the work and set them to digging another ditch a few yards further up the river, claiming that what had been done previously was valueless and, with that, the corn sown was lost and he spent seven months and used all the workmen in the new ditch.

Not a grain of corn was gathered and they got a little over four hundred bushels of barley. Because of the folly of this man, a great part of the wheat was lost in the fields. Less than four hundred bushels were obtained, when to be conservative we should have expected more than five hundred. But finally the water was extracted that same year in the month of December. From then on the mission has had irrigation. Thanks be to God!

This year there were only twenty-four baptisms and seventeen marriages. We sowed in a proper manner for the

Year 1782

Towards the end of the past year, thirty-one bushels of barley were sown and fifty-three of wheat. The barley was planted where the water could not reach it and as the drought was great, it was lost. This had never happened before in the case of this grain. We gathered only one hundred seven bushels.

The wheat which was irrigated did well but less was harvested than in the preceding year for the same reason and there were large stretches of sown land where [the major domo] did not attempt to gather a single head. There was a task that they were completing in less than an hour and, to make it shorter, they gathered only the tall ears and even so it took them a long time. A great many of the people got sick and the [steward] asked permission to betake himself to Mission San Luís Obispo, because they had sent to tell him that he was needed there. Leaving the wheat in the fields and the people down he departed and never returned.

The harvested wheat threshed out at four hundred fifty bushels. There were twenty-seven bushels of garden vegetables and one hundred sixty of Indian corn. These are the results of the first year of irrigation and such an intelligent steward.

In things spiritual it was better. We had one hundred and one baptisms and twenty-three marriages. The people gradually improved in health, even though some of them died, and without any steward, good or bad, we sowed for the

Year 1783

We can consider this the happiest year of the mission because the number of baptisms was one hundred seventy-five and of marriages thirty-six.

The sowing of all grains amounted to eighty-four bushels, eight pecks. This included one bushel and a half of wheat, half a bushel of corn, and two pecks of beans, which were sown for the [Lower] California Indians, who had moved here and were married in this mission.

And the harvest, less the amount of forty-seven bushels which belonged to these Indians and other concessions made to the people such as a portion of the barley which they might reap and some twenty bushels of wheat from the chaff of the threshing, which was stored in the mission granaries amounted to twenty-six hundred fourteen and a half bushels, that is, of measured barley six hundred seventy bushels, eight hundred thirty-five of wheat, only two hundred according to our estimate are kept in the ear. There were nine hundred seventy-one bushels of corn of both kinds according to our estimate, sixty-three bushels of peas, sixteen bushels of horse beans, four bushels of lentils, and fifty-three bushels of various kinds of beans.

Today the new Christians of this mission number six hundred fourteen living persons, even though some of them take a leave of absence from time to time. They have been maintained and are maintained without any scarcity and we supplied the quartermaster of the presidio of San Carlos with one hundred thirty bushels of Indian corn; because they did not ask for more, also with thirty bushels of beans. The escort of this mission, at the request of the ensign quartermaster, received rations in these two kinds of grain. There have not been other deliveries of consequence so that in our prudent judgment of the two chief commodities, wheat and corn, about half the amount harvested may still remain.

The value of the food supplied to the presidio has been paid already in cloth, which now covers the Indians who grew the crops, but at that we are still distressed at the sight of so much nudity among them.

We do not get clothing now from the soldiers, as we did formerly, not even from those who have debts to us no matter how small. The wool, which in some of the missions is enough to cover Indian nakedness, here has not been any help to us so far, because the thefts of sheep are so numerous that already for more than three years, we can not exceed two hundred head between goats and sheep, and from shearing the few that we have we get nothing worthwhile.

The condition, then, of the Mission in things spiritual is that up to this day in this Mission:

Baptisms	1,006
Confirmations	936
And since those of the other missions belong in some way to this it is noted in passing that their number is	5,307
Marriages in this mission	259
Burials	356

The number of Christian families living at the mission and eating jointly, as well as widowers, single men, and children of both sexes, is evident from the enclosed census lists and so is omitted here.

They pray twice daily with the priest in the church. More than one hundred twenty of them confess in Spanish and many who have died used to do it as well. The others confess as best they can. They work at all kinds of mission labor, such as farm hands, herdsmen, cowboys, shepherds, milkers, diggers, gardeners, carpenters, farmers, irrigators, reapers, blacksmiths, sacristans, and they do everything else that comes along for their corporal and spiritual welfare.

The work of clearing the fields once, sometimes twice, or even three times a year, is considerable because the land is very fertile. When we clear new land great hardship is required. Altogether there is sufficient land cleared for sowing more than one hundred bushels of wheat, and it is sowed in that grain, barley, vegetables, and corn. Every year we clear a little more.

To the seven months' work required to take water from the river for irrigation, as mentioned above, we must add the labor of bringing it to the lagoon near the mission residence. In some years, this lagoon used to be dry. Now it is always full, making it a great convenience and a delight to the mission. Some salmon have been placed in the pool and so we have it handy.

The timber palisade was inadequate to protect the seed grain because they steal the paling for firewood. So we dug a circular trench many thousands of varas[10] long. This was a two years' labor and withal nothing sufficed to prevent losses every year.

Some of the land which we cleared for farming was not only covered with long tough grasses and thickets but also with great trees, willows, alders, and so forth, and it has been hard work, as we have

[10] The Spanish *vara* was equivalent to about 2.8 feet.

already noted, but we hope that it will pay off at a profit. We also have a sizable walled garden [which produces] abundant vegetables and some fruit.

MISSION BUILDINGS

In the first few years we worked hard and well on the church and the rest of the buildings. [They were made] of paling with flat earthen roofs to minimize fire danger, but no matter what we did they always leaked like a sieve and between that and the humidity everything would rot. So we decided to build of adobe and thus today all buildings are [of that material] They are as follows:

An adobe church, forty by eight varas, with a thatched roof.

Likewise, the three-room residence of the three priests. One [room is] large, with an alcove for a bed. The floor is plain earth and the roof thatched.

Also, a granary about twenty varas long with several small compartments, a porch, and a thatched roof.

Likewise, another granary about thirty varas long with its porch and four wooden barred windows. The floor is plain earth and the roof thatched.

Also, another adobe house, thirty varas long, divided for the present into only three sections: one serves as a storeroom, another at the opposite end is used as a dormitory for the girls; the center section is a large room with two barred windows and doors. It is white-washed and clean and is used as a guest chamber for the ships' officers and for some other occasions. It is going to be divided into two rooms for which we already have the two doors with their hinges.

Likewise, another adobe building with an earthen roof and with its own shed and key. It houses the forge where the blacksmith works. It has a porch and window.

Also, next to this building is another which we call the carpenter shop. It has a room with a separate door and key for safeguarding the tools. It has two windows with bars and a door.

Likewise, another building next to the ones just mentioned where the women grind [grain], make cheese, and where different tools are kept.

Also, another building, larger than the preceding ones, where for the present the family of the Mexican blacksmith lives.

Likewise, four adobe buildings a little further on, which are [a place for] five carts, the wood shed, kitchen, and a hen house.

Also, there is a serviceable adobe corral with sections for sheep and goats and next to this a separate pen for pigs. The rest of the corrals for horses and cattle, with their corresponding stud and bull stalls, are all made of paling and from time to time give us quite a bit of repair trouble.

THE ANIMALS

number today:

Cattle, large and small	500
Sheep and goats, about the same number of each	220
Riding and draft mules	18
Tame and broken horses	20
Four herds of mares with their colts	90
Also with them, two young mules from the time we had a jack	
One old ass that may be with foal	1
Pigs	25

ACCOUNTS

Regarding the remainder of the status of the mission, [we note] that when the vessels arrive from Mexico with the supplies we know whether we have credits or debits from our stipends. This year the [boats] have not yet reached here, so we do not have this information.

We know of no local debts but there may be some hidden or unexpected debt like those we have had in the past.

The mission paid Lieutenant Ortega[11] eighteen pesos for a tent from the King's stores, which was given the father president for use when he was at San Buenaventura Mission, and while he assisted at the foundation of the new presidio of Santa Barbara. He did not think such a debt existed until they came to collect it.

Not long ago this mission paid fifteen pesos as a donation for the war, more than a year after the conflict ended,[12] as a result of misinformation given the commandancy general to the effect that the father president had excluded from the count some Indians who had run away from the mission after the lists had been completed. This was not true, for when we made the lists everyone of them had been apostates for at least two years and some for more than three. He mentioned them only as an incentive so that they might return them [to the mission] for me.

---

11 José Francisco Ortega (d. 1798) was a Mexican-born soldier who rose to the rank of brevet captain in the Spanish colonial forces.

12 The preliminary articles of peace between Great Britain and Spain were signed on January 20, 1783.

We did not even think about mentioning those who ran away, nor those who died, after the lists were made, nor did we discount them, but just the same we paid the fifteen pesos and the [entire] donation amounted to over one hundred pesos, the sum they finally asked for. At the beginning of the year when the governor showed me these [directions for] reports, inventories, and census lists, of the missions [that were] to be sent to the commandancy general, I told him that I would care for it gladly, since the reverend father guardian of my holy college[13] had given me the same order.

But, that it had to be on condition, that the papers and letters for those documents would be post free, for I had received a letter from the commander general of much less bulk than any of these reports and it bore the notation: eleven reales. What would so many papers cost?

He answered me that yes [they were post free] and, in fact, the ensign always urged me to accept [such] letters saying, even in writing, that the figures in question had reference to other accounts and that I would not have to pay it.

With that assurance, I went ahead certain that the envelope which came from San Gabriel entitled: "Reports, Inventories, and Census List of San Gabriel Mission" [was free even though] there was a notation, twenty reales, which I have kept by accident. Despite this, a few days ago we received a bill from the quartermaster for twenty-five pesos, two reales for [postage on] letters sent to the mission. They were the creditors and they collected. All we need now is some other arbitrary debt unknown to us.

What we get in the annual distributions purchased in Mexico with our stipends is known already. After using enough for our clothing, chocolate, wine, and candles for Mass, and some minor objects for the church, the rest goes for the Indians, especially for clothing to cover them. So far as we can see, nothing more need be said on this point.

If anything else should be made known about the administration and state of the mission, it can be asked of us specifically and with assurance that we will hide nothing, for thanks to the goodness of God we do not fear the light, and, since what has been said so far is true, we the ministers of the mission sign it, July 1, 1784.

Fray Junípero Serra — Fray Mathías Antonio de Santa Cathalina Noriega [rubrica].

---

13 The College of San Fernando in Mexico City had been formally established in 1733.

THE FRENCH COLONIES

16. "Instructions for the Fathers of Our Society Who Shall be Sent to the Hurons," by Jean de Brébeuf, S.J., 1637

ONE of the most resplendent periods in the history of French Catholicism occurred in the seventeenth century, and no finer pages in that history have been written than those which describe the heroic sacrifices made by the French Récollets, Jesuits, and other missionary priests in their efforts to win the Indians of France's North American colonies to the Catholic faith. That effort began in what is today Canada, but as time went on it was extended to areas south and west that embraced large sections of the present United States. Among the leaders of the Jesuits was an intrepid Norman, Jean de Brébeuf (1593–1649), who entered upon his extraordinary missionary career in 1625 at the age of thirty-two, and who persisted amid almost incredible suffering and privation until he was captured, tortured, and put to death in 1649 by a roving band of Iroquois in a raid on St. Ignatius and St. Louis Missions near Georgian Bay. Brébeuf had worked with the Huron Indians for several years and he could thus enlighten his confreres as to how they should conduct themselves among the savages. The following account was written in 1637 and foreshadowed the life of self-denial that awaited the missionaries. It was incorporated into the relation for 1637 by Paul le Jeune, S.J. St. Jean de Brébeuf was canonized by Pope Pius XI in 1930, along with seven of his fellow Jesuit martyrs of North America, of whom three met their deaths within the area of the present Diocese of Albany, New York. Source: Reuben Gold Thwaites (Ed.), *The Jesuit Relations and Allied Documents* (Cleveland: Burrows Brothers Co., 1898), XII, 117–123.

The Fathers and Brethren whom God shall call to the Holy Mission of the Hurons ought to exercise careful foresight in regard to all the hardships, annoyances, and perils that must be encountered in making this journey, in order to be prepared betimes for all emergencies that may arise.

You must have sincere affection for the Savages, — looking upon them as ransomed by the blood of the son of God, and as our brethren with whom we are to pass the rest of our lives.

To conciliate the Savages, you must be careful never to make them wait for you in embarking.

You must provide yourself with a tinder box or with a burning mirror, or with both, to furnish them fire in the daytime to light their pipes, and in the evening when they have to encamp; these little services win their hearts.

You should try to eat their sagamité or salmagundi in the way they prepare it, although it may be dirty, half-cooked, and very tasteless. As to the other numerous things which may be unpleasant, they must be endured for the love of God, without saying anything or appearing to notice them.

It is well at first to take everything they offer, although you may not be able to eat it all; for, when one becomes somewhat accustomed to it, there is not too much.

You must try and eat at daybreak unless you can take your meal with you in the canoe; for the day is very long, if you have to pass it without eating. The Barbarians eat only at Sunrise and Sunset, when they are on their journeys.

You must be prompt in embarking and disembarking; and tuck up your gowns so that they will not get wet, and so that you will not carry either water or sand into the canoe. To be properly dressed, you must have your feet and legs bare; while crossing the rapids, you can wear your shoes, and, in the long portages, even your leggings.

You must so conduct yourself as not to be at all troublesome to even one of these Barbarians.

It is not well to ask many questions, nor should you yield to your desire to learn the language and to make observations on the way; this may be carried too far. You must relieve those in your canoe of this annoyance, especially as you cannot profit much by it during the work. Silence is a good equipment at such a time.

You must bear with their imperfections without saying a word, yes, even without seeming to notice them. Even if it be necessary to criticise anything, it must be done modestly, and with words and signs which evince love and not aversion. In short, you must try to be, and to appear, always cheerful.

Each one should be provided with half a gross of awls, two or three dozen little knives, called jambettes (pocket-knives), a hundred fishhooks, with some beads of plain and colored glass, with which to buy fish or other articles when the tribes meet each other, so as to feast the Savages; and it would be well to say to them in the beginning, "Here is something with which to buy fish." Each one will try, at the portages, to carry some little thing, according to his strength; however little one carries, it greatly pleases the Savages, if it be only a kettle.

You must not be ceremonious with the Savages, but accept the comforts they offer you, such as a good place in the cabin. The greatest conveniences are attended with very great inconvenience, and these ceremonies offend them.

Be careful not to annoy anyone in the canoe with your hat; it would be better to take your nightcap. There is no impropriety among the Savages.

Do not undertake anything unless you desire to continue it; for example, do not begin to paddle unless you are inclined to continue paddling. Take from the start the place in the canoe that you wish to keep; do not lend them your garments, unless you are willing to surrender them during the whole journey. It is easier to refuse at first than to ask them back, to change, or to desist afterwards.

Finally, understand that the Savages will retain the same opinion of you in their own country that they will have formed on the way; and one who has passed for an irritable and troublesome person will have considerable difficulty afterwards in removing this opinion. You have to do not only with those of your own canoe, but also (if it must be so stated) with all those of the country; you meet some to-day and others to-morrow, who do not fail to inquire, from those who brought you, what sort of man you are. It is almost incredible, how they observe and remember even the slightest fault. When you meet the Savages on the way, as you cannot yet greet them with kind words, at least show them a cheerful face, and thus prove that you endure gayly the fatigues of the voyage. You will thus have put to good use the hardships of the way, and already advanced considerably in gaining the affection of the Savages.

This is a lesson which is easy enough to learn, but very difficult to put into practice; for, leaving a highly civilized community, you fall into the hands of barbarous people who care little for your Philosophy or your Theology. All the fine qualities which might make you loved and respected in France are like pearls trampled under the feet of swine, or rather of mules, which utterly despise you when they see that you are not as good pack animals as they are. If you go naked, and carry the load of a horse upon your back, as they do, then you would be wise according to their doctrine, and would be recognized as a great man, otherwise not. Jesus Christ is our true greatness; it is He alone and His cross that should be sought in running after these people, for, if you strive for anything else, you will find naught but bodily and spiritual affliction. But having found Jesus Christ in His Cross, you have found the roses in the thorns, sweetness in bitterness, all in nothing.

17. "How Father Jogues was Taken by the Hiroquois, and What He Suffered on his First Entrance into Their Country," by Jerome Lalemant, S.J., 1647

AMONG the most famous of the Jesuit missionaries in colonial times was St. Isaac Jogues (1607–1646). In his search for Indian converts Jogues became one of the first white men to penetrate inland as far as Sault Ste. Marie on Lake Superior where in October, 1641, he and Charles Raymbault, S.J., preached to the savages. Upon his return to the west after a visit to Quebec, Jogues was captured by the Mohawks in August, 1642, and for over a year he was forced to endure almost superhuman tortures at their village of Ossernenon near the present Auriesville, New York. Through the intervention of the Dutch he was finally released and taken to New Amsterdam and thus became the first Catholic priest to visit the future New York City. After some months in his native France the missionary returned to the New World in the spring of 1644. In spite of warnings about the dangers due to the restive state of the western tribes, he undertook another missionary journey westward in the autumn of 1646. He was captured by the Iroquois and once more taken to Ossernenon where after further cruelties he was put to death on October 18, 1646. One of his confreres, Jerome Lalemant, incorporated the following vivid description of Jogues' sufferings and martyrdom in the account which he forwarded to the Jesuit superior in 1647. Source: Reuben Gold Thwaites (Ed.), *The Jesuit Relations and Allied Document* (Cleveland: Burrows Brothers Co., 1898), XXXI, 17–119.

Father Isaac Jogues had sprung from a worthy family of the City of Orleans. After having given some evidences of his virtue in our Society, he was sent to New France, in the year 1636. In the same year, he went up to the Hurons, where he sojourned until the thirteenth of June in the year 1642, when he was sent to Kebec [Quebec] upon the affairs of that important and arduous Mission.

From that time until his death, there occurred many very remarkable things, — of which one cannot, without guilt, deprive the public. . . .

The Reverend Father Miersome L'alemant [*sic*], at that time Superior of the Mission among the Hurons . . . sent for him, and proposed to him the journey to Kebec, — a frightful one, on account of the difficulty of the roads, and very dangerous because of the ambuscades of the Hiroquois, who massacred, every year, a considerable number of the Savages allied to the French. Let us hear him speak upon this subject and upon the result of his journey. "Authority having made me a simple proposition, and not a command, to go down to Kebec, I offered myself with all my heart. . . . So there we were, on the way and in the dangers all at once. We were obliged to disembark forty times, and forty times to carry our boats and all our baggage amid the currents and waterfalls that one encounters on this journey of about three hundred leagues. . . . At last, thirty-five days after our departure from the Hurons, we arrived, much fatigued, at Three Rivers; thence we went down to Kebec. . . . Our affairs being finished in fifteen days, we solemnly observed the feast of St. Ignace; and the next day, the first of August in the same year 1642, we left Three Rivers, in order to go up again to the country whence we came. The first day was favorable to us; the second caused us to fall into the hands of the Hiroquois. We were forty persons, distributed in several canoes; the one which kept the vanguard, having discovered on the banks of the great river some tracks of men, recently imprinted on the sand and clay, gave us warning. A landing was made; some say that these are footprints of the enemy, others are sure that they are those of Algonquins, our allies. In this dispute, Eustache Ahatsistari . . . exclaimed: 'Be they friends or enemies, it matters not; I notice by their tracks that they are not in greater number than we; let us advance and fear nothing.' We had not yet made a half-league,[1] when the enemy, concealed among the grass and brushwood, rises with a great outcry, discharging at our canoes a volley of balls. The noise of their arquebuses so greatly frightened a part of our Hurons that they abandoned their canoes and weapons in order to escape by flight into the depth of the woods. . . . We were four French, — one of whom, being in the rear, escaped with the Hurons, who abandoned him before approaching the enemy. Eight or ten, both Christians and Catechumens, joined us . . . they oppose a courageous front to the enemy. . . . But, having perceived that another band — of forty Hiroquois, who were in ambush on the other side of the river — was coming to attack them, they lost courage; insomuch that those who were least entangled fled. . . . A Frenchman named René Goupil, whose death is precious before God . . . was surrounded and captured, along with some of the most courageous Hurons. I was watching this disaster," says the Father, "from a place very favorable for concealing me from the sight of the enemy . . . but this thought could never enter my mind. 'Could I, indeed,' I said to myself, 'abandon our French and leave those good Neophytes and those poor Catechumens, without giving them the help which the Church of my God has entrusted to me?' Flight seemed horrible to me. 'It must be,' I said in my heart, 'that my body suffer

[1] The old French *lieue,* mentioned many times in these French documents, was the equivalent of about 2.76 miles.

the fire of earth, in order to deliver these poor souls from the flames of Hell; it must die a transient death, in order to procure for them an eternal life.' My conclusion being reached without great opposition from my feelings, I call the one of the Hiroquois who had remained to guard the prisoners. . . . He advances and, having seized me, puts me in the number of those whom the world calls miserable. . . . Finally, they brought that worthy Christian Captain named Eustache, who, having perceived me, exclaimed, 'Ah, my Father, I had sworn and protested to you that I would live or die with you.' The sight of him piercing my heart, I do not remember the words that I said to him. Another Frenchman, named Guillaume Couture, seeing that the Hurons were giving way, escaped like them into the great forests; and, as he was agile, he was soon out of the enemy's grasp. But, remorse having seized him because he had forsaken his Father and his comrade, he stops quite short, deliberating aside with himself whether he should go on or retrace his steps. The dread of being regarded as perfidious makes him face about; he encounters five stout Hiroquois. One of these aims at him, but, his arguebus having missed fire, the Frenchman did not miss him, — he laid him, stone-dead, on the spot; his shot being fired, the other four Hiroquois fell upon him with a rage of Lions, or rather of Demons. Having stripped him bare as the hand, they bruised him with heavy blows of clubs. . . . In short, they pierced one of his hands with a javelin, and led him, tied and bound in this sad plight, to the place where they were. Having recognized him, I escaped from my guards and fall upon his neck. . . . The Hiroquois, seeing us in these endearments, at first remained quite bewildered, looking at us without saying a word; then, all at once, — imagining, perhaps, that I was applauding that young man because he had killed one of their Captains, — they fell upon me with a mad fury, they belabored me with thrusts and with blows from sticks and war-clubs, flinging me to the ground, half dead. When I began to breathe again, those who had not struck me, approaching, violently tore out my finger-nails; and then biting, one after another, the ends of my two forefingers, destitute of their nails, caused me the sharpest pain — grinding and crushing them as if between two stones, even to the extent of causing splinters or little bones to protrude. They treated the good René Goupil in the same way, without doing, at that time, any harm to the Hurons. . . .

"As I saw them engrossed in examining and distributing our spoils, I sought also for my share. I visit all the captives; I baptize those who were not yet baptized; I encourage those poor wretches to suffer with constancy, assuring them that their reward would far exceed the severity of their torments. I ascertained on this round of visits, that we were twenty-two captives, without counting three Hurons killed on the spot. . . . So there we were, on the way to be led into a country truly foreign. Our Lord favored us with his Cross. It is true that, during the thirteen days that we spent on that journey, I suffered in the body torments almost unendurable, and, in the soul, mortal anguish; hunger, the fiercely burning heat, the threats and hatred of those Leopards, the pain of our wounds, — which, for not being dressed, became putrid even to the extent of breeding worms, — caused us, in truth, much distress. But all these things seemed light to me in comparison with an inward sadness which I felt at the sight of our earliest and most ardent Christians of the Hurons. I had thought that they were to be the pillars of that rising Church, and I saw them become the victims of death. The ways closed for a long time to the salvation of so many peoples, who perish every day for want of being succored, made me die every hour, in the depth of my soul. . . .

"Eight days after our departure from the shores of the great river of the saint Lawrence, we met two hundred Hiroquois, who were coming in pursuit of the French, and of the Savages, our allies. At this encounter we were obliged to sustain a new shock. It is a belief among those Barbarians that those who go to war are the more fortunate in proportion as they are cruel toward their enemies; I assure you that they made us thoroughly feel the force of that wretched belief.

"Accordingly, having perceived us, they first thanked the Sun for having caused us to fall into the hands of their Fellow-countrymen. . . . That done, they set up a stage on a hill; then, entering the woods, they seek sticks or thorns, according to their fancy. Being thus armed, they form in line, — a hundred on one side, and a hundred on the other, — and make us pass, all naked, along that way of fury and anguish. . . . I had not accomplished the half of this course when I fell to the earth under the weight of that hail and of those redoubled blows. . . . Seeing, then, that I had not fallen by accident, and that I did not rise again for being too near death, they entered upon a cruel compassion; their rage was not yet glutted, and they wished to conduct me alive into their country. . . . I would be too tedious if I were to set down in writing all the rigor of my sufferings. . . .

"I had always thought, indeed, that the day on which the whole Church rejoices in the glory of the blessed Virgin — her glorious and triumphant Assumption — would be for us a day of pain. . . . We arrived on the eve of that sacred day at a little river, distant from the first village of the Hiroquois about a quarter of a league. We found on its banks, on both sides, many men and youth, armed with sticks which they let loose upon us with their accustomed rage. . . .

"After they had glutted their cruelty, they led us in triumph into that first village; all the youth were outside the gates, arranged in a line, — armed with sticks and some with iron rods, which they easily secure, on account of their vicinity to the Dutch. . . . We were following one another at an equal distance; and, that our executioners might have more leisure to beat us at their ease, some Hiroquois thrust themselves into our ranks in order to prevent us from running and from avoiding any blows. . . . Such was our entrance into Babylon. . . .

"Evening having come, they made us descend, in order to be taken into the cabins as the sport of the children. They gave us for food a very little Indian corn, simply boiled in water; then they made us lie down on pieces of bark, binding us by the arms and the feet to four stakes fastened in the ground in the shape of St. Andrew's Cross. . . . Oh, my God, what nights! To remain always in an extremely constrained position; to be unable to stir or to turn, under the attack of countless vermin which assailed us on all sides; to be burdened with wounds, some recent and others all putrid; not to have sustenance for the half of one's life; in truth, these torments are great, but God is infinite. At Sunrise they led us back upon our scaffold, where we spent three days and three nights in the sufferings that I have just described.

"The three days having expired, they paraded us into two other villages, where we make our entrance as into the first . . . these villages are several leagues distant from one another. . . . The sentence decreed in the Council is intimated to me; the following night is to be (as they say) the end of my torments and of my life. My soul is well pleased with these words, but not yet was my God, — he willed to prolong my martyrdom. Those Barbarians reconsidered the matter, exclaiming that life ought to be spared to the Frenchmen, or rather, their death postponed. They thought to find more moderation in our forts, on account of us. . . ."

When these poor captives had recovered a little of their strength, the principal men of the country talked of conducting them back to Three Rivers, in order to restore them to the French. . . . But, as their captors could not agree, the Father and his companions endured, more than ever, the pangs of death. Those Barbarians are accustomed to give prisoners, whom they do not choose to put to death, to the families who have lost some of their relatives in war. These prisoners take the place of the deceased, and are incorporated into that family, which alone has the right to kill them or let them live . . . but when they retain some public prisoner, like the Father, without giving him to any individual, this poor man is every day within two fingerlengths of death. . . .

The young Frenchman who was the Father's companion was accustomed to caress the little children, and to teach them to make the sign of the Cross. An old man, having seen him make this sacred sign upon the forehead of his grandson . . . said to a nephew of his: "Go and kill that dog . . . that act will cause some harm to my grandson." Father Jogues . . . wished to forewarn and strengthen his poor companion. He leads him to a grove near the village, and explains to him the dangers in which they stood. . . . While they were returning . . . the nephew of that old man, and another Savage, armed with hatchets and watching for an opportunity, go to meet them. Having approached them, one of these men says to the Father, "March forward," and at the same time he breaks the head of poor René Goupil, who, on falling and expiring, pronounced the Holy Name of Jesus. . . . "Give me a moment's time," the Father said to them, supposing that they would accord him the same favor as to his companion. . . . "Get up," they reply; "thou wilt not die this time. . . ."

That young man, or that blessed martyr, being thus slain, the Father returns to his cabin; his people apply their hands to his breast, in order to feel whether fear did not agitate his heart. Having found it steady, they said to him: "Do not again leave the village, unless thou art accompanied by some one of us; they intend to beat thee to death; look out for thyself. . . ."

They gave their poor Father to some families, to serve them as a menial in their hunts; he follows them at the approach of Winter and makes thirty leagues with them, serving them through two months, as a slave. All his clothes sheltered him no more than would a shirt and sorry pair of drawers; his stockings and his shoes made like tennis slippers, and of a leather just as thin, without any soles, — in a word, he was all in rags. . . . As they did not account him fit for hunting, they gave him a woman's occupation, — that is, to cut and bring the wood to keep up the cabin fire. The chase beginning to furnish supplies, he could to some extent repair his strength, — meat not being stinted to him; but when he saw that they were offering to the Demon of the chase all that they took, he told them plainly that he would never eat of flesh sacrificed to the devil. He therefore contented himself with a little very thin sagamité, that is to say with a little indian meal boiled in water; and even then he had it but seldom, because, gorged with meat, they despised their dry cornmeal. . . .

From the month of August to the end of March, the Father was every day in the pains and terrors of death. A lesser courage had died a hundred times, from apprehension. It is easier to die all at once than to die a hundred times. Toward the end of April, a Savage Captain from the country of the Sokokuois appeared in the land of the Hiroquois, laden with presents, which he came to offer for the ransom and deliverance of a Frenchman named Ondesson, — thus the Hurons and the Hiroquois named Father Jogues. . . . This embassy gave some credit to the Father, and caused him to be regarded for a short time with more compassionate eyes; but those Barbarians, having accepted the gifts, nevertheless did not set him at liberty, — violating the law of nations, and the law accepted among all these tribes. . . .

About that time, — some Hiroquois Captains going to visit some small nations which are, as it were, tributary to them, in order to get some presents, — that man who had the Father in custody, being of the party, led him in his train; his design was to display the triumphs of the Hiroquois over even the nations which are in Europe. . . . The Father's fatigues in that journey of more than eighty leagues were fully soothed and rewarded by the salvation of his Benefactor. . . .

Upon the return from this journey, they command the Father to go and accompany some fishermen, who conducted him 7 or 8 leagues below a Dutch settlement. While he was engaged in that exercise, he learned from the lips of some Hiroquois who came to that quarter that they were awaiting him in the village to burn him. This news was the occasion of his deliverance. . . . The Dutch having given him the opportunity to enter a ship, the Hiroquois complained of it; — he was withdrawn thence and conducted to the house of the Captain, who gave him in custody to an old man, until they should have appeased those Barbarians. . . . Now, while they were awaiting the opportunity to send him back to Europe, he remained six weeks under the guard of that old man, who was very miserly, and lodged him in an old garret. . . . [Here follows a description of Jogues's journey to and stay at New Amsterdam.]

Finally, the Governor of the country, sending a bark of one hundred tons to Holland, sent the Father back at the beginning of the month of November . . . [and] on the fifth of Janaury in the year 1644, in the morning, he was knocking at the door of our College at Rennes. . . . He made no long sojourn in France; the Spring of the year 1644, having come, he betook himself to la Rochelle in order to cross back to the country of his martyrdom, — where, having arrived, he was sent to Montreal. . . . Peace being made with the Hiroquois . . . the Father was taken from Montreal, to go and lay the foundations of a Mission in their country, which was named "The Mission of the martyrs." . . . On the sixteenth of May, 1646, this good Father left three rivers in company with Sieur Bourdon, the engineer of Monsieur the Governor. . . . Sieur Bourdon has told me that this good Father was indefatigable; that they suffered extremely on that road of iron. In short, they arrived at three rivers, — having accomplished their embassy, — on the day of Saint Peter and Saint Paul, the 29th of the month of June.

Hardly had the poor Father been refreshed among us two or three months, when he recommenced his expeditions; on the twenty-fourth of September in the same year, 1646, he embarks with a young Frenchman, in a canoe conducted by some Hurons, in order to return to the land of his crosses. He had strong premonitions of his death. . . . We have learned that he was slain directly upon his entrance into that country full of murder and blood: here follows a letter announcing this, from the Governor of the Dutch to Monsieur the Chevalier de Mont-Magny. . . .

"For the rest, I have not much to tell you, except how the French arrived, on the 17th of this present month of October, 1647, at the fort of the Maquois. . . . The very day of their coming, they began to threaten them, — and that immediately, with heavy blows of fists and clubs, saying: 'You will die tomorrow: be not astonished. But we will not burn you; have courage; we will strike you with the hatchet and will set your heads on the palings,' (that is to say, on the fence above their village) 'so that when we shall capture your brothers they may still see you.' You must know that it was only the nation of the bear which put them to death; the nations of the wolf and the turtle did all that they could to save their lives, and said to the nation of the bear: 'Kill us first.' But, alas! they are not in life for all that. Know, then, that on the 18th, in the evening, when they came to call Isaac to supper, he got up and went away with that Barbarian to the lodge of the bear. There was a traitor with his hatchet behind the door, who, on entering, split open his head; then immediately he cut it off, and set it on the palings. The next day, very early, he did the same to the other man, and their bodies were thrown into the river. Monsieur, I have not been able to know or to learn from any Savage why they have killed them. . . ."

Such is, word for word, what the Dutch have written concerning the death of Father Isaac Jogues. . . .

18. France's Representatives Take Formal Possession of the Western Country, June 4, 1671

IN THE late seventeenth century the colonial rivalry of the European powers had grown more pronounced in North America as it had elsewhere. As a consequence France decided to tighten its hold upon the western reaches of its empire, and in June, 1671, an elaborate ceremony was held at Sault Ste. Marie which signalized the new policy of the French government. The ceremony was likewise intended to impress the native peoples with the power and majesty of King Louis XIV. Claude Dablon, S.J. (1618–1697), the superior of the Jesuit missions, was, of course, aware of the significance of all this, and in the report which he submitted for that year he gave a description of the share which the famous missionary, Claude Allouez, S.J. (1620–1689), had in the Sault Ste. Marie ceremony with extracts from his confrere's speech to the Indians on that occasion. It affords an interesting example, among other things, of the united action of Church and State in the French colonies of the seventeenth century. Source: Reuben Gold Thwaites (Ed.), *The Jesuit Relations and Allied Documents* (Cleveland: Burrows Brothers Co., 1899), LV, 105–115.

It is not our present purpose to describe this ceremony in detail, but merely to touch on matters relating to Christianity and the welfare of our Missions, which are going to be more flourishing than ever after what occurred to their advantage on this occasion.

When Monsieur Talon, our Intendant, returned from Portugal, and after his shipwreck, he was commanded by the King to return to this country; and at the same time received his Majesty's orders to exert himself strenuously for the establishment of Christianity here, by aiding our Missions, and to cause the name and the sovereignty of our invincible Monarch to be acknowledged by even the least known and the most remote Nations. These commands, reinforced by the designs of the Minister, — who is ever equally alert to extend God's glory, and to promote that of his King in every land, — were obeyed as speedily as possible. Monsieur Talon had no sooner landed that he considered means for insuring the success of these plans, — choosing to that end sieur de Saint Lusson, whom he commissioned to take possession, in his place and in his Majesty's name, of the territories lying between the East and the West, from Montreal as far as the South sea, covering the utmost extent and range possible.

For this purpose, after wintering on the Lake of the Hurons, Monsieur de saint Lusson repaired to sainte Marie du Sault early in May of this year, sixteen hundred and seventy one. First, he summoned the surrounding tribes living within a radius of a hundred leagues, and even more; and they responded through their Ambassadors, to the number of fourteen Nations. After making all necessary preparations for the successful issue of the whole undertaking to the honor of France, he began, on June fourth of the same year, with the most solemn ceremony ever observed in these regions.

For, when all had assembled in a great public council, and a height had been chosen well adapted to his purpose, — overlooking, as it did, the Village of the people of the Sault, — he caused the Cross to be planted there, and then the King's standard to be raised, with all the pomp that he could devise.

The Cross was publicly blessed, with all the ceremonies of the Church, by the Superior of these Missions; and then, when it had been raised from the ground for the purpose of planting it, the *Vexilla* was sung. Many Frenchmen there present at the time joined in this hymn, to the wonder and delight of the assembled Savages; while the whole company was filled with a common joy at the sight of this glorious standard of JESUS CHRIST which seemed to have been raised so high only to rule over the hearts of all these poor peoples.

Then the French Escutcheon, fixed to a Cedar pole, was also erected, above the Cross, while the *Exaudiat* was sung, and prayer for his Majesty's Sacred person was offered in that far-away corner of the world. After this, Monsieur de saint Lusson, observing all the forms customary on such occasions, took possession of those regions, while the air resounded with repeated shouts of "Long live the King!" and with the discharge of musketry, — to the delight and astonishment of all those peoples, who had never seen anything of the kind.

After this confused uproar of voices and muskets had ceased, perfect silence was imposed upon the whole assemblage; and Father Claude Allouez began to Eulogize the King, in order to make all those Nations understand what sort of a man he was whose standard they beheld, and to whose sovereignty they were that day submitting. Being well versed in their tongue and in their ways, he was so successful in adapting himself to their comprehension as to give them such an opinion of our incomparable Monarch's greatness that they have no words with which to express their thoughts upon the subject.

"Here is an excellent matter brought to your attention, my brothers," said he to them, — "a great and important matter, which is the cause of this council. Cast your eyes upon the Cross raised so high above your heads; there it was that JESUS CHRIST, the Son of God, making himself man for the love of men, was pleased to be fastened and to die, in atonement to his Eternal Father for our sins. He is the master of our lives, of Heaven, of Earth, and of Hell. Of him I have always spoken to you, and his name and word I have borne into all these countries. But look likewise at that other post, to which are affixed the armorial bearings of the great Captain of France whom we call King. He lives beyond the sea; he is the Captain of the greatest Captains, and has not his equal in the world. All the Captains you have ever seen, or of whom you have ever heard, are mere children compared with him. He is like a great tree, and they, only like little plants that we tread under foot in walking. You know about Onnontio, that famous Captain of Quebec. You know and feel that he is the terror of the Iroquois, and that his very name makes them tremble, now that he has laid waste their country and set fire to their Villages. Beyond the sea there are ten thousand Onnontios like him, who are only the Soldiers of that Great Captain, our Great King, of whom I am speaking. When he says, 'I am going to war,' all obey him; and those ten thousand Captains raise Companies of a hundred soldiers each, both on sea and on land. Some embark in ships, one or two hundred in number, like those you have seen at Quebec. Your Canoes hold only four or five men — or, at the very most, ten or twelve. Our ships in France hold four or five hundred, and even as many as a thousand. Other men make war by land, but in such vast numbers that, if drawn up in double file, they would extend farther than from here to Missisaquenk, although the distance exceeds twenty leagues. When he attacks, he is more terrible than the thunder; the earth trembles, the air and the sea are set on fire by the discharge of his Cannon; while he has been seen amid his squadrons, all covered with the blood of his foes, of whom he has slain so many with his sword that he does not count their scalps, but the rivers of blood which he sets flowing. So many prisoners of war does he lead away that he makes no account of them, letting them go about whither they will, to show that he does not fear them. No one now dares make war upon him, all nations beyond the sea having most submissively sued for peace. From all parts of the world people go to listen to his words and to admire him, and he alone decides all the affairs of the world. What shall I say of his wealth? You count yourselves rich when you have ten or twelve sacks of corn, some hatchets, glass beads, kettles, or other things of that sort. He has towns of his own, more in number than you have people in all these countries, five hundred leagues around; while in each town there are warehouses containing enough hatchets to cut down all your forests, kettles to cook all your moose, and glass beads to fill all your cabins. His house is longer than from here to the head of the Sault," — that is, more than half a league, — "and higher than the tallest of your trees; and it contains more families than the largest of your villages can hold."

The Father added much more of this sort, which was received with wonder by those people, who were all astonished to hear that there was any man on earth so great, rich, and powerful.

Following this speech, Monsieur de Saint Lusson took the word, and stated to them in martial and eloquent language the reasons for which he had summoned them, — and especially that he was sent to take possession of that region, receive them under the protection of the great King whose Panegyric they had just heard; and to form thenceforth but one land of their territories and ours. The whole ceremony was closed with a fine bonfire, which was lighted toward evening, and around which the *Te Deum* was sung to thank God, on behalf of those poor peoples, that they were now the subjects of so great and powerful a Monarch.

19. The Conversion and Holy Death of Catharine Tegahkouita, 1676–1680

THE strenuous efforts put forth by the missionaries to win the Indians to Christianity more frequently than not met with failure. Occasionally, however, they encountered souls of rare virtue, and of none was this more true than Catharine Tegahkouita (1656–1680), the Mohawk maiden, who was received into the Church by Jacques de Lamberville, S.J. (1641–1710), in 1676, at the Mohawk village near present-day Fonda, New York. Catharine spent her last years at La Prairie de la Madeleine, a Christian Indian village in Canada, and died a holy death there in 1680. Her cause has been introduced at Rome for beatification. The following biographical sketch of Catharine was written by a French Jesuit whose work was first published in 1744. He gathered the facts from accounts left by some of his confreres, Jacques de Lamberville. Claude Chauchetière, and Pierre Cholenec, who either knew her personally or were contemporaries. Source: John Gilmary Shea (Ed.), Pierre François Xavier Charlevoix, S.J., *History and General Description of New France* (New York: John Gilmary Shea, 1870), IV, 283–296.

New France has had her apostles and her martyrs, and has given the church saints in all conditions, and I do not hesitate to say that they would have done honor to the primitive ages of Christianity.

Several I have made known so far as the course of this history permitted me. The lives of some have been published; but God, who exalted his glory during their life-time by the great things which he effected through them; by the lustre which their sanctity has diffused over this vast continent; by the courage with which he inspired them to found with untold toil a new Christiandom amid the most fearful barbarism, and to cement it with their blood, chose none of these to display on their tombs, all the riches of his power and mercy; but conferred this honor on a young neophyte, almost unknown to the whole country during her life. For more than sixty years she has been regarded as the Protectress of Canada, and it has been impossible to oppose a kind of *cultus* publicly rendered to her.

This holy virgin, so celebrated under the name of Catharine Tegahkouita, was born in 1656, at Gandahouhagué [Fonda, New York], a town in the Mohawk canton, of a heathen Iroquois father and a Christian Algonquin mother. She lost her mother at the age of four, and was still quite young when her father died, leaving her to the care of one of her aunts, and under the control of an uncle who had the chief authority in his village. The smallpox which she had in her infancy having weakened her sight, she was long compelled as it were to remain in the corner of a cabin, her eyes being unable to stand the light, and this retirement was the first source of her happiness. What she did at first from necessity, she continued to do from choice, thereby avoiding whatever could cause her to lose that moral purity so hard to preserve amid idolatrous and then very dissolute youth.

As soon as she saw herself of age to act, she took on herself all the toil of the household; and this shielded her from two dangers, fatal to most Indian girls; I mean, private conversations and idleness. Her relatives however wished her to use the decorations common to young persons of her sex, and although she yielded from simple compliance with their wishes, and with all possible repugnance, it was a matter of much scruple to her, when, favored by the light of faith, she learned how dangerous it is to seek to please men.

The first knowledge that she acquired of Christianity, was imparted by some missionaries sent to the Iroquois after M. de Tracy's expedition.[1] On their way they passed through the town where she lived and were received at her cabin. She was appointed to take care of

[1] The French Commander, Alexandre de Prouville, Marquis de Tracy (1603–1670), had cleared the way for the missionaries by a western military expedition against the hostile Iroquois in 1666.

them, and waited on them in a manner that surprised them. She had herself, on beholding them, been moved by an impulse that excited sentiments in her heart, regarded subsequently by her as the first sparks of the heavenly fire, by which she was in the sequel so completely inflamed. The fervor and recollection of those religious in their devotions, inspired her with the desire of praying with them, and she informed them of it. They understood much more than she expressed; they instructed her in the Christian truth, as far as the short stay which they made in that town permitted them, and left her with a regret that on her side was heartily reciprocated. Some time after, a marriage was proposed to her; as she showed strong opposition, her relatives did not press it; but they soon returned to the charge, and to save themselves the trouble of overcoming her resistance, they, without mentioning it to her, betrothed her to a young man, who at once went to her cabin and sat down beside her. To ratify the marriage, it only required that she should remain near the husband selected for her, such being the way of these tribes; but she abruptly left the cabin, and protested that she would not return till he withdrew. This conduct drew on her much ill treatment, which she endured with unalterable patience. She was more sensible to the reproach made that she had no affection for her kindred, that she hated her tribe, and gave all her attachment to that to which her mother belonged. Nothing however could overcome her repugnance for the state of life in which they sought to involve her.

Meanwhile Father James de Lamberville arrived at Gandahouhagué, with orders to found a mission there. Tegahkouita then felt her former desires to become a Christian revive; but she was still for some time without mentioning it, either from respect to her uncle, who did not relish our religion, or from simple timidity. At last an opportunity came for avowing her conviction, and she was not wanting. A wound in the foot which she had received, kept her in the cabin, while all the other women were busy harvesting the Indian corn. Father de Lamberville, compelled to suspend his public instructions, which no one would attend, took this time to visit the cabins, and instruct those whom age or infirmity detained there. One day he entered that where Tegahkouita was.

Unable to dissemble the joy which this visit caused her, she did not hesitate to open her mind to the missionary in the presence of two or three women, who were in company with her, on her design of embracing Christianity. She added that she would have great obstacles to overcome, but that nothing appalled her. The energy with which she spoke, the courage she displayed, a certain modest yet resolute air, that lighted up her countenance, at once told the missionary that his new proselyte would not be an ordinary Christian. He accordingly carefully taught her many things, which he did not explain to all preparing for baptism. God doubtless infuses into hearts, of which he has especially reserved possession, a sort of purely spiritual sympathy, forming even in this life the sacred bond which will unite them hereafter in the abode of glory. Father de Lamberville, whom I knew well, was one of the most holy missionaries of New France, where he died, at Sault Saint Louis, spent with toil and austerity, and, if I may use the expression, in the arms of Charity. He often declared that in his first interview with Tegahkouita, he thought he could discern that God had great designs as to that virgin; yet he would not exercise any haste in conferring baptism on her, and he adopted in her case all the precautions that experience has counselled as necessary, to make sure of the Indians, before administering the sacrament of regeneration.

The whole winter was spent in these trials, and on her side the young catechumen employed this precious time in rendering herself worthy of a grace, whose importance she fully comprehended. Before granting it to adults, the missionaries took great pains to inquire privately into their conduct and morality. Father de Lamberville asked all who knew Tegahkouita, and was greatly surprised to find that there was not one, even among those who had given her most to suffer, but sounded her praises. This was all the more glorious for her, as Indians are much given to slander, and naturally inclined to put an evil interpretation on the most innocent actions. The missionary accordingly no longer hesitated to grant her what she solicited with such earnestness. She was baptized on Easter Sunday, 1676, and received the name of Catharine.

The grace of the sacrament received into a heart which her uprightness and innocence had so well prepared, produced wondrous effects. Whatever idea the missionary had already conceived of the young Iroquois maiden, he was astonished to find in her, immediately after baptism, not a neophyte needing to be confirmed in the faith, but a soul filled with the most precious gifts of heaven, and whom he too would have to guide in the most sublime spiritual ways. In the outset her virtue excited the admiration of those even who were least inclined to imitate her, and those on whom she depended, left her free to follow every impulse of her zeal, but this did not last long. The innocence of her life, the precautions which she took to avoid all that could in the least affect it, and especially her extreme reserve as to whatever could in the slightest degree offend purity, appeared to the young men of her village as a reproach on the dissolute life they led, and many laid snares with the sole view of dimming a virtue which dazzled them.

On the other hand, although she had relaxed nothing in her domestic occupations, and was ever found ready to give her services to all, her relatives were displeased to see her give to prayer all the time left her, and to prevent her suspending on Sundays and holidays the work which the church forbids on those days consecrated to the Lord, they made her pass them without food. Seeing, however, that they gained nothing by this course, they had recourse to still more violent means; they often ill-treated her in a most unbecoming manner; when she went to the chapel, they sent young men to pursue her with hooting and pelt her with stones; men either really drunk or pretendedly drunk rushed upon her, as though they designed to take her life; but, undismayed by these artifices and acts of violence, she continued her devotions as though she enjoyed the most perfect liberty.

One day when she was in her cabin, a young man entered abruptly, with flashing eyes, brandishing his hatchet as if intending to tomahawk her. At this sight she displayed no emotion, and bowed down her head to receive the blow; but the madman, seized at the instant by a panic fear, fled as precipitately as though pursued by a war-party. These first storms were succeeded by a still more dangerous persecution. Catharine's aunt was a woman of morose disposition, who was displeased with all that her niece did to satisfy her, for the simple reason that she could find nothing to reprove. One day the virtuous neophyte happened to call the husband of this woman by his own name, instead of calling him Father, as usual; her aunt imagined, or pretended to believe, that this familiar mode of speaking showed an improper connection between the uncle and the niece, and she hastened on the spot to Father de Lamberville to assert that she had surprised Catharine soliciting her husband to sin. The missionary promised to examine the case, and when he learned on what this atrocious accusation rested, he gave the slanderer a rebuke that covered her with confusion; but which ultimately increased the annoyance of the innocent girl.

Had all this involved merely suffering, than which nothing was more to her taste, she would never have thought of changing her position; but she feared that she could not always hold firm against the seduction of bad example, or escape being overcome gradually by human respect, so powerful in the Indian mind. She accordingly began to look for an asylum, where her innocence and religion would be shielded from danger. La Prairie de la Magdeleine, where several Iroquois Christians began to settle, seemed to her well adapted, and she felt an ardent desire to remove thither; but this was not easily done.

Her uncle beheld with great displeasure the depopulation of his canton, and he declared himself the avowed enemy of all who contributed to it. It was therefore apparently impossible to obtain his consent, and it was not easy for Catharine to leave him without it. But God, who had destined her to be the example and ornament of this transplanted Christian colony, facilitated what had at first seemed impossible. She had an adopted sister, a neophyte like herself, married to a Christian very zealous for the conversion of his countrymen. This man had already taken up his abode at La Prairie de la Magdeleine, and he was one of those who under various pretexts, traversed the Iroquois towns in order to make proselytes. He knew that the greatest favor he could do to Catharine would be to take her to his home: he spoke of the matter to his wife, who confirmed him in his design, and earnestly exhorted him to give her sister this consolation.

He resolved on the project, and to effect it more surely, he pretended to go hunting with one of his friends in the direction of New York, and set out, after warning Tegahkouita to hold herself in readiness at a fixed time. Fortunately for her her uncle was away, though not far distant, and he was almost at once informed of his niece's departure. Without losing a moment he set out in pursuit bent on bringing her back dead or alive, and on tomahawking the first who resisted him. He soon overtook the two hunters, but not finding his niece with them, because, whenever they halted, they took the precaution to conceal her in the woods, he thought that he had been misinformed; accordingly, without avowing his purpose, he conversed for a time on different topics and left them, convinced that Catharine had taken some other route and followed other guides.

The holy virgin, rescued from this peril, gaily pursued her journey, and at last reached the bourne which had been the object of her prayers. This was in the month of October, 1677. Her sister had not yet a cabin to herself, and dwelt with her husband in that of a fervent Christian woman named Anastasia, whose sole employment it was to prepare persons of her own sex for baptism. A hostess of this character and such exercises were greatly to the taste of Catharine. She was, moreover, charmed with all that she beheld done in the village, nor could she sufficiently admire the omnipotence of grace, which could transform wolves into lambs, nor chant the mercies of the Lord, to see men now dwelling in the purity of gospel morality, whose debauchery had more than once paralyzed her with horror.

Animated by new fervor at this sight, she gave herself unreservedly to God, renouncing in future the least thought of self, and began to run with great steps in the career of sanctity. Prayers, toil, spiritual conversation, was henceforth her sole occupation; and after the example of Saint Anthony, she made it a duty to imitate every edifying trait that she perceived in those who composed this new church. She spent at the foot of the altar all her spare time; she lived solely by her own labor, and busied as she might be exteriorly, her heart was ever in constant communion with God.

She had not yet made her first communion when she arrived in the colony, and it is not usual in these missions to grant this favor to neophytes till after long trials. Catharine was fearful that she would be subjected to this rule, but her virtue, far more than her repeated entreaties, soon induced her director to make an exception in her favor; nor had he any reason to repent. The frequent communions, which she was permitted to receive, did not diminish in the least her fervor in preparing for them. It was enough to see her in her most ordinary actions to be roused to devotion; but when she partook of the divine mysteries, it was impossible to be near her, and not be filled with the most tender love for God.

When she was obliged to go with a hunting party, the distraction inseparable from that time deranged in nothing her interior life; she built an oratory within her heart which she never quitted. She avoided company as much as she could, and when she could not, she imparted her recollectedness to others much more than she took part in their amusements. Yet there was nothing constrained in her manners, and her devotion was neither forbidding nor troublesome. She was ever wonderfully dexterous in concealing her private practices of piety, and her austerities, which were great. One of her most common was to mingle earth with all she ate, and very few perceived it. . . .

She was seen to advance visibly in virtue. Already naught was spoken of in the country except her eminent sanctity. The people were never weary of admiring the secret spring of Divine Goodness, which, from amid a nation the most hostile to the establishment of Christianity, had drawn forth a young virgin, to make her a perfect model of all Christian virtues.

There then reigned in the mission of Sault Saint Louis a spirit of mortification which went to great length. These neophytes had just been declared, by all the Iroquois cantons, enemies of their country, and they confidently expected that after this outburst, all who fell into the hands of their idolatrous brethren, would be given over without mercy to the most fearful tortures. Hence they thought only of preparing for martyrdom by all the means that austerity can suggest for chastising the flesh. Men, women, and even children, in this manner proceeded to excesses which the missionaries would never have permitted had they been fully informed in regard to them.

Catharine more fully possessed the interior spirit than all the others, was too the most unsparing to herself of all. She consulted naught but her fervor, and believed herself in no wise bound to depend in this on her director as formerly, believing that this general concert of the whole village could not be unknown to him, and that his silence in regard to it was a consent. She was accordingly soon reduced to a state of languor and suffering from which she never recovered. Some time after she paid a visit to Montreal, where the sight of the Hospital Nuns, whom she had never even heard mentioned, increased her desire to consecrate herself to God by the vow of chastity; she renewed her entreaties to her confessor, who judged it his duty no longer to withhold his consent. She accordingly took the long desired vow, with a joy that seemed to revive all her strength, and she was the first of her tribe who took upon herself such an engagement with heaven.

The heavenly spouse of chaste souls was not slow in giving her manifest proofs that he had accepted her sacrifice, and in treating her as His well-beloved spouse. She, on her side, exerted herself to correspond to His caresses and the internal communications with which He favored her, by perfect fidelity and unreserved love. But her strength could not long sustain its ardor, and the flesh soon gave way beneath the efforts of the spirit. She fell into a dangerous disease, which left her only a lingering existence subject to constant pain. In this state she united herself more and more to Jesus Christ by meditating on His death and sufferings, and the frequent reception of the sacraments. She could no longer endure human conversation; Anastasia and Teresa were the only two persons with whom she retained any kind of intimacy, because they spoke to her only of God.

She felt well only at the foot of the altar, buried in profound contemplation, and shedding torrents of tears, whose inexhaustible fountain was His love and the wound it had inflicted on her heart, she often so forgot the wants of her body, as not even to feel the cold, with which her whole frame was benumbed. She always came from this contemplation with renewed love of suffering, and it is unconceivable [*sic*] how ingenious her mind was in inventing means to crucify her flesh. Sometimes she walked barefooted on the ice and snow, till she lost all feeling. Sometimes she strewed her couch with thorns. She rolled for three days in succession on branches of thorns, which pierced deeply into her flesh, causing inexplicable pain. Another time she burned her feet, as is done to prisoners, wishing thus to give herself the stamp and mark of a slave of Christ; but what attests far better the solidity of her virtue, is the unalterable gentleness, patience, joy even, manifested by her in the sufferings which she experienced toward the close of life. . . .

She was at last attacked by a malady, which was at once deemed mortal; and that at a time when the labors in the field so engaged all, that she could scarcely expect care from any one. She remained alone whole days with a platter of Indian corn, and a little water beside her bed. Delighted to behold herself thus forsaken of men, she communed constantly with her God, and found the days only too short. On Tuesday in Holy Week, 1678 [1680], she grew worse and received Holy Viaticum. The missionary wished also to administer Extreme Unction at once, but she assured him that it could be deferred till next day. She spent all the ensuing night in a loving colloquy with her divine Saviour, and with His Holy Mother, whom she had always singularly honored, regarding herself as a spouse of Christ, and as attached to the retinue of the Queen of Virgins.

On Wednesday morning she received the sacred anointing, and about three o'clock in the afternoon she expired after a gentle agony of half an hour, retaining her complete consciousness and sound judgment till her last sigh. . . . Her countenance, extremely attenuated by austerity and by her last illness, suddenly changed as soon as she ceased to live. It was seen assuming a rosy tint that she had never had; nor were her features the same. Nothing could be more beautiful, but with that beauty which love of virtue inspires. The people were never weary gazing on her, and each retired, his heart full of the desire to become a saint. As a distinction her body was placed in a coffin, and her tomb soon became celebrated by the concourse of the faithful, who flocked from all parts of Canada, and by the miracles wrought there. . . .

20. The French Récollets in the Illinois Country, 1680

EVERY religious order that engaged in missionary activities in colonial North America had its toll of martyrs. From the time when Juan de Padilla, O.F.M., the protomartyr of the United States, was murdered c. 1542 by the Plains Indians of the Southwest, the sons of St. Francis continued to give their lives in pursuit of their high ideal of converting the savages. As friends of the remarkable explorer, René-Robert Cavelier, Sieur de La Salle (1643–1687), the French Franciscans, or Récollets, played a prominent role in his far-flung expeditions in the Mississippi Valley. Thus we find two of these friars, Zénobe Membré (1645–1689) and Gabriel de la Ribourde (d. 1680), carrying on their missionary labors in 1680 at Fort Crêvecoeur near present-day Peoria, Illinois. An outbreak of war between the Iroquois and the Illinois compelled the French to abandon the area, and the description which Membré wrote of their experiences combined an explanation of why the missionaries had made so few converts with a touching account of the murder of his confrere which took place in September, 1680, at a point along the Illinois River some distance west of the present town of Seneca, Illinois. Membré himself met a violent death in January, 1689, along with his fellow religious, Maxim Le Clercq, when they were murdered by Karankawa Indians at Fort St. Louis near Matagorda Bay, Texas, where they had accompanied La Salle on his fatal expedition of 1684. Source: John Gilmary Shea (Ed.), *Discovery and Exploration of the Mississippi Valley* (New York: J. S. Redfield, 1852), pp. 152–153, 157–159.

Meanwhile, from the flight and desertion of our men about the middle of March to the month of September, Father Gabriel and I devoted ourselves constantly to the mission. An Illinois named Asapista, with whom the sieur de la Salle had contracted friendship, adopted Father Gabriel as his son, so that that good father found in his cabin a subsistence in the Indian fashion. As wine failed us for the celebration of the divine mysteries, we found means, toward the close of August, to get wild grapes which began to ripen, and we made very good wine which served us to say mass till the second disaster, which happened a few days after. The cluster of these grapes are of prodigious size, a very agreeable taste, and have seeds larger than those of Europe.

With regard to conversions, I can not rely on any. During the whole time Father Gabriel unraveled their language a little, and I can say that I spoke so as to make myself understood by the Indians on all that I wished; but there is in these savages such an alienation from the faith, so brutal and narrow a mind, such corrupt and anti-christian morals, that great time would be needed to hope for any fruit. It is, however, true that I found many of quite docile character. We baptized some dying children, and two or three dying persons who manifested proper dispositions. As these people are entirely material in their ideas, they would have submitted to baptism, had we liked, but without any knowledge of the sacrament. We found two who had joined us, and promised to follow us everywhere; we believed that they would keep their word, and that by this means we would insure their baptisms; but I afterward felt great scruples when I learned that an Indian named Chassagonaché, who had been baptized, had died in the hands of the medicine-men, abandoned to their superstitions, and consequently doubly a child of hell.

During the summer, we followed our Indians in their camps, and to the chase. I also made a voyage to the Myamis to learn something of their dispositions; thence I went to visit other villages of the Illinois all, however, with no great success, finding only cause for chagrin at the deplorable state and blindness of these nations. It is such that I can not express it fully. . . . [Shortly thereafter war broke between the Iroquois and the Ilinois and the French had to flee]. The reverend father Gabriel, the sieur de Tonty,[1] the few French who were with us, and myself, began our march on the 18th of September, without provisions, food, or anything, in a wretched bark canoe, which breaking the next day, compelled us to land about noon to repair it. Father Gabriel seeing the place of our landing fit for walking in the prairies and hills with little groves, as if planted by hand, retired there to say his breviary while we were working at the canoe all the rest of the day. We were full eight leagues from the village ascending the river. Toward evening I went to look for the father seeing that he did not return; all our party did the same; we fired repeatedly, to direct him, but in vain; and as we had reason to fear the Iroquois during the night, we crossed to the other side of the river and lit up fires which were also useless. The next morning at daybreak, we returned to the same side where we were the day before, and remained till noon, making all possible search. We entered the wood, where we found several fresh trails, as well as in the prairie on the bank of the river. We followed them one by one without discovering anything, except that M. de Tonty had ground to believe and fear that some hostile parties were in ambush to cut us all off, for seeing us take flight, the

---

[1] Henri de Tonty (1650–1704), French explorer, established Arkansas Post at the mouth of the Arkansas River in 1686, the earliest French settlement in the lower Mississippi Valley.

savages had imagined that we declared for the Ilinois. I insisted on staying to wait for positive tidings; but the sieur de Tonty forced me to embark at three o'clock, maintaining that the father had been killed by the enemy, or else had walked on along the bank, so that following it constantly, we should at last infallibly meet him. We got, however, no tidings of him, and the more we advanced, the more this affliction unmanned us, and we supported this remnant of a languishing life by the potatoes and garlick, and other roots, that we found by scraping the ground with our fingers.

We afterward learned that we should have expected him uselessly, as he had been killed soon after landing. The Kikapous, a little nation you may observe on the west, quite near the Winnebagoes, had sent some of their youth in war-parties against the Iroquois, but learning that the latter were attacking the Ilinois, the war-party came after them. Three braves who formed a kind of advanced guard having met the good father alone, although they knew that he was not an Iroquois, killed him for all that, cast his body into a hole, and carried off even his breviary, and diurnal, which soon after came to the hands of a Jesuit father. They carried off the scalp of this holy man, and vaunted of it in their village as an Iroquois scalp. Thus died this man of God by the hands of some mad youths. We can say of his body what the Scripture remarks of those whom the sanguinary Herod immolated to his fury, "Non erat qui sepeliret." Surely he deserved a better fate, if, indeed, we can desire a happier one before God, than to die in the exercise of the apostolic functions, by the hands of nations to whom we are sent by God. He had not been merely a religious of common and ordinary virtue; it is well known that he had in Canada, from 1670, maintained the same sanctity of life which he had shown in France as superior, inferior, and master of novices. He had for a long time in transports of fervor acknowledged to me the profound grief which he felt at the utter blindness of these people, and that he longed to be an anathema for their salvation. His death, I doubt not, has been precious before God, and will one day have its effect in the vocation of these people to the faith, when it shall please the Almighty to use his great mercy. . . .

21. Louis Hennepin's Description of the Difficulties Encountered in Trying to Convert the Indians, 1697

THE French Récollets inaugurated their labors in North America in 1615. Among the most colorful — and controversial — of these friars was Louis Hennepin (c. 1640–c. 1701), a native of the Low Countries. Hennepin was one of the most widely traveled of all the colonial missionaries and he later wrote extensively — although not always accurately — of his experiences. He was with La Salle on the famous voyage of the *Griffon* westward through the Great Lakes in 1679, and in 1680 it was Hennepin who discovered and named St. Anthony Falls at the present site of Minneapolis. The following account describes the intellectual difficulties encountered in trying to win the Indians to the Catholic faith, and the chief obstacles mentioned by Hennepin, *mutatis mutandis,* were found among practically all the native tribes. Source: Reuben Gold Thwaites (Ed.), *Louis Hennepin, A New Discovery of a Vast Country in America* (Chicago: A. C. McClurg & Co., 1903), II, 457–474.

CHAP. XII

What Method is most proper to convert the Savages; what Manner of Persons they are that ought not to be baptized.

Our ancient Missionary Recollects of *Canada,* and those that succeeded them in that work, have always given it for their opinion, and I now own 'tis mine, that the way to succeed in converting the Barbarians, is to endeavour to make them men before we go about to make them Christians. Now in order to civilize them, 'tis necessary that the *Europeans* should mix with them, and that they should dwell together, which can never be done for certain till the Colonies are augmented: but it must be acknowledged, that the Company of *Canada* Merchants, have made great Obstacles to the increasing of the Colonies; for out of greediness to keep all the Trade in their own hands, these Gentlemen would never permit any particular Society to settle themselves in the Country, nor suffer the Missionaries to perswade [*sic*] the Barbarians to dwell constantly in a place. Yet before this be done, there's no way to convert these Unbelievers. Thus the covetousness of those who are for getting a great deal in a short time, has mightly retarded the establishment of the Gospel among the Savages.

Hence 'tis manifest, that the office of a Missionary is very troublesome and laborious amongst these numerous Nations, and it must be granted that 'tis necessary to spend many Years, and undergo a great deal of pains to civilize People so extremely stupid and barbarous.

And therefore, one would not venture without much caution, to administer the Sacraments to adult Persons, who pretend themselves Converts; for we see that after so many Years of Mission, there has been but little progress made, though no pains have been wanting on the Missionary's hands.

So that Christianity is not like to gain much ground among the Savages, till the Colonies are strengthened by a great Number of Inhabitants, Artisans and Workmen, and then the Treaty betwixt the Barbarians and us should be freer, and extended to all *Europeans:* But chiefly it should be endeavour'd to fix the Barbarians to a certain dwelling Place, and introduce our Customs and Laws amongst them, further'd by the Assistance of zealous People in *Europe,* Colleges might be founded to breed up the young Savages in the Christian Faith, which might in time contribute very much to the Conversion of their Country-men. This is a very proper Method without doubt, to strengthen the Temporal and Spiritual Interests of the Colonies; but the generality of Mankind are bent upon Gain and Traffick, and are little concern'd to procure God's Blessing upon them, and endeavour the advancement of his Glory.

God is often pleas'd to prove his Children, and amongst 'em those that employ themselves in saving Souls, by those means that most afflict them, but Dangers, Labors, Sufferings, and even Death it self would be welcome to them, provided in sacrificing themselves for the Salvation of their Brethren, God would afford them the Consolation to see their Undertakings Crown'd with success to his Glory, and the Conversion of Infidels.

It is impossible for us to look upon so great a Number of People as this relation mentions, and consider the little progress Religion has made among the Savages of these vast Countries, but we must needs admire the inscrutable Decrees of God, and cry out with the Apostle, *O the Depth of the Riches of the Wisdom and Knowledge of God!* a great Number of learned secular Priests, and zealous Religious men of our Order, have carried the Light of the Gospel into all Parts of the Earth, and labour'd hard in the Lord's Vineyard. But God would have us know, that the Conversion of Souls is the Work of his Grace, the blessed Moments of which are not yet come. . . .

These miserable dark Creatures listen to all we say concerning our Mysteries, just as if 'twere a Song; they are naturally very vitious, and addicted to some Superstitions that signifie nothing; there Customs are savage, brutal and barbarous; they will suffer themselves to be baptized ten times a Day for a Glass of Brandy, or a Pipe of Tobacco, and offer their Children to be baptiz'd, but without any Religious Motive. Those that one takes the pains to instruct, for a Winter together, as I my self taught some of them while I dwelt at Fort *Frontenac,* give no better sign of Edification, than others in our Articles of Faith: so wrapt up are they in Insensibility, to what concerns Religion, which occasion'd terrible Checks of Conscience in our Religious, in the beginning of their Mission among the People of *Canada;* they saw that the few Persons of years of Discretion that they had instructed, and afterwards admitted to Baptism, soon fell again into their ordinary indifference for Salvation, and that the Children follow'd the unhappy Example of their Parents, insomuch that 'twas no better than a plain of profanation of Baptism to administer it to them. . . .

CHAP. XIII

The Barbarians of North-America *don't acknowledg any God. Of the pretended Souls of terrestrial Animals.*

Our antient Missionaries Recollects were acquainted with several different Nations within the compass of 600 leagues in *North-America;* and I have been among many more, because I went farther than any of them, having made a Voyage all along the River of St. *Lawrence,* and *Meschasipi.* I observed, as my Predecessors, that the Savages don't want good Sense in which concerns the general and particular Interest of their Nation. They pursue their Point, and take right Methods to come to the end of their designs; but 'tis what I am astonished at, that whilst they are so clear sighted in their common Affairs, they should have such extravagant notions of the concerns of Religion, the Manners, Laws, and Maxims of Life.

We must all of us own, that almost all the Savages in general have no Belief of a Deity, and that they are incapable of the common and ordinary Arguments and Reasonings that the rest of Mankind are led by upon this Subject; so dark and stupid are their Understandings. At the same time we may acknowledg, that now and then in some of them we discover some glimmerings of a confus'd Notion of God. Some will confess, but very cloudily, that the Sun is God: Others say, 'tis a Genius that rules in the Air: Some again look upon the Heavens as a kind of Divinity. But these only make a shew of believing something that we can hardly guess at: we can't fix them to any settled

Principle. The Nations Southward seem to believe an Universal Spirit that governs all: they imagine after a fashion, that there's a Spirit in every thing, even in those that are inanimate; and they address themselves to it sometimes, and beg something of it; as we took notice of one Barbarian, who made a kind of Sacrifice upon an Oak, at the Cascade of St. *Anthony* of *Padua,* upon the River *Meschasipi.*

All these Nations don't profess their Belief of a Deity out of any respect to Religion: They talk of it ordinarily, as a thing they were prepossessed with; or frolicksomly, not regarding any thing they say themselves, any otherwise than as a kind of a Fable. They have no outward Ceremony to signify that they worship any Deity: There's no Sacrifice, Priest, Temple, nor any other Token of Religion amongst them.

Their Dreams are to them instead of Prophecy, Inspiration, Laws, Commandments, and Rules, in all their Enterprizes, in War, Peace, Commerce, and Hunting: They regard them as Oracles. The Opinion they have of their Dreams draws them into a kind of necessity to be ruled by them; for they think 'tis an Universal Spirit, that inspires them by Dreams, and adviseth them what to do: And they carry this so far, that if their Dream orders them to kill a Person, or commit any other wicked Action, they presently execute it, and make satisfaction for it afterwards, as we shall show anon. The Parents dream for their Children, the Captains for their Village. There are some among them, that take upon them to interpret Dreams, and explain them after their own fancy or inclination; and if their Interpretations don't prove true, they are not lookt upon as Cheats ere the more for that.

Some have taken notice, that when they meet with any Cascade or Fall or Waters, which is difficult to cross, and apprehend any danger, they throw a Bever's [*sic*] skin, Tobacco, Porcelain, or some such matter into it by way of Sacrifice, to gain the Favor of the Spirit that presides there.

There's no Nation but what have their Jugglers, which some count Sorcerers: but 'tis not likely that they are under any Covenant, or hold communication with the Devil. At the same time, one may venture to say, that the evil Spirit has a hand in the Tricks of these Jugglers, and makes use of them to amuse these poor People, and render them more incapable of receiving the Knowledge of the true God. They are very fond of these Jugglers, tho they cozen them perpetually.

These Impostors would be counted Prophets, who fortel things to come: they would be look'd upon as having almost an infinite Power: they boast that they make Rain or fair Weather, Calms and Storms, Fruitfulness or Barrenness of the Ground, Hunting lucky or unlucky. They serve for Physicians too, and frequently apply such Remedies, as have no manner of virtue to cure the Distemper.

Nothing can be imagined more horrible than the Cries and Yellings, and the strange Contortions of these Rascals, when they fall to juggling or conjuring; at the same time they do it very cleverly. They never cure any one, nor predict any thing that falls out, but purely by chance: mean time they have a thousand Fetches to bubble (*i.e.* cheat) the poor people, when the accident does not answer their Predictions and Remedies; for, as I said, they are both Prophets and Quacks. They do nothing without Presents or Reward. 'Tis true, if these Impostors are not very dexterous at recommending themselves, and bringing themselves off, when any person dies under their hands, or Enterprizes do not succeed as they promis'd, they are sometimes murdered upon the place, without any more Formality.

These blind Wretches are wedded to many other Superstitions, which the Devil makes use of to delude them: They believe that several kinds of Animals have a reasonable Soul: They have an unaccountable Veneration for certain Bones of Elks, Bevers, and other Beasts; they never throw these to their Dogs, which are the only Domestick Animals they keep, because they serve for Hunting: So they preserve these precious Bones, and are very unwilling to cast them into the River. They pretend, that the Souls of these Animals come back into the World to see how they treat their Bodies, and give notice accordingly to the rest of the Beasts both dead and living: and that if they should find they are ill us'd, the Beasts of that kind would never let themselves be taken, neither in this World nor the next.

One may say, that the Corruption of Sin has spread a strange Darkness in the Souls of these unhappy people, and a perfect Insensibility to all Religion; insomuch that they are not to be match'd in any History. 'Tis true, they are obstinately superstitious in some things; and yet at the same time, they are not mov'd by any principle of Religion. 'Tis nothing but strong Prejudice and Imagination. When we dispute with them, and put them to a nonplus, they hold their tongues; their Minds are stupid, their Faculties are besotted. If we propose our Mysteries to them, they heed them as indifferently as their own nonsensical Whimsies. I have met with some of them, who seem to acknowledge that there is one first Principle that made all things; but this makes but a slight Impression upon their Mind, which returns again to its ordinary Deadness, and former Insensibility.

CHAP. XIV

Of the great difficulty in converting the Savages. Of the Prayers they get by rote; and of Martyrdom.

The great Insensibility of these Barbarians is caused principally by their Carelessness and neglect to be thoroughly instructed. They come to us, and attend to what we say, purely out of Idleness, and natural Curiosity to converse with us, as we with them; or rather they are tempted to follow us, by the Kindness and Flatteries we express towards them, or because of the Benefit their Sick receive from us, or out of hope to gain by trafficking with us; or lastly, because we are Europeans, and they think us stouter than themselves, and hope we will defend them from their Enemies.

We teach them Prayers; but they repeat them like Songs, without any distinction by Faith. Those we have catechized a long time, are very wavering, except some few: They renounce all, return into their Woods, and take up their old Superstitions upon the least Crotchet that comes into their Heads.

I don't know whether their Predecessors had any Knowledge of a God; but 'tis certain their Language, which is very natural and expressive in every thing else, is so barren on this Subject, that we can't find any expression in it to signify the Deity, or any one of our mysteries, not even the most common: this gives us great perplexity when we would convert them.

Another great Obstacle to their Conversion is this: Most of them have several Wives; and in the Northern parts they change them as often as they please: They can't conceive how people can tie themselves indissolubly to one person in Marriage. See how silly you are, cry they, when we argue with them about it. My Wife is uneasy to me, I am so to her; she'll agree very well with such a one, who is at odds with his Wife: now why should we four lead a miserable Life all our days?

Another hinderance lies in a Custom of theirs, not to contradict any Man; they think every one ought to be left to his own Opinion, without being thwarted: they believe, or make as if they believed all you say to them; but 'tis their Insensibility, and Indifference for every thing, especially Matters of Religion, which they never trouble themselves about.

America is no place to go out of a desire to suffer Martyrdom, taking the Word in a Theological Sense: The Savages never put any Christian to death upon the score of his Religion; they leave every body at liberty in Belief: They like the outward Ceremonies of our Church, but no more. These Barbarians never make War, but for the Interest of their Nation; they don't kill people, but in particular Quarrels, or when they are brutish, or drunk, or in revenge, or infatuated with a Dream, or some extravagant Vision: they are incapable of taking away any Person's Life out of hatred to his Religion.

They are brutish in all their Inclinations; they are naturally Gluttons, and know no other Happiness in this Life, but the pleasure of eating and drinking: This is remarkable in their very eyes, and their Diversions, which are always begun and ended with feasting.

The Passion of Revenge which they are possessed with, is another great Obstacle to Christianity: They are very tender and affectionate to their own Nation, but cruel and revengeful beyond imagination towards their Enemies: They are naturally Inconstant, Revilers, Scoffers, and Lascivious. In short, among all the Vices they are addicted to, we can perceive no Principle of Religion or Morality: and to be sure this must needs render their Conversion extremely difficult.

To persuade them to any thing, and dispose them to the Faith, 'tis requisite to make them familiar with us, and contract a good acquaintance with them; but this is not to be done presently, because first of all the Colonies ought to be multiplied, and planted every where. When they have passed away a few Weeks with the Europeans, they are obliged to go to War, Hunting, or Fishing, for their Subsistence, and this depraves 'em extremely. They should be fix'd, inticed to clear the Ground, and cultivate it, and work at several Trades, as the Europeans do; and then we should see 'em reform their barbarous Customs, and become more civiliz'd, as well towards one another as us. . . .

22. The Quebec Seminary Priests in the Mississippi Valley, 1700, and the Installation of the First Pastor at Mobile, September 28, 1704

WHEN the Holy See erected the Vicariate Apostolic of New France into the Diocese of Quebec in 1674 it was made to embrace all the territories of North America then claimed by the French crown. Canonically speaking, therefore, the Church in the Mississippi Valley was under the jurisdiction of the Bishop of Quebec and remained so until after the American Revolution. In 1665 François de Montmorency de Laval (1623–1708), first Bishop of Quebec, had affiliated his infant seminary to the Seminary of Foreign Missions at Paris, and the missionary spirit was strong among the graduates of the Quebec institution. In time they sought to enter the western mission field and in May, 1698, they received authorization to do so, with the result that at mission stations among the Tamarois, Cahokias, and other tribes along the Mississippi friction developed between them and the Jesuits who had previously been on the scene. Apart, however, from the differences between the two groups over the missions to the Indians — wherein both did notable work — the secular priest performed valuable service by ministering to the French inhabitants of the scattered western settlements. To them was entrusted the first canonically erected parish in the western country when, on July 20, 1703, Bishop Jean Baptiste de la Croix de Saint Vallier (1653–1727) performed that action for the Church of the Immaculate Conception at Fort Louis, the forerunner of the present city of Mobile, Alabama. The first two documents that follow are excerpts from letters which Father Jean Bergier (d. 1707), a seminary priest, addressed to the Bishop of Quebec from the Tamarois post, the first in late February, 1700, the second dated June 14, 1700. The third document describes the formal installation of the first pastor by Father Antoine Davion with the civil officials in attendance and attesting the act. Sources: Edward Joseph Fortier, "The Establishment of the Tamarois Mission," *Transactions of the Illinois State Historical Society,* No. 13 (1909), 236–237; John Gilmary Shea, *History of the Catholic Church in the United States* (New York: John G. Shea, 1886), I, 547–548.

At the Tamarois, February, 1700.

I related to your highness our trip to the Illinois, from which place I wrote you all I had found out about the condition of the missions and that which concerns the government of your church. There remains but to inform you of the condition of the latter.

I arrived there the 7th of this month with young Mr. de St. Cosme. I have counted there a hundred cabins in all, or thereabouts, of which nearly half are vacant because the greater part of the Cahokias are still in winter quarters twenty or twenty-five leagues from here up the Mississippi.

The village is composed of Tamarois, Cahokias, some Michigans and Peorias. There are also some Missouri cabins, and shortly, there are to come about thirty-five cabins of this last named nation who are winterquartering, some ten or fifteen leagues from here below the village, on the river. We must not, however, count this nation as forming part of the village and of the Tamarois mission, because it remains there only a few months to make its Indian wheat, while awaiting a day to return to its village, which is more than a hundred leagues away, upon the shores of the Missouri river. This it has not dared to undertake for the last few years for fear of being surprised and defeated on the way by some other hostile nation.

The Tamarois and the Cahokias are the only ones that really form part of this mission. The Tamarois have about thirty cabins and the Cahokias have nearly twice that number. Although the Tamarois are at present less numerous than the Cahokias, the village is still called Tamaroa, gallicized "Des Tamarois," because the Tamarois have been the first and are still the oldest inhabitants and have first lit a fire there, to use the Indian expression. . . .

At the Tamarois, June 14, 1700.

We have frequent alarms here and we have several times been obliged to receive within our walls nearly all the women and children of the village. Pentecost Sunday there was one [alarm] which was not without consequence. Four Sioux on the edge of the woods of the Tamarois, in plain sight of the village, cut off the neck of a slave belonging to a Frenchman; stabbed two women to death and scalped them; wounded a girl with a knife and crushed another under foot. They were all picking strawberries. We were about to finish singing compline when the chief ran to our door to warn us that the Sioux were killing them. He threw himself into Mr. de St. Cosme's canoe, with some Indians and Frenchmen to reconnoitre, partly by water and then by land. Great excitement prevailed. Finally the Sioux were discovered and three were captured, killed, burned and eaten. . . . The last of these three Sioux, who was burned only the next day was baptized by F. Pinet who made use of the "Lorrain" as an interpreter. . . .

One may say that we are "inter lupos, in medio nationis pravae et perversae." Their greatest and most universal passion is to destroy, scalp and eat men, that, is all their ambition, their glory; an essential drawback to Christianity, as long as it will last. But the mercy of Jesus Christ is all powerful. Beseech him that he diffuse it very abundantly over this mission and over the missionaries and that he make them 'Prudentes ut serpentes, simplices ut comumbat [*sic*] — Amen.'

I, undersigned, Priest and Missionary Apostolic, attest to all whom it may concern that in the year of our salvation 1704, on the 28th of the month of September, by virtue of letters of provision and collation granted and sealed on the 20th of July of last year, by which Monseigneur the most Illustrious and most Reverend Bishop of Quebec erects a parish church in the place called Fort Louis de la Louisiane, and the cure and care of which he gives to Mr. Henry Roulleux de la Vente, Missionary Apostolic of the diocese of Bayeux, I have placed the said priest in actual and corporal possession of said parish church and of all the rights thereto belonging, after observing the accustomed and requisite ceremonies, namely, the entry into the church, the sprinkling of holy water, the kissing of the high altar, the touching of the missal, the visit to the Blessed Sacrament of the altar, the ringing of the bells, which taking of possession I attest that no one opposed.

Given in the parish church of Fort Louis, the day of the month and year aforesaid, in presence of John Baptiste de Bienville, Lieutenant of the King, and Commander of the said fort; of Peter du Quay de Boisbriant, major; Nicolas de la Salle, scribe and acting commissary of the Marine.

Davion, Bienville, Boisbriant, de la Salle.

23. The Government's Provision for Capuchin Missionaries in French Louisiana, May 16, 1722

FRANCE staked its claim to possession of the Mississippi Valley on the Jolliet-Marquette expedition of 1673. In the late seventeenth century the rivalry between Spain, France, and England for the western country grew keener, and after the efforts of a number of individual Frenchmen to settle the area had failed the French government determined upon turning over responsibility for the task to a commercial company. As a consequence, the Company of the West (later called the Company of the Indies) was formed in August, 1717. The company was anxious to have the participation of the Church in its undertaking and, therefore, the council of the company — with the consent of the Bishop of Quebec — divided the Province of Louisiana into three ecclesiastical districts which were assigned to the Carmelites, the Jesuits, and the Capuchins. The question of ecclesiastical jurisdiction caused a great deal of friction and after a brief time the Carmelites withdrew. But the Capuchins remained on in Louisiana from their advent in 1722 down to and beyond the purchase of the colony by the United States in 1803. From the outset these friars were entirely dependent upon the government as is evident in the provisions made for them by the council of the company in the document which follows. It provides a further example of the close union of Church and State which obtained in Louisiana all through the colonial era. Source: Claude L. Vogel, O.F.M.Cap., *The Capuchins in French Louisiana (1722–1766)* (Washington: The Catholic University of America Press, 1928), pp. 25–26.

His Majesty, having granted Letters Patent of August 1717, the colony of Louisiana to the Company of the West, now Company of the Indies, on condition that the said Company build churches at its own expense in the places where it forms settlements and maintain there the necessary number of ecclesiastics to work for the salvation of the inhabitants, French, Indian and Negro, and having accorded to the Company the right of patronage and the faculty to name the pastors and other ecclesiastics as shall be suitable to establish within the colony, We are informed that hitherto the Company has not taken the proper measures to fulfill that which in this matter is the intention of His Majesty; and it being necessary to make provisions to this end, We have believed that, to establish religion solidly in the colony and to work there successfully for the glory of God, We cannot make a better choice than the Capuchin Fathers of the Province of Champagne, who have shown so much zeal for that mission that We cannot doubt that they will acquit themselves most worthily and will furnish the necessary number of religious. Wherefore, We have agreed upon and have accepted Father Bruno of Langres, Father Christopher of Chaumont, Father Philibert of Viander and Brother Eusebius of Chaumont, to establish under the authority of the Bishop of Quebec a convent of their order at New Orleans, situated on the St. Louis River [Mississippi] in the land of Louisiana, to perform through the superior of the convent the pastoral functions in the town; to send to all the Company's settlements, extending from the mouth of the river unto and comprising the bank of the Wabash [Ohio], religious who shall be demanded from him by the Council of the colony; to conduct there the divine service and to administer the sacraments in the capacity of pastors and according to the faculties given him by the Bishop of Quebec; to have jurisdiction over the other ecclesiastics who shall be in the parts established along the river or its affluents and, in general, to do through the superior of the convent all that he shall judge necessary for the good and advancement of the Roman, Catholic and Apostolic Religion, and for the salvation of souls. We order the commanders and the directors of the colony to install the Capuchin Fathers as explained above, to aid and protect them with all their power in the exercise of their functions both as regards their rule and their Apostolic and parochial ministry. We order, therefore, that there be constructed in New Orleans at the expense of the Company a parish church of convenient size, with an adjoining house for four religious, in order to put the Capuchins in possession there; that they be given in the same place sufficient ground for a garden and poultry yard, and that in whatever place of the colony they may be established, the Company shall furnish them lodging and all that shall be necessary for divine service.

We also order that for their maintenance, they be provided by the Company with the necessary clothing according to their Rule, and for their sustenance, namely, for each religious, one cask of Bordeaux wine, two quarts of flour, one half quart of bacon, one half quart of beef, one half quart (ancre) of brandy, twenty-five pounds of large beans, or like quantity of peas and kidney beans, eight pounds of Holland or *Gruyere* cheese, twenty-four pounds of candles, one half pound of pepper, twenty pots of vinegar, twenty-five pounds of salt and twelve pounds of olive oil.

We also expect that they be provided from the magazines of the Company with household utensils and with whatever tools may be necessary for their houses, on condition that all they shall receive in this way from the Company shall be held only for use, and that they shall not cultivate more land than is required for the needs of their houses in the colony. We finally enjoin the Directors of the colony to keep and send annually to the Company a particular account of that which shall be furnished the Capuchin Fathers, in which account shall be noted the value of the furniture in money at the rate of its worth in the market of the country.

Given at Paris, May 16, 1722, *Signed:* Jagon de Mauhault, Ougran, Fontaineu.

24. The Banishment of the Jesuits From Louisiana and the Illinois Country According to François Philibert Watrin, S.J., September 3, 1764

THE current of opinion in the countries of Europe was often felt with real force in their distant American colonies. By the mid-eighteenth century the Society of Jesus had attained great strength and influence in France, but it had also acquired many powerful enemies among the disciples of the Enlightenment, the nobility, and even so highly placed a figure as Jeanne Poisson, Marquise de Pompadour, the mistress of Louis XV. This enmity finally triumphed over the Jesuits and their supporters and in 1762 there began the systematic suppression of their society. The French Jesuits had been evangelizing the Illinois Country ever since Jacques Marquette, S.J., had introduced Christianity to the Mississippi Valley at the Mission of the Immaculate Conception which he established among the Kaskaskia Indians at one of their villages on the Illinois River in the spring of 1675. Moreover, they had been steadily at work in Louisiana since the founding of their first mission in that colony in 1725. But the action taken in France against the Jesuits soon found a counterpart in the colonies and on July 9, 1763, the superior council of Louisiana decreed the suppression of the society in that colony and the Illinois Country. It need hardly be emphasized what a blow this proved to the Church's missions in those vast areas. François Philibert Watrin, S.J. (1697–1771), was superior of the Illinois mission at the time, a man who had spent thirty years in Louisiana. After his banishment to Europe he wrote an account of the Jesuits' last days in the colony and gave details of the brutal manner in which the missionaries' work was brought to an abrupt close. Source: Reuben Gold Thwaites (Ed.), *The Jesuit Relations and Allied Documents* (Cleveland: Burrows Brothers Co., 1900), LXX, 212–301.

. . . In the month of June, 1763, the Jesuits of New Orleans, the capital of Louisiana, were still between hope and fear as to their future fate. As early as the preceding year, they had seen their enemies distribute with a triumphant air, manuscript copies of the decree given by the Parliament of Paris, August 6, 1761. But people worthy of respect had calmed their fears. They were expecting a great deal from the information given in their favor, and above all, from the petition addressed to the King by the bishops of France. They finally learned what they were to expect, at the arrival of the ship, which brought, with the news of peace, orders for their destruction. . . .

Proceedings were begun. It was decreed that the Institute of the Jesuits should be brought to the council, to be examined. It was a great undertaking for this tribunal. All the judges who composed it ought at least to have studied theology, and civil and ecclesiastical law. But, above all, they ought to have understood the language in which the institute is written. Now, this is not the kind of knowledge that is required from judges of colonies. In selecting them, search is not made for pupils of universities, but those among the inhabitants who show some capacity for business are chosen. Accordingly, one finds in these councils elderly shopkeepers, physicians, and officers of troops. . . .

For these reasons we are justified in saying that it was a great undertaking for the council of New Orleans to pronounce upon the Institute of the Jesuits. . . .

The decree was declared on the 9th of July. It was said that the Institute of the Jesuits was hostile to the royal authority, the rights of the bishops, and the public peace and safety; and that the vows uttered according to this institute were null. It was prohibited to these Jesuits, hitherto thus styled, to take that name hereafter, or to wear their customary garb, orders being given them to assume that of secular ecclesiastics. Excepting their books and some wearing apparel which was allowed to them, all their property, real and personal, was to be seized and sold at auction. It was ordained that the chapel ornaments and the sacred vessels of New Orleans should be delivered up to the Reverend Capuchin Fathers; that the chapel ornaments and sacred vessels of the Jesuits living in the country of the Illinois should be delivered up to the Royal Procurator for that country, and that the chapels should then be demolished; and that, finally, the aforesaid Jesuits, so-called, should return to France, embarking upon the first ships ready to depart, — prohibiting them, meanwhile, from remaining together. A sum of six hundred livres was assigned to pay each one's passage, and another, of 1,500 francs, for their sustenance and support for six months. They were enjoined to present themselves, after that term, to Monsieur the duke de Choiseul, secretary of State in the department of marine, to ask him for the pensions which would be assigned from the proceeds of the sale of their property. . . .

. . . It is time to speak of the execution of the decree; it was to be carried out first at New Orleans, and afterward in the Illinois country, at a distance of four or five hundred leagues. There was in that country, as has been said above, a mission of the Jesuits, established at four different posts. They were not forgotten, and a courier was sent to carry the decree of destruction. Meanwhile, it was executed promptly against those of New Orleans. Their establishment was quite near this town, and proportioned to the needs of twelve missionaries; there was quite a large gang of slaves for cultivating the land, and for plying other trades, as is the custom in the colonies; there were also various buildings, with herds of cattle and suitable works. Everything was seized, inventoried, and sold at auction, and this execution lasted a long time; those who were employed therein took their meals in the house. These were the higher officers of justice, with the lesser agents; it is right to suppose that the former kept themselves within the decent behavior that beseemed them, but the others did not consider themselves obliged to assume any disguise. They found themselves well feasted and they were sure that their employment was a lucrative one; so they did not dissemble their feelings. The superior of the Jesuits was obliged to be present at the great feasts which were given at his house during the depredation, and he saw the joy that was shown there. After the sale of the real and personal property, there remained the chapel, with its ornaments and sacred vessels: it was stated in the decree that these effects should be taken to the Reverend Capuchin Fathers; this was done, and it was the least objectionable use that could be made of them. After that, the chapel was razed to the ground; and the sepulcher of the bodies buried for thirty years in this place, and in the neighboring cemetery, remained exposed to profanation. The Jesuits who came back from Louisiana to France have often been asked the reason for this proceeding; they have been told what astonishment and horror was felt at this event; it has been said to them that this was only to be expected from open enemies of the Catholic religion; the Jesuits could only answer these sayings by silence.

The execution of the decree lacked nothing, save to send back the condemned to France; those who were at New Orleans did not wait to be notified of the order to depart. Father Carette embarked to cross over to San Domingo; Father Roy took refuge at Pensacola, at the very time when the English entered this port to take possession of it, and the Spaniards evacuated it by virtue of the treaty of peace; he entered the ship which was to bear the Governor of that place to Vera Cruz. The Father was welcomed there, by the Spanish Fathers of the college, with the greatest kindness; a little while afterward he was made an associate in the province that the Jesuits have in Mexico, by Father François Zéballos, superior of that province. His letter written upon this subject expressed most generous and most Christian sentiments, and all the Jesuits banished from the lands under French domination were invited thither to the same refuge.

Father Le Prédour was among the Alibamons, at a distance of about two hundred leagues, and much time was necessary for transmitting a copy of the decree to him. Then, after he had received it, he was obliged to await an opportunity to reach the fort of Mobile, and from that place, New Orleans; we have recently learned that he has returned to France. There were no more to send away, then, but Father Baudoin, superior of all missions; but he was seventy-two years old, and infirm, — as one may expect of a man who had passed thirty-five years in Louisiana, and of those thirty-five years about twenty in the midst of the forests, with the Chactas; he had no relatives in France, nor was he accustomed to this country; as he was born in Canada, he was permitted to remain. He was assigned a pension of nine hundred livres, which would be equivalent in France to the sum of three or four hundred francs. Monsieur Boré, an old resident of the country, offered him an asylum with himself, upon his estate, and thus proved the sincerity of the friendship which he had always shown toward the Jesuits.

Meanwhile the courier despatched to Illinois to bear the decree arrived on the night of September 23, at fort Chartres, distant six leagues from the residence of the Jesuits. He delivered to the procurator of the king the commission which charged him to execute the decree; and on the next day, about eight or nine o'clock in the morning, that officer of justice repaired to the house of the Jesuits, accompanied by the registrar and the baliff of that jurisdiction. Some days afterward, he tried to turn to account the moderation that he used in not arriving during the night, "as his orders directed," said he; with that exception, they ought to have been satisfied with his exactness. He read to Father Watrin, the superior, the decree of condemnation, and, having given him a copy of it, he made him at once leave his room to put the seal upon it; the same thing was done with the other missionaries who happened to be in the house. There remained one hall where they could remain together, although with great inconvenience; but this favor was refused them, because the guards placed in custody of the property seized opposed this; they were unwilling that the Jesuits should be able to watch their conduct so closely. The procurator of the King feared to displease these guardians, and would not permit the Jesuits even to remain at the house of one of their confrères, — who, being curé of the place, had his private lodging near the parish church; they did not put the seal thereon, because they knew there was nothing to seize. The missionaries, driven from their own house, found quarters as best they could. The superior, sixty-seven years old, departed on foot to find a lodging, a long league away, with a confrère of his, a missionary to the savages; and the French who met him on this journey groaned to see persecution begin with him.

As soon as the savages learned that he had arrived among them, they came to show to him and to Father Meurin, his associate, the share which they took in the distress of their Fathers; the news of their condemnation had already caused many tears to be shed in the village. They were asked why they were thus treated, especially in a country where so many disorders had been so long allowed. The old missionary, after several repeated interrogations, finally replied: *Arechi Kiécouègane tchichi ki canta manghi, — It is because we sternly condemn their follies.* They comprehended the meaning of this answer, — indeed they knew that the Jesuits, in whatever place they may be established, consider themselves bound by their profession to combat vice; and that, in fighting it, they make enemies for themselves.

The Christian savages proposed to send their chief men to Monsieur Neyon, commandant, and to Monsieur Bobé, subdeputy-commissary of the country, to ask that at least Father Meurin, their missionary, be kept in this mission. The two Jesuits told them plainly to do nothing of the kind, because this proceeding would be scoffed at and ineffectual, as having been suggested. They wished, then, to ask that at least the chapel and the house of the missionary be preserved, in order that the best instructed person among them might assemble the children and repeat prayers to them; and that every Sunday and feast-day he might summon those who prayed, that is to say, the Christians, — by the ringing of the bell, to fulfill as well as possible the duties of religion. They did, in fact, make such a request, and obtained what they asked.

Meanwhile, the Procurator of the King relaxed a little in his severity. About the same time he received in a single day four letters from Monsieur Bobé, the commissary, who begged him to moderate his zeal, and allowed the Jesuits to live together with their brethren, the curés of the French. They were closely crowded there, in a house that was built for only one man. Their rooms had been opened, in order that each might be able to take out his mattress and blankets, which they spread upon the floor in the house of the curé. This way of taking their rest, which lasted nearly a month, prepared them for the voyage which they were soon to make upon the Mississippi, for upon the banks of that river one encamps in hardly other fashion. The Jesuits were also permitted to take their clothes and their books, which the decree had left to them. At last, the support of these Fathers was provided for until the time when they should embark to go down to New Orleans. The greater part of the food that was found in their house, was given up to them, and this provision was, in fact, sufficient for the rest of the time that they passed in Illinois.

Finally, it came to making the inventory; time was necessary to collect and put in order the furniture of a large house, the chattels of an important estate, and the cattle scattered in the fields and woods. Besides, there was reason for not hurrying too much; the longer the delays the better they paid those who were employed in that task. . . .

Meanwhile, the auction was finished; the house, the furniture, the cattle, the land had been sold; the slaves were to be taken to New

Orleans, to be sold there for the benefit of the king; and the chapel was to be razed by the man to whom the house had been adjudged. The Jesuits were then permitted to reenter their former home, the use of which was, by a clause inserted in the bill of sale, reserved to them until their embarkation. They found it well cleared; nothing was left except the bedsteads and the straw mattresses; and, in order to lodge there they were obliged to borrow from their friends each a chair and a little table. They found their chapel in a still more melancholy condition; after the sacred vessels and the pictures had been taken away, the shelves of the altar had been thrown down; the linings of the ornaments had been given to negresses decried for their evil lives; and a large crucifix, which had stood above the altar, and the chandeliers, were found placed above a cupboard in a house whose reputation was not good. To see the marks of spoliation in the chapel, one might have thought that it was the enemies of the Catholic religion who had caused it. . . .

Finally the day set for the embarkation came; it was the 24th of November. The baggage of the Jesuits did not embarrass the vessel in which they had taken their passage; they had only their beds and their clothes in small quantities, with some provisions which they had saved for the voyage; this food served not only for them, but for forty-eight negroes embarked with them. These slaves no longer belonged to the Jesuits, having been confiscated for the benefit of the King. But their former masters always preserved the same care in regard to them, and shared quite willingly with these wretches the provisions which they had saved. . . .

The voyage, which might have been very long, lasted only twenty-seven days, because the weather was not so bad as it usually is at that season. The Jesuits found means to say mass every Sunday and every feast-day. . . . Finally, at seven or eight leagues from New Orleans, they reached the estate of Monsieur de Maccarty, former lieutenant of the King in that city, who by his kind attentions recalled . . . the benevolence he had always shown at Illinois. . . . But on departing from that estate, they found themselves in great perplexity. They saw that they were about to enter New Orleans, and they did not know where they could lodge; they were unable to enter their old house, knowing well that it was sold and occupied by other masters. . . . Meanwhile the Reverend Capuchin Fathers, hearing of the arrival of the Jesuits, had come . . . to the landing-place to manifest to them their intention of rendering them all the kind offices that they could . . . and during the six weeks which elapsed before they embarked, there were no marks of friendship which they did not receive from these Reverend Fathers. . . .

However, the Jesuits perceived that their departure was desired. The season was disagreeable, it being still the month of January, the time of rough seas. But an entirely new and well-built ship presented itself; it was the *La Minerve,* of Bayonne, commanded by Monsieur Balanquet, a famous shipowner in the last war, and very much esteemed for his integrity. These reasons determined the Jesuits to embark upon this ship. There were two, however, out of this band of six, who parted from them. Father de la Morinie, remembering that he had suffered upon the sea every evil that can be felt there, almost to death itself, postponed his departure until spring . . . and Father Meurin asked the Gentlemen of the Council for permission to return to the Illinois. This was a brave resolution, after the sale of all the property of the Jesuits: he could not count upon any fund for his subsistence, the French were under no obligation to him, and the savages have more need of receiving than means for giving. . . . His request was granted, and a promise was given to him that a pension of six hundred livres would be asked for him at the court. . . .

THE ENGLISH COLONIES

25. The Charter of Maryland, June 20, 1632

SIR GEORGE CALVERT (c. 1580–1632), one of the chief secretaries and favorites of King James I of England, belonged to that rather rare breed of men who do not hesitate to forfeit a promising political career when it conflicts with their religious convictions. After his conversion to Catholicism in 1625, Calvert resigned his royal secretaryship, although he continued to employ the favor which he retained at court to secure a haven of religious peace in the English colonies for his harassed coreligionists. Attempts to establish a settlement in Newfoundland and Virginia having failed, the first Baron of Baltimore died before he could fulfill his dream. But in June, 1632, Charles I redeemed his father's promises by issuing a generous charter to Baltimore's son, Cecilius Calvert. In view of the anti-Catholic laws of the mother country, and the hostility and suspicion that permeated the government of Charles I in all that related to Catholicism, it is not suprising to find the charter encouraging the erection of churches in the colony which were to be "dedicated and consecrated according to the Ecclesiastical Laws of our Kingdom of England. . . ." In actual fact, however, religious toleration for all Christians was preserved by Calvert, and by reason of the tact and common sense of the proprietor and his Catholic representatives in the colony that policy endured until it was abolished in 1654 by the Puritans who had overthrown Baltimore's government. Source: Francis Newton Thorpe (Ed.), *The Federal and State Constitutions* (Washington: Government Printing Office, 1909), III, 1677–1686.

. . . II. Whereas our well beloved and right trusty Subject Caecilius Calvert, Baron of Baltimore, in our Kingdom of Ireland . . . being animated with a laudable, and pious Zeal for extending the Christian Religion, and also the Territories of our Empire, hath humbly besought Leave of Us, that he may transport, by his own Industry, and Expense, a numerous Colony of the English Nation to a certain Region, herein after described, in a Country hitherto uncultivated, in the Parts of America, and partly occupied by Savages, having no Knowledge of the Divine Being, and that all that Region, with some certain Privileges, and Jurisdiction, appertaining unto the wholesome Government, and State of his Colony and Region aforesaid, may by our Royal Highness be given, granted, and confirmed unto him, and his Heirs.

III. Know Ye, therefore, that We . . . by this our present Charter

. . . do Give, Grant, and Confirm, unto the aforesaid Caecilius, now Baron of Baltimore, his Heirs, and Assigns, all that Part of the Peninsula, or Cherosonese, lying in the Parts of America, between the Ocean on the East, and the Bay of Chesapeake on the West . . .

IV. Also We do Grant . . . unto the said Baron of Baltimore . . . all Islands and Islets within the Limits aforesaid, all and singular Islands and Islets, from the Eastern Shore of the aforesaid Region, towards the East, which have been, or shall be formed in the Sea, situate within Ten marine Leagues from the said Shore . . . And furthermore the Patronages, and Advowsons of all Churches which (with the increasing Worship and Religion of Christ) within the said region . . . hereafter shall happen to be built, together with Licence, and Faculty of erecting and founding Churches, Chapels, and Places of Worship, in convenient and suitable places, within the Premises, and of causing the same to be dedicated and consecrated according to the Ecclesiastical Laws of our Kingdom of England, with all, and singular such, and as ample Rights, Jurisdictions, Privileges, Prerogatives, Royalties, Liberties, Immunities, and royal Rights, and temporal Franchises whatsoever, as well by Sea as by Land, within the Region . . . aforesaid, to be had, exercised, used, and enjoyed, as any Bishop of Durham, within the Bishoprick or County Palatine of Durham, in our Kingdom of England, ever heretofore, hath had, held, used, or enjoyed or of Right could, or ought to have, hold, use, or enjoy.

V. And we do by these Presents . . . Make, Create, and Constitute Him, the now Baron of Baltimore, and his Heirs, the true and absolute Lords and Proprietaries of the Region aforesaid, and of all other the Premises (except the before excepted) saving always the Faith and Allegiance and Sovereign Dominion due to Us . . . To Hold of Us . . . as of our Castle of Windsor, in our County of Berks, in free and common Soccage, by Fealty only for all Services, and not in Capite, nor by Knight's Service, Yielding therefore unto Us . . . Two Indian Arrows of these Parts, to be delivered at the said Castle of Windsor, every Year, on Tuesday in Easter Week: And also the fifth Part of all Gold and Silver Ore, which shall happen from Time to Time, to be found within the aforesaid Limits.

VI. Now, That the aforesaid Region . . . may be eminently distinguished above all other Regions of that Territory . . . Know Ye, that . . . We do . . . Erect and Incorporate the same into a Province, and nominate the same Maryland, by which Name We will that it shall from henceforth be called.

VII. And . . . We . . . do grant unto the said now Baron . . . and to his Heirs, for the good and happy Government of the said Province, free, full, and absolute Power, by the tenor of these Presents, to Ordain, Make, and Enact Laws, of what kind soever, according to their sound Discretions, whether relating to the Public State of the said Province, or the private Utility of Individuals, of and with the Advice, Assent, and Approbation of the Free-Men of the same Province, or of the greater Part of them, or of their Delegates or Deputies, whom We will shall be called together for the framing of Laws, when and as often as Need shall require, by the aforesaid now Baron of Baltimore . . . and in the Form which shall seem best to him . . . and duly to execute the same upon all Persons, for the Time being, within the aforesaid Province, and the Limits thereof, or under his or their Government and Power . . . by the Imposition of Fines, Imprisonment, and other Punishment whatsoever; even if it be necessary, and the Quality of the Offence require it, by Privation of Member, or Life . . . So, nevertheless, that the Laws aforesaid be consonant to Reason and be not repugnant or contrary, but (so far as conveniently may be) agreeable to the Laws, Statutes, Customs and Rights of this Our Kingdom of England.

XVII. Moreover, We will, appoint, and ordain, and by these Presents, for Us, our Heirs and Successors, do grant unto the aforesaid now Baron of Baltimore, his Heirs and Assigns, from Time to Time, forever, shall have, and enjoy the Taxes and Subsidies payable, or arising within the Ports, Harbors, and other Creeks and Places aforesaid, for Wares bought and sold, and Things there to be laden, or unladen, to be reasonably assessed by them, and the People there as aforesaid, on emergent Occasion; to whom We grant Power by these Presents, for Us, our Heirs and Successors, to assess and impose the said Taxes and Subsidies there, upon just Cause and in due Proportion.

XVIII. And Furthermore . . . We . . . do give . . . unto the aforesaid now Baron of Baltimore . . . full and absolute Licence, Power, and Authority . . . that he assign, alien, grant, demise, or enfeoff so many, such, and proportionate Parts and Parcels of the Premises, to any Person or Persons willing to purchase the same, as they shall think convenient, to have and to hold . . . in Feesimple, or Fee-tail, or for Term of Life, Lives, of Years; to hold of the aforesaid now Baron of Baltimore . . . by . . . such . . . Services, Customs and Rents of This Kind, as to the same now Baron of Baltimore . . . shall seem fit and agreeable, and not immediately of Us. . . .

XIX. We . . . also . . . do . . . grant Licence to the same Baron of Baltimore . . . to erect any Parcels of Land within the Province aforesaid, into Manors, and in every of those Manors, to have and to hold a Court-Baron, and all Things which to a Court-Baron do belong . . .

26. Baron Baltimore's Instructions to His Colonists, November 13, 1633

THE second Baron Baltimore, Cecilius Calvert (1606–1675), was conciliatory by nature and a man of great astuteness and tact. Only twenty-seven when he launched his colony, he was mature enough to realize that the entire project might quickly be wrecked if his colonists fell to quarrelling over religion. He, therefore, counseled his deputies in a set of instructions written a few days before the party sailed to see to it that the Catholics practiced prudence and forebearance toward their Protestant associates — a numerical majority — on the subject of religion. The same spirit lay behind his instruction to have only Church of England men sent as ambassadors of peace to the Governor of Virginia and to William Claiborne, the man who was so soon to bring grief upon the colony of Maryland. It is evident, too, in Baltimore's way of stating that his first intention in founding the colony was to convert the Indians "to Christianity," and that "a church or a chapel" should immediately be built, thus avoiding any mention of a particular denomination. The proprietor's realism and political sense can likewise be seen in his demand that the colonists at once take an oath of allegiance to Charles I. Source: Clayton Colman Hall (Ed.), *Narratives of Early Maryland, 1633–1684* (New York: Charles Scribner's Sons, 1910), pp. 16, 18–21; now included in *Original Narratives of Early American History*, copyright Barnes & Noble, Inc., New York.

---

1. Inpri: His Lo^pp^ requires his said Governor and Commissioners th^t^ in their voyage to Mary Land they be very carefull to preserve unity and peace amongst all the passengers on Shipp-board, and that they suffer no scandal nor offence to be given to any of the Protestants, whereby any just complaint may heereafter be made, by them, in Virginea or in England, and that for that end, they cause all Acts of Romane Catholique Religion to be done as privately as may be, and that they instruct all the Romane Catholiques to be silent upon all occasions of discourse concerning matters of Religion; and that the said Governor and Commissioners treate the Protestants wth as much mildness and favor as Justice will permit. And this to be observed at Land as well as at Sea. . . .

4. That by the first oportunity after theyr arrivall in Mary Land

they cause a messenger to be dispatcht away to James Town such a one as is conformable to the Church of England, and as they may according to the best of their judgments trust; and he to carry his ma^{ties} letter to Sr John Harvie the Governor and to the rest of the Councell there, as likewise his Lo^{pps} letter to S^{r} Jo: Harvie, and to give him notice of their arrivall: And to have in charge, upon the delivery of the said letters to behave himself wth much respect unto the Governor, and to tell him th^{t} his Lo^{pp} had an intention to have come himself in person this yeare into those parts, as he may perceive by his ma^{ties} letter to him but finding that the setling of that business of his Plantation and some other occasions, required his presence in England for some time longer than he expected, he hath deferred his owne coming till the next years, when he will not faile by the grace of god to be there. . . .

5. That they write a letter to Cap: Clayborne as soon as conveniently other more necessary occasions will give them leave after their arrivall in the Countrey; to give him notice of their arrivall and of the Authority and charge committed to them by his L^{opp} and to send the said letter together wth his L^{opps} to him by some trusty messenger that is likewise conformable unto the Church of England, wth a message also from them to him if it be not inserted in their letter wch is better, to invite him kindly to come unto them, and to signify that they have some business of importance to speake wth him about from his L^{opp} wch concernes his good very much; And if he come unto them then that they use him courteously and well, and tell him, that his L^{opp} understanding that he hath settled a plantacion there wthin the precincts of his L^{opps} Pattent, wished them to lett him know that his L^{opp} is willing to give him all the encouragement he cann to proceede. . . .

6. That when they have made choice of the place where they intend to settle themselves and that they have brought their men ashoare wth all their provisions, they do assemble all the people together in a fitt and decent manner and then cause his ma^{ties} letters pattents to be publickely read by his L^{opps} Secretary John Bolles, and afterwards his L^{opps} Commission to them, and that either the Governor or one of the Commissioners presently after make some short declaration to the people of His L^{opps} intentions wch he means to pursue in this his intended plantation, wch are first the honor of god by endeavoring the conversion of the savages to Christianity, secondly the augmentation of his ma^{ties} Empire and Dominions in those parts of the world by reducing them under the subjection of his Crowne,

and thirdly by the good of such of his Countreymen as are willing to adventure their fortunes and themselves in it, by endeavoring all he cann, to assist them, that they may reape the fruites of their charges and labors according to the hopefulness of the thing, wth as much freedome comfort and incouragement as they cann desire. . . . And that at this time they take occasion to minister an oath of Allegeance to his ma^{tie} unto all and every one upon the place, after having first publikely in the presence of the people taken it themselves; letting them know that his Lo^{pp} gave particular directions to have it one of the first things that were done, to testify to the world that none should enjoy the benefitt of his ma^{ties} gratious Grant unto his L^{opp} of that place, but such as should give a publique assurance of their fidelity and allegeance to his ma^{tie}. . . .

9. That where they intended to settle the Plantacion they first make choice of a fitt place, and a competent quantity of ground for a fort wthin wch or neere unto it a convenient house, and a church or a chappel adjacent may be built, for the seate of his L^{opp} or his Governor or other Commissioners for the time being in his absence, both wch his L^{opp} would have them take care should in the first place be erected, in some proportion at least, as much as is necessary for the present use though not so complete in every part as in fine afterwards they may be and to send his L^{opp} a Platt of it and of the scituation, by the next oportunity, if it be done by that time, if not or but part of it nevertheless to send a Platt of what they intend to do in it. That they likewise make choice of a fitt place neere unto it to seate a towne. . . .

27. The English Jesuits Establish the Mission of Maryland, March–April, 1634

IN MANY ways the most significant Catholic mission in colonial America was that inaugurated by three English Jesuits in southern Maryland in March, 1634. These men, Fathers Andrew White (1579–1656) and John Altham (1589–1640) and Brother Thomas Gervase (1590–1637), were the pioneers of a religious enterprise that was to endure — often under severe persecution — beyond the American Revolution. From their original headquarters at St. Mary's City there sprang an unbroken succession of priests from whose number the first bishop of the United States was ultimately chosen. The English Jesuits began their American undertaking under conditions very different from those of their Spanish and French confreres. From the very outset they were entirely devoid of any temporal assistance from the government and were compelled to earn their livelihood from the land

in the same manner as the lay gentlemen adventurers; they represented a Church which had been heavily persecuted in the mother country and which within twenty years would feel the whip of penal legislation in the colony; and they were part of a colony which was composed of men of mixed religious beliefs. They had to walk circumspectly, therefore, lest their missionary zeal be the cause of creating difficulties for the lord proprietor with the Protestant government in England. The following document was written by Andrew White, S.J., from St. Mary's City late in April, 1634, to Mutius Vitelleschi, General of the Jesuits, and described the voyage and the first month in Maryland. Source: E. A. Dalrymple (Ed.), ***Narrative of a Voyage to Maryland by Father Andrew White, S.J. An Account of the Colony of the Lord Baron of Baltimore. Extracts from Different Letters of Missionaries, from the Year 1635 to the Year 1677*** **(Baltimore: Maryland Historical Society, 1874), pp. 10–43.**

On the 22nd of the month of November, in the year 1633, being St. Cecilia's day, we set sail from Cowes, in the Isle of Wight, with a gentle east wind blowing. And, after committing the principal parts of the ship to the protection of God especially, and of His most Holy Mother, and St. Ignatius, and all the guardian angels of Maryland, we sailed on a little way between the two shores, and the wind failing us, we stopped opposite Yarmouth Castle, which is near the southern end of the same Island, (Isle of Wight). Here we were received with a cheerful salute of artillery. Yet we were not without apprehension; for the sailors were murmuring among themselves, saying that they were expecting a messenger with letters from London, and from this it seemed that they were contriving to delay us. But God brought their plans to confusion. For that very night, a favorable but strong wind, arose; and a French cutter, which had put into the same harbor with us, being forced to set sail, came near running into our pinnace. The latter, therefore, to avoid being run down, having cut away and lost an anchor, set sail without delay; and since it was dangerous to drift about in that place, made haste to get farther out to sea. And so that we might not lose sight of our pinnace, we determined to follow. Thus the designs of the sailors, who were plotting against us, were frustrated. This happened on the 23d of November, St. Clement's day, who, because he had been tied to an anchor and thrown into the sea, obtained the crown of martyrdom. "And showed the inhabitants of the earth, how to declare the wonderful things of God. . . ."

Now on Sunday the 24th, and Monday the 25th of November, we had fair sailing all the time until evening. But presently, the wind getting round to the north, such a terrible storm arose, that the merchant ship I spoke of from London, being driven back on her course, returned to England, and reached a harbor much resorted to, among the Paumonians. Those on board our pinnace also, since she was a vessel of only 40 tons, began to lose confidence in her strength, and sailing near, they warned us, that if they apprehended shipwreck, they would notify us by hanging out lights from the mast-head. We meanwhile sailed on in our strong ship of four hundred tons — a better could not be built of wood and iron. We had a very skilful captain, and so he was given his choice, whether he would return to England, or keep on struggling with the winds: if he yielded to these, the Irish shore close by awaited us, which is noted for its hidden rocks and frequent shipwrecks. Nevertheless his bold spirit, and his desire to test the strength of the new ship, which he then managed for the first time, prevailed with the captain. He resolved to try the sea, although he confessed that it was the more dangerous, on account of being so narrow.

And the danger was near at hand; for the winds increasing, and the sea growing more boisterous, we could see the pinnace in the distance, showing two lights at her masthead. Then indeed we thought it was all over with her, and that she had been swallowed up in the deep whirlpools; for in a moment she had passed out of sight, and no news of her reached us for six months afterwards. Accordingly we were all of us certain the pinnace had been lost; yet God had better things in store for us, for the fact was, that finding herself no match for the violence of the waves, she had avoided the Virginian ocean, with which we were already contending, by returning to England, to the Scilly Isles. And making a fresh start from thence . . . she overtook us . . . at a large harbor in the Antilles. And thus God, who oversees the smallest things, guided, protected, and took care of the little vessel. . . .

So Tuesday, Wednesday, and Thursday passed with variable winds, and we made small progress. On Friday, a southeast wind prevailing, and driving before it thick and dark clouds, so fierce a tempest broke forth towards evening, that it seemed every minute as if we must be swallowed up by the waves. Nor was the weather more promising on the next day, which was the festival of Andrew the Apostle. . . .

At this juncture the minds of the bravest among us, both passengers and sailors, were struck with terror; for they acknowledged that they had seen other ships wrecked in a less severe storm; but now, this hurricane called forth the prayers and vows of the Catholics in honor of the Blessed Virgin Mary and Her Immaculate Conception, of Saint Ignatius, the Patron Saint of Maryland, Saint Michael, and all the guardian angels of the same country. And each one hastened to purge his soul by the Sacrament of penance. For all control over the rudder being lost, the ship now drifted about like a dish in the water, at the mercy of the winds and the waves, until God showed us a way of safety. At first, I confess, I had been engrossed with the apprehension of the ship's being lost, and of losing my own life; but after I had spent some time, in praying more fervently than was my usual custom, and had set forth to Christ the Lord, to the Blessed Virgin, St. Ignatius, and the angels of Maryland, that the purpose of this journey was to glorify the Blood of Our Redeemer in the salvation of the barbarians, and also to raise up a kingdom for the Saviour (if he would condescend to prosper our poor efforts), to consecrate another gift to the Immaculate Virgin, His Mother, and many things to the same effect; great comfort shone in upon my soul, and at the same time so firm a conviction that we should be delivered, not only from this storm, but from every other during that voyage, that with me there could be no room left for doubt. I had betaken myself to prayer, when the sea was raging its worst, and (may this be to the glory of God,) I had scarcely finished, when they observed that the storm was abating. That indeed brought me to a new frame of mind, and filled me at the same time with great joy and admiration, since I understood much more clearly the greatness of God's love towards the people of Maryland, to whom your Reverence has sent us. Eternal praises to the most sweet graciousness of the Redeemer!!

When the sea had thus immediately abated, we had delightful weather for three months, so that the captain and his men declared they had never seen it calmer or pleasanter; for we suffered no inconvenience, not even for a single hour. However, when I speak of three months, I do not mean to say we were that long at sea, but I include the whole voyage, and also the time we stopped at the Antilles. For the actual voyage occupied only seven weeks and two days: and that is considered a quick passage. . . .

. . . if you except the usual sea-sickness, no one was attacked by any disease, until the Festival of the Nativity of our Lord. In order that that day might be better kept, wine was given out; and those who drank of it too freely, were seized the next day with a fever; and of these, not long afterwards, about twelve died, among whom two were Catholics. The loss of Nicholas Fairfax and James Barefote was deeply felt among us.

[Stops were made at Barbodos and Virginia.] After being kindly treated for eight of nine days, we set sail on the third of March, and entering the Chesapeak Bay, we turned our course to the north to reach the Potomeack River. The Chesopeacke Bay, ten leagues (30 Italian miles) wide, . . . is four, five, and six fathoms deep, and abounds in fish when the season is favorable; you will scarcely find a more beautiful body of water. Yet it yields the palm to the Potomeack River, which we named after St. Gregory.

Having now arrived at the wished-for country, we allotted names according to circumstances. And indeed the Promontory, which is toward the south, we consecrated with the name St. Gregory (now Smith Point), naming the northern one (now Point Lookout) St. Michael's, in honor of all the angels. Never have I beheld a larger or more beautiful river. . . . Just at the mouth of the river, we observed the natives in arms. That night, fires blazed through the whole country, and since they had never seen such a large ship, messengers were sent in all directions, who reported that a *Canoe,* like an island had come with as many men as there were trees in the woods. We went on, however, to Herons' Islands, so called from the immense number of these birds. The first island we came to, [we called] St. Clement's Island, and as it has a sloping shore, there is no way of getting to it except by wading. Here the women, who had left the ship, to do the washing, upset the boat and came near being drowned, losing also a large part of my linen clothes, no small loss in these parts. . . .

On the day of the *Annunciation of the Most Holy Virgin* Mary in the year 1634, we celebrated the mass for the first time, on this island. This had never been done before in this part of the world. After we had completed the sacrifice, we took upon our shoulders a great cross, which we had hewn out of a tree, and advancing in order to the appointed place, with the assistance of the Governor and his associates and the other Catholics, we erected a trophy to Christ the Saviour, humbly reciting, on our bended knees, the Litanies of the Sacred Cross, with great emotion.

Now when the Governor had understood that many Princes were subject to the Emperor of the Pascatawaye, he determined to visit him, in order that, after explaining the reason of our voyage, and gaining his good will, he might secure an easier access to the others. . . . And when he had learned that the Savages had fled inland, he went on to a city which takes its name from the river, being also called Potomeack. Here the young King's uncle named *Archihu* was his guardian, and took his place in the kingdom; a sober and discreet man. He willingly listened to Father (John) Altham, (Altam, that is

Oliver) who had been selected to accompany the Governor, (for he (the Governor) kept me still with the ship's cargo.) And when the Father explained, as far as he could through the interpreter, Henry Fleet . . . the errors of the heathen, he would every little while, acknowledge his own: and when he was informed that we had come thither, not to make war, but out of good will towards them, in order to impart civilized instruction to his ignorant race, and show them the way to heaven, and at the same time with the intention of communicating to them the advantages of distant countries, he gave us to understand that he was pleased with our coming. The interpreter was one of the Protestants of Virginia. And so, as the Father could not stop for further discourse at the time, he promised that he would return before very long. "That is just what I wish," said Archihu, "we will eat at the same table; my followers too shall go to hunt for you, and we will have all things in common.". . .

Going about nine leagues (that is about 27 miles) from St. Clement, we sailed into the mouth of a river, on the north side of the Potomac, which we named after St. George. This river, (or rather, arm of the sea,) like the Thames, runs from south to north about twenty miles before you come to fresh water. At its mouth are two harbors, capable of containing three hundred ships of the largest size. We consecrated one of these to St. George: the other, which is more inland, to the Blessed Virgin Mary.

The left side of the river was the abode of King *Yaocomico* (Yaocomico.) We landed on the right-side, and going in about a mile from the shore, we laid out the plan of a city, naming it after St. Mary. And, in order to avoid every appearance of injustice, and afford no opportunity for hostility, we bought from the King thirty miles of that land, delivering in exchange, axes, hatchets, rakes, and several yards of cloth. This district is already named *Augusta Carolina.* The *Susquehanoes,* a tribe inured to war, the bitterest enemies of King *Yaocomico,* making repeated inroads, ravage his whole territory, and have driven the inhabitants, from their apprehension of danger, to seek homes elsewhere. This is the reason why we so easily secured a part of his kingdom: God by this means opening a way for His own Everlasting Law and Light. They move away every day, first one party and then another, and leave us their houses, lands and cultivated fields. Surely this is like a miracle, that barbarous men, a few days before arrayed in arms against us, should so willingly surrender themselves to us like lambs, and deliver up to us themselves and their property. The finger of God is in this, and He purposes some great benefit to this nation. Some few, however, are allowed to dwell among us until next year. But then the land is to be left entirely to us. . . .

They live in houses built in an oblong, oval shape. . . . Their kings . . . and chief men have private apartments, as it were, of their own, and beds, made by driving four posts into the ground, and arranging poles above them horizontally. One of these cabins has fallen to me and my associates, in which we are accommodated well enough for the time, until larger dwellings are provided. You would call this the first chapel of Maryland, though it is fitted up much more decently than when the Indians lived in it. At the next voyage, if God favors our undertaking, our house shall not be destitute of those things, which are found useful in others.

The race are of a frank and cheerful disposition, and understand any matter correctly when it is stated to them: they have a keen sense of taste and smell, and in sight too, they surpass the Europeans. They live, for the most part, on a kind of paste, which they call *Pone,* and *Omini,* both of which are made of Indian corn; and sometimes they add fish, or what they have procured by hunting and fowling. They are especially careful to refrain from wine and warm drinks, and are not easily persuaded to taste them, except some whom the English have corrupted with their own vices. With respect to chastity, I confess that I have not yet observed, in man or woman, any act which even savored of levity, yet they are daily with us and among us, and take pleasure in our society. They run to us of their own accord, with a cheerful expression on their faces, and offer us what they have taken in hunting or fishing sometimes also they bring us food, and oysters boiled or roasted . . . and this they do, when invited in a few words of their own language, which we have hitherto contrived to learn by means of signs. They marry several wives, yet they keep inviolate their conjugal faith. The women present a sober and modest appearance.

They cherish generous feelings towards all, and make a return for whatever kindness you may have shown them. They resolve upon nothing rashly, or while influenced by a sudden impulse of the mind, but they act deliberately, therefore, when anything of importance is proposed at any time, they think it over for a while in silence; then they speak briefly for or against it: they are very tenacious of their purpose. Surely these men, if they are once imbued with Christian precepts, (and there seems to be nothing to oppose this, except our ignorance of the language spoken in these parts,) will become eminent observers of virtue and humanity. They are possessed with a wonderful longing for civilized intercourse with us, and for European garments. And they would long ago have worn clothing, if they had not been prevented by the avarice of the merchants, who do not exchange their cloth for anything but beavers. But everyone cannot get a beaver by hunting. God forbid that we should imitate the avarice of these men!

On account of our ignorance of their language, it does not yet appear what ideas they have besides, about Religion. We do not put much confidence in the Protestant interpreters: we have (only) hastily learned these few things. They acknowledge one God of Heaven, yet they pay him no outward worship. But they strive in every way to appease a certain imaginary spirit, which they call *Ochre,* that he may not hurt them. They worship corn and fire, as I hear, as Gods that are very bountiful to the human race. Some of our party report that they saw the following ceremony in the temple at (of?) *Barchuxem.* On an appointed day, all the men and women of every age, from several districts, gathered together round a large fire; the younger ones stood nearest the fire, behind these stood those who were older. Then they threw deer's fat on the fire, and lifting their hands to heaven, and raising their voices, they cried out *Yaho! Yaho!* Then making room, someone brings forward quite a large bag: in the bag is a pipe and a powder which they call *Potu.* The pipe is such a one as is used among us for smoking tobacco, but much larger; then the bag is carried round the fire, and the boys and girls follow it, singing alternately with tolerably pleasant voices, *Yaho, yaho.* Having completed the circuit, the pipe is taken out of the bag, and the powder called *Potu* is distributed to each one, as they stand near; this is lighted in the pipe, and each one, drawing smoke from the pipe, blows it over the several members of his body, and consecrates them. They were not allowed to learn anything more, except that they seem to have had some knowledge of the Flood, by which the world was destroyed, on account of the wickedness of mankind.

We have been here only one month, and so the remaining particulars must be kept for the next voyage, but this I do say that the soil seems remarkably fertile: in passing through the very thick woods, at every step we tread on strawberries, vines, sassafras, acorns, and walnuts. The soil is dark and not hard, to the depth of a foot, and overlays a rich, red clay. There are lofty trees everywhere, except where the land has been cultivated by a few persons. Numerous springs furnish a supply of water. No animals are seen except deer, beavers and squirrels, which are as large as the hares of Europe.

There is an infinite number of birds of various colors, such as eagles, cranes, swans, geese, partridges and ducks. From these facts, it is inferred that the country is not without such things, as contribute to the prosperity or pleasure of those, who inhabit it.

28. The State of Catholicism in Maryland, 1638

IN THE first years of their mission in the colony of Maryland the Jesuits were hampered from carrying out their desire to convert the Indians by the hostile acts of neighboring tribes and of the Puritans from Virginia, the reluctance of the colonial officials to run the risk of losing their priests, and the necessity of establishing themselves on the land as their sole source of income. But their religious ministrations to the colonists bore fruitful results as can be seen from the following account embodied in the *Annual Letter* for 1638 which reveals a healthy state of religion among the Maryland Catholics, progress in converting some Protestants, and comfort afforded to a number of Catholics among the indentured servants of Virginia. At the time the letter was written there were three Jesuit priests in Maryland: Andrew White, John Altham, and Thomas Copley. If the original letter carried the name of the author it was eliminated by the Jesuit editor in England before it was sent on to the Jesuit headquarters in Rome. Source: E. A. Dalrymple (Ed.), *Narrative of a Voyage to Maryland by Father Andrew White, S.J. An Account of the Colony of the Lord Baron of Baltimore. Extracts from Different Letters of Missionaries, from the Year 1635 to the Year 1677* (Baltimore: Maryland Historical Society, 1874), pp. 54–62.

Four Fathers gave their attention to this Mission, with one assistant in temporal affairs; and he, indeed, after enduring severe toils for the space of five years, with the greatest patience, humility, and ardent love, chanced to be seized by the disease prevailing at the time, and happily exchanged this wretched life for an immortal one.[1]

He was also shortly followed by one of the Fathers,[2] who was young indeed, but on account of his remarkable qualities of mind, evidently of great promise. He had scarcely spent two months in this mission, when, to the great grief of all of us, he was carried off by the common sickness prevailing in the Colony, from which no one of the three remaining priests has escaped unharmed; yet we have not ceased to labor, to the best of our ability among the neighboring people.

[1] Brother Thomas Gervase (1590–1637), who had come out with the original colonists.

[2] John Knowles (1607–1637).

And though the rulers of the Colony have not yet allowed us to dwell among the savages, both on account of the prevailing sickness, and also, because of the hostile disposition which the barbarians evince towards the English, they having slain a man from this Colony, who was staying among them for the sake of trading, and having also entered into a conspiracy against our whole nation; yet we hope that one of us will shortly secure a station among the barbarians. Meanwhile, we devote ourselves more zealously to the English; and since there are Protestants as well as Catholics in the Colony, we have labored for both, and God has blessed our labors.

For, among the Protestants, nearly all who have come from England, in this year 1638, and many others, have been converted to the faith, together with four servants, whom we purchased in Virginia, (another Colony of our Kingdom), for necessary services, and five mechanics, whom we hired for a month, and have in the meantime won to God. Not long afterwards, one of these, after being duly prepared for death, by receiving the sacraments, departed this life. And among these persons hardly anything else worth mentioning has occurred. . . .

Besides these, one of us, going out of the Colony, found two Frenchmen, one of whom had been without the sacraments of the Catholic Church for three entire years; the other, who was already near death, having spent fifteen whole years among Heretics, had lived just as they do. The Father aided the former with the sacraments and confirmed him in the Catholic faith as much as he could. The latter he restored to the Catholic Church, and, administering all the sacraments, prepared him for dying happily.

As for the Catholics, the attendance on the sacraments here is so large, that it is not greater among the Europeans, in proportion to the number of Catholics. The more ignorant have been catechised, and Catechetical Lectures have been delivered for the more advanced every Sunday; but, on Feast days sermons have been rarely neglected. The sick and the dying, who have been very numerous this year, and who dwelt far apart, we have assisted in every way, so that not even a single one has died without the sacraments. We have buried very many, and baptized various persons. And, although there are not wanting frequent occasions of dissension, yet none of any importance has arisen here in the last nine months, which we have not immediately allayed. By the blessing of God, we have this consolation, that no vices spring up among the new Catholics, although settlements of this kind are not usually supplied from the best class of men.

We bought off in Virginia, two Catholics, who had sold themselves into bondage, nor was the money ill-spent, for both showed themselves good Christians: one, indeed, surpasses the ordinary standard. Some others have performed the same duty of Charity, buying thence Catholic servants, who are very numerous in that country. For every year, very many sell themselves thither into bondage, and living among men of the worst example, and, being destitute of all spiritual aid, they generally make shipwreck of their souls.

In the case of one, we adore the remarkable providence and mercy of God, which brought a man encompassed in the world with very many difficulties, and now at length living in Virginia, almost continually without any aid to his soul, to undertake these exercises, not long before his death. This design a severe sickness prevented, which he bore with the greatest patience, with a mind generally fixed on God; and at length having properly received all the sacraments in the most peaceful manner, beyond what is usual, renders back to the Creator the breath of the life that remained, which had been so full of troubles and disquietudes. . . .

29. Virginia's Act Against Catholics and Priests, March, 1642

FROM the foundation of Virginia as a colony a strong hostility toward Catholics had been evident. When the first Baron of Baltimore visited there in October, 1629, with a view to finding a place for his coreligionists to settle, he was at once confronted by a demand that he take the oath of supremacy recognizing the king as head of the Church. By 1640 matters had become critical again for the Catholics in England and in the years 1641–1642 eleven priests were put to death. This situation was reflected in Virginia with attacks upon the neighboring colony of Maryland, and the passage of an act by the Virginia assembly in March, 1642, which sought to seal off the colony from affording refuge to those who might secretly be Catholics by exacting the oath of supremacy, as well as from giving any stay or comfort to refugee priests. Source: William Waller Hening (Ed.), *The Statutes at Large; Being a Collection of all the Laws of Virginia* (Richmond: Samuel Pleasants, Jr., 1809), I, 268–269.

Whereas it was enacted at an Assembly in January 1641, that according to a statute made in the third year of the reigne of our sovereign Lord King James of blessed memory, that no popish recusants should at any time hereafter exercize the place or places of secret councellors, register, comiss: surveyors or sheriffe, or any other publique place, but he utterly disabled for the same, And further it was enacted that none should be admitted into any of the aforesaid offices or places before he or they had taken the oath of allegiance and supremacy, And if any person or persons whatsoever should by sinister or corrupt meanes assume to himselfe any of the aforesaid places of any other publique office whatsoever and refuse to take the aforesaid oaths, he or they so convicted before an Assembly should be dismissed of his said office, And for his offence therein forfeit one thousand pounds of tobacco to be disposed of at the next Assembly after conviction, And it is further enacted by the authoritie aforesaid that the Statute in force against the popish recusants be duely executed in this government, And that it should not be lawfull under the penaltie aforesaid for any popish priest that shall hereafter arrive to remaine above five days after warning given for his departure by the Governour or commander of the place, where he or they shall bee, if wind and weather hinder not his departure, And that the said act should be in force ten days after the publication thereof, at James City, this present Grand Assembly to all intents and purposes doth hereby confirm the same.

30. Massachusetts Bay Passes an Anti-Priest Law, May 26, 1647

IT DID not need the example of Virginia in 1642, the religious bitterness of the Thirty Years' War in Europe, and the proximity of the French Catholics with their missionaries in present-day Maine and Nova Scotia to alarm the Puritans of Massachusetts Bay over the prospects of what might happen if a Catholic priest were to settle in their midst. Actually some of the Puritans believed that were were disguised priests at work in the colony. These circumstances served, therefore, as an occasion for the passage of a law in May, 1647, that would bar the presence of priests in the future. Source: Nathaniel B. Shurtleff (Ed.), *Records of the Governor and Company of the Massachusetts Bay in New England* (Boston: William White, 1854), III, 112.

This Court, taking into consideration the great warrs & combustions which are this day in Europe, & that the same are obserued to be cheifly raysed & fomented by the secrit practises of those of the Jesuiticall order, for the prevention of like euills amongst o[r]selues, its ordred, by the authorities of this Court, that no Jesuit or ecclesiasticall pson ordayned by ye authoritie of the pope shall henceforth come w[th]in o[r] jurisdiction; & if any pson shall give any cause of suspision that he is one of such societie, he shalbe brought before some of the magists, & if he cannot free himselfe of such suspitiō, he shalbe comitted or bound on to the next Court of Assistants, to be tried & proceeded with by banish[nt] or otherwise, as the Court shall see cause, & if any such pson so banished shalbe taken the 2d time w[th]in this jurisdiction, he shall vppon lawfull triall & conviction, be put to death; pvided this law shall not extend to any such Jesuit as shalbe cast vppon o[r] shores by shippwrack or other accydent, so as he contynew no longer then he may haue opptunitie of passage for his departure, nor to any such as shall come in company w[th] any messenger sent hither vppon publick occasions, or any marchant or master of any shipp belonging to any place not in enmitie w[th] the state of England or o[r]selves, so as they depart agayne w[th] the same messenger, marchant, or m[r], & behaue themselues inoffenciuely duringe their abode here.

31. Maryland's Act of Religious Toleration, April 21, 1649

AMONG the famous documents of American religious liberty Maryland's bill of April, 1649, entitled "An Act Concerning Religion," deserves a prime place, even though it was not included among the documents carried on the Freedom Train in 1947. From the very beginning of the colony Cecilius Calvert, the second Baron of Baltimore (1606–1675), and his lieutenants had maintained religious freedom for all the inhabitants; thus the assembly's action of 1649 in no way constituted a new policy for Maryland. But with the current running strongly in favor of Cromwell in England, the Puritans who had found a refuge in Maryland from oppression in Virginia and elsewhere grew bolder in attacks upon their Catholic neighbors. Baltimore sought, therefore, to insure religious peace by a specific enactment. The fact that he acted from motives of expediency, as well as from personal conviction, should not be permitted to deprive the lord proprietor and his assembly of credit for a remarkably broad grant of religious toleration for the mid-seventeenth century; nor should it be forgotten that the Protestants in the assembly joined with their Catholic colleagues to pass the measure. Source: William Hand Browne (Ed.), *Archives of Maryland. Proceedings and Acts of the General Assembly of Maryland, January 1637/38–September 1664* (Baltimore: Maryland Historical Society, 1883), I, 244–247.

---

fforasmuch as in a well governed and Xpian Com̄on Weath matters concerning Religion and the honor or God ought in the first place to bee taken into serious consideratōn and endeavoured to bee settled. Be it therefore ordered and enacted . . . That whatsoever pson or psons within this Province . . . shall from henceforth blaspheme God . . . or deny our Saviour Jesus Christ to bee the sonne of God, or shall deny the holy Trinity the ffather sonne and holy Ghost, or the Godhead of any of the said Three psons of the Trinity or the Unity of the Godhead . . . shalbe punished with death and confiscatōn or forfeiture of all his or her lands and goods to the Lord Proprietary and his heires. . . . And bee it also Enacted by the Authority and with the advise and assent aforesaid. That whatosever pson or psons shall from henceforth use or utter any reproachfull words or Speeches concerning the blessed Virgin Mary the Mother of our Saviour or the holy Apostles or Evangelists or any of them shall in such case for the first offence forfeit to the Lord Proprietary and his heires . . . the sume of ffive pound Sterling or the value thereof to be Leveyed on the goods and chattells of every such pson soe offending. . . . And be it also further Enacted by the same authority. . . . that whatsoever pson or psons shall from henceforth uppon any occasion of Offence or otherwise in a reproachful manner or Way declare call or denoniminate any pson or psons whatsoever inhabiting . . . within this Province . . . an heritick, Scismatick, Idolator, puritan, Independant, Prespiterian popish prest, Jesuite, Jesuited papist, Lutheran, Calvenist, Anabaptist, Brownist, Antinomian, Barrowist, Roundhead, Sepatist, or any other name or terme in a reproachfull manner relating to matter of Religion shall for every such Offence forfeit and loose so̅me or tenne shillings sterling or the value thereof to bee leveyed on the goods and chattels of every such Offender. . . . And whereas the inforceing of the conscience in matters of Religion hath frequently fallen out to be of dangerous Consequence in those commonwealthes where it hath been practised, And for the more quiett and peaceable government of this Province, and the better to pserve mutuall Love and amity amongst the Inhabitants thereof. Be it Therefore . . . enacted (except as in this psent Act is before Declared and sett forth) that noe person or psons whatsoever within this Province, or the Islands, Ports, Harbors, Creekes, or havens thereunto belonging professing to beleive in Jesus Christ, shall from henceforth bee any waies troubled, Molested or discountenanced for or in respect of his or her religion nor in the free exercise thereof within this Province or the Islands thereunto belonging nor any way compelled to the beleife or exercise of any other Religion against his or her consent, soe as they be not unfaithfull to the Lord Proprietary, or molest or conspire against the civill Governemt established or to bee established in this Province under him or his heires. And that all & every pson or psons that shall presume Contrary to this Act and the true intent and meaning thereof directly or indirectly either in person or estate willfully to wrong disturbe trouble or molest any person whatsoever within this Province professing to beleive in Jesus Christ for or in respect of his or her religion or the free exercise thereof within this Province other than is provided for in this Act that such pson or psons soe offending, shalbe compelled to pay trebble damages to the party soe wronged or molested, and for every such offence shall also forfeit 20^{s} sterling in money or the value therof. . . . Or if the ptie soe offending as aforesaid shall refuse or bee unable to recompense the party so wronged, or to satisfy such ffyne or forfeiture, then such Offender shalbe severly punished by publick whipping & imprisonmt during the pleasure of the Lord Proprietary, or his Lieuetenãt or cheife Governor of this Province for the tyme being without baile or maineprise. . . .

32. Disfranchisement of Catholics in Maryland, October 20, 1654

FOR years William Claiborne (c. 1587–c. 1677), a leader of the Puritan element in Virginia, has been feuding with the Calvert regime in Maryland over the possession of Kent Island and other matters. The victory of Cromwell, therefore, gave Claiborne and his followers a pretext for an all-out assault in which they succeeded in overthrowing the government of Governor William Stone (c. 1603–c. 1660) and imposing their own rule upon Maryland. Claiborne was, of course, bitterly anti-Catholic and one of the first things which he did was to put through the assembly an act disfranchising Catholics. Thus the toleration practiced since 1634, and made the subject of special legislation in 1649, was abolished. Source: William Hand Browne (Ed.), *Archives of Maryland. Proceedings and Acts of the General Assembly of Maryland, January 1637/38–September 1664* (Baltimore: Maryland Historical Society, 1883), I, 340–341.

It is Enacted and Declared in the Name of his Highness the Lord Protector with the Consent and by the Authority of the present Generall Assembly That none who profess and Exercise the Popish Religion Commonly known by the Name of the Roman Catholick Religion can be protected in this Province by the Lawes of England formerly Established and yet unrepealed . . . but are to be restrained from the

Exercise thereof, Therefore all and Every person or persons Concerned in the Law aforesaid are required to take notice

Such as profess faith in God by Jesus Christ (though Differing in Judgment from the Doctrine worship & Discipline publickly held forth shall not be restrained from but shall be protected in the profession of the faith) & Exercise of their Religion so as they abuse not this Liberty to the injury of others The Disturbance of the publique peace on their part, Provided that this Liberty be not Extended to popery or prelacy nor to such as under the profession of Christ hold forth and practice Licentiousness

33. Persecution of the Maryland Catholics, 1656

OLIVER CROMWELL'S triumph over the Stuart monarchy in England was seized upon by the Puritans in Virginia — abetted by Puritans from that colony who had been afforded a refuge in Maryland — to overthrow Baron Baltimore's government and to impose upon the colony a regime that quickly reversed the policy of religious toleration and disfranchised the Catholics. With the exception of the interval of the Stuart restoration, the Catholics experienced from 1654 on to the American Revolution almost as harsh a penal code as that imposed on their coreligionists in England. The Jesuits, needless to say, were among the first to feel the hatred of Maryland's new masters, and the *Annual Letter* for 1656 which follows relates the story of their hardships during the previous year, a theme which found frequent repetition in their annual reports to the superiors in the years ahead. Source: E. A. Dalrymple (Ed.), *Narrative of a Voyage to Maryland by Father Andrew White, S.J. An Account of the Colony of the Lord Baron of Baltimore. Extracts from Different Letters of Missionaries from the Year 1635 to the Year 1677* (Baltimore: Maryland Historical Society, 1874), pp. 91–93.

In Maryland, during the year last past, our people have escaped grievous dangers, and have had to contend with great difficulties and straits, and have suffered many unpleasant things as well from enemies as from our own people. The English who inhabit Virginia had made an attack on the colonists, themselves Englishmen too; and safety being guarantied on certain conditions, received indeed the governor of Maryland, with many others in surrender; but the conditions being treacherously violated, four of the captives, and three of them catholics, were pierced with leaden balls. Rushing into our houses, they demanded for death the impostors, as they called them, intending inevitable slaughter to those who should be caught. But the fathers, by the protection of God, unknown to them, were carried from before their faces: their books, furniture, and whatever was in the house, fell a prey to the robbers. With almost the entire loss of their property, private and domestic, together with great peril of life, they were secretly carried into Virginia; and in the greatest want of necessaries, scarcely, and with difficulty, do they sustain life. They live in a mean hut, low and depressed, not much unlike a cistern, or even a tomb, in which that great defender of the faith, St. Athanasius, lay concealed for many years. To their other miseries this inconvenience was added, that whatever comfort or aid this year, under name of stipend, from pious men in England, was destined for them, had been lost, the ship being intercepted in which it was carried. But nothing affects them more than that there is not a supply of wine, which is sufficient to perform the sacred mysteries of the altar. They have no servant, either for domestic use, or for directing their way through unknown and suspected places, or even to row and steer the boat, if at any time there is need. Often, over spacious and vast rivers, one of them, alone and unaccompanied, passes and repasses long distances, with no other pilot directing his course than Divine Providence. By and by the enemy may be gone and they may return to Maryland; the things which they have already suffered from their people, and the disadvantages which still threaten are not much more tolerable.

34. New York's Grant of Religious Toleration, October 31, 1683

ON TWO occasions in American colonial history Catholics held the office of governor of a colony. In both instances religious toleration was granted to all Christians. We have already seen how the early Calverts made provision for such toleration in Maryland. The second case was in New York under Colonel Thomas Dongan (1634–1715), appointed governor in 1682 by the Duke of York, the future James II, himself a Catholic. The new governor summoned the first representative assembly in the history of the colony in October, 1683, and sponsored the passage by that body of the Charter of Liberties and Privileges. Dongan's broad grant of religious freedom endured in New York until 1688 when James II lost his throne, the governor was recalled, and Jacob Leisler's usurping government disfranchised the Catholics. Source: Hugh Hastings (Supervisor), *Ecclesiastical Records of the State of New York* (Albany: James B. Lyon, 1901), II, 864–865.

. . . that no person or persons, which profess faith in God by Jesus Christ, shall at any time, be any ways molested, punished, disquieted, or called in question for any difference in opinion or matter of religious concernment, who do not actually disturb the civill peace of the Province, but that all and every such person or persons may, from time to time, and at all times freely have and fully enjoy his or their judgements or consciences in matters of religion throughout all the Province, they behaving themselves peaceably and quietly and not using this liberty to Licentiousnesse nor to the civill injury or outward disturbance of others

Provided always, that this liberty, or anything conteyned therein to the contrary, shall never be construed or improved to make void the settlement of any public Minister on Long Island, whether such settlement be by two thirds of the voices in any Towne thereon, which shall always include the minor part; or by subscriptions of perticuler inhabitants in said townes; Provided, they are the two thirds thereof: Butt thatt all such agreements, covenants and subscriptions thatt are there already made and had, or thatt hereafter shall bee in this manner consented to, agreed and subscribed shall att all time and times hereafter, bee firm and stable:

And in confirmation hereof, it is enacted by the Governor Councell, and Representatives: That all such sums of money so agreed on, consented to, or subscribed as aforesaid, for maintenance of said public ministers, by the two thirds of any towne on Long Island, shall always include the minor part, who shall bee regulated thereby: and also such subscriptions and agreements as are beforemenconed, are and shall be always ratifyed, performed and payed, and if any towne of said Island, in their public capacity of agreement with any such minister or any perticuler persons, by their private subscriptions aforesaid, shall make default, deny, or withdraw from such payments so covenanted to, agreed upon, and subscribed thatt in such case, upon complaint of any Collector appointed and chosen by two thirds of such towne upon Long Island, unto any Justice of that County, upon his hearing the same, he is hereby authorized, empowered, and required to issue out his warrant unto the constable or his deputy or any other person appointed for the collection of said rates or agreement, to levy upon the goods and chattells of the said delinquent or defaulter, all such sums of money so covenanted and agreed to be paid, by distresse, with costs and charges, without any further suit in law, any lawe, custom or usage to the contrary in any wise notwithstanding; provided always, the said sum or sumes be under forty shillings, otherwise to be recovered as the law directs.

And whereas all the respective Christian Churches now in practice within the City of New York, and the other places of this Province, do appear to be privileged [*sic*] Churches, and have been soe established and confirmed by the former authority of this Government; Bee it hereby enacted by this present Generall Assembly, and by the Authority thereof, That all the said respective Christian Churches be hereby confirmed therein, and thatt they and every of them shall from henceforth, forever, be held and reputed as privileged Churches, and enjoy all their former freedoms of their religion in Divine Worship and Church Discipline; and thatt all former contracts made and agreed on for the maintenances of the several ministers of the said Churches, shall stand and continue in full force and vertue, and thatt all Contracts for the future to be made, shall be of the same power; and all persons that are unwilling to perform their part of the said contract shall be constrained thereunto by a warrant from any Justice of the Peace; Provided it be under forty shillings, or otherwise, as the law directs; Provided also That all other Christian Churches that shall hereafter come and settle within this Province, shall have the same privileges.

35. An Act Against Jesuits and Popish Priests in Massachusetts, June 17, 1700

THE Treaty of Ryswick in September, 1697, brought no settlement of the rival claims of England and France in North America, and in the interval which led up to England's renewal of war against France in May, 1702, the border warfare between the two powers took an increasing toll in lives and property. In 1697 Richard Coote, the Earl of Bellomont (1636–1701), a son of the notorious Richard Coote who had committed so many outrages against the Catholic population of Ireland under Cromwell, was appointed Governor of New York, Massachusetts, and New Hampshire. Bellomont was himself fiercely anti-Catholic, and the widespread belief that Catholic missionaries were stirring up the Indians to attack the English made it an easy matter for him to put through anti-priest laws in both Massachusetts and New York within a few months' time. The Massachusetts law of 1700 was broader in application than that of 1647 and its terms were more severe. Source: *The Acts and Resolves, Public and Private, of the Province of the Massachusetts Bay* (Boston: Wright & Potter, 1869), I, 423–424.

Whereas divers Jesuits, priests and popish missionaries have of late come, and for some time have had their residences in the remote parts of this province, and other his majesty's territories near adjacent, who by their subtile insinuations industriously labour to debauch, seduce and withdraw the Indians from their due obedience unto his majesty, and to excite and stir them up, to sedition, rebellion and open hostility against his Majestie's government; for prevention whereof, —

Be it enacted by His Excellency the Governour, Council, and Representatives in General Court assembled, and it is enacted by the authority of the same

[Sect. 1] That all and every Jesuit, seminary priest, missionary, or other spiritual or ecclesiastical person made or ordained by any authority, power or jurisdiction derived, challenged or pretended from the pope or see of Rome, now residing within this province or any part thereof, shall depart from and out of the same at or before the tenth day of September next, in this present year one thousand and seven hundred.

And be it further enacted by the authority aforesaid,

[Sect. 2] That all and every Jesuit, seminary priest, missionary or other spiritual or ecclesiastical person made or ordained by any authority, power or jurisdiction, derived, challenged or pretended, from the pope or see of Rome, or that shall profess himselfe or otherwise appear to be such by practising and teaching of others to say any popish prayers, by celebrating masses, granting of absolutions, or using any other of the Romish ceremonies and rites of worship, by or of what name, title or degree soever such person shall be called or known, who shall continue, abide, remain or come into this province, or any part thereof, after the tenth day of September aforesaid, shall be deemed and accounted an incendiary and disturber of the publick peace and safety, and an enemy to the true Christian religion, and shall be adjudged to suffer perpetual imprisonment; and if any person, being so sentenced and actually imprisoned, shall break prison and make his escape, and be afterwards re-taken, he shall be punished with death.

And further it is enacted

[Sect. 3] That every person which shall wittingly and willingly receive, relieve, harbour, conceal, aid or succour any Jesuit, priest, missionary or other ecclesiastical person of the Romish clergy, knowing him to be such, shall be fined two hundred pounds, one moiety therof to be unto his majesty for and towards the support of the government of this province, and the other moiety to the informer; and such person shall be further punished by being set in the pillory on three several days, and also be bound to the good behaviour at the discretion of the court. . . .

And further be it enacted by the authority aforesaid,

[Sect. 5] That it shall and may be lawful to and for every justice of the peace to cause any person or persons suspected of being a Jesuit, seminary priest, or of the Romish clergy, to be apprehended and convented before himself or some other or his majestie's justices; and if such person do not give satisfactory account of himselfe, he shall be committed to prison in order to a tryal. Also it shall and may be lawful to and for any person or persons to apprehend without a warrant any Jesuit, seminary priest, or other of the Romish clergy as aforesaid, and to convent him before the governour or any two of the council, to be examined and imprisoned in order to a tryal, unless he give a satisfactory accompt of himselfe. And as it will be esteemed and accepted as a good service done for the king by the person who shall seize and apprehend any Jesuit, priest, missionary, or Romish ecclesiastic as aforesaid, so the governour, with the advice and consent of the council, may suitably reward him as they shall think fit; *provided,* this act shall not extend or be construed to extend to any of the Romish clergy which shall happen to be shipwrackt, or through other adversity shall be cast on shore, or driven into this province, so as he continue or abide no longer within the same than until he may have opportunity of passage for his departure; so also as such person immediately upon his arrival shall forthwith attend the governour, if near to the place of his residence, or otherwise on one or more of the council or next justices of the peace, and acquaint them with his circumstances, and observe the directions which they shall give him, during his stay in the province.

36. The Coming of the Acadians to Massachusetts, November, 1755–August, 1756

THE largest number of Catholics to come to colonial America were the conservatively estimated 6000 Acadians who were exiled by the British to the thirteen colonies in 1755–1756. These simple people were caught in the war between France and England for the mastery of North America, and they were bewildered by the contrary advice of their priests concerning the oath of allegiance demanded of them by their British conquerors. Their circumstances were extremely pitiful, and it is small wonder that some of them responded to the spirit of resistance encouraged by the Abbé Jean Louis Le Loutre at Beauséjour and the Abbé Henri Daudin at Annapolis Royal and Piziquid. Yet the author of a recent scholarly and sympathetic account of their exile has stated: "Indeed, one may say with confidence that had the Acadians determinedly followed the example and wise counsel of such worthy and venerable priests among them as Father Desenclaves

(Deseuclaves) and Chauvreux, rather than the exhortations to desperate measures of Le Loutre and his pupil Daudin, misfortunes would never have been heaped upon them" (Lawrence Henry Gibson, *The Great War for the Empire. The Years of Defeat, 1754–1757* [New York, 1946], p. 285). As a consequence of their refusal to renounce their loyalty to France, they were seized, transported, and landed along the American coasts where, by reason of their religion, political sympathies, and the trouble they occasioned, they received a generally hostile reception. Between November, 1755, and August, 1756, over 3000 Acadians were landed in Massachusetts. Many of these, it is true, were later sent south, but as late as 1763 there were still over 1000 of the exiles in that colony. Their best friend in Massachusetts was Thomas Hutchinson (1711–1780), a member of the provincial council and later governor. It was Hutchinson who wrote the first general history of the colony, and in the final volume, finished in 1778, he included the following vivid picture of the Acadians' fate in Massachusetts. Source: Thomas Hutchinson, *The History of the Colony and Province of Massachusetts-Bay,* edited by Lawrence Shaw Mayo (Cambridge: Harvard University Press, 1936), III, 28–31.

The French forts at Beau Sejour, Bay Vert, and the river St. John, in Nova Scotia, had been recovered. The state of that province was, notwithstanding, deemed very insecure; many thousand French inhabitants still continued in it. They had been admitted by lieutenant-governor Armstrong, after that province was reduced in the reign of Q. Ann, to such a sort of oath, as to consider themselves rather in a neutral state between England and France, than in subjection to either, and from thence they took the name of French neutrals. Being all Roman catholicks and great bigots, and retaining the French language, they were better affected to the French than to the English. In civil matters, they had been more indulged by the English than they would have been by the French, being in a manner free from taxes; and a great part of them were so sensible of it, that they wished to avoid taking part on one side or the other. But the Indians, who were engaged on the part of the French, had constant intercourse with them, their houses being scattered, and where there were any number together to form a village, open to both French and Indians from Canada, without any sort of defence. And it was the general opinion, that, if an attempt should be made by the French to recover the province of Nova Scotia, the whole body of the Acadians, some from inclination, others from compulsion, would join in the attempt.

The commander-in-chief of his majesty's ships, then at Halifax, as well as the governor of the province, supposed that the principle of self-preservation would justify the removal of these Acadians; and it was determined to take them by surprise, and transport them all, men, women, and children, to the English colonies. A few days before the determination was executed, notice was given to the governors of the several colonies to prepare for their reception. The greatest part by far were accordingly seized by the king's troops, which had remained in the province, and hurried on board small vessels prepared to receive them, with such part of their household goods as there was room for; the remainder, with their stock of cattle, the contents of their barns, their farm utensils, and all other moveables, being left behind, and never recovered, nor any satisfaction made for them.

In several instances, the husbands who happened to be at a distance from home, were put on board vessels bound to one of the English colonies, and their wives and children on board other vessels, bound to other colonies remote from the first. One of the most sensible of them, describing his case, said, "it was the hardest which had happened since our Saviour was upon earth."

About a thousand of them arrived in Boston, just in the beginning of winter, crowded almost to death. No provision was made, in case government should refuse to take them under its care. As it happened, the assembly was sitting when they arrived; but several days were spent without any determination, and some aged and infirm persons, in danger of perishing, were received on shore in houses provided for them by private individuals. At length, the assembly passed a resolve, that they should all be permitted to land, and that they should be sent to such towns as a committee appointed for that purpose should think fit; and a law of the province was passed, to authorize justices of the peace, overseers of the poor, &c., to employ them in labour, bind them out to service, and, in general, provide for their support, in like manner as if they had been indigent inhabitants of the province.

Favour was shewn to many elderly people among them, and to others who had been in circumstances superior to the rest, and they were allowed support without being held to labour. Many of them went through great hardships, but in general they were treated with humanity. They fared the better, because the towns where they were sent, were to be reimbursed out of the province treasury, and the assembly was made to believe the province would be reimbursed by the crown; but this expectation failed. It was proposed to them to settle upon some of the unappropriate lands of the province, and to become British subjects, but they refused. They had a strong persuasion, that the French king would never make peace with England, unless they were restored to their estates. A gentleman who was much affected with their sufferings,[1] prepared a representation proper for

[1] This was Hutchinson himself.

them to make to the British government, to be signed by the chief of. them in behalf of the rest, praying that they might either have leave to return to their estates, or might receive a compensation; and he offered to put it into the hands of a proper person in England to solicit their cause. They received the proposal thankfully, took the representation to consider of, and, after some days, returned it without having signed it. They were afraid of losing the favour of France, if they should receive or solicit for compensation from England. Despair of the free exercise of their religion was another bar to every proposal tending to an establishment.

The people of New England had more just notions of toleration than their ancestors, and no exception was taken to their prayers in their families, in their own way, which, I believe, they practised in general, and sometimes they assembled several families together; but the people would upon no terms have consented to the publick exercise of religious worship by Roman catholick priests. A law remained unrepealed, though it is to be hoped it would never have been executed, which made it a capital offence in such persons to come within the province.[2] It was suspected that some such were among them in disguise; but it is not probable that any ventured. One of the most noted families, when they were dissuaded from removing to Quebec, lest they should suffer more hardship from the French there, than they had done from the English, acknowledged they expected it; but they had it not in their power since they left their country, to confess and to be absolved of their sins, and the hazard of dying in such a state distressed them more than the fear of temporal sufferings.*

* When these unhappy persons despaired of being restored to their own estates, they began to think of a removal to places where they might find priests of their own religion, and other inhabitants of their own language. Many hundreds went from the New England colonies to Hispaniola, where, in less than a year, by far the greatest part died. Others went to Canada, where they were considered as an inferior race of Frenchmen, and they were so neglected, that some of them wrote to a gentleman in Boston who had patronized them, they then wished to return. In 1763, Monsieur Bougainville[3] carried several families of them, who had found their way to France, to the Malouines, or Falkland's Islands, where they remained but a short time, being turned off by Mr. Byron.[4] Bougainville says, "they are a laborious intelligent set of men, who ought to be dear to France, on account of the inviolate attachment they have shewn as honest but unfortunate

[2] Hutchinson was referring here to the anti-priest law of May, 1647 (No. 30).

[3] Louis Antoine de Bougainville (1729–1811) was an aide-de-camp of Montcalm at Quebec who later was given command of a fleet to found a French colony in the Falkland Islands.

[4] John Byron (1723–1786) was a British naval officer.

citizens." Thus they were dispersed through the world, until they were in a manner extinct, the few which remained being mixed with other subjects in different parts of the French dominions.

37. Bishop Challoner on Ecclesiastical Jurisdiction in the British Colonies, September 14, 1756

FROM 1631 to 1685 there was no Catholic bishop in England. Faculties for the first missionaries who came to Maryland were secured, therefore, from the Jesuit General by a special privilege granted by Gregory XIII in 1579. In the very year that the Holy See appointed four vicars apostolic to rule over the English Catholics, 1688, James II lost his throne and a systematic persecution of the Church began which lasted for almost a century. In these circumstances — aggravated by intermittent wars, infrequent communication over immense distances, and the constant feuds between the secular and regular clergy in England — it is small wonder that the question of ecclesiastical jurisdiction over the colonial Catholics should at times have become confused. After 1688 the Vicar Apostolic of the London District was the official to whom application for faculties was normally made, although the system seems never to have become regularized in a satisfactory way. One of those who tried repeatedly to have a bishop appointed for the colonies, or to have the Bishop of Quebec administer confirmation to them, was Richard Challoner (1691–1781), who served as coadjutor to old Bishop Benjamin Petre in London from 1741 to 1758, and as vicar apostolic from the latter date to his death in 1781. But nothing came of Challoner's efforts, and his death some months before the Battle of Yorktown prompted his biographer to say that "his jurisdiction over his American priests and people remained the only remnant of authority in the hands of an Englishman that was still recognised in America" (p. 148). In the following letter of September 14, 1756, to Dr. Christopher Stonor, agent of the English clergy at Rome, Challoner revealed the lack of clarity about ecclesiastical jurisdiction, mentioned the need for a bishop in America, and reflected something of the secular clergy's bias against the Jesuits in the American missions. Source: Edwin H. Burton, *The Life and Times of Bishop Challoner (1691–1781)* (New York: Longmans, Green and Co., 1909), II, 125–127.

As to the state of religion in our American settlements; the best account I can give is: —

1. There are no missioners in any of our colonies upon the continent, excepting Mariland and Pensilvania; in which the exercise of the Catholic religion is in some measure tolerated. . . . [Then follows a paragraph on the missions in the West Indies.]

3. All our settlements in America have been deemed subject in spirituals to the ecclesiastical Superiors here, and this has been time

out of mind, even, I believe, from the time of the Archpriests. I know not the origin of this, nor have ever met with the original grant. I suppose they were looked upon as appurtenances or appendixes of the English Mission. And, after the division of this kingdom into four districts, the jurisdiction over the Catholicks in those settlements has followed the London district (as they are all reputed by the English as part of the London diocese); I suppose because London is the capital of the British Empire; and from hence are the most frequent opportunities of a proper correspondence with all those settlements. Whether the Holy See has ordered anything in this regard, I cannot learn. But all the missioners in those settlements do now, and have, time out of mind, applied to the Vicar Apostolic here for their faculties, which is true of the *padri* also [the Jesuits] in Mariland and Pennsilvania; at least from the time of the Breve of Innocent XII. in 1696, only that they used rather to ask for approbation, but now also for faculties.

4. Some have wished, considering the number of the faithful, especially in those two provinces, destitute of the sacrament of confirmation, and lying at so great a distance from us, that a bishop or vicar apostolic should be appointed for them. But how far this may be judged practicable by our superiors I know not: especially as perhaps it may not be relished, by those who have engrossed that best part of the mission to themselves, and who may, not without show of probability, object that a novelty of this kind might give offence to the governing part there; who have been a little hard upon them of late years. . . .

38. The Missionaries' Reasons for Not Wanting a Bishop, April 22, 1773

ENGLAND'S victory over France in the Seven Years' War brought more American possessions under the British flag and thus caused renewed emphasis on the need for a bishop. The Congregation of Propaganda Fide was aware of the situation, but knowing the hostility of the British government toward the Church, the Roman officials were uncertain how to proceed. When requested by Propaganda for his views, Bishop Challoner had replied on August 2, 1763, as follows:

"It is to be desired that provision should be made for so many thousand Catholics as are found in Maryland and Pennsylvania, that they may receive the Sacrament of Confirmation, of the benefit of which they are utterly deprived. Now that Canada and Florida are brought under the

> English sway, the Holy Apostolic See could easily effect this, a Bishop or a Vicar Apostolic being established at Quebec or elsewhere, with the consent of our Court, by delegating jurisdiction to him throughout all the other English colonies and islands of America. This would be far from displeasing to us, and would redound greatly to the advantage of those colonies" (*American Catholic Historical Researches,* XII [January, 1895], 44–45).

But Challoner's letter got lost, further delays ensued, and in 1771 Propaganda suggested to Joseph-Olivier Briand (1715–1794), Bishop of Quebec, that he undertake the responsibility. Briand, in turn, asked Bernard Well, a Jesuit missionary in Canada, to inquire of his confreres about the prospects for a bishop in the American colonies. In the absence of John Baptist Diderich, S.J., then on the Pennsylvania missions, Well's letter was answered by Ferdinand Farmer, S.J. (1720–1786), who summarized conditions among the Catholics and gave reasons why he thought it would be unwise to send a bishop. It was a view which the Jesuits continued to hold until the late 1780's when their suspicions of opposition from the American government, and of what a bishop might mean to their property interests, were finally dissipated. Source: *American Catholic Historical Researches,* XXI (July, 1904), 118–120.

Philadelphia, 22nd April, 1773.

Reverend Father in Christ,

P.C. (Pax Christi)

Your Reverence's most welcome letter, dated February 15, was delivered to me on the 17th of April. In the absence of Rev. Father Diderick I opened it, according to directions given in the address. The above mentioned Father had been in one of the Pennsylvania Missions, a hundred or more miles distant from Philadelphia; having, in a private discussion with a non-Catholic man, made use of some rather harsh and insulting words, he came nigh being killed, a musket having been twice discharged by night on his dwelling or chapel. Wherefore he was obliged to remove to the Missions in the Province of Maryland. I shall, in due time, send him your Reverence's letter. Your Reverence desires to know the state of our Missions. I shall describe them briefly. In only two of the several English Provinces or Colonies is the Catholic Religion tolerated, namely in Maryland and Pennsylvania; in the latter in virtue of a Royal Charter given to the founder of the Colony; in the former, more from ancient possession than owing to any right. In Pennsylvania, by virtue of a Royal deed, all religions are tolerated, not that each one is free to publicly perform the rites of his religion, but in this sense that he may accomplish them in private, and that he may be in no wise compelled by anyone to share in any exercise whatsoever of another Religion than his own.

As, however, the oath must be exacted of all such as desire to be numbered among the born subjects of the Kingdom, or who hold divers offices in the Commonwealth, contains a renunciation of the Catholic religion, none of our faith can obtain the like favors. In Pennsylvania there are presently five Missionaries, one Englishman and four Germans, who attend with no mean labor to small congregations of men nearly all poor and widely scattered throughout the Province. In Philadelphia, however, where reside two missionaries, there is a greater number of souls comprising men of different nationalities. In Maryland, there are both more missionaries and a greater and better number of faithful, but, as I already mentioned, they enjoy less liberty than that which we here enjoy. All of these Missionaries are of our Society; the Superior resides in Maryland. I shall have to consult him regarding the matter treated in your Reverence's letter. But as a prompt answer is requested, until the Reverend Father Superior can examine the question and advise thereon, I beg to express my own sentiment.

From the foregoing it is easy to see that the Catholic Religion is practised with far greater authority and freedom in Canada than in our own country. Wherefore it is most certain that the advent in our midst of the Right Reverend and Illustrious [Bishop of Quebec] would create great disturbances, with the danger of depriving us of the paltry privileges we are now enjoying, especially in Maryland, where, as already mentioned, the exercise, even in private, of our Religion rests upon no authority. For the same reason, when several years ago, the Vicar Apostolic of London intended to send some one hither for the purpose either of visiting or of giving Confirmation, the gentlemen of Maryland placed under our care, by a letter to the Right Reverend Vicar, informed him of the danger to which they were exposed; wherefore the aforesaid Vicar, under whom are all these colonies, gave up his intention.

I do not wish you to understand by this that we are not greatly desirous of having Confirmation administered to those of our flock born in this country, but that it is plain to our eyes, being given especially the character of Americans, that such rite could not safely be conferred by a person established in dignity. For it is incredible how hateful to non-Catholics in all parts of America is the very name of Bishop, even to such as should be members of the Church which is called Anglican. Whence many considered it a most unworthy measure that a Bishop be granted to the Canadians; and, as for several years past the question is being agitated in England of establishing in these Provinces a Protestant Bishop of the Anglican Communion, so many obstacles were found, due especially to the character of the Americans (of whom most of the early colonists were dissidents from the Anglicans, not to mention such as left our own faith) that nothing has as yet been effected. Hardly I can persuade myself that the Right Reverend (Bishop) might succeed in obtaining from the Governor of Canada or from the King, the faculty of exercising his power beyond the limits of the Provinces belonging formerly to the Canadian government, and lately ceded by treaty to the English.

From Europe we have received no letters for several months past, so that we are ignorant as to what may be the state of our society. However, from what we learned last year from Ours, and also from what the newspapers announce, we justly infer that our interests in Rome are not succeeding favourably, though that doth succeed favourably whichsoever it pleaseth Divine Providence to ordain.

Your Reverence will excuse me for not having written this more neatly, as in this city, especially at the present time, we are very busy with the various labors of our ministry. I urgently recommend myself in all holy intentions.

Of Your Reverence,
The most humble servant in Christ,
FERDINAND FARMER, S.J.

P.S. — My Reverend colleague, Father Robert Mollineux [*sic*], most cordially greets your Reverence. Should it please ye to send me other letters, they may be addressed as follows:

To Mr. Ferdinand Farmer,
Walnut Street,
Philadelphia.

39. Charles Carroll's Defense of His Religious Beliefs, 1773

IN THE struggle for American independence the Catholics joined with their fellow countrymen without reserve. Among their number no one played a more prominent and honorable role than Charles Carroll of Carrollton (1737–1832), signer of the Declaration of Independence, who from the time he entered politics in 1773 until his retirement in 1800 filled a number of important state and federal offices. The occasion which brought him to public notice was the appearance on February 4, 1773, of the first of a series of letters when he published in the *Maryland Gazette* over the pen name of "First Citizen." Carroll had been roused by Daniel Dulany's ("Antillon") attempt to defend the arbitrary action of Governor Robert Eden in proroguing the Maryland assembly and reaffirming by proclamation officers' fees and stipends for the clergy of the established church. With the development of the debate the argument broadened and in the end Carroll's effective polemics not only vanquished Dulany but helped to swing the Maryland election of May, 1773, in favor of the patriot party who had opposed the royal governor. In the course of the exchange Dulany sought to discredit Carroll by an attack on his religion. This appeal to prejudice angered the Catholic statesman and he struck back in defense of his political and religious beliefs. The excerpts from his letters of May 16 and July 1, 1773, which follow illustrate Carroll's method of meeting the insinuations against his religious faith. Source: Kate Mason Rowland, *The Life of Charles Carroll of Carrollton, 1737–1832, With His Correspondence and Public Papers* (New York: G. P. Putnam's Sons, 1898), I, 284–285, 316, 359.

Maryland Gazette, May 6, 1773.

In vindication of his conduct, Antillon has not endeavoured to convince the minds of his readers by the force of reason, but *"in the favourite method of illiberal calumny, virulent abuse and shameless asseveration to affect their passions"* has attempted to render his antagonist ridiculous, contemptible and odious; he has descended to the lowest jests on the person of the Citizen, has expressed the utmost contempt of his understanding, and a strong suspicion of his *political and religious principles.* What connection, Antillon, have the latter with the Proclamation? Attempts to rouse popular prejudices, and to turn the laugh against an adversary, discover the weakness of a cause, or the inabilities of the advocate, who employs ridicule, instead of argument. *"The Citizen's patriotism is entirely feigned";* his reasons must not be considered, or listened to, because his *religious principles* are not to be trusted. Yet if we are to credit Antillon, the Citizen is so little attached to these principles, *"That he is most devoutly wishing for the event,"* which is to free him from their shackles. What my speculative notions on religion may be, this is neither the place nor time to declare; my political principles ought only to be questioned on the present occasion; surely they are constitutional, and have met, I hope, with the approbation of my countrymen; if so Antillon's aspersions will give me no uneasiness. He asks, who is this Citizen? A man, Antillon, of an independent fortune, one deeply interested in the prosperity of his country: a friend to liberty, a settled enemy to lawless prerogative. . . .

. . . I comprehend fully, Antillon, your threats thrown out against certain religionists; to shew the *greatness of your soul,* and your utter detestation of malice, I shall give the public a translation of your

Latin sentence; the sentiment is truly noble, and reflects the highest lustre on its author or adopter; *Eos tamen laedere non exoptemus, qui nos laedere non exoptant,* we would not wish to hurt those who do not wish to hurt us; — in other words, "I cannot wreak my resentment on the Citizen, without involving all of his religion in one common ruin with him; they have not offended me, it is true, but it is better that ninety-nine just should suffer, than one guilty man escape — a thorough paced politician never sticks at the means of accomplishing his ends; why should I, who have so just a claim to the character?" These, Antillon, are the sentiments and threats, couched under your Latin phrase, which *you even* were ashamed to avow in plain English. . . .

Ibid., July 1, 1773.

. . . The Citizen did not deliver his sentiment only but likewise the sentiment of others. We Catholics, who think we were hardly treated on occasion, *we* still remember the treatment though our resentment hath entirely subsided. It is not in the least surprising that a man incapable of forming an exalted sentiment, should not readily comprehend the force and beauty of one. . . . To what purpose was the threat thrown out of enforcing the penal statutes by proclamation? Why am I told that my conduct is very inconsistent with the situation of one, who "owes even the *toleration* he enjoys to the favour of government"? If by instilling prejudices into the Governor, and by every mean and wicked artifice you can rouse the popular resentment against certain religionists, and thus bring on a persecution of them, it will then be known whether the toleration I enjoy, be due to the favour of government or not. . . .

40. The Quebec Act Grants Religious Freedom to the Catholics of Canada, June 22, 1774

BY THE spring of 1774 the angry temper of the American colonists made it evident to the government in London that something should be done to insure the loyalty of its Canadian subjects to the crown. The result was the Quebec Act by which French law was restored in the colony, its boundaries were given a broad extension to the west and north, and the Catholic Church was guaranteed its freedom. All these features of the bill were resented by the Canadian's southern neighbors, and none to a great degree than the privileged status accorded to the Catholic religion. The act's provision for the French Catholics to take a simple oath of allegiance to the

king put no strain upon their religious beliefs as the exaction of the oath of supremacy would have done. In the crisis of the Revolution the Catholics of Canada remained steadfast in their loyalty to Britain despite the blandishments — and force — used by the Americans to win them to their side. Source: Adam Shortt and Arthur G. Doughty (Eds.), *Documents Relating to the Constitutional History of Canada, 1759–1791,* 2 rev. ed. (Ottawa: Historical Documents Publication Board, 1918), Pt. I, 570–576.

And whereas the Provisions, made by the said Proclamation, in respect to the Civil Government of the said Province of *Quebec* and the Powers and Authorities given to the Governor and other Civil Officers of the said Province, by the Grants and Commissions issued in consequence thereof, have been found, upon Experience, to be inapplicable to the State and Circumstances of the said Province, the Inhabitants whereof amounted, at the Conquest, to above Sixty-five thousand Persons professing the Religion of the Church of *Rome*. . . .

And for the more perfect Security and Ease of the Minds of the Inhabitants of the said Province, it is hereby declared, That His Majesty's Subjects, professing the Religion of the Church of *Rome* of and in the said Province of *Quebec,* may have, hold, and enjoy, the free Exercise of the Religion of the Church of *Rome,* subject to the King's Supremacy, declared and established by an Act, made in the First Year of the Reign of Queen *Elizabeth,* over all the Dominions and Countries which then did, or thereafter should, belong to the Imperial Crown of this Realm; and that the Clergy of the said Church may hold, receive, and enjoy their accustomed Dues and Rights, with respect to such Persons only as shall profess the said Religion.

Provided nevertheless, That it shall be lawful for His Majesty, His Heirs or Successors, to make such Provisions out of the rest of the said accustomed Dues and Rights, for the Encouragement of the Protestant Religion, and for the Maintenance and Support of a Protestant Clergy within the said Province, as he or they shall, from Time to Time, think necessary or expedient.

Provided always, and be it enacted, That no Person professing the Religion of the Church of *Rome,* and residing in the said Province, shall be obliged to take the *Oath* required by the said Statute passed in the First Year of the Reign of Queen *Elisabeth,* or any other Oaths substituted by any other Act in the Place thereof; but that every such Person who, by the said Statute is required to take the Oath therein mentioned, shall be obliged, and is hereby required, to take and subscribe the following Oath before the Governor, or such other Persons in such Court of Record as His Majesty shall appoint, who are hereby authorized to administer the same; *videlicet.* [Then follows the form of an oath of simple allegiance to the king with a promise to report all treasonable conspiracies to the authorities.]

And be it further enacted by the Authority aforesaid, That all His Majesty's *Canadian* Subjects, within the Province of *Quebec,* the religious Orders and Communities only excepted, may also hold and enjoy their Property and Possessions, together with all Customs and Usages relative thereto, and all their other Civil Rights. . . .

Provided also, That no Ordinance touching Religion, or by which any Punishment may be inflicted greater than Fine or Imprisonment for Three Months, shall be of any Force or Effect, until the same shall have received His Majesty's Approbation. . . .

41. John Adams' Impressions of a Catholic Service, October 9, 1774

MOST of the founding fathers of the Republic had been nourished on a deep prejudice against the Catholic Church, and whatever tolerance some of them later displayed sprang from a belief in the necessity of religious toleration as a public policy for all rather than from any softening of their attitude toward Catholicism. During the sessions of the Continental Congress John Adams (1735–1826), a delegate from Massachusetts, at times found his official duties very dull. He enlivened one day, therefore, by visiting some of Philadelphia's churches with George Washington. The letter which he wrote to his wife Abigail on October 9, 1774, contained a vivid impression of his reactions after a visit to St. Mary's Church during an afternoon service. Source: Charles Francis Adams (Ed.), *Familiar Letters of John Adams and His Wife Abigail, During the Revolution* (New York: Hurd and Houghton, 1876), pp. 45–46.

I am wearied to death with the life I lead. The business of the Congress is tedious beyond expression. . . .

This day I went to Dr. Allison's meeting in the forenoon, and heard the Dr.; a good discourse upon the Lord's supper. . . . This is a Presbyterian meeting. I confess I am not fond of Presbyterian meetings in this town. . . . And I must confess that the Episcopal Church is quite as agreeable to my taste as the Presbyterian. They are both slaves to the domination of the priesthood. I like the Congregational way best, next to that Independent.

This afternoon, led by curiosity and good company, I strolled away to mother church, or rather grandmother church. I mean the Romish chapel. I heard a good, short moral essay upon the duty of parents to their children, founded in justice and charity, to take care of their interests, temporal and spiritual. This afternoon's entertainment was to me most awful and affecting; the poor wretches fingering their beads, chanting Latin, not a word of which they understood; their pater nosters and ave Marias; their holy water; their crossing themselves perpetually; their bowing to the name of Jesus, whenever they hear it; their bowings, kneelings and genuflections before the altar. The dress of the priest was rich white lace. His pulpit was velvet and gold. The altar-piece was very rich, little images and crucifixes about; wax candles lighted up. But how shall I describe the picture of our Saviour in a frame of marble over the altar, at full length, upon the cross in the agonies, and the blood dropping and streaming from his wounds! The music, consisting of an organ and a choir of singers, went all the afternoon except sermon time, and the assembly chanted most sweetly and exquisitely.

Here is everything which can lay hold of the eye, ear, and imagination — everything which can charm and bewitch the simple and ignorant. I wonder how Luther ever broke the spell. Adieu.

42. Reactions of the Continental Congress to the Quebec Act, September 17–October 26, 1774

AS THE break of the American colonies from Great Britain grew closer the delegates to the Continental Congress determined upon more energetic measures. On September 9, 1774, a convention in Suffolk County, Massachusetts, had adopted a set of resolutions which summarized the principal colonial grievances against the mother country. These so-called Suffolk Resolves were immediately sent to Philadelphia and on September 17 the more radical delegates in the Continental Congress succeeded in having them adopted by that body. On October 21 the congress issued an address to the British people which was followed five days later by an address to the French Canadians and a petition to King George III. All these documents — except that to the Canadians — reflected the resentment felt at Britain's grant of freedom to the Catholic Church in Canada by the Quebec Act which had become law on the previous June 22. In fact, that measure was judged one of the chief sources of grievance against the British crown. It should hardly have surprised the Continental Congress to find that their appeal to the Canadians for assistance had fallen on deaf ears, for the French Catholic leaders knew the true opinions of most Americans about their religious faith, even if they were not aware at the time of the striking contradiction in sentiment between the address sent to them on October 26 and that directed to the British people five days before. The following excerpts from the documents relate to the Catholic Church. Source: Worthington Chauncey Ford (Ed.), *Journals of the Continental Congress, 1774–1789* (Washington: Government Printing Office, 1904).

Suffolk County Resolutions Adopted by the Continental Congress, September 17, 1774:

10. That the late act of parliament for establishing the Roman Catholic religion and the French laws in that extensive country, now called Canada, is dangerous in an extreme degree to the Protestant religion and to the civil rights and liberties of all America; and, therefore, as men and Protestant Christians, we are indispensably obliged to take all proper measures for our security. (*Ibid.,* I, 34–35).

Address to the People of Great Britain, October 21, 1774:

Know then, That we consider ourselves, and do insist, that we are and ought to be, as free as our fellow-subjects in Britain, and that no power on earth has a right to take our property from us without our consent. . . .

That we think the Legislature of Great-Britain is not authorized by the constitution to establish a religion, fraught with sanguinary and impious tenets, or, to erect an arbitrary form of government, in any quarter of the globe. . . .

And by another Act the dominion of Canada is to be so extended, modelled, and governed, as that by being disunited from us, detached from our interests, by civil as well as religious prejudices, that by their numbers daily swelling with Catholic emigrants from Europe, and by their devotion to Administration, so friendly to their religion, they might become formidable to us, and on occasion, be fit instruments in the hands of power, to reduce the ancient free Protestant Colonies to the same state of slavery with themselves. This was evidently the object of the Act: — And in this view, being extremely dangerous to our liberty and quiet, we cannot forbear complaining of it, as hostile to British America. . . . Nor can we suppress our astonishment, that a British Parliament should ever consent to establish in that country a religion that has deluged your island in blood, and dispersed impiety, bigotry, persecution, murder and rebellion through every part of the world. (*Ibid.,* I, 82–83; 88.)

Address to the Inhabitants of the Province of Quebec, October 26, 1774:

We, the Delegates of the Colonies . . . having accordingly assembled and taken into consideration the state of public affairs on this continent, have thought proper to address your province, as a member therein deeply interested. [Then follows a summary of the rights for which they are fighting.]

. . . These are rights *you* are entitled to and ought at this moment in perfection, to exercise. And what is offered to you by the late Act of Parliament in their place? Liberty of conscience in your religion? No. God gave it to you; and the temporal powers with which you have been and are connected, firmly stipulated for your enjoyment of it. If laws, divine and human, could secure it against the despotic caprices of wicked men, it was secured before. . . .

We are too well acquainted with the liberality of sentiment distinguishing your nation, to imagine, that difference of religion will prejudice you against a hearty amity with us. You know, that the transcendent nature of freedom elevates those, who unite in her cause, above all such low-minded infirmities. The Swiss Cantons furnish a memorable proof of this truth. Their union is composed of Roman Catholic and Protestant States, living in the utmost concord and peace with one another, and thereby enabled, ever since they bravely vindicated their freedom, to defy and defeat every tyrant that has invaded them. . . .

We do not ask you, by this address, to commence acts of hostility against the government of our common Sovereign. We only invite you to consult your own glory and welfare. . . .

That Almighty God may incline your minds to approve our equitable and necessary measures, to add yourselves to us . . . and may grant to our joint exertions an event as happy as our cause is just, is the fervent prayer of us, your sincere and affectionate friends and fellow-subjects. (*Ibid.,* I, 105–106, 108, 112–113.)

Petition to the King, October 26, 1774:

We your majesty's faithful subjects of the colonies . . . by this our humble petition, beg leave to lay our grievances before the throne. . . .

In the last sessions of parliament, an act was passed for blocking up the harbour of Boston; another, empowering the governor of the Massachusetts-bay to send persons indicted for murder in that province to another colony or even to Great Britain for trial whereby such offenders may escape legal punishment; a third, for altering the chartered constitution of government in that province; and a fourth for extending the limits of Quebec, abolishing the English and restoring the French laws, whereby great numbers of British freemen are subjected to the latter, and establishing an absolute government and the Roman Catholick religion throughout those vast regions, that border on the westerly and northerly boundaries of the free protestant English settlements; and the fifth for the better providing suitable quarters for officers and soldiers in his majesty's service in North America. . . . (*Ibid.*, I, 115–117.)

43. George Washington Bans Guy Fawkes Day in the Army, November 5, 1775

THE American Revolution served to dissipate to some extent the prejudices which had operated so strongly against Catholics all through the colonial period. Among the many indignities which they had had to suffer was to witness in most of the principal towns on November 5 of each year a commemoration of the fateful attempt of Guy Fawkes to blow up the houses of parliament at London in 1605. At these colonial celebrations one of the principal attractions was the burning of the pope in effigy. Washington's sense of decency put a stop to this practice among the troops under his command at the siege of Boston. His general orders were written while the Commander in Chief was still seemingly confident that the effort to bring the French Catholics of Canada in on the side of the revolting colonies would succeed, and he used that as his main motive for issuing the order. Source: John C. Fitzpatrick (Ed.), *The Writings of George Washington* (Washington: United States Government Printing Office, 1931), IV, 64–65.

GENERAL ORDERS

Head Quarters, Cambridge, November 5, 1775.

As the Commander in Chief has been apprized of a design form'd for the observance of that ridiculous and childish custom of burning the Effigy of the pope — He cannot help expressing his surprise that there should be Officers and Soldiers in this army so void of common sense, as not to see the impropriety of such a step at this Juncture; at a Time when we are solliciting, and have really obtain'd, the friendship and alliance of the people of Canada, whom we ought to consider as Brethren embarked in the same Cause. The defence of the general Liberty of America: At such a juncture, and in such Circumstances, to be insulting their Religion, is so monstrous, as not to be suffered or excused; indeed instead of offering the most remote insult, it is our duty to address public thanks to these our Brethren, as to them we are so much indebted for every late happy Success over the common Enemy in Canada.

44. The Dawn of Religious Freedom for American Catholics, 1776–1791

THE approach of American independence brought to the Catholics in a number of the new states quick relief from the laws that had penalized them through most of the colonial period. But the action of the individual states differed very widely in this respect, and in some cases the legal disabilities lasted well into the nineteenth century. Virginia led the way by its adoption of a bill of rights on June 12, 1776, which embodied the principle of religious freedom, and Pennsylvania and Maryland followed suit before the end of that year. In the constitutions of New York and Massachusetts, however, the old prejudices against Catholics lingered in certain clauses. Meanwhile the general government had agreed to the Articles of Confederation on November 15, 1777, and they went into force on March 1, 1781. Once the Constitution was adopted on September 17, 1787, and its first ten amendments were put into effect on December 15, 1791, it pointed the way for similar action in those states which had hitherto withheld full religious liberty from all their citizens. The following excerpts from the state constitutions were chosen to illustrate the varied action taken by several of the more important states where Catholics were either most numerous or were destined to become so. These are followed by those articles in the two federal instruments of government which pertained in any way to religion. Source: Francis Newton Thorpe (Ed.), *The Federal and State Constitutions* (Washington: Government Printing Office, 1909).

PENNSYLVANIA: Declaration of Rights adopted September 28, 1776.

II. That all men have a natural and unalienable right to worship Almighty God according to the dictates of their own consciences and understanding: And that no man ought or of right can be compelled to attend any religious worship, or erect or support any place of worship, or maintain any ministry, contrary to, or against, his own free will and consent: Nor can any man, who acknowledges the being of a God, be justly deprived or abridged of any civil rights as a citizen, on account of his religious sentiments or peculiar mode of religious worship: And that no authority can or ought to be vested in, or assumed by any power whatever, that shall in any case interfere with, or in any manner controul, the right of conscience in the free exercise of religious worship. (*Ibid.,* V, 3082.)

MARYLAND: Declaration of Rights adopted November 11, 1776.

XXXIII. That, as it is the duty of every man to worship God in such manner as he thinks most acceptable to him; all persons, professing the Christian religion, are equally entitled to protection in their religious liberty; wherefore no person ought by any law to be molested in his person or estate on account of his religious persuasion or profession, or for his religious practice; unless, under colour of religion, any man shall disturb the good order, peace or safety of the State, or shall infringe the laws of morality, or injure others, in their natural, civil, or religious rights; nor ought any person to be compelled to frequent or maintain, or contribute, unless on contract, to maintain any particular place of worship, or any particular ministry; yet the Legislature may, in their discretion, lay a general and equal tax, for the support of the Christian religion; leaving to each individual the power of appointing the payment over of the money, collected from him, to the support of any particular place of worship or minister, or for the benefit of the poor of his own denomination, or of the poor in general of any particular county: but the churches, chapels, glebes, and all other property now belonging to the church of England, ought to remain to the church of England forever. And all acts of Assembly, lately passed, for collecting monies for building or repairing particular churches or chapels of ease, shall continue in force, and be executed, unless the Legislature shall, by act, supersede or repeal the same: but no county court shall assess any quantity of tobacco, or sum of money, hereafter, on the application of any vestrymen or churchwardens; and every encumbent of the church of England, who hath remained in his parish, and performed his duty, shall be entitled to receive the provision and support established by the act, entitled "An act for the support of the clergy of the church of England, in this Province," till the November court of this present year, to be held for the county in which his parish shall lie, or partly lie, or for such time as he hath remained in his parish, and performed his duty. (*Ibid.*, III, 1689–1690.)

NEW YORK: Constitution adopted April 20, 1777.

XXXVIII. And whereas we are required, by the benevolent principles of rational liberty, not only to expel civil tyranny, but also to guard against that spiritual oppression and intolerance wherewith the bigotry and ambition of weak and wicked priests and princes have scourged mankind, this convention doth further, in the name and by the authority of the good people of this State, ordain, determine, and declare, that the free exercise and enjoyment of religious profession and worship, without discrimination or preference, shall forever hereafter be allowed, within this State, to all mankind: *Provided,* That the liberty of conscience, hereby granted, shall not be so construed as to excuse acts of licentiousness, or justify practices inconsistent with the peace or safety of this State.

XXXIX. And whereas the ministers of the gospel are, by their profession, dedicated to the service of God and the care of souls, and ought not to be diverted from the great duties of their functions; therefore, no minister of the gospel, or priest of any denomination whatsoever, shall, at any time hereafter, under any pretence or description whatever, be eligible to, or capable of holding, any civil or military office or place within this State.

XLII. And this convention doth further, in the name and by the authority of the good people of this State, ordain, determine, and declare that it shall be in the discretion of the legislature to naturalize all such persons, and in such manner, as they shall think proper: *Provided,* All such of the persons so to be by them naturalized, as being born in parts beyond the sea, and out of the United States of America, shall come to settle in and become subjects of this State, shall take an oath of allegiance to this State, and abjure and renounce all allegiance and subjection to all and every foreign king, prince, potentate, and State in all matters, ecclesiastical as well as civil. (*Ibid.,* V, 2636–2638.)

MASSACHUSETTS: Constitution ratified by popular vote June 7, 1780.

II. It is the right as well as the duty of all men in society, publicly, and at stated seasons, to worship the SUPREME BEING, the great Creator and Preserver of the universe. And no subject shall be hurt, molested, or restrained in his person, liberty, or estate, for worshipping God in the manner and season most agreeable to the dictates of his own conscience; or for his religious profession of sentiment; provided he doth not disturb the public peace, or obstruct others in their religious worship.

III. As the happiness of a people, and the good order and preservation of civil government, essentially depend upon piety, religion and morality; and as these cannot be generally diffused through a community but by the institution of the public worship of God, and of public instructions in piety, religion and morality; Therefore, to promote their happiness, and to secure the good order and preservation of their government, the people of this commonwealth have a right to invest their legislature with power to authorize and require the several towns, parishes, precincts and other bodies politic, or religious societies, to make suitable provision, at their own expense, for the institution of the public worship of GOD, and for the support and maintenance of public Protestant teachers of piety, religion, and morality, in all cases where such provision shall not be made voluntarily.

And the people of this commonwealth have also a right to, and do, invest their legislature with authority to enjoin upon all the subjects an attendance upon the instructions of the public teachers aforesaid, at stated times and seasons, if there be any on whose instructions they can conscientiously and conveniently attend. . . .

And all moneys paid by the subject to the support of public worship, and of the public teachers aforesaid, shall, if he require it, be uniformly applied to the support of the public teacher or teachers of his own religious sect or denomination, provided there be any on whose instructions he attends; otherwise it may be paid towards the support of the teacher or teachers of the parish or precinct in which the said moneys are raised. (*Ibid.,* III, 1889–1890.)

ARTICLES OF CONFEDERATION: Agreed to by Congress November 15, 1777; ratified and in force March 1, 1781.

III. The said States hereby severally enter into a firm league of friendship, with each other, for their common defence, the security of their liberties, and their mutual and general welfare, binding themselves to assist each other, against all force offered to, or attack made upon them, or any of them, on account of religion, sovereignty, trade, or any other pretence whatever (*Ibid.,* I, 10).

CONSTITUTION: Adopted September 17, 1787; government inaugurated April 30, 1789; first ten amendments in effect December 15, 1791.

VI. No religious Test shall ever be required as a Qualification to any Office of public Trust under the United States (*Ibid.,* I, 27).

I. (Amendments) Congress shall make no law respecting an establishment of religion, or prohibiting the free exercise thereof. (*Ibid.,* I, 29.)

45. Father Gibault Lends Assistance to the American Cause, 1778–1780

ONE of the last of the seminary priests of Quebec to serve in the Illinois Country was Pierre Gibault (1737–1804) who began his missionary career there in 1768. After the outbreak of the American Revolution a group of Virginia militia led by George Rogers Clark (1752–1818) determined upon capturing the British forts in the area. They surprised and took Kaskaskia on July 4, 1778, where Father Gibault was then stationed. Won by Clark's friendly treatment of the French Catholic settlers, the priest volunteered to help when he learned the Americans intended to advance on Vincennes. The leader of the little party was Jean Baptiste Laffont, the village doctor at Kaskaskia, since it was Gibault's wish to keep in the background. The effort was entirely successful and Vincennes and the neighboring Indian tribes declared for the Americans. For this action Gibault won the praise of Governor Patrick Henry of Virginia and a resolution of thanks from the legislature in 1780. But to his superior, Bishop Briand of Quebec, who was intent upon keeping his flock loyal to the British following their generous treatment of the Church in the Quebec Act, Gibault's action was anything but pleasing, and the British authorities themselves regarded him as a traitor. Sensing their reactions from the outset, Gibault kept his hand as hidden as possible and he later denied that he had done more at Vincennes than to counsel peace. The first of the two letters that follow gives Laffont's account of the episode, while the second shows Gibault's warmth toward the American cause as well as revealing something of the confused situation of the Church on the Illinois frontier during the war. Source: Clarence Walworth Alvord (Ed.), *Kaskaskia Records, 1778–1790* (Springfield: Illinois State Historical Library, 1909), pp. 50–51, 518–519.

To Colonel George Roger Clark, present.

I cannot but approve that which M. Gibault said in the contents of his journal. [Even] if he did omit some historical truths which might have been worthy of narration, that which he said is the pure truth. All that he has begged me to add and which he will tell to you, and has asked me to be present (and which he forgot) is that in all the civil affairs, not only with the French but with the savages, he meddled with nothing, because he was not ordered to do so and it was opposed to his vocation; and that I alone had the direction of the affair, he himself having confined himself towards both French and Indians solely to exhortation tending towards peace and union and to the prevention of bloodshed; and so, sir, for the temporal affairs with which I am wholly entrusted, I hope to have all the satisfaction possible, for I acted in all things with an irreproachable integrity.

My zeal and my sincerity persuade me that you will have, sir, the kindness to accept the good wishes which I have the honor to make to you, and to believe me, with a most respectful regard,

Your very humble and very obedient servant,
Laffont.

Kaskaskia, August 7th. 1778
Mr. G. R. Clark,
Sir,

We have been greatly disappointed in not having the pleasure of seeing you in our village. The joy was general when we knew that you were so near us. The kindness and benefits you showed us during your stay here gave us the promise of the same when you should return. I was not one of those who desired you with the least ardor. You know my heart; and, if the public affairs of my ministry did not demand my presence, I should have given myself the pleasure and honor of making you a visit in your new establishment; but I hope that it is only a postponement and that another opportunity will find me less occupied. We are very poor and destitute of all things. We are impatiently expecting the village boats. We fear the savages and the evilly disposed people who are urging them to kill us. In a word we are truly in a sad situation. In spite of this we are of good courage and are so good Americans that we are ready to defend ourselves to the death against any who attack us. I pray you to accept my respects and to employ me in any way in my power for your service. I always have true pleasure in being useful to you and in calling myself with all possible consideration

Your very humble and obedient servant,
P. Gibault, Priest.

Kaskaskia, May 10, 1780.

46. John Carroll Is Appointed Superior of the American Missions, June 9, 1784

THE recognition of American independence by Great Britain in the provisional treaty of November 30, 1782, confronted the Holy See with a difficult and unprecedented situation. Obviously the jurisdiction of the Vicar Apostolic of the London District over American Catholics could no longer be exercised and some substitute would have to be found. But an overseas republic with a strong tradition of hostility toward the Church, wherein the priests themselves were known to oppose the appointment of a bishop, did not offer a promising prospect for direct negotiations. In his perplexity, therefore, Lorenzo Cardinal Antonelli (1730–1811), Prefect of Propaganda, turned to France, the new republic's ally, for guidance. He first raised the question with the nuncio at Paris on January 15, 1783, and for the next year and a half the correspondence continued and ultimately involved a number of officials, including Benjamin Franklin, the American Minister to France. Finally Propaganda reached a decision by naming John Carroll (1735–1815) as superior of the American missions with very limited faculties. Thus did there come about the first step toward giving a form and government to the Church in the United States. The following letter of Antonelli to Carroll informed him of his appointment, acknowledged that it was only a temporary arrangement, and asked for more information on the state of Catholicism in the new country. Source: Latin text in Donald C. Shearer, O.F.M.Cap. (Ed.), *Pontificia Americana. A Documentary History of the Catholic Church in the United States, 1784–1884* (Washington: The Catholic University of America Press, 1933), pp. 58–59; English translation by John Gilmary Shea, *History of the Catholic Church in the United States* (New York: John G. Shea, 1888), II, 243–245.

Rome, June 9, 1784.

Very Rev. Sir:

In order to preserve and defend Catholicity in the Thirteen United States of North America, the Supreme Pontiff of the Church Pius VI., and this sacred Congregation, have thought it extremely proper to designate a pastor who should, permanently and independently of any ecclesiastical power, except the same Sacred Congregation, attend to the spiritual necessities of the Catholic flock. In the appointment of such a pastor, the Sacred Congregation would have readily have cast its eyes on the Rev. John Lewis if his advanced age and the labors he has already undergone in the vineyard of the Lord, had not deterred it from imposing on him, a new and very heavy burden; for he seems to require repose rather than arduous labor. As then, Rev. Sir, you have given conspicuous proofs of piety and zeal, and it is known that your appointment will please and gratify many members of that republic, and especially Mr. Franklin, the eminent individual who represents the same republic at the court of the Most Christian King, the Sacred Congregation, with the approbation of his Holiness, has appointed you Superior of the Mission in the thirteen United States of North America, and has communicated to you the faculties, which are necessary to the discharge of that office; faculties which are also communicated to the other priests of the same States, except the administration of confirmation, which is reserved for you alone, as the enclosed documents will show.

These arrangements are meant to be only temporary. For it is the intention of his Holiness soon to charge a Vicar-Apostolic, invested with the title and character of bishop, with the care of those states, that he may attend to ordination and other episcopal functions. But, to accomplish this design, it is of great importance that we should be made acquainted with the state of the orthodox religion in those thirteen states. Therefore we request you to forward to us, as soon as possible, a correct report, stating carefully the number of Catholics in each state; what is their condition, their piety and what abuses exist; also how many missionary priests labor now in this vineyard of the Lord; what are their qualifications, their zeal, their mode of support. For though the Sacred Congregation wish not to meddle with temporal things, it is important for the establishment of laborers, that we should know what are the ecclesiastical revenues, if any there are, and it is believed there are some. In the meantime for fear the want of missionaries should deprive the Catholics of spiritual assistance, is has been resolved to invite hither two youths from the states of Maryland and Pennsylvania, to educate them at the expense of the Sacred Congregation in the Urban College; they will afterwards, on returning to their country, be substitutes in the mission. We leave to your solicitude the care of selecting and sending them. You will make choice of those who have more promising talents and a good constitution, who are not less than twelve, nor more than fifteen years of age; who by their proficiency in the sanctuary may give great hopes of themselves. You may address them to the excellent archbishop of Seleucia, Apostolic Nuncio at Paris, who is informed of their coming. If the young men selected are unable to defray the expenses of the voyage, the Sacred Congregation will provide for them: we even wish to be informed by you frankly and accurately of the necessary traveling expenses, to serve as a rule for the future. Such are the things I had to signify to you; and whilst I am confident you will discharge the office committed to you with all zeal, solicitude and fidelity, and more than answer the high opinion we have formed of you, I pray God that he may grant you all peace and happiness.

L. Card. Antonelli,
Prefect.

Stephen Borgia,
Secretary.

47. Carroll Answers an Attack Upon the Catholic Faith, 1784

ONE of the most unpleasant duties which John Carroll, first superior of the American Catholics, had to perform in the year of his appointment was to answer an attack made upon the Catholic faith by an apostate priest. Charles H. Wharton (1748–1833) was a Maryland-born ex-Jesuit like Carroll himself who had served for some years as chaplain to the Catholics in Worcester, England. After his return to the United States he had published at Philadelphia in the early summer of 1784 *A Letter to the Roman Catholics of the City of Worcester.* The following excerpts from Carroll's reply indicate something of his method as well as the method used by Wharton in his efforts to justify his action. Carroll was a warm admirer of the religious toleration which was then becoming a reality in the United States and he was pained at the prospect of disrupting the present harmony between Americans of different religious beliefs by engaging in religious controversy. The priests of that day were accustomed to charges against the Church, but by reason of the nature and source of Wharton's publication they felt it could not be ignored, and they were agreed that Carroll was the man to answer it. Source: *An Address to the Roman Catholics of the United States of America.* By a Catholic Clergyman [John Carroll] (Annapolis: Frederick Green, 1784), pp. 59–60, 113–115.

I will not deny, that I was surprised when I read the first passage cited by the Chaplain; it appeared so opposite to the principles which St. Chrysostom had laid down in several parts of his works. It was a mortifying circumstance, that I could not conveniently have recourse to that holy doctor's writings, nor minutely examine the passage objected, together with its context. I procured a friend to examine the edition of Chrysostom's works, belonging to the public library at Annapolis; he has carefully and repeatedly read the 49th homily on St. Matthew; and not one syllable of the Chaplain's citation is to be found in it. After receiving this notice, I was for some time doubtful, whether it might not be owing to a difference in the editions. I could not persuade myself, that he, who so solemnly calls heaven to witness for the impartiality and integrity of his inquiry, would publicly expose himself to a well-grounded imputation of unpardonable negligence, in a matter of such serious concern. But I have now the fullest evidence, that the passage, for which Chrysostom on Matthew, hom. 49, is quoted, is not taken from that father. It is extracted from a work of no credit, supposed to be written in the 6th century, entitled, *The unfinished work on Matthew.* But had it ever been fairly quoted from him, the Chaplain would not have had so much cause for triumph as he imagines. For the passage, he adduces, carries with it equal condemnation of the protestant and catholic rule of faith. . . .

I have now gone through a task, painful in every point of view, in which I could consider it. To write for the public eye, on any occasion whatever, is neither agreeable to my feelings, my leisure, or opportunities; that it is likewise disproportioned to my abilities, my readers, I doubt [not], will soon discover. But if reduced to the necessity of publishing, I would wish that my duty led me to any species of composition, rather than that of religious controversy. Mankind have conceived such a contempt for it, that an author cannot entertain a hope of enjoying those gratifications, which in treating other subjects may support his spirits and enliven his imagination. Much less could I have a prospect of these incitements in the prosecution of my present undertaking. I could not forget, in the beginning, progress, and conclusion of it, that the habits of thinking, the prejudices, perhaps even the passions of many of my readers, would be set against all the arguments, I could offer; and that the weaknesses, the errors, the absurdities of the writer would be imputed to the errors and absurdity of his religion. But of all considerations the most painful was, that I had to combat him, with whom I had been connected in an intercourse of friendship and mutual good offices; and in connection with whom I hoped to have consummated my course of our common ministry in the service of virtue and religion. But when I found these expectations disappointed; when I found that he not only had abandoned our faith and communion, but had imputed to us doctrines foreign to our belief, and having a natural tendency to embitter against us the minds of our fellow-citizens, I felt an anguish too keen for description; and perhaps the Chaplain will experience a similar sentiment, when he comes coolly to reflect on this instance of his conduct. It did not become the friend of toleration to misinform, and to sow in minds so misinformed, the seeds of religious animosity.

Under all these distressful feelings, one consideration alone relieved me in writing; and that was, the hope of vindicating your religion to your own selves at least, and preserving the steadfastness of your faith. But even this prospect should not have induced me to engage in the controversy, if I could fear that it would disturb the harmony now subsisting amongst all christians in this country, so blessed with civil and religious liberty; which if we have the wisdom and temper to preserve, America may come to exhibit a proof to the world, that general and equal toleration, by giving a free circulation to fair argument, is the most effectual method to bring all denominations of christians to a unity of faith.

The motives, which led the Chaplain to the step he has taken, are known best to God and himself. For the vindication of his conduct, he appeals to the dictates of conscience with a seriousness and solemnity, which must add greatly to his guilt, if he be not sincere. He is anxious to impress on his readers a firm conviction, that neither views of preferment or sensuality, had any influence on his determination. He appears to be jealous, that suspicions will arise unfavourable to the purity of his intentions. He shall have no cause to impute to me the spreading of these suspicions. But I must entreat him with an earnestness suggested by the most perfect good will and zealous regard for his welfare, to consider the sanctity of the solemn and deliberate engagement, which at an age of perfect maturity he contracted with Almighty God. . . .

48. The First American Report to Propaganda on Catholicism in the United States, March 1, 1785

FATHER JOHN CARROLL did not find his appointment as superior of the American Catholic missions to his liking, but from the time he received word of it in late November, 1784, he set about to fulfill the duties of the office as efficiently as he possibly could. One of his most pressing tasks was to furnish Propaganda with the data they had requested concerning the condition of the Church in the United States. For that purpose Carroll turned to the twenty-four priests then in the country and asked them to supply him with the facts on their missions. From the reports submitted to him, and from his own knowledge, he composed the document which follows. It has interest as being the most authentic account of the state of the Church at that time, as well as being the first of a lengthy series of reports on American Catholicism which found their way into Propaganda's archives from 1784 until 1908 when the American Church was removed from the jurisdiction of that congregation. Source: The original Latin was published from a photostat of the document in the archives of the Congregation de Propaganda Fide by Peter Guilday, *The Life and Times of John Carroll, Archbishop of Baltimore, 1735–1815* (New York: Encyclopedia Press, 1922), I, 223–225; the translation is taken from John Gilmary Shea, *History of the Catholic Church in the United States* (New York: John G. Shea, 1888), II, 257–261.

Report for the Eminent Cardinal Antonelli

Concerning the State of Religion in the United States of America.

1. On the Number of Catholics in the United States.

There are in Maryland about 15,800 Catholics; of these there are about 9,000 freemen, adults or over twelve years of age; children under that age, about 3,000; and above that number of slaves of all ages of African origin, called negroes. There are in Pennsylvania about 7,000, very few of whom are negroes, and the Catholics are less scattered and live nearer to each other. There are not more than 200 in Virginia who are visited four or five times a year by a priest. Many other Catholics are said to be scattered in that and other States, who are utterly deprived of all religious ministry. In the State of New York I hear that there are at least 1,500. (Would that some spiritual succor could be afforded them!) They have recently, at their own expense, sent for a Franciscan Father from Ireland, and he is said to have the best testimonials as to his learning and life; he had arrived a little before I received the letters in which faculties were transmitted to me, communicable to my fellow-priests. I was for a time in doubt whether I could properly approve this priest for the administration of the sacraments. I have now, however, decided, especially as the feast of Easter is so near, to consider him as one of my fellow-priests, and to grant him faculties, and I trust that my decision will meet your approbation. As to the Catholics who are in the territory bordering on the river called Mississippi and in all that region which following that river extends to the Atlantic Ocean, and from it extends to the limits of Carolina, Virginia and Pennsylvania, — this tract of country contains, I hear, many Catholics, formerly Canadians, who speak French, and I fear that they are destitute of priests. Before I received your Eminence's letters there went to them a priest, German by birth, but who came last from France; he professes to belong to the Carmelite order: he was furnished with no sufficient testimonials that he was sent by his lawful superior. What he is doing and what is the condition of the Church in those parts, I expect soon to learn. The jurisdiction of the Bishop of Quebec formerly extended to some part of that region; but I do not know whether he wishes to exercise any authority there now, that all these parts are subjects to the United States.

2. On the Condition, Piety, and Defects, etc., of Catholics.

In Maryland a few of the leading more wealthy families still profess the Catholic faith introduced at the very foundation of the province by their ancestors. The greater part of them are planters and in Pennsylvania almost all are farmers, except the merchants and mechanics living in Philadelphia. As for piety, they are for the most part sufficiently assiduous in the exercises of religion and in frequenting the sacraments, but they lack that fervor, which frequent appeals to the sentiment of piety usually produce, as many congregations hear the word of God only once a month, and sometimes only once in two months. We are reduced to this by want of priests, by the distance of congregations from each other and by difficulty of travelling. This refers to Catholics born here, for the condition of the Catholics who in great numbers are flowing in here from different countries of Europe, is very different. For while there are few of our native Catholics who do not approach the sacraments of Penance and the Holy Eucharist, at least once a year, especially in Easter time, you can scarcely find any among the newcomers who discharge this duty of religion, and there is reason to fear that the example will be very pernicious especially in commercial towns. The abuses that have grown among Catholics are chiefly those, which result with unavoidable intercourse with non-Catholics, and the examples thense derived: namely more free intercourse between young people of opposite sexes than is compatible with chastity in mind and body; too great fondness for dances and similar amusements; and an incredible eagerness, especially in girls, for reading love stories which are brought over in great quantities from Europe. Then among other things, a general lack of care in instructing their children and especially the negro slaves in their religion, as these people are kept constantly at work, so that they rarely hear any instructions from the priest, unless they can spend a short time with one; and most of them are consequently very dull in faith and depraved in morals. It can scarcely be believed how much trouble and care they give the pastors of souls.

3. On the number of priests, their qualifications, character and means of support.

There are nineteen priests in Maryland and five in Pennsylvania. Of these two are more than seventy years old, and three others very near that age: and they are consequently almost entirely unfit to undergo the hardships, without which this Vineyard of the Lord cannot be cultivated. Of the remaining priests some are in very bad health, and there is one recently approved by me for a few months only, that in the extreme want of priests I may give him a trial: for some things were reported of him, which made me averse to employing him. I will watch him carefully, and if anything occurs unworthy priestly gravity I will recall the faculties granted, whatever inconvenience this may bring to many Catholics: for I am convinced that the Catholic faith will suffer less harm, if for a short time there is no priest at a place, than if living as we do among fellow-citizens of another religion, we admit to the discharge of the sacred ministry, I do not say bad priests, but incautious and imprudent priests. All the other clergymen lead a life full of labour, as each one attends congregations far apart, and has to be riding constantly and with great fatigue, especially to sick calls. Priests are maintained chiefly from the proceeds of the estates; elsewhere by the liberality of the Catholics. There is properly no ecclesiastical property here: for the property by which the priests are supported, is held in the names of individuals and transferred by will to devisees. This course was rendered necessary when the Catholic religion was cramped here by laws, and no remedy has yet been found for this difficulty, although we made an earnest effort last year.

There is a college in Philadelphia, and it is proposed to establish two in Maryland, in which Catholics can be admitted, as well as others, as presidents, professors and pupils. We hope that some educated there will embrace the ecclesiastical state. We think accordingly of establishing a Seminary, in which they can be trained to the life and learning suited to that state.

John Carroll.

March 1, 1785.

49. Lay Trusteeism in New York, January 25. 1786

THE most serious trouble that confronted the Catholic Church in the United States after the Revolution arose from the abuse of lay trusteeism. The root causes of the difficulty were: an imperfect knowledge, on the part of both clergy and laity, of the canon law pertaining to the holding and administration of church property; small groups of laymen imbued with the heady wine of their newly won religious freedom, and the example of their Protestant neighbors who had the dominant voice in ruling their congregations; wayward priests who for selfish reasons abetted the laymen's ambitions to govern the congregations; and a mounting antagonism among Catholics of varying national backgrounds. All the principal elements were present at St. Peter's Church, New York City, in the 1780's, plus the frustration suffered by John Carroll as ecclesiastical superior due to his limited faculties to deal with situations of this kind. St. Peter's got its start with an Irish-born Capuchin, Charles Whelan, who arrived in 1784, but with the appearance of another Irish Capuchin, Andrew Nugent, in 1785, quarrels arose and the congregation was soon divided between warring factions with the trustees finally casting Whelan out and going over to Nugent as the better preacher. Carroll was appealed to and in his reply to the trustees he cogently set forth the chief issues involved. The ugly affair eventually resulted in schism and it was only with the coming of Father

William V. O'Brien, O.P. (1740–1816), in October, 1787, that peace was restored. Carroll's letter is included here to illustrate the nature of an evil that would plague the American Church in one form or another until near the middle of the nineteenth century. Source: *American Catholic Historical Researches,* XVII (January, 1900), 1–4.

R.C. [Rock Creek] near Georgetown, Jan. 25, 1786.
Gentlemen:

I was honored yesterday at the same time with your letters of Dec. 22, 1785, and January 11, 1786. You did me justice in supposing that the former was delayed on its way or had miscarried; for certainly I should not have failed in my duty of immediately answering so respectable a part of the congregation. You will however readily conceive, that this is not an easy nor, allow me to say, a very agreeable office in the present instance. One circumstance indeed gives me comfort; you profess to have no other views than for the service and credit of religion; and as I make it my endeavor to be influenced solely by the same motive, I trust that proposing to ourselves the same end we shall likewise agree in the means of obtaining it.

The first advices of any disturbances among you, were transmitted to me in letters from Messrs. Whelan and Nugent which I answered on the 17th and 18th inst. Both these gentlemen represented the steps taken as extreme and improper. I spoke of them therefore in the same manner in my answers, and the more freely as neither of them mentioned the name of one single person concerned. Having now received a communication of your sentiments, I shall likewise deliver mine with the respect due to your representations, and with the freedom and plainness becoming the responsible and burdensome office, of which I feel myself every day more unworthy, in proportion as the duties and the weight of it grow upon me.

But I must first state to you the previous information I had received: 1st, that the trustees denied having agreed to the articles, of which I left a copy with Mr. Whelan; and which to my best apprehension had been adopted at the meeting I had the honor of having with those gentlemen. 2d, that an opinion was formed and propagated of the congregation having a right not only to choose such parish priest as is agreeable to them, but discharging him at pleasure, and that after such election, the bishop or other ecclesiastical superior cannot hinder him from exercising the usual functions. 3dly, that two of the congregation (by whose orders I am not informed) on Sunday, December 18th, after Divine Service and in the face of all present in the chapel, seized in a tumultuary manner and kept possession of the collection then made. The first part of this intelligence shocked me very much both because it reflected on my veracity which in this instance I will steadily assert and because I considered the matters then agreed on as right in point of justice as the renewal of confidence and foundation of future union. The next point of intelligence was still more important. If ever the principles then laid down should become predominant, the unity and catholicity of our Church would be at an end; and it would be formed into distinct and independent societies, nearly in the same manner as the congregational Presbyterians of our neighboring New England States. A zealous clergyman performing his duty courageously and without respect of persons would be always liable to be the victim of his earnest endeavors to stop the progress of vice and evil example, and others more complying with the passions of some principal persons of the congregation would be substituted in his room; and if the ecclesiastical superior has no control in these instances, I will refer to your own judgment what the consequences may be. The great source of misconception in this matter is that an idea appears to be taken both by you and Mr. Whelan that the officiating clergyman at New York is a parish priest, whereas there is yet no such office in the United States. The hierarchy of our American Church not being yet constituted, no parishes are formed, and the clergy coming to the assistance of the faithful, are but voluntary laborers in the vineyard of Christ, not vested with ordinary jurisdiction annexed to their office, but receiving it as delegated and extra hierarchical commission. Wherever parishes are established no doubt, a proper regard (and such as is suitable (?) to our governments) will be had to rights of the congregation in the mode of election and representation; and even now I shall ever pay to their wishes every deference consistent with the general welfare of religion: of which I hope to give you proof in the sequel of this letter. The third article of my information was particularly mortifying; for I could not but fear, that a step so violent, at such a time and place, and probably in the presence of other religionists would breed disunion among yourselves and make a very disadvantageous impression, to the prejudice of the Catholic cause, so soon after the first introduction of public worship into your city.

I now return to the contents of your letters, and observe that after stating some censurable instances of Mr. Whelan's conduct, you desire me to remove him, and imply a desire that Mr. Nugent, as being very acceptable, may succeed to his office. I can assure you, Gentlemen, that I have a very advantageous opinion of Mr. Nugent's abilities, and he shewed me very good testimonials of his zeal and virtue. I repeatedly told him, as I did to many of yourselves, that nothing but my own want of sufficient authority prevented me from giving him every power requisite for the exercise of his ministry. I hoped before this to have that restriction of my authority removed, but as it is not, it remains still out of my power to employ him agreeably to your and my desires. If I am ever able to do it, I will certainly remember my assurances to him. But in the mean time what can I do? Can I revoke Mr. Whelan's faculties and leave so great a congregation without assistance? Can I deprive him, when neither his morals, his orthodoxy, or his assiduity have been impeached? especially while I am uncertain whether his removal be desired by a majority of the congregation? For I have received assurances very much to the contrary. But even if a considerable part are still attached to him, would the great object of unanimity be obtained by his removal? Would not his adherents consider Mr. Nugent as coming in upon the ruins of his predecessor and consequently would they not keep alive the spirit of discord? Upon these considerations I have taken a resolution which will, I hope, meet your wishes, as well as of every part of the congregation. As soon as I am at liberty to grant them, Mr. Nugent shall have powers from me [to] act as your joint-chaplain; for the idea of parish-priest is not admissible. He has repeatedly assured me he never will accept of an appointment to the exclusion of his brother: in his letter he says a sufficient maintenance of both may be obtained. In the mean time he has full authority to announce the word of God, and I promise myself he will do it with effect, especially by including the great duty of charity and unanimity. He and Mr. Whelan will concur in recommending this characteristic virtue of christianity, by their examples as well as advice. Educated in the same school of religion, and connected by special ties to the same order, they will assist each other in the work of the ministry and every part of the congregation will have it in their power to apply to him of the two, in which they have the greatest confidence. I must not omit taking notice of Mr. Whelan's address to the congregation inclosed in your last. I greatly disapprove it, and shall so inform him. When I wrote the letter to which he refers, I had heard nothing from New York concerning your uneasiness. I lamented that my hands being still tied, I was prevented from giving full employment to Mr. Nugent's zeal; and I must add, for Mr. La Valinère's[1] credit, that when I declined granting him leave to administer the Sacraments to the Canadian refugees, it was for the same reason, because I had no power to do it. Otherwise I have such a conviction of his many qualities, that I should gladly have indulged the wishes of those good people who solicited [this power] and of this I beg to inform him.

[At the close?] of your last letter you make some mention of eventually having recourse to legal means to rid yourselves of Mr. Whelan. The insinuation makes me very unhappy. I cannot tell what assistance the laws might give you; but allow me to say that you can take no step so fatal to that respectability, in which as a religious Society you wish to stand, or more prejudicial to the Catholic cause. I must therefore entreat you to decline a design so pernicious to all your prospects; and protesting against measures so extreme, I explicitly declare, that no clergyman, be he who he may, shall receive any spiritual powers from me who shall advise or countenance so unnecessary . . . [the copy breaks off at this point].

50. Thomas FitzSimons Urges Pennsylvania's Early Ratification of the Constitution, September 29, 1787

IN THE convention that drafted the federal Constitution at Philadelphia in May-September, 1787, there were two Catholic delegates: Thomas FitzSimons of Pennsylvania and Daniel Carroll of Maryland. FitzSimons (1741–1811) had early won prominence as a member of both the Pennsylvania legislature and the congress established under the Articles of Confederation, and from 1789–1795 he served as a member of the national House of Representatives. He was active in the debates of the constitutional convention in behalf of a strong national government and, therefore, when the Constitution was laid before the legislature and a threat of delay developed, FitzSimons vigorously contended that neither the old congress nor the state legislatures had any right to make the decision; that right, said FitzSimons, rested with the people in an election for delegates to a ratifying convention. FitzSimons belonged to the Federalist group of delegates from Philadelphia and the commercial towns who were intent upon quick ratifica-

[1] Pierre Huet de la Valinière (1732–1806), a French-born Sulpician, who had incurred the displeasure of both Bishop Briand and the British authorities in Canada during the Revolution because of his flirtations with the Americans. He was a rather erratic fellow whose many wanderings seemed to bring him little peace of mind.

tion lest the anti-Federalist forces of the German farmers and Scotch-Irish frontiersmen be given time to crystallize. His speech in the legislature on September 29, 1787, helped to hasten action and in the squel Pennsylvania was the second state to ratify the Constitution on December 12, 1787. FitzSimons was one of Philadelphia's most outstanding citizens, filling for many years such posts as president of the Chamber of Commerce, trustee of the University of Pennsylvania, trustee of the Bank of North America, and founder and director of the Insurance Company of North America. He was always a devout Catholic and was the largest single contributor to St. Augustine's Church in Philadelphia. Source: *Proceedings and Debates of the General Assembly of Pennsylvania* (Philadelphia: Daniel Humphreys, 1787), I, 131–132.

I think too highly of the good sense of this House, to suppose it necessary to say anything to prove to them, that their *agreement* to calling a convention is *not unfederal,* as every member must have fully considered the point before this time; now I do not think a single gentleman supposes, that it would be unfederal. Though the member from Westmoreland has taken some pains to persuade us, that Pennsylvania has been hitherto a federal state, and that we are about to depart from that conduct, and to run before even prosperity itself — I think it greatly to the honor of Pennsylvania that she deserves the gentleman's commendation, by having always stood foremost in support of federal measures, and I think it will redound still more to her honor, to enter foremost into this new system of confederation, seeing the old is so dissolved or rotten as to be incapable of answering any good purpose whatsoever. Has the gentleman ever looked at the new constitution? If he has, he will see it is not an alteration of an article in the old, but that it departs in every principle from the other. It presupposes, Sir, that no confederation exists; or if it does exist, it exists to no purpose, as it can answer no useful purpose; it cannot provide for the common defense, nor promote the general welfare — Therefore, arguments that are intended to reconcile one with the other, or make the latter an appendage to the former, are but a mere waste of words. Does the gentleman suppose that the convention thought themselves acting under any provision made in the confederation for altering its articles? No, Sir, they had no such idea. They were obliged, in the first instance, to begin with the destruction of its greatest principle, *equal representation.* They found the confederation without vigor, and so decayed, that it was impossible to graft a useful article upon it; nor was the *mode,* Sir, prescribed by that confederation, which requires alterations to originate with Congress. They found at an early period, that no good purpose could be effected by making such alterations, as were provided by the first articles of union. They also saw, that what alterations were necessary could not be ratified by the legislatures, as they were incompetent to ordaining a form of government. They knew this belonged to the people only, and that the people only would be adequate to carry it into effect. What have Congress and the legislature to do with the proposed constitution? Nothing, Sir — they are but the mere vehicles to convey the information to the people. The convention, Sir, never supposed it was necessary to report to Congress, much less to abide their determination: they thought it decent to make the compliment to them of sending the result of their deliberations — concluding the knowledge of that would be more extensively spread through their means — not that I would infer there is the least doubt of the most hearty concurrence of that body. But, should they decline, and the State of Pennsylvania neglect calling a convention, as I said before, the authority is with the people, and they will do it themselves: but there is a propriety in the legislatures, providing the mode by which it may be conducted in a decent and orderly manner.

The member from Westmoreland agrees that a convention ought to take place. He goes further, and declares that it must and will take place, but assigns no reason why it should not early take place. He must know that any time after the election will be proper, because at that time the people, being collected together, have full opportunity to learn each other's sentiments on this subject. Taking measures for calling a convention is a very different thing from deciding on the plan of government. The sentiments of the people, so far as they have been collected, have been unanimously favorable to its adoption, and its early adoption, if their representatives think it a good one; if we set the example now, there is a great prospect of its being generally come into; but if we delay, ill consequences may arise. And I should suppose, if no better arguments are offered for the delay than what has been advanced by the gentleman on the other side of the house, that we will not agree to it. As to the time for election, that has been all along conceded, and gentlemen will propose such time as they think proper.

51. Daniel Carroll Argues for Marylanders to Ratify the Constitution, October 16, 1787

DANIEL CARROLL (1730–1796), brotner of the first Archbishop of Baltimore, served the nation in a number of important offices, viz., as delegate to both the Continental Congress and the Constitutional Convention, United States Senator from Maryland, and as one of the three commissioners appointed by President Washington to survey the federal district. Like his fellow Catholic in the convention that drafted the Constitution, FitzSimons of Pennsylvania, Carroll was intent that the new government should be a strong one. When Samuel Chase, writing over the pen name of "Caution," counseled his fellow Marylanders to delay action, Carroll as "A Friend to the Constitution" came forward with a persuasive appeal urging a speedy ratification. Source: *Maryland Journal,* October 16, 1787.

To the Inhabitants of Baltimore Town:

You have been addressed in the last Friday's Paper, by a writer under the signature of Caution, who would persuade you that you ought to withhold your approbation at the time, from the Federal Constitution recommended by the Convention.

This writer may have the best intention in the world toward the PUBLIC WELFARE, and the PROSPERITY of Baltimore; but every one must perceive that he is an enemy to the proposed Constitution, and wishes to prevent you from expressing yourselves in its favor, not only AT THIS TIME, but at any future time.

Mr. C—— is said to be the author of this admonition; but that this is a malicious insinuation, aimed at his sincerity, will appear by considering his recent promise on this subject, signed and published by himself, in reference with the resolution of the Convention, upon which that promise is founded. I shall date both the resolution and promise, that you may judge for yourselves.

The resolve of the Convention declares, that the Constitution should be submitted to a Convention of Delegates, chosen in each State by the people, under the recommendation of its legislature, for their assent and ratification.

Mr. C—— being called upon, before his election, to declare himself on this point, promised to the people, "that he will use his endeavors, if elected to call a Convention."

I would just observe on this resolve and promise: — First, that the resolve make it an absolute condition that the legislature recommend a Convention TO ASSENT TO AND RATIFY THE CONSTITU-

TION. Secondly — that the promise made by Mr. C—— is obligating upon him to use his endeavors to procure a Convention FOR THIS PURPOSE.

Another remark which occurs on this occasion, is that Mr. C—— could not mean that a Convention ought to be called FOR ANY OTHER PURPOSE than to assent and ratify the Constitution; for it is absurd to suppose he meant the Convention should be authorized by the legislature TO PROPOSE AMENDMENTS OR ALTERATIONS, that being CONTRARY to the declared intention of the resolution, and the Sense which his friends entertained of his engagement at the time he entered into it: Mr. C—— therefore (without presuming him capable of doing the greatest violence to his promise) strenuously, though indirectly, against adopting the Constitution.

From the brief view of the nature and intention of the resolve, I think it is evident that the people ought WITHOUT DELAY, to signify their approbation of the Constitution by a PETITION TO THE LEGISLATURE, to this end that the legislature, which is called upon by the Convention, and Congress to recommend to the people to choose Delegates to ratify it, may have the authority of this largest and most promising commercial and manufacturing Town in the State to countenance so important a recommendation. But Caution thinks a petition improper and unnecessary because says he "Your Delegates will move for and exert themselves to procure the calling a Convention." Admitting your Delegates to move to have a Convention called, does it follow that they will add to the motion these essential words, to confirm and ratify the Constitution. Does it not rather appear, from the tenor of this writer's remarks that your Delegates ought to leave these words out of their motion? But the propriety and necessity of a petition does not depend on what your Delegates may or may not do. It is PROPER at this time because the Constitution meets your approbation. It is NECESSARY at this time, because wanted as an inducement to the legislature to call upon the people to appoint a Convention to carry into effect the object of the resolution. In other words, as the recommendation for a. Convention involve the legislature in a complete approbation of the Constitution, there is the greatest propriety and necessity for your telling the legislature that it meets your approbation.

I am sorry to find, by Caution's publication and insinuations, which I am told are circulated with great industry, that an opposition is opened against the Constitution. I did not, I confess, expect to see it adopted without some opposition, but I could not bring myself to believe, that this opposition could have originated in Baltimore, which is so peculiarly interested in its speedy adoption. But what I intended to say on this point, is so well expressed in a late speech of Mr. Wilson,[1] to the people of Philadelphia, previous to their election for representation, that I shall take the liberty of closing with it.

"After all, my fellow-citizens (says this excellent politician) it is neither extraordinary nor unexpected that the Constitution offered to your consideration should meet with opposition. It is the nature of man to pursue his own interest in preference to the PUBLIC GOOD; and I do not mean to make any personal reflection when I add, that it is the interest of a very numerous, powerful and respectable body to counteract and destroy the excellent work produced by the late convention. All the offices of government, and all the appointments for the administration of justice, and the collection of the public revenue, which are transferred from the individual to the aggregate sovereignty of the States, will necessarily turn the stream of influence and emolument into a new channel. EVERY PERSON, therefore, who either enjoys, or expects to enjoy, a place of profit under the present establishment, will object to this proposed innovation, not in truth because it is injurious to the liberties of his country; but because it effects his schemes of wealth and consequences. I will confess, indeed, that I am not a blind admirer of this plan of government, and that there are some parts of it, which if my wish had prevailed, would certainly have been altered. But, when I reflect how widely men differ in their opinions, and that every man (and the observation applies likewise to every state) has an equal pretension to assert his own, I am satisfied that anything nearer to perfection could not have been accomplished. If there are errors, it should be remembered, that the seeds of reformation are sown in the work itself, and the concurrence of two thirds of the Congress may, at any time, introduce alterations and amendments. Regarding it then, in every point of view, with a candid and disinterested mind, I am bold to assert, that it is the best form of government which has ever been offered to the world."

A FRIEND TO THE CONSTITUTION.

---

[1] James Wilson (1742–1798) of Pennsylvania, one of the best informed and most influential members of the convention that drafted the Constitution.

52. The Foreshadowing of Trusteeism in the First National Parish of the United States, 1787

THE most important group of Catholics in the thirteen original colonies — aside from those of English and Irish extraction — were the Germans who had begun immigrating in the early eighteenth century to Philadelphia and the rural settlements west of the city where in time they had developed relatively flourishing congregations. In 1741 two German Jesuits, Theodore Schneider and William Wappeler, came from Europe to minister to these families, and when Robert Harding, S.J., reported a census of the Catholics in Pennsylvania in April, 1757, he gave the total as 1365 of whom 949 were Germans. Motivated by the recent grant of religious liberty and by their nationalist sentiments, in 1787 a group of German laymen in Philadelphia decided to erect a church for those of their own nationality. In spite of the opposition of Fathers Robert Molyneux and Francis Beeston, who were in charge of St. Mary's Church, they persisted and asked John Carroll for permission to proceed. Carroll gave a somewhat reluctant consent; the laymen secured legal incorporation in October, 1788; elected as their own pastor John Charles Helbron, a German Capuchin; and on November 22, 1789, Holy Trinity Church was opened for services. This first national parish in the United States contained all the elements of the later widespread abuse of trusteeism: laymen acting in church affairs on their own initiative, abetted by vagrant priests who had no regard for ecclesiastical authority, appeals to the civil law, etc. In fact, Holy Trinity Church ultimately went into schism in September, 1796, and the trustees did not finally yield to Carroll's authority until January, 1802. The documents which follow are the laymen's original request to Carroll (undated, late in 1787) and his letter of November 24, 1787, in which he refused to concede their right to choose Helbron in place of Father Laurence Graessl whom he had designated to be their priest. Source: Martin I. J. Griffin, "The Church of the Holy Trinity, Philadelphia," *Records of the American Catholic Historical Society of Philadelphia*, XXI (1910), 9–11.

[late in 1787]

To the Right Reverend Father in God, John Carroll.

Right Reverend Sir: We the subscribers duly appointed by a respectable German Catholic Congregation in and about Philadelphia to wait on your Right Reverence with a memorial, humbly set forth:

Whereas by the late glorious revolution in this part of the globe Heaven has blessed with liberty and free and uninterrupted exercise of our most holy Religion, and is the more fully confirmed by the new Federal Constitution, and whereas the German Catholic congregation in and about Philadelphia has largely increased and is dayly more and more increasing, that the new chappel in Fourth Street is, as it is well known, too small to accommodate conveniently and hold such great number of people of all nations at the time of divine service.

Therefore your humble memorialists, warm wishers to keep up their respective nation and Language, have the honor to inform your Right Reverence that they have concluded and by the divine assistance of Allmighty God and your Right Reverence's gracious approbation are fully determined to build and erect another new place of divine worship for the better convenience and accommodation of Catholics of all nations, particularly the Germans under whose direction the aforesaid new building is to be constructed, they have already bought and deeded a fine and commodious piece of ground situated on the corner of Spruce and Sixth streets.

Your humble memorialists would rather preferred a lot more up town, but it could not be had at so moderate a price as the aforesaid lot bought, the difference of price is near two thousand pounds. They have the pleasure further to acquaint your Right Reverence that they already opened a subscription and with good success, they find great incouragement by all denominations. The inclosure is the preamble of the subscription handed about, which to meet with your Right Reverence's kind approbation is their ardent wish and sanguine hope. Your humble memorialists have made several applications to the Rev. Mr. Molyneux for his concurrence but his kind answer and injunction was, to apply, pray for, and obtain your Right Reverence's liberal approbation which would suffice and compleat the whole.

Therefore your humble and dutifull memorialists earnestly beg your Right Reverence as to deign their undertaking with your most kind and gracious approbation and concurrence, which will give Life and Sanction to their true minded endeavor, for such great favor they will ever pray and with the greater acknowledgment and submission they have the honor to call themselves

Right Reverend Father in God,

Your most humble and most dutiful Children,

Jacob Cline,

George Lechler, Sen.,

Adam Premir *et al*

[November 24, 1787]

Carroll to Joseph Cauffman:

Sir: I have received a petition or remonstrance last night signed by yourself, Mess[rs] Oellers and Premir, and as requested direct my answer to you. As the Congregation of this place never before had the nomination of the Clergymen appointed to serve I now see no reason why I should depart from a right which has been always exercised by my predecessors. I am governed by important and weighty considerations of justice, prudence and gratitude so that I cannot make my determination agreeable to the wishes of the petitioners & of the Gentlemen who wrote the remonstrance of last night. This congregation has ever flourished & drawn on itself the admiration of all, who have visited Phil[a] and I trust in God it ever will unless it be disturbed by an interference, that has never been exercised before. In my way to New York I was requested to procure a German Clergyman. This I promised to do as soon as in my power, & informed the Gentlemen, who did me the honour of calling on me, that I expected Mr. Cresler [Graessl] to come expressly for Philad[a] with which they were much satisfied. I now see no sufficient reason for changing his destination.

With great respect I have the honour to be, sir,
Y[r] most obed[t] Ser[t],
J. Carroll.

Be pleased to communicate this to Messrs. Premir & Oellers.

THE NATIONAL PERIOD

53. The Brief *Ex hac apostolicae* of Pope Pius VI Erecting the Diocese of Baltimore and Appointing John Carroll as the First Bishop, November 6, 1789

WHEN the subject of a Catholic bishop for the new United States was first raised the clergy had opposed the idea out of fear of incurring the displeasure of the civil authorities, as well as from an uneasiness lest the coming of a bishop affect adversely the property interests of the suppressed Society of Jesus. Such was the unanimous opinion of the priests at their general meeting at Whitemarsh, Maryland, in October, 1784, and for the next few years they continued to hold that view. But in time the clergy changed their minds. The change was due chiefly to the rise of serious problems among the American Catholics which Carroll found himself unable to handle with his limited faculties as superior of the missions, to the growing experience of religious freedom which became more general and real, and to the action of the Protestant Episcopalians who in November, 1784, had a bishop consecrated for their church with no untoward results from the government. The priests met again in March, 1788, and this time they drew up a petition to Pope Pius VI (1775–1799) in which they stated the need for a bishop with full status of an ordinary, and they asked for permission to be allowed, at least for the first time, to choose him themselves. The Holy See acted favorably on their request and after learning of the priests' choice of Baltimore for the site of the new see and the virtually unanimous election of John Carroll, the formal bull erecting the Diocese of Baltimore and appointing Carroll as its first bishop was issued. Source: Latin text in Donald C. Shearer, O.F.M.Cap. (Ed.), *Pontificia Americana. A Documentary History of the Catholic Church in the United States, 1784–1884* (Washington: The Catholic University of America Press, 1933), pp. 81–84; English translation by John Gilmary Shea, *History of the Catholic Church in the United States* (New York: John G. Shea, 1888), II, 337–343.

When from the eminence of our apostolical station, we bend our attention to the different regions of the earth, in order to fulfill, to the utmost extent of our power, the duty which our Lord has imposed upon our unworthiness of ruling and feeding his flock; our care and solicitude are particularly engaged that the faithful of Christ, who, dispersed through various provinces, are united with us by Catholic communion, may be governed by their proper pastors, and diligently instructed by them in the discipline of evangelical life and doctrine. For it is our principle that they who, relying on the divine assistance, have regulated their lives and manners agreeably to the precepts of Christian wisdom, ought so to command their own passions as to promote by the pursuit of justice their own and their neighbor's spiritual advantage; and that they who have received from their bishops, and by checking the intemperance of self-wisdom, have steadily adhered to the heavenly doctrine delivered by Christ to the Catholic Church, should not be carried away by every wind of doctrine, but, grounded on the authority of divine revelation, should reject the new and varying doctrines of men which endanger the tranquillity of government, and rest in the unchangeable faith of the Catholic Church. For in the present degeneracy of corrupt manners into which human nature, ever resisting the sweet yoke of Christ, is hurried, and in the pride of talents and knowledge which disdains to submit the opinions and dreams of men to the evangelical truth delivered by Jesus Christ, support must be given by that heavenly authority which is entrusted to the Catholic Church, as to a steady pillar and solid foundation which shall never fail; that from her voice and instructions mankind may learn the objects of their faith and the rules of their conduct, not only for the obtaining of eternal salvation, but also for the regulation of this life and the maintaining of concord in the society of this earthly city. Now, this charge of teaching and ruling first given to the apostles, and especially to St. Peter, the Prince of the Apostles, on whom alone the Church is built, and to whom our Lord and Redeemer entrusted the feeding of his lambs and of his sheep, has been derived in due order of succession to Bishops, and especially to the Roman Pontiffs, successors of St. Peter and heirs of his power and dignity, that thereby it might be made evident that the gates of hell can never prevail against the Church, and that the divine founder of it will ever assist it to the consummation of ages; so that neither in the depravity of morals nor in the fluctuation of novel opinions, the episcopal succession shall ever fail or the bark of Peter be sunk. Wherefore, it having reached our ears that in the flourishing commonwealth of the Thirteen American States many faithful Christians united in communion with the chair of Peter, in which the centre of Catholic unity is fixed, and governed in their spiritual concerns by their own priests having care of souls, earnestly desire that a Bishop may be appointed over them to exercise the functions of episcopal order; to feed them more largely with the food of salutary doctrine, and to guard more carefully that portion of the Catholic flock.

We willingly embraced this opportunity which the grace of Almighty God has afforded us to provide those distant regions with the comfort and ministry of a Catholic Bishop. And that this be effected more successfully, and according to the rules of the sacred canons, We commissioned our venerable Brethren the Cardinals of the holy Roman Church, directors of the Congregation 'de propaganda fide,' to manage this business with the greatest care, and to make a report to us. It was therefore appointed by their decree, approved by us, and published the twelfth day of July of the last year, that the priests who lawfully exercise the sacred ministry and have care of souls in the United States of America, should be empowered to advise together and to determine, first, in what town the episcopal see ought to be erected, and next, who of the aforesaid priests appeared the most worthy and proper to be promoted to this important charge, whom We, for the first time only, and by special grace permitted the said priests to elect and to present to this apostolic See. In obedience to this decree the aforesaid priests exercising the care of souls in the United States of America, unanimously agreed that a bishop with ordinary jurisdiction, ought to be established in the town of Baltimore, because this town situate in Maryland, which province the greater part of the priests and of the faithful inhabit, appeared the most conveniently placed for intercourse with the other States, and because from this province Catholic religion and faith had been propagated into the others. And at the time appointed for the election, they being assembled together, the sacrifice of holy Mass, being celebrated, and the grace and assistance of the Holy Ghost being implored, the votes of all present were taken, and of twenty-six priests who were assembled twenty-four gave their votes for our beloved Son, John Carroll, whom they judged the most proper to support the burden of episcopacy, and sent an authentic instrument of the whole transaction to the aforesaid Congregation of Cardinals. Now all things being materially weighed and considered in this Congregation, it was easily agreed that the interests and increase of Catholic religion would be greatly promoted if an episcopal see were erected at Baltimore, and the said John Carroll were appointed the Bishop of it. We, therefore, to whom this opinion has been reported by our beloved son, Cardinal Antonelli, Prefect of the said Congregation, having nothing more at heart than to ensure success to whatever tends to the propagation of true religion, and to the honor and increase of the Catholic Church, by the plenitude of our apostolical power, and by the tenor of these presents, do establish and erect the aforesaid town of Baltimore into an episcopal see forever, for one Bishop to be chosen by us in all future vacancies; and We, therefore, by the apostolical authority aforesaid, do allow, grant and permit to the Bishop of the said city and to his successors in all future times, to exercise episcopal power and jurisdiction, and every other episcopal function which Bishops constituted in other places are empowered to hold and enjoy in their respective churches, cities and dioceses, by right, custom, or by other means, by general privileges, graces, indults and apostolical dispensations, together with all pre-eminences, honors, immunities, graces and favors, which other Cathedral Churches, by right or custom, or any other sort, have, hold and enjoy. We moreover decree and declare the said Episcopal see thus erected to be subject or suffragan to no Metropolitan right or jurisdiction, but to be forever subject, immediately to us and to our successors the Roman Pontiffs, and to this Apostolical See. And till another opportunity shall be presented to us of establishing other Catholic Bishops in the United States of America, and till other dispositions shall be made by this apostolical See, We declare, by our apostolical authority, all the faithful of Christ, living in Catholic communion, as well ecclesiastics as seculars, and all the clergy and people dwelling of the aforesaid United States of America, though hitherto they may have been subject to other Bishops of other dioceses, to be henceforward subject to the Bishop of Baltimore in all future times; And whereas by special grant, and for this first time only, we have allowed the priests exercising the care of souls in the United States of America, to elect a person to be appointed Bishop by us, and almost all their votes have been given to our beloved Son, John Carroll, Priest; We being otherwise certified of his faith, prudence, piety, and zeal, forasmuch as by our mandate he hath during the late years directed the spiritual government of souls, do therefore by the plenitude of our authority, declare, create, appoint and constitute the said John Carroll, Bishop and Pastor of the said Church of Baltimore, granting to him the faculty of receiving the rite of consecration from any Catholic bishop holding communion with the apostolical see, assisted by two ecclesiastics, vested with some dignity, in case that two bishops cannot be had, first having taken the usual oath according to the Roman Pontifical.

And we commission the said Bishop elect to erect a church in the said city of Baltimore, in form of a Cathedral Church, inasmuch as the times and circumstances may allow, to institute a body of clergy deputed to divine worship, and to the service of said church, and moreover to establish an episcopal seminary, either in the same city or elsewhere, as he shall judge most expedient, to administer ecclesiastical incomes, and to execute all other things which he shall think in the Lord to be' expedient for the increase of Catholic faith and the augmentation of the worship and splendor of the new erected church. We moreover enjoin the said Bishop to obey the injunctions of our venerable brethren, the Cardinals Directors of the Sacred Congregation 'de propaganda fide,' to transmit to them at proper times a relation of his visitation of his church, and to inform them of all things which he shall judge to be useful to the spiritual good and salvation of the flock trusted to his charge. We therefore decree that these our letters are ever and ever shall be firm, valid and efficacious, and shall obtain their full and entire, effect; and be observed inviolable by all persons whom it now doth or hereafter may concern; and that all judges ordinary and delegated, even auditors of causes of the sacred apostolical palace, and Cardinals of the holy Roman Church, must thus judge and define, depriving all and each of them of all power and authority to judge or interpret in any other manner, and declaring all to be null and void, if any one, by any authority should presume, either knowingly or unknowingly, to attempt anything contrary thereunto. Notwithstanding all apostolical, general or special constitutions and ordinations, published in universal, provincial and synodical councils, and all things contrary whatsoever.

Given at Rome at St. Mary Major, under the Fisherman's Ring, the 6th day of November, 1789, and in the fifteenth year of our Pontificate.

54. The Beginnings of the First Catholic College in the United States, 1789

BY REASON of the penal legislation against Catholics in colonial America it had never been possible to have a Catholic school. The brief existence of the furtive little academy at Bohemia Manor was but the exception that proved the rule. But with the coming of religious liberty the Catholics were free to have a school of their own, and John Carroll took the lead among the clergy in urging its establishment. At a meeting of the priests on May 15, 1789, it was agreed to issue a prospectus which would explain the nature of the school they had in mind and to solicit subscriptions. The following document was printed later that year and the work got under way. After some delays caused by lack of funds Georgetown Academy opened in November, 1791, with William Gaston of North Carolina, future associate justice of the state's supreme court, as the first student. As will be noted, the academy welcomed students of all religious faiths. Thus was begun the institution from which there developed the first Catholic college in the United States. Source: John Gilmary Shea, *Memorial of the First Centenary of Georgetown College, D.C., Comprising a History of Georgetown University* (New York: P. F. Collier, 1891), pp. 12–13.

PROPOSALS TO ESTABLISH AN ACADEMY AT GEORGE TOWN, PATOWMACK RIVER, MARYLAND.

The object of the proposed Institution is to unite the means of communicating Science with an effectual provision for guarding and preserving the Morals of Youth. With this View, the Seminary will be superintended by those who, having had Experience in similar Institutions, know that an undivided Attention may be given to the Cultivation of Virtue and literary Improvement, and that a System of Discipline may be introduced and preserved incompatible with Indolence and Inattention in the Professor, or with incorrigible habits of Immorality in the Student.

The Benefit of this Establishment should be as general as the Attainment of its Object is desirable. It will therefore receive Pupils as soon as they have learned the first Elements of Letters, and will conduct them through the several Branches of Classical Learning to that Stage of Education from which they may proceed with Advantage to the Study of higher Sciences in the University of this or those of the neighboring States. Thus it will be calculated for every Class of Citizens; — as Reading, Writing, Arithmetic, the earlier Branches of the Mathematics, and the Grammar of our native Tongue, will be attended to no less than the learned Languages.

Agreeably to the liberal Principal of our Constitution, the Seminary will be open to Students of every religious profession. They, who, in this Respect differ from the Superintendent of the Academy, will be at Liberty to frequent the places of Worship and Instruction appointed by their Parents; but with Respect to their moral Conduct, all must be subject to general and uniform Discipline.

In the choice of Situation, Salubrity of Air, Convenience of Communication and Cheapness of Living have been principally consulted, and George Town offers these united Advantages.

The Price of Tuition will be moderate; in the Course of a few

Years it will be reduced still lower, if the System formed for this Seminary be effectually carried into execution.

Such a plan of Education solicits, and, it is not presumption to add, deserves public Encouragement. The following gentlemen, and others that may be named hereafter will receive subscriptions and inform the subscribers to whom and in what proportion payments are to be made. In Maryland, the Hon. Charles Carroll of Carrollton; Henry Rozer, Notley Young, Robert Darnall, George Digges, Edmond Plowden, Esq'rs, Mr. Joseph Millard, Captain John Lancaster, Mr. Baker Brooke, Chandler Brent, Esq., Mr. Bernard O'Neill and Mr. Marsham Waring, merchants; John Darnall and Ignatius Wheeler, Esq., on the western shore; and on the eastern, Rev. Mr. Joseph Mosley, John Blake, Francis Hall, Charles Blake, William Matthews and John Tuitte, Esq'rs. In Pennsylvania, George Mead and Thomas Fitzsimmons, Esq'rs, Mr. Joseph Cauffman, Mr. Mark Wilcox and Mr. Thomas Lilly. In Virginia, Colonel Fitzgerald and George Brent, Esq'rs, and at New York, Dominick Lynch, Esq.

Subscriptions will also be received and every necessary Information given by the following Gentlemen, Directors of the Undertaking: The Rev. Messrs. John Carroll, James Pellentz, Robert Molyneux, John Ashton and Leonard Neale.

55. The Catholics' Congratulations to President Washington, 1789, and His Reply, March 12, 1790

EARLY in his first administration President Washington received congratulatory messages from a number of American religious groups. Late in 1789 the Catholics sent such a message signed by John Carroll for the clergy and by four prominent laymen in the name of the laity. The Catholics alluded to the participation of their coreligionists in the struggle that had won national independence and the full rights of citizenship which it had won them in some states, to which they added their expectation of the same rights from those states that still withheld them from Catholics. Washington, who had abolished the army's commemoration of Guy Fawke's Day out of consideration for Catholic sensibilities, had known at firsthand the patriotic role that had been played by Catholics like Stephen Moylan (1737–1881), mustermaster general of the forces, and others. In his reply, therefore, he expressed the belief that as mankind became more liberal all worthy citizens would be admitted to equal treatment by civil governments, and he presumed that non-Catholic Americans would not forget the patriotic part which Catholics had played in the Revolution and in the establishment of

the government, as well as the assistance which the revolutionary cause had received from Catholic France. Source: Washington Papers, 334, Division of Manuscripts, Library of Congress.

[undated, late in 1789]

To George Washington
President of the United States of America.
Sir,

We have been long impatient to testify our joy and unbounded confidence in your being called, by an unanimous vote, to the first station of a country, in which that unanimity could not have been obtained without the previous merit of unexampled services, of eminent wisdom, and unblemished virtue. Our congratulations have not reached you sooner, because our scattered situation prevented the communication, and the collection of those sentiments, which warmed every breast. But the delay has furnished us with the opportunity, not merely of presaging the happiness to be expected under your administration, but of bearing testimony to that which we experience already. It is your peculiar talent, in war and in peace, to afford security to those, who commit their protection into your hands. In war, you shield them from the ravages of armed hostility: in peace you establish public tranquillity by the justice and moderation, not less than by the vigour, of your government. By example as well as by vigilance, you extend the influence of laws on the manners of our fellow-citizens. You encourage respect for religion, and inculcate, by words and actions, that principle, on which the welfare of nations so much depends, that a superintending providence governs the events of the world, and watches over the conduct of men. Your exalted maxims and unwearied attention to the moral and physical improvement of our country have produced already the happiest effects. Under your administration, America is animated with zeal for the attainment and encouragement of useful literature. She improves her agriculture, extends her commerce, and acquires with foreign nations a dignity, unknown to her before. From these happy events, in which none can feel a warmer interest than ourselves, we derive additional pleasure by recollection, that you, Sir, have been the principal instrument to effect so rapid a change in our political situation. This prospect of national prosperity is peculiarly pleasing to us on another account; because whilst our country preserves her freedom and independence, we shall have a well founded title to claim from her justice equal rights of citizenship, as the price of our blood spilt under your eyes, and of our common exertions for her defence, under your auspicious conduct, rights rendered more dear to us by the remembrance of former hardships. When we pray for the preservation of them, where they have been granted; and expect the full extension of them from the justice of those States, which still restrict them; when we solicit the protection of Heaven over our common country: we neither omit nor can omit recommending your preservation to the singular care of divine providence; because we conceive that no human means are so available to promote the welfare of the United States, as the prolongation of your health and life, in which are included the energy of your example, the wisdom of your counsels, and the persuasive eloquence of your virtues.

J. Carroll, in behalf of the Roman Catholic Clergy
Charles Carroll of Carrollton, Daniel Carroll,
Thos. FitzSimons, Domk. Lynch.[1] — in behalf
of the Roman Catholic Laity.

To the Roman Catholics in the United States of America.

Gentlemen, — While I now receive with much satisfaction your congratulations on my being called, by an unanimous vote, to the first station in my country; I cannot but duly notice your politeness in offering an apology for the unavoidable delay. As that delay has given you an opportunity of realizing, instead of anticipating, the benefits of the general government; you will do me the justice to believe that your testimony of the increase of the public prosperity enhances the pleasure which I should otherwise have experienced from your affectionate Address.

I feel that my conduct in war and in peace has met with more general approbation than could reasonably have been expected: and I find myself disposed to consider that fortunate circumstance, in a great degree, resulting from the able support and extraordinary candor of my fellow-citizens of all denominations.

The prospect of national prosperity now before us is truly animating, and ought to excite the exertions of all good men to establish and secure the happiness of their Country, in the permanent duration of its freedom and independence. America, under the smiles of a Divine Providence — the protection of a good government — the cultivation of manners, morals and piety, can hardly fail of attaining an uncom-

---

[1] The Irish-born Dominik Lynch (1754–1825) was the leading Catholic layman of New York at the time. The other laymen have been identified in previous notes.

mon degree of eminence in literature, commerce, agriculture, improvements at home, and respectability abroad.

As mankind become more liberal, they will be more apt to allow, that all those who conduct themselves as worthy members of the community are equally entitled to the protection of civil government. I hope ever to see America among the foremost nations in examples of justice and liberality. And I presume that your fellow-citizens will not forget the patriotic part which you took in the accomplishment of their Revolution, and the establishment of their government; or the important assistance which they received from a nation in which the Roman Catholic religion is professed.

I thank you, Gentlemen, for your kind concern for me. While my life and my health shall continue, in whatever situation I may be, it shall be my constant endeavor to justify the favorable sentiments you are pleased to express of my conduct. And may the members of your Society in America, animated alone by the pure spirit of christianity, and still conducting themselves as the faithful subjects of our free government, enjoy every temporal and spiritual felicity.

(March 12, 1790) G. Washington.

56. Bishop Carroll's Sermon on Taking Possession of His See, St. Peter's Pro-Cathedral, Baltimore, December 12, 1790

THE consecration of John Carroll took place at Lulworth Castle, England, on August 15, 1790, and was performed by Bishop Charles Walmesley, O.S.B. (1722–1797), Vicar Apostolic of the Western District. Upon the new bishop's return to the United States in early December the task that awaited him was truly frightening, for, as he said, everything had to be raised from its foundations in a diocese which comprised the entire country. How well he conceived the immensity of his task, how clearly he envisioned from the outset the need for a school, a seminary, native priests, spiritual aid for the Catholics in distant and scattered settlements, and the danger to his tiny flock from doctrinal errors — all these were before Carroll's mind in his first sermon as an American bishop. His manly piety directed him to put his confidence in God, and how splendidly he fulfilled his difficult mission the history of the next quarter century would tell. Source: Peter Guilday, *The Life and Times of John Carroll, Archbishop of Baltimore, 1735–1815* (New York: Encyclopedia Press, 1922), I, 384–385.

In this, my new station, if my life be not one continued instruction and example of virtue to the people committed to my charge, it will become, in the sight of God, a life not only useless, but even pernicious. It is no longer enough for me to be inoffensive in my conduct and regular in my manners. God now imposes a severer duty upon me. I shall incur the guilt of violating my pastoral office, if all my endeavours be not directed to bring your lives and all your actions to a conformity with the laws of God; to exhort, to conjure, to reprove, to enter into all your sentiments; to feel all your infirmities; to be all things to all, that I may gain all to Christ; to be superior to human respect; to have nothing in view but God and your salvation; to sacrifice to these health, peace, reputation, and even life itself; to hate sin, and yet love the sinner; to repress the turbulent; to encourage the timid; to watch over the conduct of even the ministers of religion; to be patient and meek; to embrace all kinds of persons; these are now my duties — extensive, pressing, and indispensable duties; these are the duties of all my brethren in the episcopacy, and surely important enough to fill us with terror. But there are others still more burdensome to be borne by me, in this particular portion of Christ's church which is committed to my charge, and where everything is to be raised, as it were, from its foundation; to establish ecclesiastical discipline; to devise means for the religious education of Catholic youth — that precious portion of pastoral solicitude; to provide an establishment for training up ministers for the sanctuary and the services of religion, that we may no longer depend on foreign and uncertain coadjutors; not to leave unassisted any of the faithful who are scattered through this immense continent; to preserve their faith untainted amidst the contagion of error surrounding them on all sides; to preserve in their hearts a warm charity and forebearance toward every other denomination of Christians, and at the same time to preserve them from that fatal and prevailing indifference which views all religions as equally acceptable to God and salutary to men. Ah! when I consider these additional duties, my heart sinks almost under the impression of terror which comes upon it. In God alone can I find any consolation. He knows by what steps I have been conducted to this important station, and how much I have always dreaded it. He will not abandon me unless I first draw upon His malediction by my unfaithfulness to my charge. Pray, dear brethren, pray incessantly, that I may not incur so dreadful a punishment. Alas! the punishment would fall on you as well as on myself; my unfaithfulness would rebound on you and deprive you of some of the means of salvation. . . .

57. John Carroll's Prayer for the Civil Authorities, November 10, 1791

LESS than a year after returning from his consecration Bishop Carroll assembled the clergy at his residence in Baltimore on November 7–10, 1791, for the holding of the first diocesan synod of the American Church. During those days the bishop and his twenty-two priests framed twenty-four decrees to regulate and render uniform such matters as the administration of the sacraments, divine services, the conduct of the clergy, and the support of the churches. Among the regulations for divine services it was stated that after the gospel in Masses on Sundays and feast days there should be read the prayer prescribed "for all the ranks of society and for the welfare of the Republic." In this session of November 10 the synod adopted the beautiful prayer which Carroll had composed for the civil authorities and which revealed the combination of piety and patriotism which was so characteristic of him, as well as showing his charity for the welfare of all his fellow citizens, regardless of their religious faith. The prayer is still used in Catholic churches in the United States on occasions of a national character. Source: Peter Guilday, *The Life and Times of John Carroll, Archbishop of Baltimore, 1735–1815* (New York: Encyclopedia Press, 1922), II, 432.

We pray Thee, O almighty and eternal God! Who through Jesus Christ hast revealed Thy glory to all nations, to preserve the works of Thy Mercy, that Thy Church, being spread through the whole world, may continue with unchanging faith in the confession of Thy name.

We pray Thee, Who alone art good and holy, to endow with heavenly knowledge, sincere zeal, and sanctity of life, our chief bishop, N.N., the vicar of Our Lord Jesus Christ, in the government of His Church; our own bishop, N.N. (or archbishop); all other bishops, prelates, and pastors of the Church; and especially those who are appointed to exercise amongst us the functions of the holy ministry, and conduct Thy people into the ways of salvation.

We pray Thee, O God of might, wisdom, and justice! through Whom authority is rightly administered, laws are enacted, and judgment decreed, assist with Thy holy spirit of counsel and fortitude the President of the United States, that his administration may be conducted in righteousness, and be eminently useful to Thy people over whom he presides; by encouraging due respect for virtue and religion; by a faithful execution of the laws in justice and mercy; and by restraining vice and immorality. Let the light of Thy divine wisdom direct the deliberations of Congress, and shine forth in all the proceedings and laws framed for our rule and government, so that they may tend to the preservation of peace, the promotion of national happiness, the increase of industry, sobriety, and useful knowledge; and may perpetuate to us the blessing of equal liberty.

We pray for his excellency, the Governor of this State, for the members of the Assembly, for all judges, magistrates, and other officers who are appointed to guard our political welfare, that they may be enabled, by Thy powerful protection, to discharge the duties of their respective stations with honesty and ability.

We recommend likewise, to Thy unbounded mercy, all our brethren and fellow citizens throughout the United States, that they may be blessed in the knowledge and sanctified in the observance of Thy most holy law; that they may be preserved in union, and in that peace which the world can not give; and after enjoying the blessings of this life, be admitted to those which are eternal.

Finally, we pray to Thee, O Lord of mercy, to remember the souls of Thy servants departed who are gone before us with the sign of faith, and repose in the sleep of peace; the souls of our parents, relatives, and friends; of those who, when living, were members of this congregation, and particularly of such as are lately deceased; of all benefactors who, by their donations or legacies to this church, witnessed their zeal for the decency of divine worship and proved their claim to our grateful and charitable remembrance. To these, O Lord, and to all that rest in Christ, grant, we beseech Thee, a place of refreshment, light, and everlasting peace, through the same Jesus Christ, our Lord and Saviour. Amen.

58. The French Sulpicians and St. Mary's Seminary, Baltimore, April 23, 1792

THE arrival in Baltimore on July 10, 1791, of four French Sulpicians and five seminarians for the purpose of inaugurating a seminary for the training of priests for the United States proved to be a singular blessing to the American Church. For 150 years the Sulpicians had been among the most prominent and successful trainers of the priests of France. The establishment of their first American seminary — financed entirely by themselves — was, needless to say, a tremendous boon to the infant Diocese of Baltimore. These priests not only provided a faculty for St. Mary's Seminary which began classes in October, 1791, in a building called the One Mile Tavern, but they likewise accepted assignment to take charge of missions in Maryland

and in places as far distant as Illinois and Michigan. The first years of the new seminary were exceedingly trying ones and for a time there was serious discussion of its abandonment. But the seven students of 1791 had increased by 1810 to twenty-four, and by the time Archbishop Carroll died in 1815 thirty priests had been ordained from this mother seminary. In the following letter Carroll expressed to Cardinal Antonelli, Prefect of Propaganda, what the coming of the Sulpicians meant to him and to his impoverished diocese. Source: Peter Guilday, *The Life and Times of John Carroll, Archbishop of Baltimore, 1735–1815* (New York: Encyclopedia Press, 1922), II, 470–471.

It is already known to the Sacred Congregation how singular a blessing has come to us from the disorders that threaten religion in France, since on account of the same has arisen the opportunity of sending thither some priests from the Seminary of St. Sulpice, at Paris. While I was in London, this matter was seriously considered as I have already made known to the Sacred Congregation; after my return to my diocese, the plan was fully decided upon, and in July of last year four priests with five clerics, students of philosophy and theology, reached this port, led by the Venerable Nagot,[1] formerly Superior of the Seminary of St. Sulpice. . . . The establishment of a seminary is certainly a new and extraordinary spectacle for the people of this country; the remarkable piety of these priests is admirable, and their example is a stimulant and spur to all who feel themselves called to work in the vineyard of the Lord. Such are the great and remarkable effects of God's bounty. But what is still more important is that, owing to the establishment of this seminary, the clergy will be brought up in the purity of faith and in holiness of conduct. All our hopes are founded on the Seminary of Baltimore. Since the arrival of the priests of St. Sulpice, the celebration of the offices of the Church and the dignity of divine worship have made a great impression, so that, though the church of Baltimore is hardly worthy of the name of cathedral, if we consider its style and its size, it may be looked upon as an episcopal church in view of the number of its clergy.

[1] François Charles Nagot (1734–1816), the first superior of the Sulpicians in the United States, had been one of the most prominent members of the society in France, being vice superior of the Seminary of St. Sulpice in Paris and a member of the superior-general's council at the time of his appointment to Baltimore.

59. Religious Conditions in Louisiana, November 1, 1795

THE first Bishop of Louisiana and the Two Floridas, a diocese which had been erected on April 25, 1793, was a Cuban-born priest, Luís Ignacio Maria de Peñalver y Cardenas (1749–1810). Upon Peñalver's arrival in New Orleans in July, 1795, he found religious conditions at a very low ebb. On November 1, 1795, the bishop made a report to the Spanish government which described not only the spiritual abuses among the populace but which also reflected the nationalist feeling between the French and Spanish colonists. Peñalver did all he could to revive religious life during his six years of residence in Louisiana, but when he left in November, 1801, to become Archbishop of Guatemala he could point to only qualified success for his efforts. Source: Charles Gayarré, *History of Louisiana. The Spanish Domination* (New York: Redfield, 1854), pp. 376–379.

Since my arrival in this town, on the 17th of July, I have been studying with the keenest attention the character of its inhabitants, in order to regulate by ecclesiastical government in accordance with the information which I may obtain on this important subject.

On the 2d of August, I began the discharge of my pastoral functions. I took possession without any difficulty of all the buildings appertaining to the church, and examined all the books, accounts, and other matters thereto relating. But as to re-establishing the purity of religion, and reforming the manners of the people, which are the chief objects El Tridentino[1] has in view, I have encountered many obstacles.

The inhabitants do not listen to, or if they do, they disregard, all exhortations to maintain in its orthodoxy the Catholic faith, and to preserve the innocence of life. But without ceasing to pray the Father of all mercies to send his light into the darkness which surrounds these people, I am putting into operation human means to remedy these evils, and I will submit to your Excellency those which I deem conducive to the interests of religion and of the state.

Because his Majesty tolerates here the Protestants, for sound reasons of state, the bad Christians, who are in large numbers in this colony, think that they are authorized to live without any religion at all. Many adults die without having received the sacrament of communion. Out of the eleven thousand souls composing this parish, hardly three to four hundred comply with the precept of partaking at least once a year of the Lord's supper. Of the regiment of Louisiana,

[1] The bishop was referring to the reform legislation of the Council of Trent.

there are not above thirty, including officers and soldiers, who have discharged this sacred duty for the last three years. No more than about the fourth part of the population of the town ever attends mass, and on Sundays only, and on those great holydays which require it imperiously. To do so on the other holydays they consider as a superfluous act of devotion to which they are not bound. Most of the married and unmarried men live in a state of concubinage, and there are fathers who procure courtezans for the use of their sons, whom they thus intentionally prevent from getting lawful wives. The marriage contract is one which, from a universal custom, admitting only a few accidental exceptions, is never entered into among the slaves. Fasting on Fridays, in Lent, and during *vigilas y temporas* [vigils of feasts and ember days], is a thing unknown; and there are other mal-practices which denote the little of religion existing here among the inhabitants, and which demonstrate that there remains in their bosoms but a slight spark of the faith instilled into them at the baptismal font.

I presume that a large portion of these people are vassals of the king, because they live in his domain, and accept his favors. But I must speak the truth. His Majesty possesses their bodies and not their souls. Rebellion is in their hearts, and their minds are imbued with the maxims of democracy; and had they not for their chief so active and energetic a man as the present governor,[2] there would long since have been an eruption of the pent-up volcano; and should another less sagacious chief ever forget the fermenting elements which are at work under ground, there can be no doubt but that there would be an explosion.

Their houses are full of books written against religion and the state. They are permitted to read them with impunity, and, at the dinner table, they make use of the most shameful, lascivious, and sacrilegious songs.

This melancholy sketch of the religious and moral customs and condition of the flock which has fallen to my lot, will make you understand the cause of whatever act of scandal may suddenly break out, which, however, I shall strive to prevent; and the better to do so, I have used and am still using some means, which I intend as remedies, and which I am going to communicate to your Excellency.

The Spanish school, which has been established here at the expense of the crown, is kept as it ought to be; but as there are others which

[2] Francisco Luís Hector, Baron de Carondelet, was Governor of Louisiana from 1791 to 1797.

are French, and of which one alone is opened by authority and with the regular license, and as I was ignorant of the faith professed by the teachers and of their morality, I have prescribed for them such regulations as are in conformity with the provisions of our legislation.

Excellent results are obtained from the Convent of the Ursulines,[3] in which a good many girls are educated; but their inclinations are so decidedly French, that they have even refused to admit among them Spanish women who wished to become Nuns, so long as these applicants should remain ignorant of the French idiom, and they have shed many tears on account of their being obliged to read in Spanish books their spiritual exercises, and to comply with the other duties of their community in the manner prescribed to them.

This is the nursery of those future matrons who will inculcate on their children the principles which they here imbibe. The education which they receive in this institution is the cause of their being less vicious than the other sex. As to what the boys are taught in the Spanish school, it is soon forgotten. Should their education be continued in a college, they would be confirmed in their religious principles, in the good habits given to them, and in their loyalty as faithful vassals to the crown. But they leave the school when still very young, and return to the houses of their parents mostly situated in the country, where they hear neither the name of God nor of King, but daily witness the corrupt morals of their parents. . . .

60. Father Badin's Description of the Church on the Kentucky Frontier, April 11, 1796

KENTUCKY entered the union in 1792 as the first state of the new West. A large immigration from the eastern states had poured into the area during the 1780's to swell the population to almost 75,000 by 1790, and among those who had made the long journey over the mountains and down the Ohio River were many Catholic families from Maryland. The first two priests sent to minister to these scattered frontier settlements proved to be rather unhappy choices, and it was only with the arrival in November, 1793, of Stephen Theodore Badin (1768–1853) that the Kentucky missions received continuous and proper attention. Badin was the first priest to be ordained in the United States on May 25, 1793. This remarkable man was to serve the Catholics of Kentucky and other western states as an itinerant missionary off and on for nearly sixty years. He was a wonderfully zealous priest to whom many souls in the West owed, under God, their salvation,

[3] Cf. No. 61.

but he was of a somewhat exacting and contentious disposition with the result that his lengthy career was marked by many stormy episodes. In the letter which follows Badin gave Bishop Carroll a vivid description of the state of the Church in this distant part of his diocese after the missionary had been on the scene for about two years and a half. Source: Edward I. Devitt, S.J. (Ed.), "Letters from the Baltimore Archives," *Records of the American Catholic Historical Society of Philadelphia,* XIX (1908), 258–264.

Priestland, Harden's Creek, Washington County,
April 11th, 1796.

My Lord

I wrote to you last month, and a few days afterwards Mr. Sanders brought me the letters which you sent by him. Last fall and winter I wrote you several letters which you have not answered, doubtless for the reason that they were lost or intercepted during the journey, which frequently happens. In them I proposed some cases of conscience and asked for several dispensations; I therein exposed to you the needs of my congregations and especially my own; would that you could know them, Monseigneur, as I know them — although even I know them imperfectly; — you would be deeply afflicted, your charity for the people and priests of whom you are the pastor would rend your fatherly heart, because there is no pasturage in Kentucky for the souls that, as you assured me when I was leaving Baltimore, you tenderly love. Probably there is not in all your diocese as large congregations as are those of Kentucky, and they are increasing from day to day; there is not a Catholic here that does not bitterly lament at finding himself deprived of those means of salvation that were to be had in Maryland &c. I can assure you, Monseigneur, and you will be touched to hear it, that some among them are so afflicted as to lose their mind. Faith yet sustains me, thanks be to God, but I am as worried as any among them, since I share the troubles of each; but no one can share mine, or at least the only person in Kentucky who could share them makes himself incapable of doing so.[1] I shall keep silence until I am better informed.

You speak to me of French priests: I entreat you, my Lord, to send me at least one whose virtue is known to you. I would willingly decide to send him my horse were it not imprudent to deprive myself of it for I have no other of my own in Kentucky, and I often need it

---

[1] Badin was apparently referring here to Father William de Rohan, a somewhat erratic priest who had come to Kentucky c. 1790, and who was responsible for the state's first Catholic church, that of Holy Cross at Pottinger's Creek, built in 1792.

in order to visit the sick, by day and by night. In my present abandonment I am utterly incapable, my lord, of fulfiling the heavy charge of the ministry. I have neither the virtue nor the bodily strength necessary: If I had at least one priest to consult with me, to advise and encourage me! If I walked with a firmer footstep myself, I might, with God's grace, guide those whom I ought to direct in the path of salvation. I once more beseech you, my lord, to look with an eye of pity on the poor priests of Kentucky, and on the other faithful, of whom you are the father, and who depend, after God, upon your charity in order to obtain a favorable entrance to the mansions of eternity. . . .

The faithful Scot [*sic*] county are forsaken and disheartened: last year there was some difference of opinion between them about the land which was bought for the support of their priests. It is situated about four miles from the chapel, and is today in the midst of Catholic plantations which have extended since peace was concluded with the Indians. All the Fenwick families, who incontestably are the most prominent, were united for the success of this business. The heads of only two rich families sought to place obstacles to it, because they considered it too far away, under present circumstances, from the resident of the priest: another motive may have influenced their opposition, — the rich are not always the most disposed to make sacrifices. The poorer families were now of one opinion now of another, according as they listened to the arguments of the prejudiced and considered the distance at which they lived from the chapel or from the priest's land. It seems to me that this congregation has not always followed the natural law of prudence; when they resolved to build a chapel, before my coming to Kentucky, land was very cheap; they could have and should have purchased enough of it to make a good plantation which would have in a few years brought more than the cost of the purchase and would have enabled them to cover the expense of a chapel &c. They did quite the contrary; and moreover the priest will have the trouble of travelling to the chapel which at present is located almost at the extreme end of their plantations. The congregations at Nelson and Washington bought the land for the priest in Washington when they built their chapel at a distance of two miles and a half, near the frontier of Nelson [County]. During the four months that Mr. Barriere[2] stayed in Kentucky he changed his mag-

[2] Father Michel Bernard Barrière, a French-born priest, had come to Kentucky with Badin in 1793, but had left in the spring of 1794 for Spanish Louisiana.

nificent plans several times, and finally adopted one which causes us some embarrassment at present: he gave power of attorney to Mr. J. Lancaster[3] which to me seems about as valid as the powers of the vicar general with which he claimed to have invested me; Mr. Lancaster could act independently of the priests who were serving Kentucky, and consequently a rectory was begun; the purchase and the payment for the ground and for several negroes, the salary of Mr. Roan [*sic*], some other expenditures by Mr. Barriere, building and furnishing the chapel &c. have made it impossible for us now even to put under roof this immense presbtery. *Quis volens turrim aedificare non p. ejus computat. . . .* About six months after the departure of Mr. Barriere I engaged a score of men to build a cabin, which although but a cabin, is one of the best residences to be found among the congregation. During my absence, the work was interrupted and the laborers were discouraged because they were not working for Mr. Barriere's orders: I took the inertness of Mr. R [B.?] for humility: but, after all, when I settled here last year, I took half of a little house that I had not had built for myself. The bad management of affairs and my occupations caused a lack of any harvest for me, so I am reduced this year to beggary; and the country seems to have suffered a genuine famine this summer. Divine Providence had perhaps allowed this as a punishment of their indolence.

After what I said, my lord, you can judge of what was told you also by Mr. D. McCarthy. Mr. Joseph Fenwick is now on the way to the Illinois, where he thinks of establishing himself with his family, in order to procure for them the advantages of religion. Another Catholic from Nelson undertook a like journey last Christmas, but without any success, because there was no land to buy, and the Indians of the Spanish side of the Mississippi kill and rob Americans although they leave the French unmolested.

I informed you last winter, my lord, in one of my letters that Mr. Dubois[4] wished to come to Kentucky and had commissioned several of his friends to buy him some land. They tell me that Mr. Thomas Yates procured for him some of his on Cartwright's creek, near the chapel which is being built there, about eight miles from here. I am sure that Mr. George Hamilton will devote to a rectory two or

---

[3] John Lancaster (d. 1838) was a leader of the group of Maryland Catholics who came to Kentucky in 1788. He became one of the most prominent Catholics in Kentucky and served for several terms in the legislature. He was the grandfather of John Lancaster Spalding (1840–1916), first Bishop of Peoria.

[4] Jean Dubois (1764–1842), the future third Bishop of New York, was a missionary in Maryland at the time.

three hundred acres of land, about 80 miles from here on the Green river. His plan is to help a Catholic settlement and to sell them a portion of the land that he bought there. Those [Catholics] in Scot can never be as numerous as in the other counties for the reason that land there sells for six, eight or even ten times higher; they are also much richer, and more favored as to commerce, manufactures, education &c. But I will add also that luxury and vice are more general there — I can not be everywhere at once; they are nearly all discontented; and where I am I do very little good and undoubtedly much harm; the people do not always like my principles, or rather the principles of my ritual *videat autem diligenter Sacerdos* &c. You were right, my lord, when you complained in your letter to me some four months ago that the rules of theology are not always followed. I am in charge of all general confessions, and I do not suffice: I have so little courage, my lord! Can't you send us Mr. Thayer[5] or Mr. F. Neale?[6] I would even venture to ask you for both of them and others beside; would that you might listen to me! At least I shall ask God for a good French priest who may save one soul and most likely many another. He will have an opportunity to learn English quickly in Kentucky, and at all events it is not essential to know English in order to celebrate the divine Mysteries, to edify the people, to baptize, to absolve the dying, to direct me &c. Please, I beg of you, have compassion on me.

I am told that Mr. Henry Jarber [Jarboe?] of St. Inigoes, left in his will a sum of money for the Church in Kentucky. If you can get it, my lord, it might be of some service to the priest you intend for here. I mentioned in one of my letters that my faculties expire the third of September. I suppose I should repeat this fact, because my letter might not have reached you: I have so often acknowledged to you my difficulties and incapacity that you will readily conclude that I have no pretentions to new powers. I trust in the goodness of the Lord that before that time there will be worthy laborers to cultivate the soil that at present lies almost fallow because of my cowardice.

I asked you some time ago to have sixty Masses said; I must now ask you to attend to more than thirty intentions. . . .

. . . I hope that my anxieties will not be of long duration, and that good priests who may be favorably inclined to serve in your

---

[5] John Thayer (1758–1815), a Boston-born convert priest, came to Kentucky in 1799 but left after four years of rather unsatisfactory service.

[6] Francis Neale (1755–1837) was on the Maryland missions at the time; he was later prominent in the restored Society of Jesus and served as president of Georgetown College, 1810–1812.

diocese will hasten to follow your wishes and those of the people of Kentucky. Mr. Wm. Hamilton who carries my letters can tell you in person how much they suffer.

I am very grateful for the trouble you take to keep me informed about the general conditions in France. They tell me that the city in which I was born has been consigned to the flames by a philanthropic decree of the legislators. I have reason to believe that my relations [or parents] were included in the decree for I have received no letters from them for several years.

Let me observe in regard to the coming of priests to Kentucky that they will not have to face the dangers to which they would have been exposed in preceding years, as peace has been concluded with the Indians.

I have the honor to be &c &c &c.

Etienne Theodore Badin

P.S. — The holy oils that I brought with me to Kentucky need to be renewed. The ritual asserts that clerics should carry them wherever there is need; I hope that you will give them to one or more priests. Mr. Hamilton should return here next July; he would be a very suitable companion for them [the priests] if they have not already started before that time.

61. President Jefferson Reassures the Louisiana Ursulines About Their Future Under the American Government, May 15, 1804

IN AUGUST, 1727, a little band of eleven Ursuline nuns arrived in Louisiana from France to open the first convent of religious women in what was later to be the United States. All through the eighteenth century they persisted — often under the greatest handicaps — with their teaching the young, nursing the sick, and other works of charity. The sisters witnessed the colony change hands several times, and in 1803 they found themselves citizens of the United States. The anxiety which they felt about their property rights and status under the American regime were conveyed by their superior to both Bishop Carroll and President Jefferson. In his reply Jefferson set their fears at rest about the future and assured them of the appreciation which Americans of all religious faiths felt for the charitable labors which they had carried on in Louisiana for so many years. Source: Henry C. Semple, S.J. (Ed.), *The Ursulines in New Orleans and Our Lady of Prompt Succor. A Record of Two Centuries, 1727–1925* (New York: P. J. Kenedy & Sons, 1925), facsimile facing p. 60.

Washington May the 15, 1804

To the Soeur Therese de St. Xavier Farjon, Superior; and the Nuns of the Order of St. Ursula at New Orleans.

I have received, holy sisters, the letter which you have written me, wherein you express anxiety for the property vested in your institution by the former government of Louisiana. The principles of the Constitution and government of the United States are a sure guarantee to you that it will be preserved to you sacred and inviolate, and that your institution will be permitted to govern itself according to it's own voluntary rules, without interference from the civil authority, whatever diversity of shade may appear in the religious opinions of our fellow citizens, the charitable objects of your institution cannot be indifferent to any; and it's furtherance of the wholesome purposes of society, by training up it's younger members in the way they should go, cannot fail to ensure it the patronage of the government it is under. Be assured that it will meet with all the protection which my office can give it.

I salute you, holy sisters, with friendship and respect,

Th. Jefferson

62. The United States Government Declines to Commit Itself on a Bishop for Louisiana, November 17–20, 1806

AT THE time that Louisiana was transferred by France to the United States in December, 1803, the Church in that colony was riddled by dissension. The *marguilliers* or trustees of St. Louis Cathedral in New Orleans supported Antonio de Sedella (1748–1829), a refractory Spanish Capuchin, against the authority of Fathers Thomas Hassett and Patrick Walsh whom Bishop Peñalver had left as administrators of the see when he departed in 1801. A schism in the cathedral congregation finally resulted and an intrigue was set on foot to have Sedella named bishop through the intervention of Emperor Napoleon. News of the trouble reached the Holy See and on September 20, 1805, Bishop Carroll was named administrator of the Diocese of Louisiana and the Two Floridas. Carroll fully realized the practical impossibility of his being able to settle the difficulties satisfactorily at so great a distance. Moreover, his awareness of the resentment of many of the French and Spanish inhabitants at the cession of their colony to the Americans gave him additional worry. In his perplexity Carroll turned to James Madison (1751–1836), Secretary of State in Jefferson's cabinet, to inquire if there would be any objection to his recommending a French priest to be the bishop of Louisiana. The following exhange of letters reveals, first, Carroll's patriotic

feeling and his reluctance to make any recommendation that might jeopardize American interests in Louisiana and, second, Jefferson's and Madison's scrupulous care to keep the government clear of the charge of meddling in religious matters, as well as their high personal confidence and esteem for Carroll. Sources: John Gilmary Shea, *History of the Catholic Church in the United States* (New York: John G. Shea, 1888), II, 591–592; *Records of the American Catholic Historical Society of Philadelphia,* XX (1909), 63–64.

November 17, 1806.

. . . I was not so satisfied with the accounts of Louisiana, of the clergymen living there, as would justify a recommendation of any of them for the important trust, which requires not only a virtuous but very prudent conduct, great learning, especially in matters of a religious nature, and sufficient resolution to remove gradually the disorders which have grown up during the relaxed state of civil and ecclesiastical authority. I therefore directed my views to two others, who, tho' Frenchmen, have been long resident in this country and steady in their attachment to it. But the removal of either of them to Louisiana was rendered impracticable, and circumstances have since occurred which perhaps makes it unadviseable in the opinion of this government, to nominate for the bishop of that country any native of France or Louisiana. I therefore declined hitherto taking any concern in this business, tho' the situation of the church there has long required, and requires now more particularly a prompt interference, not only for the interests of religion, but likewise for quieting and composing the minds of the inhabitants. You will observe that my first commission to take a provisional charge of the diocese of N. Orleans was received long before the intermeddling of the Emperor Napoleon. This has been procured, as I am credibly informed from N.O. by a mission to Paris from a Mr. Castillon,[1] who is at the head of the municipality, and an artful Spanish friar, Antonio de Sedilla [*sic*], the intimate friend of the Marquis of Caso [*sic*] Calvo.[2] This mission was entrusted to a certain Castanedo,[3] who was furnished with $4,000 to obtain a recommendation from the Emperor Napoleon for the immediate nomination of de Sedilla to the bishopric: but the attempt was completely miscarried, as you will see by the duplicate copy of the commission sent to me, &c. To this commission allow me to join

---

[1] Jean-Baptiste-Victor Castillon was president of the *marguilliers* of St. Louis Cathedral in New Orleans.

[2] Sebastián de la Puerta y O'Farril, Marquis de Casa Calvo, had been acting Governor of Spanish Louisiana for some months in 1799.

[3] Jean Castanedo was a member of the board of the cathedral *marguilliers.*

an extract from a letter of Card. Pietro, prefect of the Congreg. de Prop. fide at Rome, which I received at the same time. He says, &c. . . . From which it appears, that the acquiescence of our government is necessary with respect to the measures to be adopted for settling the ecclesiastical state of Louisiana. Something, as has been mentioned, is immediately necessary, before I proceed to determine on the choice of a subject fit to be recommended for the future bishop. If a native of this country, or one who is not a Frenchman, tho' well acquainted with the language, cannot be procured, would it be satisfactory to the Executive of the U.S. to recommend a native of France who has long resided amongst us, and is desirous of continuing under this government? In the meantime, as the only clergyman in Louisiana, in any degree qualified to act with vigor and intelligence in restoring order in the Cath. church, is a French emigrant priest, far from any attachment to the present system of his country, may be appointed to act as my vicar, without the disapprobation of our Executive? I have many reasons for believing that this person rejoices sincerely in the cession of that country to the United States.

Department of State
November 20th 1806.

Right Reverend Sir,

I have had the honor to receive and lay before the President your letter of the 17th inst, inclosing a duplicate of the commission which places under your care the Roman Catholic Church at New Orleans, and requesting the sentiments of the Executive on certain discretionary points affecting the selection of the functionaries to be named by you.

The delicacy towards the public authority and the laudable object which led to the enquiry you are pleased to make, are appreciated by the President, in the manner which they so justly merit. But as the case is entirely ecclesiastical it is deemed most congenial with the scrupulous policy of the Constitution in guarding against a political interference with religious affairs, to decline the explanations which you have thought might enable you to accommodate the better, the execution of your trust, to the public advantage. I have the pleasure, Sir, to add, that if that consideration had less influence, the President would find a motive to the same determination, in his perfect confidence in the purity of your views, and in the patriotism which will guide you, in the selection of ecclesiastical individuals, to such as combine with their professional merits, a due attachment to the independence, the Constitution and the prosperity of the United States.

I enclose the document which you requested might be returned, and pray you to accept assurances of the perfect respect and esteem with which,[1]

I remain,
Your most obt Servt
James Madison.

[1] In a private letter of the same date Madison told Carroll that he shared his views on Sedella, that he wished Carroll would be placed in permanent control of the Church in Louisiana, and that the "foreign interposition" of the New Orleans trustees to further the candidacy of Sedella for the bishopric was known by the government and regarded as "manifestly reprehensible." *Ibid.*, XX (1909), 64–65.

63. Mother Seton's Plans for Her Religious Community, February 9, 1809

THE founder of the first American religious congregation of women, the Sisters of Charity of St. Joseph, was Elizabeth Ann Seton (1774–1821). This convert widow of a distinguished Protestant Episcopalian family of New York laid the foundations of her community at Baltimore in 1808 under the auspices of Archbishop Carroll and the Sulpicians. In the summer of 1809 she moved to Emmitsburg, Maryland, where the mother house was permanently established and where the school for small children which had been begun in Baltimore was continued. Mother Seton's sisters increased in number and within six months after her death they had schools in Philadelphia, New York, and Baltimore. In the following letter to Filippo Filicchi she described the plans of herself and her advisers for the future of the infant community. Mother Seton's cause for beatification is now being studied by the Congregation of Rites. Source: Annabelle M. Melville, *Elizabeth Bayley Seton, 1774–1821* (New York: Charles Scribner's Sons, 1951), pp. 145–146.

My dear Filicchi,[1] you will think, I fear, that the poor little woman's brain is turned who writes you so often on the same subject, but it is not a matter of choice on my part, as it is my indispensable duty to let you know every particular of a circumstance which has occurred since I wrote you last week relative to the suggestions so strongly indicated in the letters I have written both yourself and your Antonio[2] since my arrival in Baltimore. Some time ago I mentioned to you the

[1] Filippo Filicchi, a well-to-do merchant of Leghorn, Italy, had long been a friend of the Seton family. He had assisted and encouraged Mrs. Seton in becoming a Catholic.

[2] Antonio was the brother of Filippo Filicchi.

conversion of a man of family and fortune in Philadelphia.[3] This conversion is as solid as it was extraordinary, and as *the person* is soon to recieve [*sic*] the Tonsure in our seminary, in making the disposition of his fortune he had consulted our Rd. Mr. Dubourg,[4] the Prest. of the College on the plan of establishing an institution for the advancement of Catholick female children in habits of religion and giving them an education suited to the purpose. He also desires extremely to extend the plan to the reception of the aged and also uneducated persons who may be employed in spinning, knitting, etc., etc., so as to found a Manufactory on a small scale which may be very beneficial to the poor. You see I am bound to let you know the disposition of Providence that you may yourself judge how far you may concur with it. Dr. Matignon[5] of Boston to whom Mr. Cheverus[6] the Bishop elect and Antonio referred me on every Occasion, [*sic*] had suggested this plan for me before the gentleman in question ever thought of it. I have invariably kept in the background and avoided even reflecting voluntarily on anything of the kind, knowing that Almighty God alone could effect it if indeed it will be realized. Father Mr. Dubourg has always said the same, be quiet, God will in his own time discover His intentions, nor will I allow one word of intreaty [*sic*] from my pen. His blessed will be done.

In my former letter I asked you if you could not secure your own property and build something for this purpose on the lot (which is an extensive one) given by Mr. Dubourg. If you will furnish the necessary expenditures for setting us off, and supporting those persons or children who at first will not be able to support themselves. Dr. Matignon will appoint a Director for the establishment which if you knew how many good and excellent souls are sighing for would soon obtain an interest in your breast, so ardently desiring the glory of God. But all is in his hands. If I had a choice and my will would decide in a moment, I would remain silent in his hands. Oh how sweet it is there to rest in perfect confidence, yet in every daily Mass and at communion I beg him to dispose of me and mine in any way which may please him. YOU are Our Father in him, thro your hands

---

[3] Samuel Sutherland Cooper (1769–1843), a convert of means who became a priest, gave financial aid to Mother Seton's community in its early years.

[4] Louis W. V. Dubourg, S.S. (1766–1833), was at the time president of St. Mary's College, Baltimore. He died as Archbishop of Besançon.

[5] François A. Matignon (1753–1818) was a French-born priest who was pastor of what was soon to become the Cathedral of the Holy Cross in Boston.

[6] Jean Cheverus (1768–1836) was the first Bishop of Boston who died as Cardinal Archbishop of Bordeaux.

we received that new and precious being which is indeed true life. And may you in your turn be rewarded with the fullness of the divine benediction. Amen a thousand times.

MEA Seton

64. Robert Walsh's Prospectus for His *American Review of History and Politics,* January 1, 1811

THE American Catholic minority had no more articulate representative in the ranks of the intellectuals of the early national period than Robert Walsh (1784–1859), even if his ideas were often at variance with many of his coreligionists. Educated at Georgetown and St. Mary's College, Baltimore, he later read law with Robert Goodloe Harper (1765–1825), son-in-law of Charles Carroll of Carrollton and a haughty Federalist of aristocratic bearing. Possessed of means, a penetrating mind, a deep love for literature and the arts, and the benefit of years of leisurely travel and study in Europe, Walsh's literary talents found an outlet in a variety of enterprises such as editing the *American Register,* contributing to the *Port Folio,* and establishing at Philadelphia the first formal quarterly review in the United States, the *American Review of History and Politics.* Due to Walsh's tenacious Federalist views in the midst of the War of 1812, the last venture lasted only two years. But he went on to become a founder of the *National Gazette and Literary Register* in 1820 and in 1827 launched the *American Quarterly Review* which for a decade held its place as one of the country's leading journals. Walsh was a striking contrast to his fellow townsman and fellow Catholic, Mathew Carey, in his execration of the Madison administration, his advocacy of Adam Smith's *laissez-faire* doctrines, his suspicion of the embryonic labor movement, and his opposition to the movement for public schools for the masses. Yet this conservative aristocrat, whose Philadelphia salon drew the city's elite, was personally a kindly and charitable man, a devoted husband to Anna Maria Moylan, niece of Stephen Moylan (1737–1811) of Revolutionary War fame, and a fond father to their twelve children. In August, 1844, Walsh was named American consul at Paris by President Tyler, a post he held until 1851. His remaining years were spent mostly in the French capital where he was on familiar and easy terms with the political and literary great. At the time that he launched the *Review* in January, 1811, his detestation of Napoleon Bonaparte was matched only by his grave misgivings over the way the Jeffersonian Republicans were running the government of the United States. These ideas, together with his reflections on the current literary trends in England and this country, were well summarized in the prospectus he wrote for the first issue of the new magazine and which is printed in the document which follows. Walsh's death took place in Paris on February 7, 1859, his last words being, "I die in the faith of my ancestors — in the faith of the Holy Catholic Church" (Sister M. Frederick Lochemes, *Robert Walsh: His Story* [New York, 1941], p. 221). Source: *American Review of History and Politics,* I (January, 1811), i–x.

This work will be conducted under adequate management, and modelled upon a plan calculated to render it extensively and permanently useful. It will embrace a review of the public occurrences of Europe, and of our own relations with that quarter of the globe, — an examination of the parliamentary history and domestic policy of this country, — an inquiry into the merits of foreign and native productions — particularly of such as profess to delineate our own condition and character; — original essays, and selections in every department of literature; — an application of the principles of political economy to the peculiar circumstances of the United States, — and a collection of state papers, in the form of an appendix — fitted to illustrate and to confirm the facts and opinions advanced in the historical and political articles.

The chief ends of this miscellany, to which the most indefatigable attention will be given, and for which ample resources will be provided, — are the propagation of sound political doctrines, and the direction and improvement of the literary taste of the American people. It has been thought advisable to adopt a plan of a nature so comprehensive as to exclude nothing which may conduce to the attainment of these ends. The preference given to a quarterly over a monthly or annual publication is founded upon the idea, that it will combine the advantages, while it obviates the inconveniences, peculiar to both, — by affording an interval of time, not so great as to divest the historical and political disquisitions of the interest of novelty, and yet sufficient for the exercise of care and discrimination in the composition, the selection, and the arrangement of materials.

Whatever maxims of wisdom applicable to our institutions the best writers either ancient or modern can afford on the science of government, will be industriously sought and quoted, as well as such cases in the history of the past, as may serve to enlighten the public opinion both with regard to our own situation and to the transactions of European powers. It will be made a principal object to furnish the readers of this miscellany with correct views of the true condition and policy of the two great belligerents by whose distant struggles our domestic peace is shaken, and in whose dispositions and projects our highest interests are deeply involved. Every document, therefore, calculated to throw light on this topic, and which an extensive correspondence and the best opportunities can yield, will be minutely examined, and rendered subservient to a purpose, on the importance of which it would be superfluous to dwell. The proceedings of congress will be vigilantly watched, and temperately discussed, — but not, however, without that degree of zeal which an ardent love of country naturally excites, and which, so far from proving an obstruction, is, in fact, auxiliary to the surest operations of the judgment. Genuine sentiment and sound policy can never be dissociated, — and it is, therefore, that full scope will be given to the natural, elevated, warm feelings, and to the vehement, unsuborned, virtuous passions, of the heart, whenever the subject of discussion shall be those schemes of profligate ambition which now menace the liberties of all mankind, and those acts of portentous corruption, — the crimes of unexampled depravity, — which assail the moral and political order of Europe — and which awaken terror while they kindle indignation in the mind of every reflecting and honest individual of every country.

The utility of the present undertaking must be too obvious to require a particular exposition, and should it be well executed — it is hoped that no necessity will arise for an elaborate appeal to the public on the score of patronage. A work of the nature now contemplated has been long desired by the most enlightened men of this country, and claims the cooperation as well as the protection of those who unite the ability with the desire of promoting the interests of freedom and of letters.

There is something in the melancholy character of the times, — in the signal and extraordinary dangers with which the United States, together with the rest of the civilized world, are threatened, — that calls loudly for the utmost activity in the defence of those institutions and that system of knowledge, which constitute our best riches, and which ennoble and decorate human nature. At a moment when the whole continent of Europe is sinking under the ascendant of a military despotism, and the same dark cloud of ignorance and tyranny is settling upon it, which a few centuries ago was dispelled by the genius of commerce, it is incumbent upon the American public to encourage the development and the application of whatever resources may be found in the faculties of individuals, in order to secure from the same fatal influence, the inestimable blessings and the pure lights which this country drew from the very fountain that is now partly, and which may be hereafter, totally choked up and polluted. . . .

Independently of such considerations as these which affect our highest interests and appeal to the nobler feelings of the breast, there are others of secondary importance, which operate as a recommendation to an undertaking like the present and are not to be overlooked. The critical examination of European works particularly of those which come to us from England, will be made to enter, as has been before stated, into the structure of this journal. Whatever may be the ability with which the English reviews are conducted, it is certain that truth in them is often distorted or wholly suppressed, — that their decisions are materially influenced by the spirit of party — the suggestions of private friendship, or the authority of popular names; and not infrequently, by the prejudices of literary patriotism and the intolerance of national pride. The formation therefore, of a domestic tribunal exempt from the operation of feelings which vitiate the taste, and mislead the judgment, and whose province it shall be both to vindicate our own merits when injuriously attacked, and to exhibit faithfully those of foreign writers when erroneously reported, cannot but be productive of the most beneficial consequences, not merely in relation to the purity of our relish for elegant literature, but also to the accuracy of our opinions on questions connected with the domestic politics of another country, of the utmost importance to our own national welfare.

Another topic which it is deemed expedient to urge in favour of a journal on the plan mentioned above, is, the apparent necessity for some such enterprize with a view to the promotion of the literary fame of this country. The period has arrived when a platform at least, should be laid, and it is in this mode only — under the peculiar circumstances of our condition — that the object can be accomplished. If the foundation were once settled, there remains no doubt but that with the scaffolding of English literature, a fabric of literary reputation might be ere long erected, of materials which both for their variety and excellence would delight and surprise the nations of Europe. It is certain that our means are not duly appreciated abroad; — that we ourselves have not done justice to our resources, either of genius or of learning. Whatever may be said by the prejudiced or the uninformed critics of Europe, there is, nevertheless, among us an ample portion of the "ethereal spirit," and an abundant store of erudition, competent to extend the limits of human knowledge and to shed lustre on the national character, — as there is, also, a solid fund of legislative wisdom and public virtue fitted to raise us to a proper standard of estimation in the eyes of the world, and to fashion and fortify this republic into a "deeplaid indissoluble state."

But through the agency of a combination of unavoidable circumstances in the one case, and of a train of unfortunate contingencies and lamentable errors in the other, all these advantages lie inert and obscure, and mankind judging only from external indications and practical results, have come to this fallacious but natural conclusion, that we are no less miserably deficient in the treasures of learning and in the powers of genius, than ridiculously weak in our public councils, and improvidently backward in the organization of our physical strength. From the actual composition of our deliberative assemblies, and the measures of our cabinet, they infer that we are altogether without that gallantry of spirit, that generous and lofty enthusiasm, the liberal studies, and enlarged "courageous wisdom" which, if they had uniformly presided over our affairs, might have given an irresistible momentum and a most imposing attitude to a nation so singularly favoured by nature and fortune. They make the rarity and insignificance of our productions in literature, the criterion of our ability to produce, and imagine that a mercenary, groveling, narrow-minded system of policy is accompanied by a correspondent poverty of conception and scantiness of knowledge.

It shall be one of the ends of this journal to refute these imputations, and it is one of its chief advantages that it may itself become a practical illustration of their falsehood. The sound doctrines and the elevated sentiments of which it may be made the receptacle, and which, together with habits of profound investigation and a rich fund of political science, belong to so many individuals in this country, may serve to convince the world that it is to causes merely accidental that we owe the coarse texture of our legislative bodies, and the abject spirit of our administration. It may be asserted without presumption that this country has not shone in periodical literature rather on account of the absence of proper excitements and of suitable repositories for the productions of taste and learning, than for any want either of capacity or leisure. The analysis of important works and the literary disquisitions which fall within the scope of the present publication, will afford an ample field for the display of ingenuity and of erudition, and should the materials of this description which may form a part of the first numbers, be wrought with skill and elegance, a spirit of emulation, the natural effect of classical models, — may be excited, so as to lead to efforts of the highest and happiest order.

In Europe, profound statesmen, eminent authors, brilliant scholars, cooperate ambitiously in journals of this nature, — and communicate to the world, through such channels, their most elaborate researches, and their most finished productions. They know that in so doing, they derogate nothing from their own dignity, while they contribute infinitely to the advantage of the public. Sound doctrines are, in this way, more widely disseminated, a more habitual and certain influence is given to the principles of taste, and a more prompt and diffusive fame secured to the labours of learning and of genius. The delicacy and solidity of the tissue which they weave, the rich and lasting colours which they employ, counteract the perishable nature of the frame in which they exhibit their productions; and it may, therefore, be asserted with confidence, that such disquisitions as those of the Edinburgh Review and the Mercure de France, will be no less durable, as they are no less elegant and instructive, than the most formal or ambitious treatises, however profound or original. The enlightened and the patriotic of every country will always zealously advance the progress of letters — and will not disdain to become, as it were, militant themselves, in a cause which is inseparable from that of pure morals, of national glory, of refined humanity, of generous and elevated sentiment, of true policy, and heroic conduct.

The illustrous example just quoted should be here imitated by those whose proper stations in our political world have been usurped by the most incapable and contemptible men that ever presumed to be ambitious; by men who are no less devoid of the accomplishments of liberal and useful science than of all the distinguishing qualifications of real statesmen; — who are not the guides but the instruments of the people; — who are at once the shame and the scourge of their country. This example may be held up to our ingenuous youth as pointing to the only mode in which they can, at this moment when the principles of natural subordination are overthrown among us, and the just correspondence and symmetry of our political system completely deranged, — gratify that avidity to serve the commonwealth — which is the passion of noble minds — and restore to liberal studies and to vigorous talents that due and wholesome preponderance of which — by the most mischievous of all kinds of oppression, — in defiance of the dispensations of divine wisdom, and in violation of the laws of true political equality as well as of the prerogatives of nature, — they are here systematically and almost universally deprived. If those who are our brightest ornaments, — our legitimate instructors — and our natural rulers, — who have from nature authentic evidence of delegation to the functions of government, who, in the possession of superior capacity, wisdom and learning, carry with them "the passport of Heaven to human place and honour," are excluded from the management of public affairs, they are not, however, absolved from the obligation of struggling for the regeneration of the state in another course of exertion which, although less direct and sure than the exercise of official authority, may nevertheless, produce the most salutary results. They still lie under engagements of interest and duty which they violate in resigning themselves to total inaction, when by the concentration of their desultory and scattered efforts in one focus, — by the speculations of the closet widely circulated, — by the admonitions of wisdom constantly reproduced, and by specimens of sound literature and chaste composition, they may finally succeed in touching the mastersprings and the nobler passions of our nature, — in refining and enlarging our habits of thought — in extending the range of our literary and scientific inquiries, and in correcting that low and degenerate fashion of argument which would sacrifice national honour to pecuniary interests, and which mistakes the suggestions of a sordid and improvident parsimony for those of genuine state economy — a principle both magnificent and prospective, and often opposed to all arithmetical calculation. . . .

This country is hideously metamorphised since the days of Washington, — but we are far from despairing of the public fortunes. It is not credulity to imagine that much of that spirit still remains which then seemed to pervade the great majority of this nation, and that to be made to reappear it needs only to be "ritually invoked." Although the repetition of enormous crimes since the commencement of the French revolution, is calculated to render the present generation callous to any excesses of profligate power, we are not without a numerous body composing the best and most efficient class of citizens, who are justly shocked at the horrible depravity of the conduct and views of the Imperial government of France, particularly as they are exemplified in the cases of Spain and Holland. Although the grossest delusions and the most pernicious errors prevail generally on the subject of France, a large proportion of the intelligent proprietaries of this country are alive to most of the dangers which impend over us from that quarter, and look with a fearful and watchful eye on the tremendous growth of her power. It shall be one of the leading objects of this journal to unfold the whole extend of those dangers, and to administer in every form and at every recurrence of opportunity, the strongest antidotes to that blind security, which we consider as the capital evil, and the most serious distemper of the state. Should this journal become what by suitable exertions it may be rendered — "a bank of deposit and a bank of circulation" for correct representations of facts, for the fundamental truths of state-policy, and for the lessons of experience, much more may be accomplished than can be now distinctly foreseen or even readily imagined. It is a remark of Bolingbroke that truth and reason when vigourously and pertinaciously maintained will often bear down all prejudices and surmount all obstacles. "Their progress," he adds, "is generally sure although "sometimes not observable by every eye. — Contrary prejudices may "seem to maintain themselves in vigour, and these prejudices may be "long kept up by passion and artifice. But when sound principles and "natural sentiments continue to be urged, a little sooner, or a little "later, and often when the revolution is least expected, the prejudices "vanish at once and give place to the dominion of wisdom and of "truth." Such should be the expectation of the enlightened and virtuous portion of our community, and upon this rational ground of hope should they persevere in combating abuses and in resisting delusions, that menace our very existence, and have already entailed upon the infancy of this republic all the marks of weakness and folly which usually accompany the dotage of governments.

65. The First Bishop of the Middle West Arrives in His See, June, 1811

ON APRIL 8, 1808, Pope Pius VII divided the original Diocese of Baltimore and erected four new sees, the only one west of the Alleghenies being the Diocese of Bardstown, Kentucky. The man appointed to rule this see in the wilderness was a French-born Sulpician, Benedict Joseph Flaget (1763–1850), who had come to the United States in 1792. After an unsuccessful attempt to escape the episcopacy Flaget was consecrated by Archbishop Carroll on November 4, 1810, but he was so poor at the time that he did not have enough money to cover his traveling expenses. It was not until May, 1811, that he was able to set out with a small party of three priests, three seminarians, and three servants. The data for the following description of their journey westward and their first days in Kentucky were gathered from various sources by Bishop Martin J. Spalding, Flaget's coadjutor, and published two years after the latter's death. Source: M. J. Spalding, *Sketches of the Life, Times, and Character of the Rt. Rev. Benedict Joseph Flaget, First Bishop of Louisville* (Louisville: Webb & Levering, 1852), pp. 68–72.

To give you a clear idea of the bishoprics of the United States, I propose to lay before you a brief statement of the condition in which I found myself, after the Holy See, on the representation of Bishop Carroll, had nominated me to the bishopric of Bardstown. I was compelled to accept the appointment, whether I would or not, I had not a cent at my disposal; the Pope and the Cardinals, who were dispersed by the revolution, were not able to make me the slightest present; and Archbishop Carroll, though he had been Bishop for more than sixteen (*twenty*) years, was still poorer than myself; for he had debts, and I owed nothing. Nevertheless, my consecration took place on the 4th of November, 1810; but for want of money to defray the expenses of the journey, I could not undertake it. It was only six months afterwards, that, through a subscription made by my friends in Baltimore, I was enabled to reach Bardstown, my episcopal see.

At length, on the 11th of May, 1811, the Bishop and his suite left Baltimore for the West. They traveled over the mountains to Pittsburg; whence they embarked on the 22d in a flat-boat, chartered especially for the purpose. They were thirteen days in descending the Ohio river to Louisville, where they arrived on the 4th of June. . . .

The boat on which we descended the Ohio became the cradle of our seminary, and of the church of Kentucky. Our cabin was, at the same time, chapel, dormitory, study room and refectory. An altar was erected on the boxes, and ornamented so far as circumstances would allow. The Bishop prescribed a regulation which fixed all the exercises, and in which each had its proper time. On Sunday, after prayer, every one went to confession; then the priests said Mass, and the others went to communion. After an agreeable navigation of thirteen days, we arrived at Louisville, next at Bardstown, and finally at the residence of the Vicar General.[1]

While we were there (in Louisville), the faithful of my episcopal city put themselves in motion to receive me in a manner conformable to my dignity. They despatched for my use a fine equipage drawn by two horses; and a son of one among the principal inhabitants considered himself honored in being the driver. Horses were furnished to all those who accompanied me, and four wagons transported our baggage.

It was then, for the first time, that I saw the bright side of the episcopacy, and that I began to feel its dangers. Nevertheless, God be thanked, if some movements of vanity glided into my heart, they had not a long time to fix their abode therein. The roads were so detestable, that, in spite of my beautiful chargers and my excellent driver, I was obliged to perform part of the journey on foot; and I should have traveled the entire way, had not one of my young seminarians dismounted and presented me his horse. . . .

The next day, the sun was not risen when we were already on our journey. The roads were much better; I entered the carriage with two of my suite. I was not the more exalted (*fier*) for all this; the

[1] Father Badin was vicar general of the new diocese.

idea that I was henceforward to speak, to write, and to act as Bishop, cast me into a profound sadness. How many sighs did I not breathe forth while traversing the four or five remaining leagues of our journey!

At the distance of a half league (a mile and a half) from town, an ecclesiastic of my Diocese, accompanied by the principal inhabitants, came out to meet me. So soon as they had perceived us, they dismounted to receive my benediction. I gave it to them, but with how trembling a hand, and with what heaviness of heart! Mutual compliments were now exchanged, and then we all together proceeded towards the town. This *cortege,* though simple and modest in itself, is something very new and extraordinary in this country. It was the first time a Bishop was ever seen in these parts (*deserts*); and it was I, the very last of the last tribe, who was to have this honor!

In entering the town, I devoted myself to all the guardian angels who reside therein, and I prayed to God, with all my heart, to make me die a thousand times, should I not become an instrument of His glory in this new Diocese. O, my dear brother, have compassion on me, overloaded with so heavy a burden, and pray fervently to God that he would vouchsafe to lighten it.

The Bishop entered Bardstown, — where there was as yet no church, — on the 9th of June; and he reached St. Stephen's, the residence of M. Badin, on the 11th. Here he was met by the clergy of his Diocese, and was greeted by a large concourse of his people, anxious to see their Bishop. The ceremony of his installation is thus described by M. Badin:

The Bishop there found the faithful kneeling on the grass, and singing canticles in English; the country women were nearly all dressed in white, and many of them were still fasting, though it was then four o'clock in the evening; they having entertained a hope to be able on that day to assist at his Mass, and to receive the holy communion from his hands. An altar had been prepared at the entrance of the first court, under a bower composed of four small trees which overshadowed it with their foliage. Here the Bishop put on his pontifical robes. After the aspersion of the holy water, he was conducted to the chapel in procession, with the singing of the Litany of the Blessed Virgin; and the whole function closed with the prayers and ceremonies prescribed for the occasion in the Roman Pontifical.

Under circumstances so simple, yet so touching, did the first Bishop of the West enter into formal possession of his see.

66. A Detroit Visitor Records His Impressions of Gabriel Richard, S.S., June, 1816

ONE of the principal gains made by the American Church among the priests who were forced into exile by the French Revolution was the Sulpician, Gabriel Richard (1767–1832). After some years on the Illinois missions Richard arrived in Detroit in June, 1798, and for the next thirty-four years his life was identified with practically every important event in Michigan. He served as missionary to the Indians, built Detroit's first schools, and introduced the first printing press whereon were printed the first books and the first newspaper in Michigan, the *Michigan Essay or Impartial Observer* (August 31, 1809). When the British took Detroit during the War of 1812 he refused to silence his American sympathies and was deported to Windsor and placed under house arrest. Richard not only carried out all his priestly duties but found time to serve as vice president of the incipient University of Michigan and to win the distinction of being the only priest ever to hold a seat in Congress as delegate of Michigan Territory. While attending the cholera victims he contracted the disease and died on September 13, 1832. During the visitation tour of Upper Canada in June, 1816, Joseph-Octave Plessis (1763–1822), Bishop of Quebec, visited Detroit and the impressions of Richard which he recorded in his journal give a good idea of the multiplicity of the priest's occupations and the place he held in the life of the community. Source: Henri Têtu (Ed.), *Journal des visites pastorales de 1815 et 1816 par Monseigneur Joseph-Octave Plessis, Evêque de Québec* (Québec, 1903); translation by Lionel Lindsay, *American Catholic Historical Researches,* XXII (July, 1905), 224–226, 228–230.

June 19 . . . .

This ecclesiastic is, moreover, thoroughly estimable on account of his regularity, of the variety of his knowledge, and especially of an activity of which it is difficult to form an idea. He has the talent of doing, almost simultaneously, ten entirely different things. Provided with newspapers (*gazettes*) well informed on all political questions, ever ready to argue on religion when the occasion presents itself, and thoroughly learned in theology, he reaps his hay, gathers the fruit of his garden, manages a fishery fronting his lot, teaches mathematics to one young man, reading to another, devotes times to mental prayer, establishes a printing-press, confesses all his people, imports carding and spinning wheels and looms, to teach the women of his parish how to work, leaves not a single act of his parochial register unwritten, invents an electric machine, goes on sick calls at a very great distance, writes letters to and receives others from all parts, preaches on every Sunday and holy-day both lengthily and learnedly, enriches his library, spends whole nights without sleep, walks for whole days, loves to converse, receives company, teaches catechism to his young parishioners, supports a girls' school, under the management of a few female teachers of his own choosing, whom he directs like a religious community whilst he gives lessons in plain-song to young boys assembled in a school he has founded, leads a most frugal life, and is in good health, as fresh and able, at the age of fifty, as one usually is at thirty. Such is the abridged portrait of this more than ordinary man; extremely appreciated by the Bishop of Quebec and his traveling companions, but having against him the great majority of his parishioners; entirely set against him, and several of whom, in their self-conceit and folly, would prefer remaining without a priest, to having that one. . . .[1]

June 24. M. Richard having paid a visit to the Bishop of Quebec on Thursday evening [June 20], it was agreed that he would introduce the latter to the American commanders, civil and military, of Detroit, whom he intended visiting on the following Monday. . . . They began by visiting the Governor,[2] who lived in a small house quite at the east or northeast extremity of the city. . . .

It would be folly on the part of the ecclesiastics to count on military honors. They should have no pretension thereto, but consent through politeness to accept them, when they are offered with good grace. It happened thus at the quarters of Major General McComb,[3] Military Commander of Detroit. He lives at the other extremity of the city, that is to say at the east or southeast. . . .

The visitors thought they had done with ceremony, at least for the remainder of that day, and hoped to dine leisurely and fraternally at M. Richard's house where they were expected. On the contrary. While they were going there by water, the Governor and the General arrived by land. . . .

The Abbé Richard, who had summoned all these guests without the participation of the Bishop of Quebec, placed him simply between the Governor and the General, and served them, on a rather badly disposed table, a dinner too abundant in meat, too scant in vegetables, in too small an apartment, whose windows he had had the precaution of removing to give more air to his company. A shower of rain

---

[1] The situation to which Bishop Plessis alluded had arisen over the refusal of certain parishioners to accept Richard's arrangements with the civil authorities for the location of a new church. Ultimately seven of the ringleaders were excommunicated and the breach was healed only by the personal visit of Bishop Flaget of Bardstown to Detroit in June, 1818.

[2] Lewis Cass (1782–1866) was Governor of Michigan Territory at the time.

[3] General Alexander Macomb was military commander at Detroit.

driven by the southerly wind, which occurred during the repast, sprinkled the chief guests. They would have desired to have the windows closed; but there were none to close, so they had to give it up.

However, the conversation was quite lively, and each one seemed to rejoice in the reunion of a company whose members, French, Canadians, Americans, English, civil, military, ecclesiastics, laymen, Catholics, Protestants, were strangers to each other.

The hour for departing had come. General McComb's band, which had followed the company, was ready to play in the adjoining room. Toasts or healths had to be drunk: the Americans attach great importance to this. The first was in the Bishop's honor. He proposed one to the President of the United States, expecting that it would be returned by another to the King of England. Not at all. Governor Cass proposed his to our Holy Father the Pope, and the General to the prosperity of the Catholic clergy. It must be remarked that these two dignitaries had quite recently received from M. Richard an honor that the Catholic clergy do not ordinarily grant to Protestants, which was that at the solemn procession of Corpus Christi, the 13th of the same month, he had invited them to hold the ribbons of the *dais* or canopy under which was the Blessed Sacrament, and had had the procession accompanied by an American regiment under arms. The parishioners had not been, in general, edified by such a mixture, and had justly complained of this novelty. The Abbé Richard justifies his conduct by what the Bishop of Baltimore had given as a principle to his clergy: to do towards the Protestants all that might draw them to the Catholic church: an excellent principle, so long as it does not violate the rules in essential points.

67. Archbishop Maréchal's Report to Propaganda, October 16, 1818

THREE years after the death of Archbishop Carroll his second successor in the See of Baltimore, the French-born Sulpician, Ambrose Maréchal (1764–1828), made a detailed report on the state of religion in the archdiocese to Lorenzo Cardinal Litta, Prefect of the Congregation de Propaganda Fide. It is an important source for the history of American Catholicism in the early nineteenth century since it covered practically all phases of the Church's activities in the large area from Maryland south to Florida and west to the Mississippi River. Maréchal not only gave an account of the priests, parishes, seminaries, religious congregations of men and women, with side lights on the religious life of the laity, but he also included some interesting

reflections on topics such as American social customs, the trustee problem in the South, and the nationalist feeling that was causing an increasing amount of friction in various Catholic congregations. Source: A Latin text was published in the *Catholic Historical Review,* I (January, 1916), 439–453, from which the translation which follows was made by the Reverend Urban J. Stang of the College of Mount Saint Joseph on-the-Ohio.

Baltimore, October 16, 1818.

Your Eminence:

Having returned to Baltimore after a visit to most of the missions in my diocese, I have undertaken to commit to writing the present status of the Catholic Church in these regions, to the extent that it is known to me, and to transmit this account to the Sacred Congregation, until the time that I may be able to submit a more accurate record.

1. In the United States of North America the Sees of Boston, New York, Pennsylvania and Bardstown have also been erected. The Diocese of Baltimore however includes the following provinces, namely, Maryland, Virginia, North and South Carolina, Georgia and that vast territory which is contained in the limits of Georgia, the Floridas, Tennessee and the Mississippi River. Before the American Revolution there were at most 10,000 Catholics in the aforesaid provinces. At present there are at least 100,000 in these same regions,[1] the greatest part of them residing in Maryland. This multitude of the faithful, favored by divine Providence, is increasing marvelously by the natural progress of generation, by the conversion of Protestants, and especially by the immense number of Europeans who immigrate to our Republic every year. In my diocese there are 52 priests exercising the sacred ministry. They have come from various nations, namely, Italians 1, Germans 3, English 4, Belgians 7, Americans 12, Irish 11, and French 14. Each of these missionaries has a church in which he celebrates the most holy sacrifice of the Mass; many of them also have two or three missions some distance removed, which they visit at least once a month. Some of these churches are built of wood, others of brick, others of polished stone; but scarcely any of them is sufficiently large to accommodate the increasing number of Catholics. And so during the coming year ten new churches will be built in the various parts of my diocese.

2. There are four churches in the city of Baltimore, namely, the

---

[1] Maréchal's figures on the Catholic population were not accurate. For a correction cf. Gerald Shaughnessy, S.M., *Has The Immigrant Kept The Faith?* (New York, 1925), pp. 69–73.

church of St. Patrick in the Eastern part of the city; the church of St. John in the central portion; the church of the Seminary to the West; there is also the old metropolitan church, dedicated to St. Peter, towards the Northern part. The latter was the only church in the city of Baltimore, when, having come over from France, I entered it in 1792. But with the growth of the city the number of the faithful increased and the church of St. Patrick was erected. It was spacious and in the beginning was large enough but now it is too small for the congregation. Later the church of St. John was built. It is frequented principally by those of German descent. The Directors of the Seminary also built a large and very beautiful chapel at their own expense. A devout multitude of the faithful flock to it on Feastdays and Sundays, allured by the majestic Gregorian chant, the splendor of the divine worship, and the ceremonies performed with the help of the seminarians. Within the past year at least 10,000 communions were distributed to the faithful in this chapel. With regard to the old metropolitan church of St. Peter, it is so small in comparison to the multitude of parishioners that it can scarcely hold one-tenth part of them; and unless many masses be celebrated successively in it on Sundays, an immense number of the faithful could not be present at the most holy Sacrifice. Weighing carefully this most grave inconvenience, my predecessor, the Most Illustrious Bishop Carroll, undertook the building of a Cathedral Church of such dimensions that the Catholics of Baltimore might easily be admitted to it. But he had scarcely finished the foundation when the work was left unfinished because of a lack of funds. However during the past year, collections and alms having been taken up here and there, it was decided, at my suggestion, to complete the work which had been begun; and such was the industry and activity of the workers that I now have a well founded hope that after about eighteen months I will be able to perform the solemn ceremony of the consecration of this Basilica. Without a doubt its size and grandeur will far surpass that of any temple built up to this time in the United States of America, whether by the Protestants or by the Catholics. Even the Protestants of Baltimore take pride in it. It is, indeed, the greatest ornament of their city. But it grieves me very much that its interior is almost completely lacking in decoration. Would that the Sacred Congregation or some noble Roman would give to us as a gift some pious statues such as may be found around Rome. Four or six would suffice and they could be sent to us easily by way of Leghorn. Such a gift would elicit the supreme gratitude of all the Catholics of the United States towards the munificent donor. In vain did I wish to buy two statues, namely one of Our Lord and Saviour and one of the Blessed Virgin to whom the Metropolitan Church will be consecrated; none whatsoever could be found in these regions and there were no workers who could make them. In the year 1792 scarcely 800 Catholics could be found in the city of Baltimore; now there are about 10,000.

3. In my diocese there are two Seminaries under the direction of the priests of St. Sulpice. These are the major Seminary of Baltimore and the minor, located near the village of Emmitsburg, which is about 15 leagues from Baltimore. In the major seminary the junior clergy apply themselves to the study of philosophy and theology, and they are educated in all the sciences and virtues which are necessary for missionaries. A spacious college is connected with this seminary. In it the sons of wealthy or noble Catholic families pursue their studies of the humanities and of letters. All the youths living within the walls of this college are industriously taught by their kind directors and are educated in the principles of the Catholic religion. Many others, and among them many Protestants, daily frequent the schools outside of the city. The legislature of Maryland has conferred upon this college the dignity of a university. The minor seminary at Emmitsburg was founded especially according to the mind of the Council of Trent, that youths might be received in it, who wished to consecrate themselves to the service of God and the church. There are about 80 young men in this seminary. Of these fifteen have already received clerical tonsure and there are also the others whose ecclesiastical vocation is not yet sufficiently manifest. These two seminaries are most precious to the Catholic religion. Upon their prosperity depends to a great extent the prosperity of our holy faith in North America. They were erected at the expense of the Society of St. Sulpice. Since their income is exceedingly meager, it has caused me to wonder just how they have been able to sustain them. May it please God to inspire American citizens, who have wealth and means at their command, to sustain from time to time, by means of pious and liberal gifts, these two venerable institutions; then there would soon be at our command a sufficient number of missionaries both for fostering and propagating our holy faith, on all sides, in the immense republic of America.

Besides these two seminaries, whose principal end is the education of the secular clergy, there is also Georgetown. It is a magnificent college, near the capital city Washington, and is directed by the Fathers of the Society of Jesus. It consists of two principal buildings.

The former is occupied by secular youths who study the humanities and letters; the latter contains the novices and scholastics of the Society. Of these there are thirty-three. It is very much to be regreted that the college is deeply in debt. However, since the Society recently recovered all their belongings and the other properties, which they possessed before the destruction of the Society, without a doubt they will soon be wealthy enough. All wonder why their superiors at Rome do not send to Georgetown six or eight religious men, outstanding for their knowledge and piety, to foster this rising institution in our regions. For there is no part of the Catholic world in which the Society of Jesus could exist more securely, spread more widely and produce more abundant fruits.

4. There are three monasteries of nuns in the diocese of Baltimore. The first is that of the Carmelites. It is not far distant from a village called Port Tobacco, high up on the bank of the Potomac River which separates Maryland from Virginia. Twenty-three nuns live there. They have a sufficiently large income. These virgins of St. Teresa live so holily, that I scarcely believe that any other house of this order exists anywhere in the Catholic world in which piety and monastic discipline flourish to the same extent. They strictly observe the cloister. The second house is that of the Visitation of Georgetown situated near Washington. It contains nearly fifty nuns. Their resources are limited but they live partly on their income and partly by the labor of their own hands. This house is certainly most pious and most holy. In it the virtues of Francis de Sales shine very brightly; never do these nuns go beyond the limits of their monastery. Near the monastery is a building in which Catholic girls reside and are educated. Some of the nuns undertake the work of giving them a pious and liberal education. Besides these there are also many younger girls, Catholic and Protestant, who come for classes at appointed hours. Every year there goes forth from this religious home a number of young ladies, who diffuse far and wide in the world the lessons of piety taught them in this school. The third house is that of the Daughters of St. Vincent de Paul.[2] Their house is not far distant from the village of Emmitsburg. They have thirty-two sisters, who live holy lives according to the rules of their Holy Founder, with the exception of the modifications demanded by American customs and dispositions. They do not take care of hospitals, nor could they since the administrators of these hospitals are Protestant. Their

[2] The Sisters of Charity of St. Joseph at Emmitsburg, founded in 1808, were not affiliated to the Daughters of Charity of St. Vincent de Paul until 1850.

principal work is the pious education of Catholic girls, those of the poor as well as those of the rich. There are about eighty young girls in the house at Emmitsburg as well as some who are destitute of parents or means. This pious institute has produced most abundant fruits of religion. So if at some time in the future, with God's favor, I may be able to collect a large enough sum of money, I intend to erect another house, besides that of Emmitsburg, and this house for girls I intend to erect at Baltimore. These three monasteries, which I have visited very recently, reflect wonderfully the greatest piety, fervor of spirit, strict discipline, and indeed all virtues. Certainly I cannot thank God enough for all this. The Protestants themselves treat them with a certain veneration. Assuredly the sisters and their work are like so many overflowing fonts of grace to water abundantly my flock. Besides these religious communities, there are, in nearly all the churches of my diocese, confraternities, whether of the scapular, or the rosary, or of the Most Blessed Sacrament, or of the Sacred Heart of Jesus. Especially noteworthy is the association in the city of Baltimore for the good that it has accomplished. It is made up of outstanding Catholic men who strive to serve God. Once every month the members of the confraternity gather together in the lower chapel of the Seminary, where they attend Mass and listen to a sermon on the dogmas of the faith and the principal moral precepts of the gospel. The purpose of this pious association is that its members should show by example the virtues of the gospel to their fellow citizens, Catholic and Protestant. Among the regulations by which they are bound, one is of the greatest importance, namely, that on four of the more solemn feast days they as a group publicly receive Holy Communion in the metropolitan church. This wonderful example of their brethren has a marvelous effect upon those who see them and drives from them that mundane fear under which many in these regions labor and which caused them to refrain from receiving the sacraments.

I will conclude this article by announcing to the Sacred Congregation that by next winter I shall have established in Baltimore free schools. The poor youths of either sex, whether Catholic or Protestant, may attend these schools free of charge, if the parents consent that they be educated in the principles of our most holy religion.

5. In the United States of America all the Protestant sects have their followers, ministers and churches. They care little about the dogmas which Luther, Calvin and Henry VIII formerly preached. There is a manifest and general tendency of all towards Socinianism. The Anglican church, which was predominant before the American

Revolution and was protected by the rule of Great Britain, has tottered and fallen to pieces everywhere, for like all other religions it is only tolerated. The Catholic Church has vindicated for herself general veneration and the Protestants turn their eyes towards her. The prejudices, with which formerly the young were imbued, have disappeared to such an extent that pseudoministers no longer dare to suggest them in their preaching; and if one of them does do so he is branded a calumniator by his hearers.[3] Many Protestants now come to our churches on Sundays and of these not a few have embraced our holy faith. I refer to this fact for it gives me the greatest consolation and proves how quickly the Catholic faith can be propagated in these regions. In the visitation of my diocese, which I undertook this year, I administered confirmation in a certain village called *Taneytown*. The pastor of this mission is a Roman priest, the Rev. D. Zocchy [*sic*].[4] At least a third part of those who received this sacrament were Protestants who had recently become converts to the Catholic religion. Americans are endowed with keen minds and the best of natural dispositions. They possess naturally the art of reasoning, even the workmen. Nearly all the citizens are engaged in commerce, agriculture, or in the mechanical arts. They strive after riches with the greatest industry of mind and body. The civil arts and delicacies of life, in which Europeans indulge, are found amongst us in abundance. But no one among them can be said to be outstanding for his knowledge. Yet it can be said truthfully that the mass of people, taken in general, far surpass the European people in education, in the politeness of their customs, and a certain cultivation of the intellect. It is almost with divine worship that they adore the liberty which they enjoy; and since there are within the limits of this Republic vast forests, which are sold at a very cheap price, it is almost impossible to believe what large number of Europeans come to this country. It is estimated that during the present year about two hundred immigrants per day came to our shores from Europe. Among these there were very many Catholics.

Among the principal vices of the Americans are the desire for unlimited riches, which seems to have seized the minds of all, and the vice of drunkenness among laborers and the lower classes. And so

[3] In view of the Nativist uprisings against Catholics in the 1830's Maréchal's remarks concerning the disappearance of Protestant prejudice were altogether too optimistic.

[4] Nicholas Zocchi (1773–1845), a member of the Fathers of the Faith, a society made up principally of ex-Jesuits, had come to the United States from Canada in 1803.

it is exceedingly difficult to provide for the sustenance of missionaries, even though the people are wealthy in earthly possessions. Whenever a church is to be built or some charitable or pious institution to be erected, each will contribute a few coins to the common fund, but seldom are their gifts exceptionally large. The men live chastely enough, especially after they are once married. Those living in the cities go to the sacraments quite frequently, much oftener in fact than those living in rural areas. The eagerness with which they listen to the divine word is almost unbelievable. Any priest of even mediocre eloquence is certain to attract to himself a multitude of eager listeners in our churches. With regard to the women of my diocese, the purity of the customs of the whites is beyond question. Adultery or fornication are crimes that are seldom, if ever committed in my diocese. Most of them frequently receive Holy Communion. They take great care in adorning themselves and making themselves appear beautiful, although with few exceptions they cultivate Christian modesty. Their clothes are so luxurious that it is difficult to distinguish the daughter of a cobbler from European ladies of rank. Those who are not dutiful eagerly read books of romance and frequent theaters and dances. However they never do so on Sundays. The civil laws forbid it and it is considered the greatest of scandals. Among the women of African descent many indeed serve God faithfully; but there are also many, even among those who are Catholic, who are ignorant of religion and live and die addicted to vice and especially that of impurity.

In the United States of America, there are, besides the Colleges and Universities, many schools of lower rank in which the pupils are taught to read and write, and there is scarcely any American who is not versed in this art. All the books, which are printed in England or France, are publicly sold here in the bookstores. Among these there are innumerable books which teach doctrines that are harmful to faith and good morals. Nor are the civil laws a remedy for this evil. Americans strenuously defend the freedom of the press. Perhaps more gazettes are published daily by the press in the state of Maryland alone, than in Italy and France taken together.

6. In the early and subsequent ages of the Church, nations were converted to Christ by the sweat and labors of missionaries from without. In like manner, the Catholic faith has been introduced into our American Union by the work and zeal of priests from Europe, and they still continue to serve and propagate the faith here. Therefore it is not surprising that the American clergy is made up chiefly of missionaries, who were born in various parts of Europe. For my

part, I will certanly leave nothing undone that will help me build up an entirely native clergy. And yet, no matter to what extent the seminaries at Baltimore and Emmitsburg may flourish now or in the future, or how great the number of novices for the Society of Jesus, which is well established at Georgetown, I can never hope that they will supply me with a sufficiently large number of missionaries, which would be necessary to preserve and extend the faith in this growing country. Placed in these circumstances, we cannot be thankful enough to God, Who has inspired many European priests to cross the ocean, to cultivate the vineyard of the Lord in these regions. American priests, who are acquainted with the customs and characteristics of their fellow citizens, are, however, of all, the most dear to them. They are acquainted with only the necessary ecclesiastical sciences. The reason for this is the fact that before their ordination they can spend only a few years in studying the humanities, letters, and theology, and afterwards they are impeded from further study because of the ever pressing need of their ministry. So they find it difficult to talk on more erudite topics. However those who have a sufficient knowledge of moral and dogmatic theology, combined with true and solid piety, produce most abundant fruits. According to the Americans, English priests are more pleasing to the citizens in these regions, and prove themselves more useful to religion. There are only four English priests in my diocese; of these three came at my suggestion last year. One of these was formerly my pupil in theology in the Seminary of Lyons.[5] When he had heard that I had been promoted to the episcopal dignity, he said farewell to his fatherland that he might live with me, and he also brought with him two friends. One exercises the sacred ministry at Baltimore; another at Richmond, which is the capital city of Virginia; the third is at Alexandria, which is also a town of Virginia; and the fourth is in the missions of Zacchia.[6] Would that I could obtain many more like them, but such is the poverty of the priests in this country, that I have no hopes of being able to bring others into my diocese. From this brief exposition it is easy to conclude, that the Sacred Congregation, in urging me to place English at the head of missions, exhorts me to do that which is altogether impossible. For besides the four aforesaid priests, I have no other, nor can I obtain others. The Belgian, French and

[5] This was James Whitfield (1770–1834) who was to succeed Marechal in 1828 as fourth Archbishop of Baltimore.

[6] The missions of what was then called Upper and Lower Zacchia embraced the area of the present parishes of Waldorf and Bryantown, Maryland.

German priests have shown themselves to be the best of missionaries. They are to be highly commended for their zeal for souls, purity of customs, learning and love of ecclesiastical discipline. Some indeed do not pronounce English perfectly; but they do announce the word of God in a manner that is not displeasing to Americans, notwithstanding the calumnies that have been uttered against them by Doctor Gallagher[7] and his impious faction. Besides it is to be very much regretted that the Sacred Congregation so readily gave ear to the accusations of these enemies of the church of Christ. If there exists any piety, love of religion and especially veneration towards the Holy See in the diocese of Baltimore, it must be referred especially to the example and untiring labors of these missionaries. The Americans love and venerate them. The Irish, who are moved by the spirit of God and imbued with truly ecclesiastical habits, serve religion fruitfully. For they are prompt in their work, speakers of no mean ability, and outstanding in their zeal for souls. Indeed, it gives me great joy that many of this race are in my diocese; I would certainly gladly receive many more like them with open arms. But alas, so many priests who have come hither from Ireland, are addicted to the vice of drunkenness, and I cannot place them in charge of souls until after a mature and thorough examination. For when they have once obtained faculties from us, it is hard to say what harm they would bring down upon the Church of God, if they should fall back into the vice of drunkenness. Nor would there be much of a remedy left to us by which we could put an end to their scandals. For if we should take away their faculties or attempt to do so, they would shake off the yoke completely and trouble the American Church with unbelievable seditions. They can do nothing among the faithful who are Americans, English, or belong to any of the European nationalities. These indeed flee from them. But it is truly surprising how much authority these drunkard priests exercise among the lowest classes of their own race. For since these consider drunkenness only a slight imperfection, they strenuously defend their profligate pastors, associate with them, and enter into and remain with them in schism. That lamentable fact is proved clearly in the history of all the dissensions that have occurred in the Church in North America, since it was established here. It was not the Americans, nor the English, nor

[7] Simon Felix Gallagher had come to the United States from Ireland in 1793 and had been assigned to St. Mary's Church, Charleston, South Carolina, where he became a key figure in the trustee war which ultimately led to a schism in the congregation.

the immigrants who came from other countries in Europe who disturbed or are disturbing the peace at Charleston, Norfolk, Philadelphia, etc., etc.; but it was those priests from Ireland who were given over to drunkenness or ambition, together with their accomplices, whom they win over to their side by means of innumerable artifices. Most recently they tried by means of various writings to persuade these ignorant people that the Bishops of Boston, Bardstown, and myself intended secretly to establish a French hierarchy in these provinces and to expel the Irish priests. They did not hesitate to broadcast this absurd calumny at Rome by means of letters and messengers. But indeed 1. Ten Irish priests received faculties from me and are exercising the sacred ministry in the missions of my diocese. 2. The greatest part of the clergy who are now studying theology in the Seminary in Baltimore, are Irish. Moreover of the fourteen French priests whom I now have here, eight exercise no functions in the missions, but live within the walls of the Seminaries of Baltimore and Emmitsburg. With the exception of the priests of the Society of Jesus, who possess many and very rich estates, all the rest of the missionaries have no other source of income but the pious and voluntary offerings of the faithful and the money which each one of the faithful pays every year for the seat he occupies in the church. Hence they live in the greatest of poverty in the country districts; in the cities, however, their sustenance is much better taken care of. They wear black clothes and in the sacrifice of the Mass they use the cassock, which comes to the ankles; but outside of the church, the vestments they wear are shorter but nevertheless modest. Nor is this surprising, since they live among Protestants and they have to ride on horseback very frequently. All administer the sacraments; every Sunday they preach the divine word. In places where it is possible for the children to gather together, they catechize them thoroughly. As far as I am concerned, I am most poor. Up till now my income has scarcely been sufficient to pay the expenses of the letters, which are sent to me from all sides (postage). I indeed have a right to receive yearly one thousand dollars Mexican; but for certain reasons, which perchance I shall at some time explain to the Sacred Congregation, it is doubtful whether this will ever be paid to me. I do not even have a secretary; and although I am weighed down by the administration of an immense diocese, I hear many confessions, administer the other sacraments, and also preach the divine word. I live in the same house with two priests who have the pastoral care of the metropolitan church and am happily destitute of all the comforts of this world.

7. There is no region in the world, where the Catholic religion can be propagated more quickly or widely and where it exists more securely than in the United States of America. Here there is no danger whatsoever that converts to the faith will suffer persecution or that their churches will be destroyed by the arbitrary command of some tyrant, as often occurs in the Chinese Empire and in the other missions of the Indes. All religious, which recognize Christ as the Saviour of the world, are tolerated here, and the laws of the Republic protect them all and most severely punish those who attempt to disturb the divine worship of any sect. And since religious liberty is the fundamental principle of the American Republic, there is no magistrate from the President to the least official, who can with impunity molest Catholics even in the slightest way. The only danger that blocks the path of our most holy religion, consists in the internal dissensions which divide the faithful against each other. The magistrates do not care about these dissensions. Only offenses which affect public peace and the liberty of the citizens are punished by the civil law. The nations which border our republic profess the Catholic religion. These are Canada, Florida and Mexico. Besides there is a very large number of Catholics in our United States. The Protestants, who constitute the greatest part of the citizens, have almost completely rejected the prejudices under which they formerly labored, and they look upon the Catholic religion with a certain amount of veneration. There is also an immense number of Europeans, who come hither daily, and among them there are many Catholics. It seems that this immigration will not be lessened for a number of years. Since the American republic possesses such an extensive territory, it might easily sustain, by the millions, those who migrate to it, and it is evident that the multitudes, who come to America from Europe, will not be quickly diminished. If the Sacred Congregation ponders over these facts it will perceive clearly that there is no region which offers a wider or more fertile field for apostolic zeal.

However, we do have many difficulties here that must be overcome:

1. *Insufficient number of missionaries.* Young American ladies, who formerly could scarcely refrain from laughing aloud when they heard Europeans telling of nuns living uninterruptedly in monasteries, now embrace the religious life so willingly, that I must needs exercise vigilance lest more than can be cared for be admitted to the monas-

teries which exist in my diocese. But it is an altogether different story with regard to youths embracing the clerical state. Some are deterred by celibacy; others are frightened away by the labors of acquiring a knowledge of the ecclesiastical sciences, for this takes a long time and must be undertaken before ordination; but most of all they are afraid of the poverty which is suffered by missionaries, who exercise the sacred ministry in the country districts. For with a little industry on their part, they can hope to live in comfort, nay even in abundance, if they engage in commerce or agriculture.

2. *Among those who otherwise wish to consecrate themselves to the service of the church, there are many who do not have the necessary funds to pay for the expenses of their own education.* The directors of the Seminaries of Baltimore and Emmitsburg have very limited incomes, and as a result they can receive only a limited number of seminarians free of charge. So until the time that divine Providence supplies me with the means with which to provide for the education of poor clerics, the number of missionaries, necessary to propagate our most holy religion, will not be sufficient.

3. *The schisms which occur very frequently in these regions.* It is of the greatest concern that the Sacred Congregation know accurately their principal cause. It should therefore be noted: — 1. that the American people pursue with a most ardent love the civil liberty which they enjoy. For the principle of civil liberty is paramount with them, so that absolutely all the magistrates, from the highest to the lowest, are elected by popular vote at determined times in the year. Likewise all the Protestant sects, who constitute the greater part of the people, are governed by these same principles, and as a result they elect and dismiss their pastors at will. Catholics in turn, living in their midst, are evidently exposed to the danger of admitting the same principles of ecclesiastical government. Clever and impious priests, who flatter them and appeal to their pride, easily lead them to believe that they also possess the right of choosing their pastors and dismissing them as they please. 2. When the Catholics in some part of my diocese become numerous enough to think that they can build a church, first of all each contributes a few coins to the common fund; and since the amount is seldom sufficient, then they select two or three men, whom they depute as their representatives to solicit contributions in the cities and villages from their fellow citizens, both Catholics and Protestants. When they have once collected enough money, then they buy a large enough tract of land upon which to build a church and priest house and to have a cemetery. However,

when they have once decided to buy this tract, sometimes they hand over to the bishop the title of possession, so that he is the true possessor of this ecclesiastical property and is considered as such by the civil tribunals. But it often happens that the legislators of the province approach and obtain from them the title of possession, upon the condition that they transmit it to four or five Caholic men, who are elected annually by the congregation. In this case, these men are not only the temporal administrators of the temporalities of the church (*marguilliers*) as they are in Europe, but they have possession and are considered the true possessors of all the temporal goods of the church in the eyes of the civil tribunals and they can with impunity exercise over them the same authority as they do over their own homes and lands. However, a schism has never taken place in those churches, of which the bishop holds the civil title; in fact, it is impossible for it to happen there. For if the priest, who is constituted the pastor of this church, is addicted to drunkenness or impurity or other scandalous vices, and will not correct his life, then the bishop, by reason of the title he possesses, can at once remove him, just as any citizen has the right of expelling those who presume to occupy his home against his will. For he could easily obtain an order of eviction from the magistrates. But if the title of possession is in the hands of the temporal administrators (*marguilliers*), then they can easily raise the flag of rebellion against the bishop. If indeed the greater part of them do not fear God and conceive a hatred for their pastor, they will continually remove him from the church, no matter how great the sanctity of his life and customs; besides they deprive the entire Catholic congregation of the use of the church. This is the state of affairs at Norfolk, where the impious Doctor Oliver Fernandez and two Irish drunkards, destitute of all religion, removed from their church a most holy man, the pastor, Mr. Lucas,[8] and all his Catholic fellow citizens. Likewise when a priest is leading a scandalous life and, instead of nourishing, is rather devastating the flock of the Lord by his bad example, if the bishop takes measures against him, or also threatens to punish him, it often happens that the temporal administrators come to his defense with cunning and impious theories, whether by maintaining that the bishop is proceeding unjustly against him, or by declaring that he has appealed to Rome, or by arguing that they, and they alone, have the natural right of selecting and removing their pastors. And if he has once been able to convince them of these

[8] James Lucas, a French-born priest, had been appointed in December, 1815, to serve the congregation at Norfolk, Virginia, by Archbishop Leonard Neale.

wicked principles, then the impious priest, protected by the temporal administrators, publicly withstands the authority of his bishop, calumniates him, sacrilegiously performs his sacred ministry, and lays waste the flock of Christ. Nor do the civil laws of the American republic offer any remedy for this great evil. Over and above, if such a priest is even more brazen and skilled in deceit, he gathers false testimony everywhere from the offscourings of the people. Then he busies himself in strengthening this testimony, by obtaining upon it the seal of Protestant magistrates, who secretly rejoice in the dissensions of this kind among Catholics. After this, having collected money here and there, he sends to Rome a messenger, who knows well how to assume a semblance of piety and to speak in a reverential manner. This was the method of procedure used by Doctor Gallaher and Mr. Browne[9] at Charleston.

In the beginning of organization here, the most illustrious Bishop Carroll, the first bishop of Baltimore, thought that the propagation of the Catholic religion would be furthered if the temporal administrators not only had charge of the administration of church property but also had the title of possession. For a number of years he defended this system.[10] However so many dissensions and schisms resulted from it, that shortly before he died he regretted very much that he had ever permitted it. Bishop Neale, his venerable successor, who was inflamed with the deepest love of God and the Church, after mature deliberation upon the evils resulting from the aforesaid system, fought it with all his strength and constantly opposed it. As far as I am concerned, it seems to me that it could be allowed without danger if the temporal administrators were restricted by means of certain clauses, either in the title of possession itself or in a contract, which they would be obliged to sign at the time of their election, so that they could not abuse the civil right entrusted to them; for example, that a pastor in his sacred functions be altogether independent of them; that if he be guilty or accused of some fault, the case be taken to the bishop and that he be considered innocent as long as the bishop has not condemned him; that they might never remove him from the church on their own private authority, that they might never permit a priest, who had been deprived of jurisdiction, to celebrate

[9] Robert Browne was an Irish-born Augustinian who was the source of considerable difficulty in the trustee troubles of congregations in Georgia and South Carolina in these years.

[10] It would be more accurate to say that Archbishop Carroll had rather tolerated and tried to work along with the lay trustee control of church properties than to say that he had defended it.

mass in a church under their care, nor retain there, against the will of the bishop a priest publicly bound by censures, etc., etc., etc.

8. In my previous letter to the Sacred Congregation, I made the observation that it would give me great joy if the provinces of the two Carolinas, Georgia, and the territory which is called Mississippi, were separated from my diocese. And since it seemed to me, as well as to other prudent and learned men, that under the present circumstances of times and conditions it would not be for the good of religion to erect immediately an episcopal see at Charleston, I humbly begged that a Vicariate Apostolic be established there for a number of years; telling them that I would help them as much as possible in this matter, I besought the Sacred Congregation to please send me the instrument, which when once handed over to a priest, chosen from among those who labor more worthily in the United States of America, he would thereby be constituted the Vicar Apostolic of the above mentioned regions. Most certainly I have never dreamed (as is gratuitously insinuated in a letter which I recently received from the Sacred Congregation) to have or wish to exercise the power of establishing a Vicariate Apostolic. I suggested this means only because it was the very one previously used by the Sacred Congregation with regard to Louisiana when the see of New Orleans was vacant. For it sent such an instrument to my predecessor, Bishop Carroll, who presented it to Bishop DuBourg and in this way he was appointed the Vicar Apostolic of Louisiana.[11] Be that as it may, an event of greatest importance, of which I wrote to the Sacred Congregation, has taken place and it demands that the episcopal see of Charleston be erected without delay. For very recently the American government began to sell at public auction the immense territory which is now called Mississippi. Besides, since the land is exceptionally fertile and most productive, innumerable Americans and Europeans, who come hither daily, are buying these lands and are going thither to cultivate them. Among them there is quite a number of Catholics. Hence the good of religion demands that there be appointed as soon as possible for these southern provinces a bishop, who can sow, foster and cultivate the seed of the Catholic faith in this territory, before the Protestant ministers can disseminate their errors there. Therefore I most humbly and eagerly beseech the Sacred Congregation to obtain from the Holy Father the erection of the episcopal see of Charleston, in South Carolina, and that as soon as possible. I regret

[11] Louis W. V. Dubourg had been appointed apostolic administrator of the Diocese of Louisiana and the Two Floridas in 1812 by Carroll.

that I know of no priest in the United States of America whom I can spontaneously recommend to occupy that see. But it seems certain to me that an English priest would be better suited for fulfilling this important office; nor is there a lack of priests in Great Britain who are outstanding for their piety, zeal, and learning. One of them would be far more acceptable to the people than a Frenchman or an Irishman or one of another nationality. Yet it would be desirable that he know how to speak French, for many inhabitants of the Mississippi territory speak French. He would prove far more useful if he were about forty years of age, since an old man cannot sustain the labors of the missions.

9. Although the most pious Mr. Clorivière[12] would be exceedingly useful to those in Charleston who are sincerely attached to the Catholic religion, and though he has gained for himself the love and veneration of all of these, yet he has been deprived of real power by the numerous calumnies and persecutions arising from the impiety of Mr. Gallaher [*sic*] and some of the Irish seduced by Mr. Gallaher, so that I finally recalled him from that city. Then I sent two outstanding priests of the Society of Jesus, one an American, the other an Irishman. I obtained them from the superior Provincial only after many negotiations. It is impossible for me to say whether these new pastors can bring back peace and some sense of religion to those wicked men. It is true that they retain the name of Catholics but they are most certainly exceedingly dangerous enemies of our holy religion. They possess the same customs, principles, and turbulent passions which imbued those impious men who tried to overthrow the altars of Christ in the abominable French Revolution (*Jacobins*). Even though they send messengers to Rome, they despise the authority of the Sacred Congregation and even of the Supreme Pontiff just as much as mine. To make this clear to the Most Eminent Fathers of the Sacred Congregation I am sending to them a little book, which these men very recently published. It is hard to say whether the impudence of the calumnies referred to are greater than the brazenness of their impiety. Nor can I here pass over the fact that these enemies of the church of Christ, led on by a fanatical spirit, have sent messengers into all the provinces of the American Union to induce all the Irish, whom they know to be given over to impiety and vice, to enter with them into a society, whose purpose is to compell the Holy

[12] Joseph Pierre Picot de Limoëlan de Clorivière (1768–1826), a French-born priest, had been sent to Charleston in 1812 by Carroll to try to heal the schism in St. Mary's Church.

See to enter into an agreement with them, in which they will be granted the right of choosing their bishops and pastors by popular vote. Perhaps it may seem strange to the Sacred Congregation that I have written to them so often about these dangers. But here we are dealing with a matter of the utmost importance. For if these impious men should again deceive the Sacred Congregation whether by threats or by means of false promises, or if it were to give them the least bit of protection, it would do more harm to religion in these regions than the labor of a thousand missionaries could accomplish for it. The vast multitude of faithful American Catholics is horrified at this impious faction, and is surprised that its messengers going to Rome from our shores have any hope of again deceiving the Sacred Congregation of the Propagation of the Faith.

With a few words I will now conclude this very long letter.

During four months I have visited all the missions of Maryland and the principal ones of Virginia, and I administered the sacrament of Confirmation in all the congregations, also taking care of other episcopal duties. It gave me great joy to see our holy religion flourishing everywhere as well as being propagated in a wonderful manner. Since the time of my consecration I have conferred on many the sacrament of Orders, namely:

first tonsure, to eight young men
minor orders 2
subdiaconate 6
diaconate 4
priesthood 4

Just a few days ago I received all the faculties which the Holy Father has kindly granted to me and which the Sacred Congregation has deigned to transmit to me; except, however, the faculty for a few cases of validating the marriage *in radice,* when the consent of both parties could not be renewed without most grave consequences. With regard to the admonition which is found at the bottom of the Baltimore calendar, it was inserted at the order of the most illustrious Bishop of St. Louis. I cannot say upon what authority he based his concession of a dispensation from the laws of fast and abstinence in his diocese at certain times of the year. However, I suspect that those derogations from the law were introduced in the Louisiana diocese because the province has been subject to Spanish rule. The entire matter will be explained better to the Sacred Congregation by the most illustrious Bishop DuBourg himself to whom I wrote very recently.

The Diocese of Philadelphia remains in the same state of widowhood. Last year it was announced that the bulls would be sent without delay, but they were never transmitted here.

This is the account of the status of the Catholic religion in the diocese of Baltimore, which, although very imperfect, I have undertaken to submit to the judgment of the Sacred Congregation. I hope that at some time I may be able to give testimony of my greatest veneration, filial love, and obedience to Their Eminences, for these are the sentiments with which I am imbued towards them all. I again most humbly commend to their kindness and good will my difficulties in the dangers which beset me. In the meanwhile prayers and sacrifices shall not be lacking, that the Pastor of Pastors, Our Lord Jesus Christ, keep you safe for many years to come.

I am, Most Eminent Cardinal,

Your most humble and devoted servant,
✠ Ambrose, Archbishop of Baltimore

68. The Abuse of Lay Trusteeism at Norfolk, Virginia, June–September, 1819

ONE of the most notorious cases of the abuse of lay trusteeism in the early nineteenth century occurred in Norfolk, Virginia, where a group of laymen gained financial control of the church in 1808. For over a decade they dominated the congregation against the pastors appointed by the Archbishop of Baltimore to the point of actual schism and an attempt to set up an independent national church, free from the "French" influence of Baltimore. Not only did the Norfolk trustees repudiate the rightful jurisdiction of the ordinary, but they appealed over his head to Pope Pius VII, the Congregation of Propaganda, the state officials of Virginia, and even to President Jefferson and the Congress. On June 14, 1819, the trustees sent a letter (given first below) to Archbishop Maréchal which affords a sample of the sort of thing with which bishops had to contend during this period. On September 28 of the same year Maréchal signed a pastoral letter to the Norfolk congregation which ran to sixty-three printed pages in which he outlined in detail the history and teaching of the Church on the question of ecclesiastical jurisdiction, and he struck especially at the trustee's pretension to the *jus patronatus* or the right of patronage. Maréchal's pastoral (in the second place below) was termed by Guilday "the historical turning-point in the schismatic movement in America of these years" (p. 123). Sources: Peter Guilday, *The Catholic Church in Virginia, 1815–1822* (New York: United States Catholic Historical Society, 1924), pp. 108–110; *Pastoral Letter of the Archbishop of Baltimore to the Roman Catholicks of Norfolk, Virginia* (Baltimore: J. Robinson, 1819), pp. 1–3, 5, 28–29, 34–38, 40–42, 44.

At a joint meeting of the Trustees of the Roman Catholic Congregation of Norfolk and Portsmouth, convened on the 14th day of June, 1819, to take into consideration a letter directed by the Rev. Archbishop of the Catholic Church of Baltimore, to the Norfolk Pastor, the Reverend Dr. Thomas Carbry,[1] dated on the 8th instant, by which the Reverend Archbishop summons the Right Reverend Pastor to appear before or to send to him the authentic Title, in virtue of which the Right Reverend Dr. Carbry is exercising the functions of Pastor in Norfolk and Portsmouth which said Reverend Archbishop calls his Diocese.

After mature consideration of the contents of the letter aforesaid, the Trustees of the Norfolk and Portsmouth congregations immediately resolved:

First that the Priest James Lucas[2] and the Reverend Archbishop Maréchal, after the resolutions passed by the Trustees of the Roman Catholic Congregation aforesaid on the 4th of Jan., 1817, and 16th of March of last year; being neither their Prelate and Pastor which resolutions were rendered public through the press; and distributed amongst the members of both Congregations, a protest shall be legally intimated to the Reverend Archbishop of the Catholic Church of Baltimore, that himself not being a lawful Prelate of this state, and still less of these congregations he has no right at all to interfere with these congregations or any of their religious matters, whatever. And likewise, with the Right Reverend Pastor thereof duly elected by the Congregation, approved of by His Holiness and communicated to us by his Eminence Cardinal Litta.[3]

Resolved that besides the right inherent in them as Christians and patrons of their churches acknowledged by the Holy See, the impertinence of the demand of the Right Reverend Archbishop of the Catholic Church of Baltimore, being a most glaring violation of their civil right and religious liberties and in direct opposition to the state

[1] Thomas Carbry, an Irish-born Dominican, went to Norfolk from New York in June, 1819, at the invitation of the trustees and assumed charge of the congregation without any authorization from the Archbishop of Baltimore.

[2] James Lucas, a French-born priest, had been appointed to Norfolk in December, 1815, by Archbishop Leonard Neale.

[3] Lorenzo Cardinal Litta, Prefect of Propaganda, with only a meager knowledge of the facts, had made the mistake of receiving one of the trustees at Rome in the summer of 1817 and of writing a letter to Fernandez on September 20, 1817, which gave them hope of attaining their objective of a separate bishopric in Virginia. When he later realized the true nature of the case Litta assured Maréchal on April 1, 1818, that nothing would be done by the Holy See without "the light of your counsel and after mature consideration" (Guilday, *op. cit.*, p. 79).

laws of Virginia, an extract of the same laws, shall be forwarded to him by which he may see, that he has no authority to meddle with the choice of our Pastors or to interfere with the exercise of his sacred functions, resolved that the Reverend Archbishop of the Catholic Church of Baltimore, be reminded of the proceedings in former times, viz:

At Rome in the African church (St. Cyprian, Lib. 2. Ep. 2)
(St. Cyprian, Lib. 1. Ep. 4)
(Conc. Carth; 4th Can. 1)

At Alex., etc., etc. [*sic*].

Likewise of the proceedings, etc., of the Archbishop of Goa towards the Catholics of Bombatin [*sic*] on the coast of Malabar and its results by Lord Minto's decision, the whole published by the House of Commons of July 13th, 1814, as well as of the sentiments of the present Pope, Pius VII, in his Bull to the Archbishop and Bishops of Ireland of the first of February, 1816, acknowledging the right of the people in the election of their Prelates, alledging [*sic*] the authority of his predecessor St. Leo the Great, viz., that no more be ordained Bishops without the consent and postulation of the flock lest an unwelcome intruder incur its contempt and hatred,[4] as it has been unfortunately the case with the Reverend Amb. Maréchall [*sic*] in this and other cities of the different states of the union.

Resolved that should said Reverend Archbishop of the Catholic Church of Baltimore, proceed (which God forbid) to any public act or calumnious deed against either the Reverend Dr. Thomas Carbry or any of the members of the congregation, all his illegal, absurd and impious proceedings, as well as the causes leading to them shall be rendered public through the press and himself held responsible to the laws of the state of Virginia.

Resolved that a copy of these resolutions signed by the President and Secretary of this board, be forwarded to the Reverend Archbishop of the Catholic Church of Baltimore.

[4] In neither Goa nor Ireland had there been a real parallel with the Norfolk situation. The British had declined to recognize the ancient Portuguese right of patronage over Catholic churches in India, and in 1720 the Portuguese clergy had been expelled from the Malabar coast as anti-British. The Portuguese, in turn, refused to relinquish their claim and thus there ensued a long period of strife involving a defiance of the British by the Archbishop of Goa and a double jurisdiction that led to endless confusion. Pius VII's letter of February, 1816, to the hierarchy of Ireland had been concerned with the proposed veto of the British government over the selection of Irish bishops and again had no true relevance in the Norfolk case.

Norfolk, June 14, 1819 and 43d year of the independence of the United States.

Thomas Reilly, President
John F. Oliveira Fernandez,
acting as secretary of the Board of the Roman Catholic Church and Congregation of Norfolk.

Beloved Brethren,

After having enjoyed the consolation of spending several days with you last year, we thought it our duty, as your first Pastor, before we left your city, to address a few words to you from the Altar, on the danger to which some of you might eventually be exposed, of being seduced from the pale of the Holy Church, in which, through the infinite mercy of God, you have been baptized and educated.

It is true, the few individuals who have brought so many calamities on your Congregation, could not hope, by their affected zeal for the cause of religion, to make any considerable impression on the minds of the great majority of you, and much less to induce you to join them in the execution of their desperate scheme. . . . We still recollect, Beloved Brethren, with feelings of admiration and gratitude, the virtuous grief you manifested, when you were informed, that relying on the impossibility of your ever recovering by legal process, the sacred property they have wrested from your hands, they rejected with stern pride, every offer of peace which was tendered to them; and particularly your consternation and tears, at hearing the impious language they employed against the Episcopal Dignity, which their religion commands them to respect, and which the laws of common decency protect from insult in every country of the civilized world. Our Protestant Brethren themselves, whom we had the pleasure of visiting in Norfolk, prompted by the spirit of benevolence and the delicacy of manners which distinguish them, were justly shocked at such excesses.

But although these pretended Catholicks, by their scandalous conduct and virulent language, must naturally have deterred you from adopting their principles and joining their party, yet we could not help apprehending, lest, by the concurrence of many unfortunate causes, some of you might be insensibly drawn over to the schismatical plan they were then meditating, and which they have since put into execution. . . . But in order to guard you, my Beloved Brethren, against their seducing language, it will be sufficient for us to recall to your minds, some of the fundamental principles of your Religion; and with these before you, to fix your attention to undeniable facts which invincibly prove the absolute vanity of their reasonings and prentensions. [Then follows an explanation of Christ's authority to His apostles based on the New Testament, the teaching of the Council of Trent, the distinction between the power of the citizens in a republican government to elect their magistrates and the lack of such power in the Church, the canon law on the right of patronage in the Middle Ages, etc.]

From this slight sketch of Canon law, you readily discover, Dealy [*sic*] Beloved Brethren, how vainly those characters, who have involved your Congregation in confusion and misery, pretend to the right of patronage, and flatter you with it. This right does not exist, and probably never will exist in the United States of America. Because it is contrary to the spirit at least of the constitution and of the laws of the land. For the government of the United States stretches indeed the shield of its protection, over every denomination of christians; but without giving the least preference to any: and surely it would be ridiculous to suppose, that following the example of Catholick powers on the other side of the Atlantic, the United States will ever shew a partiality to us, by any considerable donation to our Church. And as this alone is the groundwork of all the *concordates* between Catholick Powers and the Holy See, and of the consequent right of patronage in the nominations of Bishops, it is manifest that such a Politico-religious treaty can never take place in this country. We are grateful for the protection, which we enjoy under the equal laws of the U. States, in common with the rest of our fellow christians; but we neither wish nor expect any particular favours. . . .

Some sectarians, Dear Brethren, consider their ministers as clerical characters, not by virtue of any spiritual mission derived from the Redeemer of mankind through his Church; but in virtue only of the temporary civil contract entered upon, between them and their respective congregations. Consistently with this principle, it is evident that those who appointed them Pastors, justly dismiss them, whenever their services cease to be acceptable. But the case is very different with the clergy of the Catholick church. When a Bishop appoints a Priest Pastor of a congregation, he presents himself to all its members, under a point of view highly respectable. By the act of his institution, the faithful who are committed to his charge, become immediately and in reality his flock; and he is invested with spiritual powers in their regard, which all the world can neither give nor take away. It becomes his duty to govern, and sanctify by his instructions and example, the faithful entrusted to his pastoral solicitude . . . Enlightened and virtuous

Catholicks do not consider this Clergyman as a hireling, whom they may retain or expel at pleasure, but as an ambassador from Heaven, a minister of the altar, and an Apostle. If the Bishop be bound to impress deeply on his mind, the great obligations and responsibility, which are laid upon him, and the sublime and awful functions he has to perform, surely he is obliged likewise to admonish the Faithful, to respect, love, and obey him. And as he is prevented by his orders from any lucrative secular employment, and bound to devote himself exclusively to God, and to the good of souls, so is it the imperative duty of his flock to provide for his temporal necessities. Is this Apostolic language, Dearly Beloved, a transgression of the laws of Virginia?

In 1786, the General Assembly of that state, in order to establish religious freedom on a broad and permament basis, enacted, that *no man shall be compelled to frequent or support any religious worship, place, or ministry, whatsoever; nor shall be enforced, restrained, molested, or burthened in his body or goods, nor shall he suffer on account of his religious opinions or belief.* Such is one of the fundamental laws of Virginia. Has any Catholick clergyman ever transgressed it? Who is the man, who can say, that his Pastor has compelled him, or attempted to compel him by legal means, to frequent his Church, or support him: Not one. It is true, there is no obligation whatever, imposed upon the citizens, to support any ministers of religion, not even their own Pastors. But because there is no legal obligation of doing it, is there not a moral and religious one? Has a Christian and a Catholick no other duties to fulfil, besides those composed by the law of the land? And is it in a Pastor, a transgression of this law, to exhort his people to a performance of them? If this were a violation of the laws of Virginia, then indeed not only Catholick, but all Protestant ministers are guilty of it; for the habitual and principal subjects of their instructions and labours are to inculcate on the minds of the christian people, the moral and religious duties, proclaimed in the Gospel, on which the civil law is perfectly silent.

After having proceeded so far, and proved that neither the Catholick congregations nor their representatives, have power to elect, institute or dismiss their Pastors, it may naturally be asked whether the right, at least of election, would not prove advantageous to religion in our days?

Relying on the authority of the Catholick Church, Dear Brethren, we may without any fear of error, answer negatively to this question. For the Christians of the present age, are certainly no better than their ancestors who lived a thousand years ago; and if the Church thought it necessary, on account of the perpetual confusion and scandals which took place at these elections, to withdraw the privilege she had granted to the Faithful: can we imagine that the exercise of it would not now be attended with the same bad consequences? However let us suppose this privilege were conceded to the present generation. Who would be the electors? Would every man, who bears the name of Catholick be admitted to give in his vote, whatever may be his impiety and the immorality of his life? Or would the privilege be restrained to those only whose conduct is pious and edifying? Shall the drunkard, the impure, the professed libertine, and he who hardly knows the elements of his religion, and lives in an open transgression of her laws, be allowed to choose the ministers of Jesus Christ, together with the sober, the chaste, the enlightened and regular Catholick who punctually fulfills all the commandments of God and the Church? It is evident that in a matter of a nature so sacred, a discrimination ought to be made; and would not this first and necessary step be obnoxious to insuperable difficulties? Upon whom would the choice most probably fall? Would it fall on the modest and pious clergyman, who spends his days in instructing the poor and the ignorant; in carrying the last consolations of religion to dying christians; in reconciling repenting sinners to the offended Majesty of God in the tribunal of Penance, — who every day in his private oratory and at the altar, raises his pure hands to God, to draw down the blessing of Heaven on his flock — who mounts the pulpit, not to please his auditory and glean from the world the pitiful reward of praise; but to instruct, exhort and move — who consecrates his intervals of leisure, not to idle visits and frivolous conversation; but to meditation and studies suitable to his state of life? The merits of such a clergyman being generally unknown or not sufficiently felt, he would very likely not be elected: and yet *him has the Lord chosen.* The gay and sprightly companion — he who at home spends his time in idleness or frivolous occupations — who, in the societies of worldlings which he habitually frequents, can command their attention by some light accomplishment — who can preach a fashionable discourse, or pronounce a vapid declamation which he probably had not even the slender merit of composing, this man will unite the votes of the multitude. In vain might a few pious and sensible Catholicks raise their voices against his election; they would be drowned in the general clamour. Under such a pastor what would become of the unfortunate congregation? Instead of exhibiting the endearing spectacle of sincere religion and piety, it would soon present disgusting scenes, of irreligion and immorality. . . .

From the principles which we have laid down, Dearly Beloved Brethren, it is evident, that Rev. Thomas Carbry has no jurisdiction whatever among you, in virtue of the choice which the above mentioned writer,[1] and some other laymen have made of him for their Pastor. To cover this defect, and to compose the fear of conscientious Catholicks, it has been industriously circulated, that he has received a *secret* appointment from the Holy See, to the place which he now holds. And as this report is calculated to lead some of you astray, it is important that we should shew you, that it is absolutely unfounded and false. . . .

69. The Inauguration of the *United States Catholic Miscellany* of Charleston, June 5, 1822

THE birth of American Catholic journalism may be dated from the founding of the *United States Catholic Miscellany* by John England (1786–1842), first Bishop of Charleston. Before that there had been the brief issue of the *Michigan Essay or Impartial Observer* in August, 1809, by Gabriel Richard, S.S., in Detroit and a number of Irish papers which were edited by Catholics and contained a considerable amount of Catholic news. But the *Miscellany* was the first American Catholic newspaper properly so called. England had gained valuable experience in journalism during his time on the staff of the Cork *Mercantile Chronicle,* 1812–1817, and as a result his paper not only served admirably in answering the attacks of the nativists, but through its discussions of current problems affecting the Church in all aspects of its life the *Miscellany* was one of the leading agencies of the 1820's and 1830's in making for an informed Catholic opinion. The support England received for his paper was always meager and twice, throughout the year 1823 and again from January-July, 1826, he was compelled to suspend it. But after July, 1826, the *Miscellany* carried on unbrokenly until the disastrous Charleston fire of December, 1861, which destroyed the cathedral, bishop's house, diocesan library, and the office of the paper, put an end to it forever. Source: *United States Catholic Miscellany,* June 5, 1822.

PROSPECTUS

The object of this publication is to supply an apparent want in the United States of North America.

In these states perfect freedom of conscience exists; hence, men of various religions have fled hither as to an asylum from the per-

[1] Maréchal was referring to Dr. John F. Oliveiria Fernandez, secretary of the Board of Trustees of the Norfolk congregation, who had written several pamphlets against the archbishop's authority.

secutions of the dominant sects in other countries. Almost every division of Christians here has its peculiar publication, for the expositions of its doctrines, the communication of facts, and if necessary, the vindication of its tenets. The Roman Catholics of these states form a considerable portion of the citizens; it is natural they should be desirous of having a similar publication for like purposes.

To supply this want, the Miscellany is intended. By its means the thousands of Roman Catholics spread through these states, from Maine to Florida, and from Arkansas to the Atlantic, may hold constant communication; by its means they may also learn the state of their brethren in communion with them in the other quarters of the globe: by its means those persons who have been misled into erroneous opinions of the principles of their neighbors, will be enabled to judge correctly of their tenets, and to form rational opinions of their practices.

The principles of the publication will be candour, moderation, fidelity, charity, and diligence. Not that its conductors presume to attain the perfection of all or any of those qualities; but they will constantly keep them in view.

The topics which it will embrace are,

I. The simple explanation and temperate maintenance of the doctrines of the Roman Catholic Church; in exhibiting which, its conductors are led to hope, that many sensible persons will be astonished at finding they have imputed to Catholics doctrines which the Catholic Church has formally condemned, and imagined they were contradicting Catholics, when they held Catholic doctrine themselves.

II. The examination of history for the purpose of investigating the truth of many assertions which have been, perhaps, too lightly hazarded, and which have obtained too ready and general credence; and which have excited unfounded prejudices in the minds of many well-disposed individuals.

III. The correct statement of occurrences regarding the Catholic religion: for the purpose of better discharging which duty, communications and periodical publications from Rome, Paris, London, Dublin, Canada, South-America, the various parts of the United States, and other portions of the world will be obtained, and are solicited.

IV. Memoirs and anecdotes of the several eminent persons who have distinguished themselves in the Church, or against it, in ancient or modern times.

V. A summary of political events and domestic occurrences.

VI. Occasional reviews of religious publications.

Advertisements wll be received at the usual rates.

THE MISCELLANY will be published in the city of Charleston, S. C. weekly, on a fine sheet of paper, quarto size; containing eight pages of three columns each, so that the numbers may be bound at the end of each year.

All communications to be *post paid* and directed *"To the Editor of The Catholic Miscellany, Charleston, S. C."*

Any person wishing to receive the Paper will please to enclose his subscription, and send it *post paid,* directed as above; and give also the name of the Post Office to which his Paper may be sent.

70. Bishop England's Account of His Address Before Congress, January 29, 1826

IN THE generation after Archbishop Carroll's death the most striking public figure in the American hierarchy was John England (1786–1842), first Bishop of Charleston. This Irish-born prelate engaged actively in newspaper controversies, debates, and public addresses, but his most famous address was the speech which he delivered before Congress on Sunday, January 8, 1826, in which he discoursed for two hours on the principal doctrines of the Catholic faith. On the previous Christmas day he had preached at St. Patrick's Church, Washington, where he took occasion to answer certain charges against the Church which had been made by John Quincy Adams in 1821 when he was Secretary of State. Within a few days England was a dinner guest at the White House where he and President Adams got on in a friendly fashion and when the bishop made his appearance before Congress, Adams was there to hear him. Three weeks after the speech England wrote his impressions of the affair to William Gaston (1778–1844), the most prominent Catholic layman of North Carolina, who in 1833 was appointed associate justice of the state's supreme court where he served with distinction until his death. Source: *Records of the American Catholic Historical Society of Philadelphia,* XIX (1908), 104–106.

Fayetteville (N.C.), Jan'y 29, 1826.

My Dear Friend:

I posted a letter for you, directed to Newbern, to inform you that I was not at present sufficiently master of my own movements to delay in this State longer than until next Monday morning, when I intend leaving this place for Georgetown & Charleston, — a variety of pressing business calls me to headquarters as soon as possible. I hope to return speedily & to see you in Newbern.

I directed the publisher of the sketch of what I preached at the

Capitol to send to you & to my friend Judge Taylor[1] copies from me. You will find only what you have often heard from myself, but I thought you would like to see in print what would bear better to be heard than to be read. Perhaps I might have been the humble instrument of removing some prejudices. If so, I am more than repaid.

Without seeking for the occasion, or feeling myself upon the topics until I had gone too far to recede, & then, & only then, my eyes rested upon Mr. Adams, I on Christmas day met foot to foot the 4th of July oration in which he so unkindly assailed us four years since. I then as cooly & as firmly as I could did my utmost, & I am told by many, with sufficient success. The next Wednesday I was at his levee, where I was received in a very flattering manner, & upon my arrival at home found a card for dinner on the succeeding Saturday. We had much conversation upon several topics, & a little about yourself, in which he appeared to think it news that you were a Popish churchwarden.

On the day I filled the Speaker's chair I was indeed a show, & all Washington must have thought so, for the throng was so great that the President found it very difficult to get in, & when in, much more so to get a seat. Upon my arrival, nearly half an hour after, I found vast numbers returning without a hope of getting upstairs, so as even to see in, — & for once I must own I felt ashamed at hearing my own name proclaimed by my friends Haynes[2] & Hamilton[3] of S.C. who formed my bodyguard, whilst in all the pomp of Prelacy I struggled through and heard the proclamation renewed still to make way for me to enter. If I could blush, I am convinced I then did, because I had some unusual sensation of heart and some unwonted glow *in* my cheek & *in* my forehead. When I was done I certainly felt a very extraordinary gratification at the intense attention with which I was heard, & that every face seemed to say "go on." But I thought two hours enough for them & for me, — I made the sign of the cross, & my gratification was indeed increased by the vast & respectable portion of the assembly that exhibited its faith. You will, perhaps, smile at my saying that even elevated as I was, I could not forget that I once was an

---

[1] John L. Taylor (1769–1829), Chief Justice of the Supreme Court of North Carolina, was married to Gaston's sister, Jane.

[2] Charles Eaton Haynes (1784–1841) was a representative in Congress from Georgia, 1825–1831; 1835–1839.

[3] James Hamilton (1786–1857) was a representative in Congress from South Carolina and later governor of the state.

insignificant being, & I vouchsafed to come down from my seat to recognize the President of the U.S. & converse a little with him.

Do not think me vain or childish in this; I know you would wish to learn, even if you did not care for the individual, what was the first appearance of a Catholic clergyman before the legislature of the union, & I would not write thus to another.

I love your countrymen more as I know them better. They are a well-disposed, religiously-inclined people; there is but one true Church, & that is the Roman Catholic; but how can they believe without evidence? — they have never received it. They must be instructed, not abused. They must be expostulated with, not quarrelled with. They are not obstinate heretics — they are an enquiring, thinking, reasoning, well-disposed, I will add, a pious people, — & God will bless them & bring them to truth. I every day see abundant evidence to support me in this position, & to some of your apparently accidental remarks I owe much of the reflection which has led me to know how to appreciate their character & to aid in removing their prejudices. I hope long to profit by many more of them & for many years of more frequent intercourse.

My sister joins with me in affectionate respects to your sister, to the Judge & all the family.

Yours sincerely,

✠ John, Bishop of Charleston.

71. The Cholera Epidemic in the Diocese of Mobile, November 10, 1832

ONE of the greatest scourges in the history of American medicine struck the United States in 1832 in the form of Asiatic cholera. The losses suffered by the Catholic Church were exceedingly heavy, and among the many deaths of priests, religious, and laity which occurred during those terrible months were two notable churchmen of the Middle West who died within a few days of each other, Gabriel Richard, the heroic Sulpician missionary of the Detroit area, who succumbed on September 13, and Edward D. Fenwick, O.P. (1768–1832), first Bishop of Cincinnati, who died on September 26 at Wooster, Ohio, in the course of a diocesan visitation. All parts of the country felt the consequences of the epidemic, and in the South the effects were especially grievous. At the time the French-born priest, Mathias Loras (1792–1858), was vicar-general of the Diocese of Mobile, and in a letter to his mother in France he described the conditions in southern Alabama. Source: *Acta et Dicta,* V (July, 1917), 113–114.

College of Spring Hill, November 10, 1832.

My dear Mother:

Your dear letter, the second which you kindly sent me, came to me happily on October 28th; that of Madame Tallon of July 19th arrived on September 18th; that of Emile of May 31st, which enclosed another from Marie Richard and a "P.S." from dear Fleury, just about two months later, are also in my hands. All these writers may be sure that they have given me great pleasure and if I do not answer directly this time it is according to the words of Jesus Christ, "Do you not know that I must concern myself directly with the glory of my Father?" Will you therefore act as intermediary between me and them?

You have written about the cholera in Paris and in the Provinces. It is a small matter, compared to the terrible ravages which this disease is working in New Orleans. Here it is combined with yellow fever, small-pox and so forth. The disease broke out in New Orleans on October 24th and has brought to the grave daily nearly 200 persons. The terror is at its height; the dead are buried clothed as they are and pell-mell; it is hard to find negroes who are willing to do this work. The people of Mobile are in a state of consternation.

This plague will certainly visit us also. Our pupils are likewise filled with fear. Some of them have left the college. We who are here place ourselves in the kind hands of Divine Providence. As for me, my dear mother, I am perfectly calm; my greatest trouble is to see that this great warning which Heaven sends to us all does not make more impression upon sinners and heretics. This shows that faith is dead in their hearts, if indeed it was ever there. Nevertheless we redouble our efforts and our prayers that this fatal veil of blindness may at last be lifted. I should be only too happy to die in aiding these unfortunate people. I shall write to M. Miolland[1] after some time; he will be able to tell you what the state of affairs is here. . . .

We are seriously considering the foundation here of a community of Sisters of the Visitation for the education of girls.[2] This is one of the things which I beg to see before I die. The first is the college,

---

[1] Jean Marie Miolland was superior of the diocesan missionary band of Lyons when Loras joined it in 1827; he was Bishop of Amiens, 1838–1849, and Archbishop of Toulouse until his death in 1859.

[2] A small group of nuns from the Visitation Convent at Georgetown, D. C., arrived in Mobile in late December, 1832, to open Georgetown's first daughter house.

which exists and is flourishing;[3] the second is the establishment of several parishes in this diocese; the fourth will be to see you once more, my good, dear mother; then I shall say my "Nunc dimittis."

Excuse my brevity; you yourself suggested to me that I might be brief; and believe that nothing will ever be able to change the sentiments of most filial attachment of

Your most devoted son,
M. Loras.

P.S. We are perfectly well. Give my sincerest regards, I pray you, to all my dear brothers and sisters and my respects to my dear cousin, etc.

[3] Loras had been the founder and first president of Spring Hill College near Mobile which had its formal opening in July, 1830, with fifty students and a faculty of six professors.

72. De Tocqueville on American Catholics in Relation to Democracy, 1835

A RECENT writer has declared Alexis de Tocqueville (1805–1859) to have been "the best friend democracy ever has had, and democracy's most candid and judicious critic" (Russell Kirk, *The Conservative Mind* [Chicago, 1953], p. 179). In May, 1831, De Tocqueville arrived in the United States for a tour of investigation of the prison system. He remained in the country until February, 1832, and when the first volume of his celebrated work, *De la démocratie en Amérique,* appeared in 1835 it became obvious at once what a thorough study he had made of the American political system as well as of social institutions and customs. His observations concerning the religious beliefs of Catholics and their relation to democracy as a form of government were far different from those of most contemporary American Protestants, but the century that has passed since their publication has produced nothing that would destroy their general validity. Source: Alexis de Tocqueville, *Democracy in America,* edited by Phillips Bradley (New York: Alfred A. Knopf, Inc., 1945), I, 300–302; II, 26–30; paper-back edition by Vintage Books, Inc.

About fifty years ago Ireland began to pour a Catholic population into the United States; and on their part, the Catholics of America made proselytes, so that, at the present moment more than a million Christians professing the truths of the Church of Rome are to found in the Union.[1] These Catholics are faithful to the observances of their religion; they are fervent and zealous in the belief of their doctrines. Yet they constitute the most republican and the most democratic class

[1] De Tocqueville was in error on the number of Catholics in the United States in 1831; the best estimate for the year 1830 was 318,000.

in the United States. This fact may surprise the observer at first, but the cause of it may easily be discovered upon reflection.

I think that the Catholic religion has erroneously been regarded as the natural enemy of democracy. Among the various sects of Christians, Catholicism seems to me, on the contrary, to be one of the most favorable to equality of condition among men. In the Catholic Church the religious community is composed of only two elements; the priest and the people. The priest alone rises above the rank of his flock, and all below him are equal.

On doctrinal points the Catholic faith places all human capacities upon the same level; it subjects the wise and ignorant, the man of genius and the vulgar crowd, to the details of the same creed; it imposes the same observances upon the rich and the needy, it inflicts the same austerities upon the strong and the weak; it listens to no compromise with mortal man, but, reducing all the human race to the same standard, it confounds all the distinctions of society at the foot of the same altar, even as they are confounded in the sight of God. If Catholicism predisposes the faithful to obedience, it certainly does not prepare them for inequality; but the contrary may be said of Protestantism, which generally tends to make men independent more than to render them equal. Catholicism is like an absolute monarchy; if the sovereign be removed, all the other classes of society are more equal than in republics.

It has not infrequently occurred that the Catholic priest has left the service of the altar to mix with the governing powers of society and to take his place among the civil ranks of men. This religious influence has sometimes been used to secure the duration of that political state of things to which he belonged. Thus we have seen Catholics taking the side of aristocracy from a religious motive. But no sooner is the priesthood entirely separated from the government, as is the case in the United States, than it is found that no class of men is more naturally disposed than the Catholics to transfer the doctrine of the equality of condition into the political world.

If, then, the Catholic citizens of the United States are not forcibly led by the nature of their tenets to adopt democratic and republican principles, at least they are not necessarily opposed to them; and their social position, as well as their limited number, obliges them to adopt these opinions. Most of the Catholics are poor, and they have no chance of taking a part in the government unless it is open to all the citizens. They constitute a minority, and all rights must be respected in order to ensure to them the free exercise of their own privileges. These two causes induce them, even unconsciously, to adopt political doctrines which they would perhaps support with less zeal if they were rich and preponderant.

The Catholic clergy of the United States have never attempted to oppose this political tendency; but they seek rather to justify it. The Catholic priests in America have divided the intellectual world into two parts: in the one they place the doctrines of revealed religion, which they assent to without discussion; in the other they leave those political truths which they believe the Deity has left open to free inquiry. Thus the Catholics of the United States are at the same time the most submissive believers and the most independent citizens. . . .

I showed in the first Part of this work how the American clergy stand aloof from secular affairs. This is the most obvious but not the only example of their self-restraint. In America religion is a distinct sphere, in which the priest is sovereign, but out of which he takes care never to go. Within its limits he is master of the mind; beyond them he leaves men to themselves and surrenders them to the independence and instability that belong to their nature and their age. I have seen no country in which Christianity is clothed with fewer forms, figures, and observances than in the United States, or where it presents more distinct, simple, and general notions to the mind. Although the Christians of America are divided into a multitude of sects, they all look upon their religion in the same light. This applies to Roman Catholicism as well as to other forms of belief. There are no Roman Catholic priests who show less taste for the minute individual observances, for extraordinary or peculiar means of salvation, or who cling more to the spirit and less to the letter of the law than the Roman Catholic priests of the United States. Nowhere is that doctrine of the church which prohibits the worship reserved to God alone from being offered to the saints more clearly inculcated or more generally followed. Yet the Roman Catholics of America are very submissive and very sincere. . . .

America is the most democratic country in the world, and it is at the same time (according to reports worthy of belief) the country in which the Roman Catholic religion makes most progress. At first sight this is surprising.

Two things must here be accurately distinguished: equality makes men want to form their own opinions; but, on the other hand, it imbues them with the taste and the idea of unity, simplicity, and impartiality in the power that governs society. Men living in democratic times are therefore very prone to shake off all religious authority; but if they consent to subject themselves to any authority of this kind, they choose at least that it should be single and uniform. Religious powers not radiating from a common center are naturally repugnant to their minds; and they almost as readily conceive that there should be no religion as that there should be several.

At the present time, more than in any preceding age, Roman Catholics are seen to lapse into infidelity, and Protestants to be converted to Roman Catholicism. If you consider Catholicism within its own organization, it seems to be losing; if you consider it from outside, it seems to be gaining. Nor is this difficult to explain. The men of our days are naturally little disposed to believe; but as soon as they have any religion, they immediately find in themselves a latent instinct that urges them unconsciously towards Catholicism. Many of the doctrines and practices of the Roman Catholic Church astonish them, but they feel a secret admiration for its discipline, and its great unity attracts them. If Catholicism could at length withdraw itself from the political animosities to which it has given rise, I have hardly any doubt but that the same spirit of the age which appears to be so opposed to it would become so favorable as to admit of its great and sudden advancement.

One of the most ordinary weaknesses of the human intellect is to seek to reconcile contrary principles and to purchase peace at the expense of logic. Thus there have ever been and will ever be men who, after having submitted some portion of their religious belief to the principle of authority, will seek to exempt several other parts of their faith from it and to keep their minds floating at random between liberty and obedience. But I am inclined to believe that the number of these thinkers will be less in democratic than in other ages, and that our posterity will tend more and more to a division into only two parts, some relinquishing Christianity entirely and others returning to the Church of Rome.

73. Mathew Carey Explains How He Came to Write the *Olive Branch,* March 13, 1835

THE administrations of Jefferson and Madison marked one of the most exciting and vituperative periods in American political history. Americans were not only sharply divided between Jefferson's Republicans and the Federalists of Hamiltonian persuasion, but they likewise took violent sides between Britain and France whose renewal of war in May, 1803, ushered in over a decade of international conflict that had disastrous results for American commerce and finally led to the declaration of war on England in June, 1812. In all of this no citizen took a more lively interest than the Irish-born Mathew Carey (1760–1839) of Philadelphia who had fled Ireland in September, 1784, disguised as a woman to escape arrest for the attacks he had written in his *Volunteer's Journal* of Dublin against the government of William Pitt. Carey was a versatile fellow whose activities included a publishing business that made him the leading publisher of the nation in the first years of the nineteenth century, the founder of the Hibernian Society for relief of Irish immigrants, a director of the United States Bank, and a charter member of the Philadelphia Society for the Promotion of National Industry, for which he wrote a series of addresses that economists recognize as the classic American argument in behalf of the protective system. Moreover, Carey was a devout Catholic and the father of nine children, the oldest of whom, Henry C. Carey (1793–1879), became by the mid-century the acknowledged leader of the only American group that can lay claim to being a distinct school of political economy. The elder Carey went astray for a brief time in the lay-trustee troubles of St. Mary's Church, Philadelphia, but he soon righted his course and became a stanch defender of episcopal authority and a forthright contender for Catholic civil liberties as well. One of his most famous works was the *Olive Branch,* published in 1814, with a view to bringing peace between the embittered Federalists and Republicans. When Andrew Jackson had read the gift copy sent to him by Carey he told the latter that the book, "by unveiling the eyes of many who have been long hoodwinked by the misrepresentations of folly and falsehood, must have a most salutary effect in allaying that factious spirit which threatens so much evil to our happy government" (Jackson to Carey, Nashville, August 28, 1815, "Selections from the Correspondence of Mathew Carey," *Records of the American Catholic Historical Society of Philadelphia,* XI [1900], 347). The editor of the *New England Magazine* induced Carey to write his autobiography which was published in a series of letters in that journal (V–VII [July, 1833–December, 1834]). He explained that his aim in writing was to show an example of how a man who for years had been on the brink of bankruptcy had escaped through unflinching perseverance and industry, and of how such a man is offered an abundance of aid from others when success seems assured, although the same persons had withheld it when it was really needed. To Carey's main objectives in writing, he confessed he should add, "perhaps, a spice of vanity, from which no human being is wholly exempt" (p. 115). In the letter that follows Carey described how he came to write the *Olive Branch* and the success with which it was greeted. Source: *Mathew Carey. Autobiography* (reprint) (Brooklyn: Eugene L. Schwabb, 1942), pp. 118–122.

The publication of the Olive Branch was one of the most important incidents of my life. I proceed to state the circumstances that led to it, and the extraordinary success that attended the work.

The lawless and outrageous depredations on our commerce, by the belligerents, most of which, under pretexts the most fallacious, violated every principle of honor, honesty, justice and international law, had divided the people of the United States into two hostile parties, by which, as is the case in times of faction in all countries, the solid interests of the nation were often in some degree lost sight of.

It was on the one side asserted that Mr. Jefferson, and the administration generally, were in the interests and in the pay of the French Government — and this was as firmly believed by the mass of the party whose leaders had promulgated the idea, as if it had been judicially proved.

On the other side it was confidently asserted, and as implicitly believed, that the opposition was so blindly devoted to the interests of Great Britain, that they were ready to sacrifice those of their own country in her favour.

It is not my intention to enter into any discussion of the causes that led to the formation of those opinions, nor to the pleas on which they were grounded or defended — that would be, *renovare infandum dolorem.* It is sufficient for my purpose simply to state the facts — and that a most formidable and menacing excitement existed among our citizens.

I had watched for years the progress of this excitement in New England with the most intense anxiety. It foreboded, in my estimation, civil war and all its horrors. That we were on the verge of it can scarcely at this moment be doubted by those who have a perfect recollection of the perturbed state of the public mind at that period. I had written to Mr. Madison, between the time of his inauguration and November, 1814, at least a dozen letters, expatiating at length on the deplorable circumstances of the country, and urging him to adopt some measures to allay the popular ferment. Among the means I suggested, one was, to establish a Washington Union Society. A constitution, prepared for the purpose, is to be seen at the commencement of some editions of the Olive Branch. He objected to have any agency in the affair, on the ground that it would be improper for him, the first executive officer in the nation, to interfere in such a scheme. In the force of his reasoning I could never agree.

In the month of September, 1814, in a moment of ardent zeal and enthusiasm, I was seized with a desire of making an effort, by a candid publication of the numerous errors and follies on both sides, (to call them by no stronger names,) to allay the public effervescence and calm the embittered feelings of the parties. The idea was truly Quixotic, which nothing but the excited state of my feelings could have suggested.

I accordingly commenced about the 8th of September, and made some progress. A part of the plan was a proposition, that, for the sake of peace, and to concentrate the energies of the country, some leading federalists should be brought into the administration, or even that a total change should be made. This was in a moment of deep despondency. I thought it better to submit to such a bitter pill, than have the country torn in pieces, as appeared probable, or to lie at the mercy of a foreign enemy. I wrote twelve or fourteen pages of this tenor. To judge of this extraordinary proposition, it is necessary to reflect on the appalling state of affairs at that period, when, at home or abroad, nothing was to be discerned but the most awful prospects. It was after the shameful defeat at Bladensburg, and the Vandalic conflagration at Washington.[1] The stoutest hearts felt qualms, and were lost in suspense as to the fearful result of such an awful state of things. Those were really "times that tried men's souls." I attempt neither to palliate or justify my daring proposition. I simply state facts. But great as was my despondency, I felt dissatisfied with what I had written — tore the pages — and, for some days, relinquished the idea of pursuing the subject.

Meanwhile three events occurred, admirably calculated to raise the spirits of our citizens generally, viz; the victory of Commodore Mc-Donough [*sic*] the defeat of Prevost at Plattsburg,[2] and that of Ross in his attempt on Baltimore.[3] These exhilarating circumstances dispelled the gloom of the public mind; removed the despondence by which I had been borne down; and, on the 18th of September I commenced anew, on a different plan, abandoning the presumptuous and inadmissible idea of suggesting any change in the administration; in a word, on the plan pursued in the Olive Branch as it now stands.

But it does not require much study of human nature to know, that zeal is a quality remarkably subject to ebbs and flows; and that the higher the flow, the lower the ebb. This, at all events, I experienced.

---

[1] The defeat of the Americans at Bladensburg, Maryland, occurred on August 24, 1814, and Washington was occupied by the British immediately thereafter.

[2] Captain Thomas Macdonough's victory on Lake Champlain took place on September 11, 1814, and compelled Sir George Prevost's army to retreat from Plattsburg back to Canada.

[3] The unsuccessful attack on Baltimore led by General Robert Ross took place on September 12–14, 1814.

When the work was about two-thirds printed, my ardor began to ebb, and I was struck with dismay at the presumption of supposing, that a man in private life, wholly without influence, unsupported by party or by family connexions, could calm the raging waves of faction which threatened shipwreck to the vessel of state. At this moment, although the work, as I have said, was two-thirds printed, I felt half resolved to suppress it, and make waste paper of what was done.

This ague fit continued a few days, but was succeeded by a feverish excitement, which continued long enough to enable me to finish the work. It was begun, as I have stated, on the 18th of September; finished at press about the 6th of November; and published on the 8th; that is to say, it occupied the leisure time of six or seven weeks.

This rapid movement will appear marvellous to the reader. But the wonder will be dispelled when I state the facts of the case. The work is printed in 12mo., large type, (except public documents and other quotations) containing only 252 rather small pages, of which about 80 are public documents, which one of my daughters copied for me: so that my share of the work was only 172 pages. Moreover, as for years I had my mind engrossed by the subject, it was almost as familiar to me as the *ut re mi* of the gamut is to a practised musician. In truth, with the advantages I possessed, I might have completed it in one week, had I applied as closely to it as I have done on other occasions. It cost little more time than the mere transcription would have done.

The edition consisted of 500 copies. The reason why I published so small a number were, partly because political books or pamphlets have generally a very limited circulation, rarely ever defraying cost — and partly because, presuming that it must be imperfect, from the rapidity of its execution. I was desirous of having an opportunity of correcting it in a future edition, should one be required.

The edition was sold out in a few weeks. I sent to Washington to ascertain the success of some that had been sent there, and to order those unsold to be returned. It appeared that only *thirty-seven* copies had been sold! There were there, at that time, about 200 legislators — a number of foreign ministers — and probably two or three hundred visiters [*sic*]. That among such a number of persons, so few should have been sold, a book on such absorbing subjects, whatever might be its demerits, displays a degree of apathy not often exceeded. It was not because the work was unknown; as I had sent a few copies by the mail to members, and others, some of whom particularly Elbridge Gerry[4] and the Secretary of the Treasury, Richard Rush,[5] had written me respecting it, in encomiastic terms.

I was preparing for a new edition, when the thrice-welcome news of peace arrived — which, I thought, would render a new edition unnecessary. I was much mistaken. The demand increased daily, and I need not say that I had every motive to induce me to supply it. I used such diligence, that the second edition, of 1000 copies, was published on the 4th of January 1815, in less than two months from the appearance of the first.

This edition was greatly enlarged. . . . The demand increased, instead of diminishing. I went on adding to the quantity of matter, and published another edition of 1000 copies. This edition was in two volumes, containing 516 pages. It was published on the 10th of April 1815, in a little more than two months from the appearance of the second, and about four from that of the first.

Having reason to believe that the book was doing much good, in allaying the spirit of party, the object for which it was written — desirous to extend that beneficent result as far as possible — and being utterly regardless of pecuniary interests, so far as this work was concerned, I offered the privilege of the republication to at least eight or ten printers and booksellers. . . . *I did not require nor receive a cent for copyright.* May I not ask, is not this a case of rare occurrence? The book was at that time in high favor with a large portion of the community — in demand with both sides of the question — and bid fair to be lucrative to every man who republished it. Of course I might with propriety, according to the general practice of writers, have required payment for the privilege of reprinting it. But had I adopted this course it would have limited the circulation of the work, and so far defeated the great object I had in view. . . .

The sixth edition was published September 6, 1815; the seventh, December 20, same year; the eighth in the same month of 1816; the ninth July 9th, 1817, and the tenth, June 1818.

Thus in three years and a half it went through ten editions. The whole number sold was about 10,000 copies, a greater sale probably than any *book* ever had in this country, except some religious ones.

Various attempts were made to depreciate the work. It was asserted

[4] Elbridge Gerry (1744–1814) of Massachusetts was Vice-President of the United States at the time.

[5] Richard Rush (1780–1859) of Pennsylvania was Attorney General, not Secretary of the Treasury, in Madison's cabinet. He was later Secretary of State under Monroe.

by an influential federal printer, in New York, that he had positive proof that I had not written a line of it — that it was the production of an elevated character, who was understood to be Oliver Wolcott[6] — others asserted that there were false titles printed — that I had them prepared to suit my purpose. . . . One person, a New York bookseller, said that he supposed I kept a set of title pages to insert at pleasure; that it reminded him of a soldier who had but two shirts, and numbered them No. 19 and 20.

As this ridiculous assertion was calculated to throw doubt on my character for candor, I deemed it of sufficient importance to submit the ten editions to four respectable citizens, the Rev. James Abercrombie, D.D., Messrs. Thomas Dobson, W. W. Woodward, and A. Small, who, after due examination, testified that there was

> "Such a total difference in the arrangement of the matter, the size of the pages and types, and more particularly in the number of pages contained in them, as *to convince the most superficial observer that they were bona fide different editions.*"

This difference arose from the fact that I had not allowed any edition to go to press after the first, without making additions, alterations and improvements; as I was determined to spare neither pains nor expense to have the work as complete as was compatible with human imperfection.

M. Carey.

Philadelphia, March 13, 1835.

74. William Gaston Pleads for Complete Religious Freedom in North Carolina, June 30, 1835

ONE of the most distinguished Catholic statesmen of the early nineteenth century was William Gaston (1778–1844). He was the first student to enroll in Georgetown College when it opened in September, 1791, and in 1796 he graduated from the College of New Jersey (Princeton) with the highest honors in his class. Gaston was a Federalist in politics and he served in both the state legislature and in Congress for two terms, 1813–1817. When a vacancy occurred on the Supreme Court of North Carolina in 1832 at a time when that bench was in very low repute, Gaston was named, in spite of an article in the state constitution which forbade any person to

[6] Oliver Wolcott, Jr. (1760–1833), of Connecticut had been Secretary of the Treasury in Washington's cabinet and was president of the Bank of America in New York up to April, 1814, when he was dismissed in what he regarded as a political plot. The incident turned Wolcott from a loyal Federalist into a man of "war hawk" mentality.

be appointed to a civil office who denied the truth of the Protestant religion. Eminent lawyers, both within and without the state, including John Marshall (1755–1835), gave it as their judgment that the article in question did not bar Gaston and he was, therefore, elected by the general assembly in 1833. One of his most notable services was performed in the constitutional convention of 1835 where he made an impassioned plea to have the article on religious qualifications for office holding deleted entirely. Gaston failed of his objective but he scored, nonetheless, a real triumph in having the final draft of the controverted article substitute the word "Christian" in place of "Protestant" in the revised constitution of North Carolina. Following are excerpts from the lengthy speech which Gaston made in the convention. Source: *Proceeding and Debates of the Convention of North-Carolina, Called to Amend the Constitution of the State, Which Assembled at Raleigh, June 4, 1835* (Raleigh: Joseph Gales and Son, 1836), pp. 264–265, 283–285, 292.

Mr. Chairman — The peculiar situation in which I am known to stand with respect to the question now under consideration, and the character of the debate which has already taken place upon it, may be thought to render it indelicate in me to interfere at all in the discussion. But no considerations of delicacy ought to deter me from the full and faithful performance of my duties as a Delegate of the People of this Convention. Besides, silence is likely to subject me to much greater misconstruction than the most frank and fearless exposition of my opinions. At all events, the latter is the course to which I am prompted by inclination as well as by a sense of propriety, and therefore is it, that I must ask the patient and kind attention of this Committee. . . . I am not, indeed, aware that any one decent citizen of the State has called in question the purity of my motives or questioned the propriety of my conduct, or has expressed dissatisfaction at my course. But this is an age of detraction. Calumnies are the ordinary weapons of warfare with religious as well as political factions; and if I have not yet been assailed by slander on this subject, it is not unlikely that I soon shall be. This explanation is therefore due, not only to my character, but to the character of the State, whose honor is always involved in the fair fame of her sons. [Gaston then entered upon a detailed explanation of how he came to accept appointment to the Supreme Court of North Carolina in 1833 in view of the controverted article thirty-two of the state constitution barring those who denied the truth of the Protestant religion.]

Prejudice and cupidity are formidable foes, and will no doubt oppose an obstinate resistance to every effort which may be made to dislodge them from their hold. But we should be false to this people, if we distrusted their ability to decide correctly on this question. Lay it *fairly* before them, and no man need doubt the issue. The question is, ought there to be any Religious test in the Constitution? Shall any man be debarred from office, merely because of his *opinions* on matters of Religion? To me it seems, if there can be any certainty in moral or political science, the answer must be in the negative. It is an invasion of the right of the people to select those whom they deem worthy of confidence, and a violation of the right of the citizen to acquire the confidence of his fellow men, and to enjoy the rewards which they wish to bestow on his intelligence, industry, patriotism and virtue. In those governments which undertake to prescribe a religious faith to their subjects, and command its profession as a part of civil duty, there is at least a congruity in visiting disobedience by appropriate penalties. Incapacitation for office is *there* a punishment for disloyalty — and if it be supposed not adequate to its end, it is followed up by imprisonment, fine, confiscation, exile, torture and death. The *principle* is the same in all these grades of punishment. It is a visitation of the vengeance of the State upon those who offend against its institutions. But where a State is avowedly based on Religious Freedom, where it proclaims that every man has from nature a right, which he cannot surrender, and which none may take away — a "natural and unalienable right" to worship Almighty God according to the dictates of *his own conscience* — a right, of the correct exercise of which, his conscience is the sole judge — how can that State, without a violation of first principles, punish him by degradation because of the exercise of that very right? To this question, an answer is attempted to be given; and if the indefensible character of the cause did not forbid all wonder at any sophism that might be pressed into its defence, I should find it difficult either to restrain, or fitly to express my surprise at the nature of the pretended answer. It is very gravely said, that no man has any natural right to office, and therefore, the refusal of an office to him cannot be a punishment. . . .

Sir, I am opposed, out and out, to any interference of the State with the *opinions* of its citizens, and more especially with their opinion on Religious subjects. The good order of society requires that *actions* and *practices* injurious to the public peace and public morality, should be restrained, and but a moderate portion of practical good sense is required to enable the proper authorities to decide what conduct is really thus injurious. But to decide on the truth or error, on the salutary or pernicious consequences of *opinions,* requires a skill in dialectics, a keenness of discernment, a forecast and comprehension of mind, and above all, an exemption from bias, which do not ordinarily belong to human tribunals. The preconceived opinions of him, who is appointed to try, become the standard by which the opinions of others are measured, and as these correspond with, or differ from his own, they are pronounced true or false, salutary or pernicious. . . . Law is the proper judge of *action,* and reward or punishment its proper sanction. Reason is the proper umpire of *opinion,* and argument and discussion its only fit advocates. To denounce opinions by law is as silly, and unfortunately much more tyrannical, as it would be, to punish crime by logic. Laws [*sic*] calls out the force of the community to compel obedience to its mandates. To operate an opinion by law, is to enslave the intellect and oppress the soul — to reverse the order of nature, and make reason subservient to force. But of all the attempts to arrogate unjust dominion, none is so pernicious as the efforts of tyrannical men to rule over the human conscience. Religion is exclusively an affair between man and his God. If there be any subject upon which the interference of human power is more forbidden, than on all others, it is on Religion. Born of Faith — nurtured by Hope — invigorated by Charity — looking for its rewards in a world beyond the grave — it is of Heaven, heavenly. The evidence upon which it is founded, and the sanctions by which it is upheld, are addressed solely to the understanding and the purified affections. Even He, from whom cometh every pure and perfect gift, and to whom Religion is directed as its author, its end, and its exceedingly great reward, imposes no coercion on his children. They believe, or doubt, or reject, according to the impression which the testimony of revealed truth makes upon their minds. He causes His Sun to shine, alike on the believer and the unbeliever, and His dews to fertilize equally the soil of the orthodox and the heretic. . . . [Gaston here described the services of George Calvert, Roger Williams, and William Penn to religious freedom in colonial America, and how that principle had won out in most of the United States.] But finally, in every other of the twenty-four States of this Union, *perfect Religious Freedom,* perfect equality of sects, an entire exemption from religious tests, are now solemnly declared to be the basis on which rest all their Institutions. This salutary principle has spread across the Atlantic, and triumphed over the misrule and inveterate usages of the ancient Governments there. With scarcely an exception, it now prevails throughout *all* Europe, and Religious opinions are no longer there a qualification for, or an incapacity for Civil employment. And can it be, that *we* shall prove recreant in this noble strife for securing the sanctity of conscience and purity of religion?

Shall *we* afford to the bigots, the fanatics, and the friends of arbitrary power abroad, an apology for claiming this State as an ally in the cause of Intolerance? — I hope not. I trust that we shall act *up* to the axiom proclaimed in our Bill of Rights, and permit no man to suffer inconvenience or to incur incapacity, because of religion, whether he be Jew or Gentile, Christian or Infidel, Heretic or Orthodox. Pollute not the ark of God with unholy touch. Divine Truth *needs* not the support of human power, either to convince the understanding or to regulate the heart. Dare not to define divine truth, for it belongs not to your functions, and you may set up falsehood and error in its stead. Prohibit, restrain and punish, as offences against human society, all practices insulting to the faith, the institutions, and the worship of your people, but offer no bribes to lure men to profess a faith which they do not believe, inflict no penalties to deter them from embracing what their understandings approve, and make no distinction of ranks and orders in the community because of religious opinions. . . .

75. The Aid of the Society for the Propagation of the Faith to the Archdiocese of Baltimore, January 31, 1838

ONE of the greatest sources of financial support to the American Church throughout the nineteenth century was the Society for the Propagation of the Faith which had been organized by two priests and ten zealous laymen at Lyons, France, in May, 1822. The year after its establishment the society began its benefactions to the Archdiocese of Baltimore which were continued to 1865 when it had contributed $56,757. Equally generous sums were distributed to other American dioceses and by 1922, the centennial year of the society, a total of $6,375,218 had been sent from France to the United States. By that time American Catholics were relatively well off and had become mission-minded with the result that they had given back $10,983,452 to the society's headquarters in France to be distributed to more needy mission lands. In the following letter Samuel Eccleston, S.S. (1801–1851), fifth Archbishop of Baltimore, not only recorded his gratitude for the assistance sent to him, but he gave insights as well on the nativist movement, the problem of the slaves, and the need for more priests. Eccleston's letter is typical, not only of dozens of such reports received from bishops and religious superiors in the United States and published all through the nineteenth century in the society's annual volumes, but as well of hundreds of unpublished reports. Source: *Annales de la Propagation de la Foi,* X (1837), 494–500.

Baltimore, January 31, 1838.

Gentlemen,

I have already written to you to acknowledge the money which the Propagation of the Faith has been good enough to grant me. Today, according to your request, I am going to give you some details on the state of my diocese. There is certainly very much to say on this subject, but my many duties will not permit me to enter into all the necessary explanations. Allow me, above all, Gentlemen, to repeat my thanks in my name and in the name of my confrères in the episcopate: Oh! how I wish I could adequately express all the sentiments of gratitude and admiration which rise in my heart, when I consider the noble and truly Catholic zeal of your pious Association. A few months ago I was surrounded by the venerable Prelates of this province assembled for the last council,[1] and I had then the consolation to learn from their own lips the immense good that is being done by your means. If new churches are rising in the midst of our forests and deserts; if the Savages, who are more and more being driven back beyond our frontiers by the progress of civilization, carry with them at least the torch of the Faith; if, in a country where learning and talents are perhaps more than elsewhere exposed to the seduction of ambition and avarice, the small number of those who are called to the ecclesiastical life, find a safe shelter where they are formed to the virtues and the knowledge which the holy ministry demands; if — in a word — the Catholic religion is every day better known and as a consequence more respected from one end to the other of these vast regions, to whom do we owe it? It pleases me to say, that it is to you, Gentlemen; it is to your prayers and donations that we are for the most part indebted for these inestimable advantages. Yet, what title have we to your benefactions? Humanly speaking, and under the triple relation of country, of language, and of customs we are only strangers to you. But enlightened by the light of the Faith, you have recognized in us members of the Catholic unity, you have seen in us, brothers; you have treated us like brothers. And we also, Gentlemen, look upon you as brothers, and we cherish you like brothers. It must, however, be said, and, moreover, without it something would be lacking to your merit: your Association, excellent as it is, encounters opposition here as it undoubtedly does elsewhere. It is not that the most intelligent portion of my fellow citizens are not well disposed, or at least without animosity toward the Catholic religion; but there is among us a numerous and well organized association of religious fanatics who

[1] The Third Provincial Council of Baltimore had met April 16–22, 1837.

watch our progress with only a mortal envy: these people are your calumniators and ours.[2] While on the one hand they try to disparage our doctrines, on the other, they accuse us of lacking loyalty to our country, of distorting or exaggerating the nature and extent of the help which we receive from our brothers in the Faith; and while they waste millions to hire their emissaries and to spread their slanders under all forms, they pretend to see treason and a flagrant conspiracy in the pious liaison which we maintain with you. But their fury is the surest sign of the progress which our holy Religion is making, and therefore it should tend on one hand to stimulate your charity, and on the other to make us redouble our zeal.

My diocese comprises Maryland and the district of Columbia. I am also charged with the administration of the diocese of Richmond in the state of Virginia. Maryland contains 13,950 square miles and 450,000 inhabitants of whom 102,294 are slaves. The Catholics number 70,000.

The district of Columbia contains 100 square miles and 40,000 inhabitants of whom 10,000 are Catholics. Virginia has about 70,000 square miles and 1,220,000 inhabitants of whom 470,000 are slaves: the number of Catholics is 9,000. There are in my two dioceses 61 churches or chapels, eight of which belong to the diocese of Richmond. The churches in general are small and of a very simple construction, a few of them not even of wood. About twelve congregations or parishes have no churches and are visited only now and then by a Priest who happens to be near.

My clergy is composed of 74 Priests employed either in the missions or in the Catholic establishments: among them there are some whose parishes are 20 to 150 miles in extent; about twenty of them work in our principal towns. I do not speak of the Ecclesiastics who belong to religious communities and who also render us very great service.

Although many of the Catholic families are emigrating toward the south and west, the Faith is making solid progress in this diocese, the first one where the missionaries who came from Europe exercised in the past their apostolic zeal. As I have already mentioned, our success has roused against us the fanaticism of several sects; but it is among the Presbyterians especially that there arises the greatest

---

[2] Speaking of the American nativist reaction to the foreign missionary societies, the historian of the movement has said: "Annual reports of the Leopold Association and the Association for the Propagation of the Faith were widely published in the religious press, with warnings of the fate awaiting America if these activities were continued" (Ray Allen Billington, *The Protestant Crusade* [New York, 1938], p. 127).

animosity.[3] There is in Baltimore a class of men who are always disposed to receive avidly the most atrocious calumnies against the Catholics, and who more than once have tried to inflame the passions of the people by inflammatory pamphlets in order to destroy some of our religious establishments. Happily, the vulgar impostures which they are using are beginning to be appreciated at their face value by those who are more reasonable among our separated brethren; one may even say that this blind rage becomes for some an occasion of salvation by inspiring in them the desire to see and investigate for themselves. Not long ago a Jew from one of our southern states came to see me to ask some questions relating to the doctrines which are the object of our Faith; he told me that he had never read a Catholic book, but that the violent tone and the malignity which appeared in the Protestant treatises and pamphlets which he received every day had in the end made him suspect a cause which had recourse to such odious means of defense. He therefore decided that a religion which was attacked with such persistent hatred must be sustained by proofs that its adversaries had a thousand reasons to keep secret. I procured for him the necessary books to help him understand the basis of Catholic doctrine, and he promised that he would read them carefully: may the sincerity of his heart be rewarded by the knowledge of truth and by the sweet consolations which it alone can bring to man! Thus it is that the efforts of our adversaries by an admirable disposition of Providence turn to their own disadvantage.

It is true that round about us there are souls who will, perhaps, never be better disposed to receive favorable impressions of the true Religion. What I have had occasion to observe during the visitation of the vast territory under my jurisdiction has more and more confirmed me in this opinion; everywhere a laudable curiosity to know the doctrines of the Catholic Religion; everywhere a good number of upright men who would very probably renounce their prejudices if we had a sufficient number of Priests to attend to their conversion. But before thinking of these poor souls, there is a still more urgent duty to fulfill, and that is to procure for the Catholic population religious in-

[3] In Eccleston's see city of Baltimore two Presbyterian ministers, the Reverends Robert J. Breckinridge and Andrew B. Cross, had launched in 1835 the *Literary and Religious Magazine*, a fiery anti-Catholic journal. A few years later when the controversy between Bishop Hughes and the school authorities broke in New York the Presbyterians were again in the lead. "Nearly all of the Protestant denominations in the United States responded to this appeal but none with more enthusiasm than the Presbyterians whose heritage of antagonism toward Rome fitted them to take full advantage of the excitement over the New York controversy (Billington, *op. cit.*, p. 173).

struction and the facilities for them to receive the sacraments. They are now numerous and whole congregations who cry out to me for the bread of life and I have no one to distribute it to them. The consequences of this situation are deplorable; because, lacking the means to practice their religious duties, these Catholics end by succumbing to indifference, and their children who grow up among Protestant companions, unfortunately soon no longer distinguish between the true Church from the ephemeral sects which surrounded them.

The slaves of these states also present a vast harvest for the apostolic workers. Their souls, redeemed by the same Savior, and destined to the same blessed immortality, are not, in the eyes of God, less precious than the souls of their masters; and often in their very simplicity, they are better prepared to receive divine grace and make it bear fruit. I have done some special research on this subject, and I have constantly found that every time a Priest had given careful attention to these poor people, his zeal has soon been richly rewarded by their happy change of life, and by their edifying regularity in frequenting the sacraments. In our towns, many of the Protestant families prefer Catholic servants; in the country many of the Protestant planters who, have in their neighborhood some pious Catholic congregations, seeing how our Religion has influenced the slaves, have more than once sought to have them instructed in our salutary beliefs. I do not think that there is in this country, without excepting the Savages, any class of men among whom it would be possible to work more fruitfully. But, I repeat, far from being able to do what I should like to do for the salvation of unfortunate Negroes, I find myself unable to satisfy the thousands of whites who equally deprived of the help of Religion, feel more keenly their spiritual abandonment.

It was the opinion of my venerable predecessor, and it is also mine, that the only way to obtain a clergy sufficient for our needs, and suitable for the missions of these regions, is to found an establishment solely consecrated to the education of those who are destined for the priesthood; because our colleges, able to maintain themselves only by the number of students, are forced to receive all the youths who present themselves, Catholic or Protestant. The result is that when there are found among them several who have some inclination toward the ecclesiastical state, their contact and their necessary relations with the young men who have opposite views to theirs necessarily exposes their vocation. In order to obviate these disadvantages, there was begun a few years ago the building of a minor seminary a few miles from Baltimore.[4] The roof is covered, and the first floor is almost finished. We have done all that was in our power to finish this purely ecclesiastical college and to get it started; but the lack of funds has forced us to suspend the work, and to wait until Providence would come to our assistance. Certainly it is not for lack of effort on my part that the work remains incomplete: considering this nursery of students as the hope of my diocese, I have several times assembled the faithful in order to excite their charity; I have even gone from door to door to solicit help. Unfortunately, I have no resources of my own. Will not my cathedral furnish me with it? But it is burdened with a considerable debt, and besides it is not even finished; the walls still lack decoration and the suitable embellishments befitting such an edifice.

As to myself, thank God, I have need of little and that little I do not lack: my worries, my prayers, are for my flock. I look only for the honor of the sanctuary; I seek only to save souls redeemed by the blood of J.C., of whom one day he will ask an accounting of me.

This is, Gentlemen, the state of my dioceses, of which there has been fashioned, perhaps, in France a little different idea; however that be, I am extremely grateful for everything that you have done either for my predecessors or for myself; once more please accept my thanks. I pray the good God, Gentlemen, that he send you his most abundant graces, on all the charitable members of the Association and that he may reward you a hundredfold in this life and in the next.

Samuel Eccleston, Archbishop of Baltimore.

76. The Papacy's Relation to Temporal Affairs Explained by Bishop Kenrick, 1838

THE outstanding American Catholic theologian of the nineteenth century was Francis Patrick Kenrick (1796–1863). During the nativist agitation of the 1830's the Church was often challenged in regard to the institution of the papacy and its claims to primacy. Making a bid for unity among the Christian churches, the Protestant Episcopal Bishop of Vermont, John Henry Hopkins, published a work called *The Church of Rome in her Primitive Purity compared to the Church of Rome at the Present Day* (New York, 1835). To this Kenrick, then Coadjutor Bishop of Philadelphia, prepared

[4] St. Charles College, Ellicott City, opened with five students on November 1, 1848, under the presidency of Oliver L. Jenkins, S.S.

an answer which is generally regarded as the best of his numerous writings on theological and apologetic subjects. It first appeared in the spring of 1838, passed through numerous editions, and was translated into German in 1853. In the excerpt below Kenrick sought to explain the historical background for the papacy's exercise of jurisdiction in temporal concerns and to show the changes that had taken place in regard to that practice since the Middle Ages. He not only had in mind a reply to Hopkins but the hope of dispelling the prejudices which so many Americans entertained concerning the papacy. Source: Francis Patrick Kenrick, *The Primacy of the Apostolic See, and the Authority of General Councils, Vindicated*, 7 rev. ed. (Baltimore: John Murphy Co., 1875), p. 282.

. . . The divine law, doubtless, embraces all classes of men, princes and people, and all varieties of human actions, political as well as personal. The chief Pastor of the Church is placed on his high eminence, to proclaim the command of God, and in His name to instruct in justice those that judge the earth. As expounder of the moral law, he speaks to all with power and authority, condemning all that God has forbidden, and inculcating the observance of each divine commandment. He can cast forth from the Church every one, prince or subject, who is notoriously guilty of flagrant immorality, if he will not yield to paternal admonition. But secular concerns are not, of themselves, subject to his cognizance: and the complicated social relations which arise from the free acts of individuals, or from public law, or from the action of the civil authorities, are not the matter of his judgment, unless where they involve a violation of the great principles of Christian morality. In the Middle Ages, kings and nations implored his judgment, and consequently brought within the sphere of his authority those secular transactions and controversies, of which otherwise he might have said, in the words of our Redeemer, to those who called for his interference: "Who hath appointed me judge over you?" Whencesoever the conviction of his right to take cognizance of them may be supposed to have arisen, it was universally admitted, and it was consequently a part of the public and common law of nations. Guizot[1] testifies that it was generally believed, in the middle of the ninth century, that he was above temporal governments, even in temporal affairs, when connected with religion: he might have qualified it by adding, in their moral aspect, since he observes that it was by developing the principles of morality ecclesiastics exercised power over governments.

The key to the whole history of the Middle Ages appears to us

[1] François Guizot (1787–1874), a Protestant, was Premier of France in the last month of the reign of King Louis Philippe.

to be the sentiment then prevailing, that Christian principle should regulate all the departments of government and all the relations of life. We do not think that the authority of the Popes over sovereigns is to be accounted for, merely by reason of the relations in which they actually stood to them, or of the concessions which had been made by former princes. On the contrary, we trace those concessions and relations to the persuasion which was universal, that the head of the Christian Church was the fittest arbiter of the respective obligations of princes and their subjects, and the natural judge of all, in what regarded the application of the Christian maxims to society.

77. The Church in the Republic of Texas, April 11, 1841

EVER since the time when the Spanish Franciscans had begun their labors in Texas in 1690 that vast area had proved a difficult terrain for the Church's missionaries. In 1836 Texas broke from Mexico and declared its independence with the result that a new arrangement had to be made for spiritual care of the widely scattered Catholics. On October 24, 1839, the Holy See erected the Prefecture Apostolic of Texas and its care was entrusted to the Vincentian Fathers with John Timon (1797–1867) as first prefect. By reason of Timon's many preoccupations elsewhere the practical establishment of the Texas mission was delegated to Jean-Marie Odin (1800–1870) who was later first Vicar Apostolic of Texas, 1841–1847; first Bishop of Galveston, 1847–1861; and second Archbishop of New Orleans, 1861–1870. The following letter of Odin was written to Jean-Baptiste Etienne who was Superior-General of the Vincentians from 1843–1874. Besides the description of religious conditions, it demonstrates how primitive life was in large sections of Texas four years before it entered the American Union. Source: *Annales de la Propagation de la Foi,* XIV (1842), 453–460.

Galveston, Texas, 11 April 1841

My dear Brother,

Last year the Holy See having conferred on our Congregation the spiritual direction of the Catholics of Texas, I left the seminary of the Barrens,[1] on May 2, 1840, in order to explore this new Mission in my capacity of vice-prefect apostolic. It was not without regret that I left Missouri; to separate myself from a people who had become very dear to me, and from flourishing establishments that I had seen born, was like expatriating myself a second time.

[1] St. Mary's Seminary, Perryville, Missouri (the Barrens), had been established by the Vincentians in 1818 at the little village about eighty miles south of St. Louis.

Texas, situated between the 26th and the 35th degrees of latitude and extending from the 93rd to the 102nd of longitude, possesses vast prairies, and more abundant pasturage than any other region of America. Woods are rare here, especially in the west. Several rivers irrigate the country, but they are not large or deep enough for navigation. Although the exact figure of the population of Texas is not known, it is rather generally agreed not to exceed thirty thousand souls.

When the first Spaniards settled in Texas more than a century and a half ago, some Franciscans came and founded several Missions in order to convert and civilize the savage tribes. The most celebrated of these were: *San Antonio, de la Conception de San Jose, del Refugio,* and *San Sabas* and *Nacogdoches;* they became very flourishing and soon counted a great number of fervent neophytes. Each year the Reverend Fathers plunged into the forests, earning by their gifts and their very affable manners the confidence of the Indians, and conducting them to the stations where they fashioned them little by little to piety and work. In 1812 these precious establishments were suppressed; today they are only heaps of ruins. For the poor savages, deprived of their Fathers, were dispersed: some returned to Mexico; several succumbed under the blows of the uncivilized tribes, and others returned to their primitive state. The fervor which I have found in the small number of those who still inhabit the country clearly indicates that they had been formed to virtue by capable hands. Two churches, the only ones that have resisted the assaults of time and of the recent wars, are of a beauty which does honor to the taste and zeal of the old Missionaries. . . .

From Liunville, a small seaport where we debarked, we proceeded to Victoria. I left in that post M. l'abbé Estany,[2] and I took the route to San Antonio with M. Calvo[3] and a coadjutor brother. The distance which separates the two towns is only fifty leagues, but the numerous bands of savage *Comanches* and *Tonakanies* who roam the country without ceasing make the trip extremely perilous: it is even pretty nearly certain that one will be massacred, if one does not travel in sufficient numbers to intimidate the Indians. We therefore joined a convoy of twenty-two wagons which were transporting some merchandise. All of our companions were very well armed; but, if on the one hand the force of the caravan reassured us against the attacks of the Indians, on the other, what miseries to endure! What slowness

---

[2] Eudald Estany was a Spanish Vincentian who had accompanied Odin to Texas.

[3] Michael Calvo was another Spanish Vincentian who had come to Texas in May, 1840.

in our advance! The heat was excessive, and scarcely a bush offered itself in the shade of which we might enjoy a moment of repose. Toward sunset we moved forward; but often at first step one of our vehicles got out of order and it was necessary to pass a part of the night in repairing it. These accidents sometimes happened far from any springs or rivers; we then had to scour the wastes, very happy when after a lot of searching we found in a mudhole some drops of muddy and distasteful water. Moreover, we were very poorly provisioned, and yet we hastened to partake as brothers with our traveling companions, worse provided for than ourselves; it was even necessary to have recourse to hunting at the risk of attracting the savages by the noise of the guns.

To scarcity there was also joined the fever; I had several attacks, like the others; but some medicines which I had provided myself proved opportune, and they restored us little by little to health. The relief that I obtained for our poor sufferers gave me a reputation by which I was later often embarrassed; because some of our good wagoners recognized me under the name of the *"Father who knows how to heal,"* all the sick came to ask me for consultations and remedies. Several times along the way, the cry of *Los Indios* spread alarm in our midst: this was, I believe, only a mistake of our scouts, because we arrived at San Antonio without striking a blow.

That city, founded in 1678 by the Spaniards from the Canary Islands,[4] includes a population of two thousand souls: one notices there some houses of stone; the other houses are only miserable huts covered with rushes. It is irrigated on the east by the San Antonio river, on the west by a very small stream; in the center one finds a canal from which the abundant water fertilizes all the gardens; it was built by the Indians under the direction of the Missionaries. There is nothing more beautiful than the valley of San Antonio: agreeable climate, pure and healthful air, rich and fertile soil, all contribute to make it a delightful place, without the continual hostility of the savages, who up to the present have not permitted its immense resources to be exploited. There is not a family who does not mourn the death of a father, of a son, of a brother, or of a spouse pitilessly slaughtered by the *Comanches.* To the massacre of the colonists, these brigands add the devastation of the land and the kidnapping of the herds: thus poverty is extreme in the country, and if ever it would have been consoling to have some aid to distribute, it would un-

[4] Odin was wrong here. San Antonio had been founded in 1718 and the Canary Islanders did not arrive until 1730.

doubtedly have been at the sight of so many needy and unfortunate.

A few days after our arrival at San Antonio, there took place a ceremony which filled us with consolation in proving to us how much of the faith still lived among the Mexicans. A sick person, in danger of death, needed to receive holy viaticum; we judged it opportune to carry it to him publicly and with pomp. At the sound of the bell, the people hastened to the holy place in order to accompany Our Lord through the streets; many tears fell from the eyes of the old people who for forty years had not been witnesses of this homage rendered to our Religion. Some among them cried out that they did not fear death any longer now that heaven had sent them Fathers to assist them in their last moment.

After three months in San Antonio, seeing that, thanks to God, all went as we desired, I directed myself toward Seguin, Gonzales, and Victoria. My visit in these towns was very brief because I was not able to separate myself from my traveling companions without exposing myself to be killed by the Indians. Later I reascended alone the Lavaca river, which offers less danger, and I found on its banks seventy Catholics, formerly my parishioners at the Barrens. It was very consoling to me to see them again, and especially to convince myself that they had lost nothing of their faith and their early piety, because since their arrival in Texas they had been deprived of the aid of Religion. All of them went to confession and had the good fortune to receive holy communion.

I was able to remain with them only one week. From Lavaca I went to Austin, a powerful little town, recently designated to be the seat of the Texas government. The congress was then in session; I solicited from some of the legislators a decision which would confirm to the Catholic Church all the churches constructed by the Spaniards in former times. It is true that, with the exception of *Conception* and *San Jose,* these edifices are almost all in ruins; nevertheless they can be repaired, and considering the poverty and small number of the faithful, they can be turned to account while awaiting happier times that will give us the chance of constructing new ones. Thanks to the generous intervention of M. de Saligny,[5] chargé d'affaires of France, my request has been well received.

There still remains the eastern part of Texas to visit. What difficulties and obstacles present themselves on that long route! Sometimes it is a river there which it will be necessary to cross by swimming, some-

[5] Alphonse Dubois de Saligny was *chargé d'affaires* in Texas for the government of King Louis Philippe of France.

times a vast and desolate swamp where we will run the risk of losing our horses; here the famine and nothing to alleviate it; elsewhere torrents of rain and no shelter. Thus we proceeded from Montgomery to Huntsville, from Cincinnati to Crok and to Douglas, from Nacogdoches to San Augustine. It is true that we were well compensated for our fatigue by the eagerness to hear our instructions which was manifested by the inhabitants of these diverse localities; rarely have I seen the word of God heard with more joy and recollection. This visit, although short, has contributed not a little to dissipate the prejudice of the Protestants, and to awaken pious sentiments in the heart of the faithful.

Outside of the Catholic population of Texas, estimated to be about ten thousand souls, there are some savage tribes to which it will be urgent to apply ourselves: these are the *Comanches* to the number of 20,000; the *Tonakanies,* the *Lipans,* the *Tankanago,* the *Bidaïs,* the *Karankanags,* the *Nacoës,* etc. Most of these Indians like to eat human flesh; the feet and hands are their favorite parts. I have already made several approaches to the *Karankanags,* in order to unite them in a mission: M. Estany has also visited them, and they have expressed to him the desire to have a priest. The *Comanches* will be the most difficult to win over. From time immemorial this tribe has been constantly at war with the civilized inhabitants and the neighboring tribes. Clever horsemen, skillful thieves, they handle the spear and the lance with great dexterity; one sees them in bands of ten, twenty, thirty, or fifty, running about the country without ceasing. From the heights where they lie in wait for their prey, when they discover a convoy too feeble to resist them, they pounce on the travelers with the rapidity of lightning and they gorge themselves without pity. It would be impossible to say how many unfortunates have succumbed under their blows, how many women and children have been taken captive.

A short time after my arrival in Texas one party of five or six hundred *Comanches* penetrated almost to Liunville. The inhabitants, who were not expecting this visit, were obliged to hide themselves in the middle of the Labaca [*sic*] bay in order to protect themselves from their spears: there were eight victims; a young woman married only ten days became their prisoner after having seen her husband fall pierced in his sides. When the savages had plundered the stores and had made a minute search of all that might enrich them, they delivered the town to the flames. From Liunville they went to Victoria. The first house they attacked was the one where our confrère M. Estany lived: he had the good fortune to pass through a hail of spears without receiving any wound; but all that he possessed was taken: linens, ornaments, books, nothing was spared. There were again some murders; several women and children were carried off. Soon the alarm was spread, and they rushed forth in pursuit of the brigands and caught up with them near the *Plombereek* and *St. Marc* rivers. The battle was bloody; eighty-four *Comanches* lost their lives, without mentioning those who a short time after succumbed to wounds they had received. These unfortunates, at the approach of the Texans, sought to kill all the prisoners whom they had carried off. One poor mother who fell into their hands with her little infant, scarcely ten months old, had the anguish of seeing this innocent creature crushed under her eyes, and was herself finally pierced by several blows of the lance! I have counted, in the space of ten months, almost two hundred slaughtered by that tribe alone.

In spite of the devastation to which this country is prey, heaven has already begun to bless our feeble work. From August 1, 1840, to March 1, 1841 we have heard 911 confessions and administered 281 baptisms; there have been 478 communions. . . . The good of Religion will demand that there be erected immediately at least six chapels at the most important places of the republic; but where to find the funds? We are without resources, and the population is poor. In my travels, I pass part of the night in the woods in the open air; I cook my own food, nevertheless my traveling expenses are always considerable. Thus lately in order to have two armed men accompany me during three days of traveling, I was obliged to pay them twenty-four piasters. Schools are also necessary at San Antonio and Galveston: who will cover the first expenses? We are without lodgings, obliged to beg hospitality among the Catholics, often even with the Protestants. . . . Here one learns, indeed, how to lead the life of a Missionary: I thought that I had already made a long apprenticeship; but since my arrival in Texas I have discovered that I was not yet initiated.

Your devoted servant,
J.-M. Odin.

78. Father De Smet's Promotion of the Indian Missions of the Far West, May 1, 1841

WHEN Charles Van Quickenborne, S.J., left Whitemarsh in Maryland on April 11, 1823, as the superior of a small group to reopen Jesuit activities in the Middle West for the first time since their forcible expulsion in 1763, there was among the seven novices a Belgian-born youth, Pierre-Jean De Smet (1801–1873), who was destined to become one of the most famous promoters of Catholic missions among the American Indians. The Flathead Indians of Montana had made four different attempts at St. Louis to secure a Catholic priest, the last in the summer of 1839. De Smet's zeal was fired by this striking manifestation of faith, and after securing the permission of his superiors he set out in March, 1840, for the first of his journeys to the Rocky Mountain country. Not only did he make several trips to the Far West, but he traveled widely in both the United States and Europe — in all about 180,000 miles — begging for the Indian missions and advertising them as only he could do. If De Smet's imagination sometimes outran his practical sense, he had no peer as a propagandist of the mission cause, or as a man in whom the Indians felt complete confidence. That was witnessed by the help he gave to the peace commissioners in negotiating the peace treaty with the Sioux in July, 1868. Some months after his return to St. Louis from his first trip to the Rockies he wrote the following letter to a friend in which he showed how he was making good on his promises to the Indians of the Far West. Source: Hiram Martin Chittenden and Alfred Talbot Richardson (Eds.), *Life, Letters and Travels of Father Pierre-Jean De Smet, S.J., 1801–1873* (New York: Francis P. Harper, 1905), I, 272–274.

To the Editor of the *Catholic Herald*
Steamboat *Oceana,* Mo. River,
May 1, 1841

. . . On my arrival at St. Louis, I gave an account to my superior of my journey and of the flattering prospects which the mission beyond the Rocky Mountains held out. You will easily believe me when I tell you that my heart sank within me on learning from him that the funds at his disposal for missionary purposes would not enable him to afford me scarcely the half of what would be necessary for the outfit and other expenses of an expedition. The thought that the undertaking would have been given up, that I would not be able to redeem my promise to the poor Indians, pierced my very heart and filled me with the deepest sorrow. I would have desponded had I not already experienced the visible protection of the Almighty in the prosecution of this great work. My confidence in him was unabated. Whilst in this state of mind one of my friends encouraged me to appeal to the zealous and learned coadjutor of Philadelphia [Francis Patrick Kenrick] and to his indefatigable clergy. I immediately acted upon the thought. I did appeal and with what success the Catholic public already know. To the Bishop who gave his sanction to the plan of a general and simultaneous collection throughout his diocese; to the clergy of the different churches of the city who so kindly interested themselves in this good work and proposed it to their congregations; to the generous people of Philadelphia who so liberally responded to the call of their pastors, I return my sincere thanks and will daily beg the father of mercies to reward them with his choicest blessings.

I must not omit to make mention of other generous contributors. After having written to Philadelphia I was advised to visit New Orleans and recommend the cause of the Indians to the good Bishop [Antoine Blanc] of that city and to his clergy and people. I did so. The Bishop received me with great kindness; gave his approbation to a collection, and placed his name first on the list. His clergy followed his example. As I had only a few days at my disposal, I thought it best to solicit subscriptions through several generous ladies who offered themselves for this purpose. In the space of three or four days, they collected nearly $1,000. You have no idea with what spirit the pious portion of the people entered into the affair. Almost every moment of my stay persons came to offer me something for the Indian mission. Several ladies gave me various trinkets, such as earrings, bracelets, and ornaments of every description; others brought implements and articles, which will be of great use in the Indian country. In a word, Reverend Sir, I left New Orleans with $1,100 in cash and six boxes full of various and most useful articles. From the Reverend Mr. Durbin[1] of Kentucky I received $300, and the Reverend Jno. O'Reilly[2] remitted $140, the amount collected in St. Paul's Church, Pittsburg. St. Louis supplied the balance of what was necessary for the outfit, the expenses of the journey and the commencement of the establishment in the Indian country. To the Bishops and to the zealous clergy and laity of Philadelphia and New Orleans; to the clergy and laity of other places who aided the good cause; in a word, to all the benefactors of the mission beyond the Rocky Mountains, I again return my sincere thanks. . . .

---

[1] E. J. Durbin was stationed at Sacred Heart Church, Union County, Kentucky, at this time.

[2] John O'Reilly was pastor of St. Paul's Church, Pittsburgh.

79. Canon Salzbacher's Observations on American Catholic Colleges for Men, 1842

AMONG the principal foreign benefactors of American Catholicism in the nineteenth century was the Leopoldinen-Stiftung of Vienna which was founded in April, 1829, and which between 1830 and 1913 sent over $700,000 to the assistance of German Catholic immigrants in this country. Early in the 1840's complaints began to reach Vienna of the neglect of the German immigrants by the American bishops, and the society decided, therefore, to send the editor of its annual *Berichte,* Canon Josef Salzbacher (1790–1867) of St. Stephen's Cathedral, to investigate conditions in the United States. Salzbacher landed at New York from the *Great Western* on April 17, 1842, and during the next three months he covered about 10,000 miles and visited German Catholic immigrant groups in eleven dioceses spread over seventeen states. By the time he departed for home on July 27 he had accumulated a large body of data from which he later wrote a book. His volume was one of the most careful factual accounts ever published by a foreign visitor on the Church in the United States. Toward the end of the work the author included some general observations. The passage which follows covered the Catholic colleges for men as he saw them in 1842. Source: Josef Salzbacher, *Meine Reise nach Nord-Amerika in Jahre 1842 mit statistischen Bemerkungen über die Züstande der katholischen Kirche bis auf neuste Zeit* (Vienna: Wimmer, Schmidt & Leo, 1845), pp. 354–357.

Besides the elementary, Sunday and free-schools and orphanages the Catholic Church in America has institutions of higher learning as colleges, academies and universities which are devoted to the so-called classical studies which in America as elsewhere are the mark of the people of higher rank. The classical course, philosophy, mathematics, and sciences are about the same as in Europe and ordinarily require for their completion four years. One can assert that the instructors in many of these institutions are fully competent to teach the subjects entrusted to them. Since many Catholic youth want to obtain a higher education to become physicians, attorneys, or priests, it has long been the ambition of the bishops to erect such higher institutions of learning and to supervise them in order that these young men, who otherwise would attend the public state schools, might not go astray. Realizing that religious orders can accomplish more than individuals, the bishops have called upon the Sulpicians, Jesuits, Lazarists, etc., to conduct these institutions of higher learning. It is hardly necessary to say that the bishops and the faithful are obliged to assume the entire burden of financing these institutions. How well they have succeeded is shown by the long list of educational institutions which we have catalogued under the heading of the various dioceses. Outstanding are the Jesuit colleges at Georgetown, St. Louis, Cincinnati, and the Sulpician college, St. Mary's at Baltimore. The state governments liberally concede the privileges of universities to these schools so that they can grant their distinguished students doctor's and master's diplomas, notwithstanding the fact that these colleges are under the control of the bishops and the religious orders and the secular authorities have not the slightest authority over them. Usually, as is the case in Europe, these colleges are conducted as boarding schools. The number of the externes so-called is usually small.

Not all the students in Catholic colleges and schools are Catholics. . . . Such Protestant students are accepted by Catholic colleges because of the insufficient number of Catholic students available and because the income derived from Protestant students makes it possible for the college to provide better facilities for the students, more teachers and better equipment. Moreover, these non-Catholic students by constant association with priests and Catholic teachers lay aside their prejudices against the Catholic Church which from youth have been impressed upon them; many become Catholics; if not permitted to take this step because of the opposition of parents or relatives, they later, as men of influence, become defenders of the Church and will more readily allow their people to enter the Church.

Experience also teaches that Protestant parents place great confidence in the methods of instruction and in the competency of the Catholic instructors and, convinced of the excellence of Catholic schools, they send their children preferably to these institutions. True it is that the Protestant preachers do their utmost to prevent the attendance of Protestants at Catholic schools, and in their public addresses and sermons they inveigh bitterly against Catholic educational institutions, but their calumnies have often produced results opposite to those they intended. Many Protestants began to visit the Catholic schools, and seeing the beauty and order of such institutions, they concluded that the preachers had indulged in slanderous assertions and determined to send their children to Catholic colleges. The good order and discipline of the colleges is in no manner impaired by the presence of the non-Catholic students. Every father and mother who place their son in the college are at once made acquainted with the rules of the institution and, if they are unwilling to submit their son to such discipline, the student in question is not accepted. Non-Catholic students are not obliged to attend instruction on Catholic doctrine. Every appearance of proselytism is carefully avoided but the non-Catholic students are required to respect the Catholic exercises of religion and they are obliged to attend morning and evening devotions, to be present for the prayers before and after meals, and to participate with the Catholics in the prayers before and after each class. Attendance at divine worship is not insisted upon, however, in the case of non-Catholics. Attached to every college is a church or chapel of sufficient capacity to accommodate all the students and on all the Sundays and holy days services are held as in parish churches. All the Catholic students must attend these.

In 1844 there were twenty-four Catholic colleges for young men in the United States. Of these six are conducted by the Jesuits, three are in charge of the Lazarists, two belong to the Sulpicians, one is directed by the Eudists and one is in the hands of the Redemptorists. The others are taught by secular priests. About 3,000 young men receive instruction in these colleges. Nearly every college possesses a select library, equipment for the teaching of the sciences and a scientific laboratory. Public examinations are held each year and prizes are awarded to the best students. Without exaggeration one may say that these institutions, distinguished by the strict morality and ability of their professors, contribute much to the respect which the Catholic religion enjoys in the United States.

80. The Launching of the American Protestant Association Against the Catholic Church, November 22, 1842

AFTER 1820 the numerical strength of the Catholic Church in the United States rose rapidly by reason of immigration, and by 1840 there were estimated to be 663,000 Catholics out of a total population of 14,195,805 white Americans. This increase alarmed many American Protestants who disliked the Church and who feared, too, lest native Americans be supplanted in their jobs by the cheaper labor of Irish and German immigrants, so many of whom were Catholics. The result was an organized effort against Catholics under the banner of American nativism. The nativists needed only a very slender excuse to go into action and when Francis P. Kenrick (1796–1863), Bishop of Philadelphia, on November 14, 1842, respectfully petitioned the board of the city's public schools for redress against Catholic children having to use the King James Bible and to be present at Protestant religious exercises in the schools, an excuse was at hand. A group of the city's Protestant leaders met and on November 22 ninety-four ministers, representing twelve denominations, signed the constitution of what they called the American Protestant Association. The association was responsible for arousing antagonism between Protestants and Catholics and its agents were in good measure to blame for the public riots in May and July, 1844, in which thirteen citizens were killed, over fifty wounded, and two of Philadelphia's Catholic churches burned. The constitution of this association which follows was typical of the numerous organizations of this kind which were actively at work against the Church throughout the country up to the Civil War. Source: Ray Allen Billington, *The Protestant Crusade, 1800–1860: A Study of the Origins of American Nativism* (New York: The Macmillan Co., 1938), pp. 438–439; reissued in 1952 by Rinehart & Co., New York.

Whereas, we believe the system of Popery to be, in its principles and tendency, subversive of civil and religious liberty, and destructive to the spiritual welfare of men, we unite for the purpose of defending our Protestant interests against the great exertions now making to propagate that system in the United States; and adopt the following constitution: —

Article I. This Society shall be called the American Protestant Association.

Article II. The objects of its formation, and for the attainment of which its efforts shall be directed, are —

1. The union and encouragement of Protestant ministers of the gospel, to give to their several congregations instruction on the differences between Protestantism and Popery.

2. To call attention to the necessity of a more extensive distribution, and thorough study of the Holy Scriptures.

3. The circulation of books and tracts adapted to give information on the various errors of Popery in their history, tendency, and design.

4. To awaken the attention of the community to the dangers which threaten the liberties, and the public and domestic institutions, of these United States from the assaults of Romanism.

Article III. This Association shall be composed of all such persons as agree in adopting the purposes and principles of this constitution and contribute to the funds by which it is supported.

Article IV. The officers of the Association shall be a President, three Vice-Presidents, a treasurer, a corresponding secretary, a recording secretary, and two lay directors from each denomination represented in the Association, to be elected annually; together with all the ministers belonging to it; who shall form a Board for the transaction of business of whom any seven, at a meeting duly convened, shall be a quorum. The stated meetings of the Board to be quarterly.

Article V. The Board of managers shall, at the first meeting after their election, appoint an executive committee, consisting of a minister and layman from each of the denominations represented in the association, of which the secretaries and treasurer shall be ex-officio members. This committee to meet as often as they may find necessary for the transaction of the business committed to them, and to report quarterly to the Board of managers.

Article VI. The duties of the Board shall be, to carry out, in every way most expedient in their view, the ends and purposes for which this Association is organized; and to aid and encourage the formation of similar associations in the various parts of the United States; and to render an annual report of their proceedings to the Association, at their annual meeting on the second Tuesday in November.

Article VII. The Board of managers shall have power to enact such by-laws as may not be inconsistent with this constitution, and to fill all vacancies that may occur between the annual meetings.

Article VIII. This constitution shall be subject to amendments only at the annual meetings of the Association, by a vote of two thirds of the members present at such meeting.

81. A Rural Colonization Project for German Catholic Immigrants, October 12, 1843

BY 1840 Catholic immigrants were finding life increasingly unpleasant in the eastern cities by reason of the bitter campaigns waged by the nativists against their religion and foreign birth. As a consequence a number of Philadelphia and Baltimore families banded together to form the German Catholic Brotherhood with the idea of establishing a new home at some remote spot where they would be free from religious and racial prejudice. Their leaders purchased large tracts of land in what is today Elk County, Pennsylvania, and the arrival of the wives and children of the pioneers on December 8, 1842, prompted them to call the settlement St. Mary's. They had originally consulted with Father Alexander Czvitkovicz, C.SS.R., (1806–1883), Hungarian-born superior of the Redemptorists in the United States, who after a visit to the colony recommended that the Redemptorists invest $10,000 in the project. This was done and schools for both boys and girls were provided, but the Redemptorists lost so heavily in the undertaking that they felt compelled to withdraw in November, 1849. They were succeeded by the German Benedictines from St. Vincent's Priory in Westmoreland County who were more experienced farmers and who in time brought the mission to a flourishing state. The following letter of Czvitkovicz to the Society for the Propagation of the Faith outlined the objectives of the colonizers and vividly described the perils of life in the forests of north-

western Pennsylvania at the time. St. Mary's was typical of many rural colonization projects of the German Catholic immigrants before the Civil War, a period noted for some rather bizarre backwoods communitarian experiments as well. Source: *Annales de la Propagation de la Foi,* XVI (1844), 401–406.

Baltimore, October 12, 1843.

Dear Mr. President,

. . . After having given a mission in Detroit, I returned directly to Baltimore where there awaited me duties apparently less apostolic.

A great number of our German brothers of Baltimore and Philadelphia, seeing all the different sects with which our cities are populated, and the great danger for them and for their children of losing faith, proposed to form an exclusively Catholic community; and to that end they purchased last year at a very moderate price, a piece of waste land in the neighborhood of thirty-six thousand acres. Some of the faithful, before entering into the association, consulted me on the project, which forced me to examine the laws; and as I soon perceived that it would remain without result and that it would soon break up, I straight-forwardly said so to those who spoke to me about it, explaining to them the reasons which prompted my advice. Nevertheless, before my departure for Europe the colony seemed to make some progress; many families eagerly joined it: but soon this false appearance of success disappeared, and on my return to America, the enterprise was at the point of death. Around thirty-eight families had already quit the community; its principal members and the twenty-six families who were still there, seeing the impossibility of restoring it to life and fearing to lose all the capital they had already expended in the first tillage which would have ruined a hundred families, remembering my prediction, sent some delegates to me in order that I might aid them with my counsel and my credit.

I pitied their condition, especially since the honor of Religion was at stake, for already the heretics and the infidels triumphing at the dissolution, mocked the colonists in their newspapers. Some concluded that Catholicism was powerless to found lasting establishments, others have so little union and fraternity with our coreligionists that there is rarely found among them men with enough charity to interest themselves in the fate of their unfortunate brothers. I therefore went to the colony where I was received by the twenty-six families who had been vegetating there for a year with as much lively joy as if my presence alone was capable of changing this land of malediction into a terrestrial paradise. The next day, accompanied by all the colonists to the number of twenty-six, armed with the proper instruments for measuring the land, and with guns to procure ourselves some game and protect ourselves against the ferocious beasts, such as the wolves and bears, of which there are still great numbers in these regions, I began with the compass and map in hand, to seek out the limits of the land that had been bought. What was my surprise in soon learning that these poor people had watered with their daily sweat an unknown land that they had taken for their own! After having surveyed the ground well, I made a general demarcation; after that I divided it into portions of twenty-five, fifty, seventy-five and a hundred acres, marking out the limits by the trees. I determined the place where the village ought to be constructed; I made the plan, counseling them to group the houses instead of spreading them as they had done up to now, at two, three, four or five miles from one another.

It is impossible to give an idea of the fatigue caused by these excursions; those who have seen and inhabited these immense American forests, whose origin dates from the beginning of the world, without ever the hand of man having touched this chaos, can alone understand: one meets at almost every step thick brushwood, roots intertwined with the branches which bend to the ground, entire trees uprooted by age and the winds, heaped up here and there like impassable ramparts; moreover, since the sun is not able to penetrate beneath these vaults of foliage it is very humid, the ground is so slippery that one is never sure of his footing and has almost as many falls as steps.

The property purchased extends for nine miles. We covered scarcely the space of three miles in a day and in order to manage that we were forced to pass the night in the middle of these forests. Then at night we lighted a big fire because it was the end of October, and we were already very cold; seated around the fire we took our supper which ordinarily left the stomach pretty empty. After evening prayer, which we said in common, each made his own bed as he wished, and slept if he were able. One may well imagine that being exposed to the cold, the snow, and the rain, that we slept very little; nevertheless, I passed these nights very agreeably, occupied during my long hours of insomnia in calculating the advantages that Religion would one day derive from this civilizing work, accomplished in solitude under the eyes of God alone. It was then that I called to mind the fruitless pains that others before me, and I myself for three years, had taken to find some young Americans destined to become Missionaries of their own land; I believe that I can see in the new establishment the future refuge where this infant Christianity sheltered from the corruption of the world and perversion of heresy, will increase in knowledge without losing virtue and will furnish generous vocations among which God will be pleased to choose Apostles for America. It seems to me that thousands of Catholics will yet rally around the cross as around the religious symbol of true liberty. I already foresee a nascent congregation, a humble daughter of the universal Church, flowering in the desert beneath the divine benediction; I assist in spirit in the holy ceremonies of its solemn mysteries. There is the place, I think, that henceforth we will point out to the German Catholics who arrive on these distant shores and who remain in the cities of this country only long enough to obtain the necessary money to acquire a piece of land; it is there that they will be able to earn their living and at the same time preserve their faith and save their souls. Finally I also see there a peaceful retreat for our own Missionaries who, having spent their strength in apostolic works, will be able to settle down to the exercises of their state and the practice of their rule.

Such were my preoccupations at night, and in the morning I found myself happier than if I had enjoyed a long and comfortable sleep. With the dawn we began again as on the previous day our laborious work with the same courage, for as the days passed we felt more exhausted from the hunger and fatigue; we likewise often thought that we would faint entirely, especially when we were violently assailed by the snow, rain, and gales, then it was not only strength which failed; but what to do when the humidity and the cold seized the body and penetrated to the marrow of the bone, when the winds uprooted even the greatest trees *en masse* and the workmen had to risk being crushed in their fall.

For six weeks I lived this truly Indian life, pretty nearly like the Missionaries who live among the savages.

Before my departure from the colony I traced out once more the public roads, as they are marked by the government, so that at present those who oftentimes chance along are able to penetrate into these wastes without danger of getting lost. More than once some Catholics have already strayed for several days under the terrible dread of not being able to get out, and a Protestant minister who went hunting there disappeared forever. One still finds these remarkable forests in great numbers, even in the most civilized regions of the New World; those who wish to found new settlements ought not to plunge into these distant regions since there the prime necessities of life are naturally rarer and the dangers greater.

The land of which I speak is in Pennsylvania, the diocese of Pitsburg [*sic*]; it is fertile, it abounds in streams and springs of which the water is pure and good; the climate, so much like that of Germany, furnishes all that is necessary for a comfortable life; it is therefore a place very well chosen for a colony.

On returning to Baltimore, I found my confrères in the greatest consternation; as I had not been able to write to them during my long absence, they had made a thousand conjectures about my death; they believed it to be certain that having lost myself in the depth of the forests, I had died there of hunger, or had been eaten by the bears; so that I was received by them as one risen from the dead who was even yet only half alive. Believing myself to be in good health, I laughed at their taking me for a walking skeleton; but I soon found out that the fatigues of this trip had so exhausted me that my days of active labor seemed passed. God did not judge that this was yet enough sacrifice; after an illness of three weeks, he so restored my strength as to enable me to exercise again my missionary functions. Please Heaven that I may be able to establish similar colonies at this price! I will gladly consent to lose for each of them not only my health but even life itself.

I have the honor to be, etc.,

Alexandre Czwitkowietz [*sic*], *General Superior of the Redemptorists Missionaries in America.*

82. Bishop Spalding's Impressions of Protestant Revivalism on the Frontier, 1844

NOT long after the first Maryland Catholic families had immigrated to Kentucky in the 1780's that area was overrun by a series of Protestant revivalist meetings that created tumult on the Kentucky frontier for almost a generation. The prime motive for these unusual gatherings has been stated by one historian as follows: "When the godlessness of the backwoodsmen began to be a matter of concern to the missionaries and the circuit riders, drastic measures were used to bring conviction of sin, repentance, and conversion" (Alice Felt Tyler, *Freedom's Ferment* [Minneapolis, 1944], p. 35). The Kentucky Catholics were amazed at what they witnessed among some of their Protestant neighbors, and one of them, Martin J. Spalding (1810–1872) who died as Archbishop of Baltimore, devoted a chapter of one of his early books to a description of the strange phenomenon. Spalding had had a great deal of experience with Protestants as a religious debater and as editor of the *Catholic Advocate,* a weekly paper which he founded in February, 1835. At the time he wrote the book from which the following passage is taken he was vicar-general of the Diocese of Louisville and four years removed from his consecration as Coadjutor Bishop of Louisville. Source: M. J. Spalding, *Sketches of the Early Catholic Missions of Kentucky* (Louisville: B. J. Webb & Brother, 1844), pp. 82–83, 101, 104–106.

Before we proceed farther in our rapid sketch of the early history of the Catholic missions in Kentucky, it may be well to pause a little, in order to survey the contemporary history of the principal Protestant sects. These often came into collision, not only with each other, but with the Catholic church. Differing in almost all else, they united in the principle of hatred of the Catholic religion. And we cannot fully understand the early history of the latter, in our State, without examining the corresponding phases in the history of the former.

Our sketch, confined, as it necessarily must be, to one chapter, will be very brief and summary, embracing only some of the principal facts and features in the history of the most conspicuous among the early sects of Kentucky. We shall state nothing which is not undoubted, and little that cannot be satisfactorily proved from respectable Protestant authority. To show that we mean to be impartial, we will farther remark, that our chief authority will be a work of some antiquity, and of considerable weight among the sects themselves.[1] . . . [Spalding then treats the religious revivals among the Kentucky Protestants in the early years of the nineteenth century.]

This same great revival was truly an "astonishing and precious work" — the most astonishing perhaps, if not the most precious, that ever was witnessed in this world! It marked an era in the Protestant church history of Kentucky. It was on the whole so very singular, that we will be pardoned for dwelling on it in some detail. . . . [He then quotes from the work of the Protestant writer, William Stone,[2] who wrote critically of religious deceptions in *Matthias and His Impostures* (New York, 1835).]

To understand more fully how very "precious and astonishing" this great revival was, we must farther reflect: 1st. That it produced, not

---

[1] The book in question was *An Outline of the History of the Church in the State of Kentucky,* edited by Robert H. Bishop (Lexington, 1824), which contained the memoirs of the Reverend David Rice, a Presbyterian minister, born in Virginia, in 1733, migrated to Kentucky in 1783, and died there is 1816. Spalding's chapter quoted generously from Rice's memoirs.

[2] William L. Stone (1792–1844), journalist and historian, editor of the New York *Commercial Advertiser,* later exposed the frauds of Maria Monk in his volume, *Maria Monk and the Nunnery of the Hôtel Dieu* (New York, 1836).

a mere momentary excitement, but one that lasted for several successive years: 2ndly. That it was not confined to one particular denomination, but, to a greater or less extent, pervaded all: 3rdly. That men of sense and of good judgment in other matters, were often carried away by the same fanaticism which swayed the mob: 4thly. That this fanaticism was as wide-spread, as it was permanent — not being confined to Kentucky, but pervading most of the adjoining States and territories: and 5thly. That though some were found who had good sense enough to detect the imposture, yet they were comparatively few in number, and wholly unable to stay the rushing torrent of fanaticism, even if they had had the moral courage to attempt it.

Such are some of the leading features of a movement in religion, (!) which is perhaps one of the most extraordinary recorded in history, and to which we know of but few parallels, except in some of the fanatical doings of the Anabaptists in Germany, during the first years of their history. The whole matter furnishes one more conclusive evidence of the weakness of the human mind, when left to itself; and one more sad commentary on the Protestant rule of faith. Here we see whole masses of population, spread over a vast territory, boasting too of their enlightenment and Bible-learning, swayed for years by a fanaticism, as absurd as it was blasphemous; and yet believing all this to be the work of the Holy Spirit!! Let Protestants after this talk about Catholic ignorance and superstition! Had Catholics ever played the "fantastic tricks," which were played off by Protestants during these years, we would perhaps never hear the end of it.

The picture drawn above by Col. Stone is not only not exaggerated, but it even falls short of the original, in many of its features. Besides the "exercises" which he mentions, there was also the *jumping* exercise. Spasmodic convulsions, which lasted sometimes for hours, were the usual sequel to the *falling* exercise. Then there were the "exercises" of *screaming,* and *shouting,* and *crying.* A Camp-meeting during that day exhibited the strangest bodily feats, accompanied with the most Babel-like sounds. An eye-witness of undoubted veracity, stated to us that in passing one of the camp-grounds, he noticed a man in the "*barking* exercise," clasping a tree with his arms, and dashing his head against it until it was all besmeared with blood, shouting all the time that he had "treed his Saviour"!! Another eye-witness stated, that in casually passing by a camp in the night, while the exercises were at the highest, he witnessed scenes of too revolting a character even to be alluded to here.

One of the most remarkable features, perhaps, of these "exercises" is, the apparently well authenticated fact, that many fell into them, by a kind of sympathy, almost in spite of themselves, and some even positively against their own will! Some who visited the meetings to laugh at the proceedings, sometimes caught the contagion themselves. There seems to have then existed in Kentucky a kind of mental and moral epidemic — a short of contagious frenzy — which spread rapidly from one to another.

Yet the charm was not so strong that it could not be broken, as the following incident, related to us by a highly intelligent Protestant gentleman, clearly proves. Some young ladies of his acquaintance came from one of these meetings to pass the night at his father's house. They were laboring under great nervous excitement, and, in the course of the evening, began to *jerk* most violently. The father, one of the most intelligent men in Kentucky, severely rebuked them, and told them bluntly, that he would "have no such behavior as this in his house." The reproof was effectual, and the *jerking* spirit was exorcised! . . .

83. Samuel Mazzuchelli, O.P., on the Catholic Temperance Societies, 1844

ALTHOUGH the evangelical trends in American Protestantism of the early nineteenth century had little in common with American Catholicism, except, perhaps, during the preaching of the parish mission, they shared an interest in the eradication of the evils of intemperance. Beginning in the late 1830's Catholic temperance societies spread rapidly. The American tour (June, 1849–November, 1851) of the famous Irish Capuchin temperance crusader, Theobald Mathew (1790–1856), gave them fresh impetus, and when a national union of these groups was formed at Baltimore in February, 1872, the meeting drew delegates from over 200 societies. One of those who had great admiration for the work of the temperance societies was the remarkable missionary, Samuel Charles Mazzuchelli (1806–1864). This Italian-born Dominican came to the United States in 1828 and for nearly forty years labored tirelessly in behalf of the Indians of the Middle West, in establishing parishes for the new settlers in Iowa, Illinois, and Wisconsin, in founding a teaching sisterhood of Dominican nuns, to say nothing of building the bishop's residence in Dubuque, designing the first capitol at Iowa City, and serving as chaplain to the first territorial legislature of Wisconsin. In 1843 he made his only visit home to Milan, the city of his birth, and there in the following year he published a volume of memoirs of his American experiences with a view to acquainting Italians with the progress of the Church in the United States and of preserving certain documentary materials for its history. Mazzuchelli's appreciation of the American Catholic temperance societies was deep and sincere, even if it was too optimistic about the permanency of the results obtained. Source: *Memoirs Historical and Edifying of a Missionary Apostolic of the Order of Saint Dominic among Various Indian Tribes and among the Catholics and Protestants in the United States of America,* translated by Sister Mary Benedicta Kennedy, O.S.D. (Chicago: W. F. Hall Printing Co., 1915), pp. 282–284; copyright The Dominican Sisters of Sinsinawa, Wisconsin.

Very few persons in the United States cultivate the vine or make wine to any extent, so this beverage forms one of the objects of commerce with France, Spain and Italy, while the distance, imposition of duties, etc., render it not only costly, but also very scarce. But to supply the lack of the vine in America, extensive use is made of strong spirits extracted from Indian corn, which grows there in prodigious quantities and can be had at a very low price. Many of the people are addicted to the abuse of this strong liquor to such a degree as to fall unhappy victims of intoxication.

A great number of the emigrants from Ireland, notwithstanding the Faith, the generosity, the honesty, the industry and all the other virtues that so eminently distinguish the race, were often too weak upon this one point, giving themselves up in bondage to the vice of intemperance. The more zealous among the Protestants, especially the Presbyterians, took occasion from this to hurl bitterest reproaches and invectives against the Catholic Church, which they accused of being far from the Evangelical sanctity she professed, while she held within her own bosom so many leading scandalous lives. But God who often makes use of His very enemies as instruments to carry out the inscrutable designs of His grace, raised up our far-famed Father Matthew [*sic*] in Ireland to banish the demon of drunkenness from that island, and to enroll millions of his compatriots in the Temperance Societies by virtue of which they pledged themselves to taste no beverage that could intoxicate.

The Irish who comprise more than half of the Catholics of the United States, followed the example of their brethren in Europe, and Temperance Societies were founded in every city and village of the land. It could be asserted now that these children of that Saint Patrick to whom Ireland owes her conversion to the Faith are now with very few exceptions models of temperance. The Catholic Clergy exerted themselves to the utmost in America, to bring about a change so marvelous and so necessary to the advancement of the Faith; the Faith that had retrograded among many Catholics through the vice of intemperance. A number of the Bishops and nearly all of the Priests are zealous members of this Society. . . .

If the tree is to be judged by its fruits, there is no doubt as to the Religious influence exerted by the Temperance Society, — in truth we must ascribe thereto these wonderful effects, the conversion of a great number of sinners hardened in vice for years, who approached the tribunal of penance only after they had promised to give up entirely the use of intoxicating liquors. From the year 1839 when the Societies had become established in the various Missions recorded in these Memoirs, piety actually made visible progress from day to day, in proportion as the virtue of Temperance won its blessed victories among the people; peace and plenty reigned in the families, Catholicity won the respect and reverence of its very enemies, and the Faith spread among the more sincere of those outside the Church. Many of the Catholic Irish abandoned entirely the dangerous traffic in intoxicating drink and sought more honorable means of subsistence. . . .

84. A Report to the Ludwig-Missionsverein on Catholicism in Wisconsin, April 23, 1845

AMONG the most important agencies for financial assistance to the American Church was the Ludwig-Missionsverein, founded at Munich in December, 1838, under the patronage of King Louis I of Bavaria, from whom it derived its name. The special objects of this missionary society's benefactions in the United States were the German Catholic immigrants. No center of German Catholic activity was more prominent than the Diocese of Milwaukee which had been erected on November 28, 1843, and which included the entire state of Wisconsin with its 54,715 square miles. When John Martin Henni (1805–1881), the first Bishop of Milwaukee, arrived in his see city in May, 1844, he found only four priests to care for the 15,000 Catholics scattered throughout the state. The fact that by 1850 there were over 60,000 Catholics in Wisconsin with forty-three priests will give some idea of the rapidity of growth of the See of Milwaukee. Between 1838 and 1921 the Ludwig-Missionsverein gave nearly a million dollars to the American missions and the Diocese of Milwaukee was among its principal beneficiaries. Less than a year after his arrival Henni sent a report on religious conditions to the Reverend Joseph Mueller, general manager of the Munich society, in which he included some interesting observations on the secular scene, even to anticipating the St. Lawrence Waterway. Source: *Salesianum,* XXXVII (April, 1942), 82–85, translated by Augustine C. Breig and edited by Peter Leo Johnson.

Milwaukee, April 23rd, 1845.

I received your letter of February 17th. You may imagine how anxiously I was waiting for it for some time. I am very grateful to you for having released at least to a certain extent the suspense I was in and still partly am in on account of some intervening "difficulties" as you remark. In the meanwhile you bid me to be of good cheer. In fact I am, especially since your esteemed letter assures me of your good will towards me and also of the sincere efforts of you and of the rest of the friends in Munich in behalf of my cause, in which no one can be indifferent who has the welfare of the church in this part of America at heart. This holds good especially as far as I am concerned, for I more than others must realize the importance of this cause. I shall therefore very anxiously wait for further developments. In the meanwhile I shall leave the matter entirely to God and to the efforts and prudence of my friends in Munich.

Complying with your advice I have sent a petition directly to the board of directors, as enclosure shows. But since I presumed that the lengthy report on my diocese and my mission journeys, especially among the Indians, which I have sent at the same time to Vienna and Einsiedeln[1] and also to the Catholics of Bavaria, would become known, I have purposely avoided all repetitions and mentioned only the most pressing needs. However I did not dare to ask for a definite sum fearing that such a request might be misinterpreted by some at least. I would prefer that one or the other of my benefactors would suggest this to the board of directors.

With regard to the German-English seminary I have nothing else to add than that the proposed plan appeals to me more day by day. The establishment of such an institute in Bavaria itself should certainly not be undertaken in order to spare the young men the slur of being emissaries because it is this slur the sly bigots yell continuously into our ears. They do not write any more so strongly against the truths of our religion because here they have overcome the strongest prejudices perhaps more than in Germany. But now these people accuse us as being anti-republicans, dangerous to the state. Nothing more than this lie arouses the American, who is generally broad minded, to follow without hesitation justice and truth wherever he finds them. Just this political lie especially invites the American of all

[1] The Leopoldinen-Stiftung of Vienna, founded in April, 1829, was the Austrian counterpart to the Ludwig-Missionsverein. The Abbey of Our Lady of the Hermits at Einsiedeln, Switzerland, was generous in its help to German Catholic missions abroad; it was from Einsiedeln that several Benedictine monks founded the future St. Meinrad's Archabbey in southern Indiana in March, 1854.

classes to investigate our teachings and principles; they are the first ones who follow their conviction. For this reason, to be honest, I like them better than all other Protestants. Lately I received Dr. Hunt an excellent physician into the church. Several others are taking instructions. A good Catholic priest is certainly more respected than the numerous preachers. In spite of my poverty as bishop every one of our outstanding state officials wished to get acquainted with me.

At present I am about to arrange an old frame building for a temporary seminary. I have three seminarists, a German, an Irishman and an Italian, the latter of whom has studied for some time in America, and upon whom I will soon confer major orders. Three other clerics I expect towards the end of August from the Jesuit college in Cincinnati and a fourth one from Montreal, Canada.

Good Father Boeswald[2] is still waiting for a "German bishop" to carry out his grand plan as he lately wrote to Father Heiss.[3] Father Heiss whom I did not keep in the dark about my plans regarding the seminary made him acquainted with it. In the meanwhile I endeavor to get the Rev. Boeswald here if our plan should become a reality. I believe that he would come if he should realize that Covington has not more Germans than Milwaukee. South of the Ohio (river) among the Negroes Germans will never settle. Their main settlements in fact are in the northwestern states. Yes, the majority of the domiciled Germans are there; there only the poor farmer from Europe can acquire the desired land at a low price. It is also easier for him to come to Milwaukee from New York than to Cincinnati. Besides only two or three years may elapse till the English-shipping Well and canal will connect Quebec with Lake Erie. Then ships from Liverpool (and from the Rhein and Trieste, if you wish) shall enter the harbor of Milwaukee. Do not smile dear friend. The time when this shall happen is not far off.

However I do not wish that your box packed with the different church utensils should wait till then. Unfortunately I am not acquainted with anybody on one of the seaports to whom you could send the goods intended for me. For the present I have to ask to inquire [*sic*] of the Liguorians [Redemptorists] who certainly have shipping agents everywhere, how and to what place to send the goods. Even in New

---

[2] Charles Boeswald was pastor of Immaculate Conception Church in Louisville.

[3] The Bavarian-born Michael Heiss (1818–1890) was pastor of St. Mary's Church, Covington, Kentucky, when he volunteered to accompany Henni to Milwaukee in 1844. He later became the first rector of St. Francis Seminary, Milwaukee, 1856–1868; first Bishop of La Crosse, 1868–1880; and Henni's successor in the See of Milwaukee.

York their society might be the surest agent also for me. I shall inform the Rev. Rumpler of this.[4] But I kindly ask you not to send my goods with any belonging to them.

With joy we are looking for the arrival of the Rev. Schraudenbach.[5] Should you be able to find one or the other priest or theological student, I would be very well pleased. I need also two priests who speak French very well, for this reason I shall write to the bishop of Strassburg. Last fall I received at last from Lyons 15,000 francs. What help this was you may imagine. Perhaps you would do well to order for several 100 florins some vestments from the factory you spoke of. Should they be cheap and come up to our expectations some more could be ordered. Could you perhaps get a suitable mitre for me? For all this I authorize you to handle in my name the money granted by the board of directors.

We are informed that Europe had a very severe winter. We had hardly any snow. In fact I have never lived through a more pleasant winter. No doubt the climate here is the healthiest in the United States especially for Europeans. People who come sickly from southern regions grow here healthy and strong. I have also to confess that the spiritual life here is a comfort to me. Since the enlargement of my frame cathedral and a better arrangement of the divine services an excellent spirit manifests itself around me, even among the Protestants.

I have been informed that Miss Linder of Basle was received into the church and that she is living in Munich. Should this be the case kindly give her my best regards and tell her that that I still gratefully remember her kindness towards me. She gave me a beautiful painting representing Christ. Unfortunately I had to leave it at Cincinnati where it adorns a side altar in Holy Trinity church. If Miss Linder still devotes her time to painting I would like to ask her for a picture of St. Francis de Sales. Dear friend in doing so use your own good judgment.

May God bestow his blessing on us and grant that our friends in Munich, you yourself and canon Speth, may work for a long time for the distant missions.

---

[4] The Redemptorists first came to the United States in June, 1832, from Austria and all through the nineteenth century they continued to be one of the leading religious congregations to devote its labors to the German immigrants. Gabriel Rumpler, C.SS.R., was pastor of St. Alphonsus Church in Baltimore at this time.

[5] Charles Schraudenbach was pastor of St. Ignatius Church, Racine, Wisconsin.

85. Consecration of the Cathedral of St. Peter in Chains, Cincinnati, November 2, 1845

ONE of the evidences of the marked growth of American Catholicism in the Middle West in the mid-nineteenth century was the improved quality in both design and materials of the church buildings erected for divine services. Among the fastest growing of the western sees was Cincinnati where by 1845 there were an estimated 65,000 Catholics in a diocese served by sixty-six priests. In 1840 Bishop John B. Purcell (1800–1883) began construction of the new Cathedral of St. Peter in Chains, an edifice which was described a century later as "one of the handsomest and most monumental of Greek Revival churches" (Talbot Hamlin, *Greek Revival Architecture in America* [New York, 1944], p. 285). Hamlin stated that the architect was probably Henry Walters. The cathedral was consecrated on Sunday, November 2, 1845, by Samuel Eccleston, S.S., fifth Archbishop of Baltimore, in the presence of eight bishops and a large gathering of clergy and laity. The unusual ceremony for those days was described in Cincinnati's Catholic weekly newspaper, of which Father Edward Purcell, brother of the bishop, was editor, in an editorial entitled "Consecration of St. Peter's Cathedral." Source: *Catholic Telegraph,* November 6, 1845.

This long expected and gratifying ceremony took place on last Sunday. The clergy of the diocese had been in retreat for eight days previous, under the spiritual direction of V. Rev. Dr. Spalding[1] of Kentucky, and with very few exceptions, all the English Catholics of Cincinnati received the Holy Communion in the old Cathedral, to prepare their souls for celebrating with proper dispositions, their joyous entrance into their new and magnificent Church. The day was chilly and damp, but the crowds in attendance were very great, and the utmost decorum was observed by all, both outside as well as in the interior of the building. The most Rev. Dr. Eccleston, Arch-Bishop of Baltimore was the consecrating Prelate; when the procession entered the Church bearing the relics, the following Bishops attended their metropolitan, The Rt. Rev. Dr. Flaget, Bishop of Louisville; Rt. Rev. Dr. Portier, Bishop of Mobile; Rt. Rev. Dr. Chabrat, Co-adjutor Bishop of Louisville; Rt. Rev. Dr. Henni, Bishop of Milwaukie [*sic*]; Rt. Rev. Dr. Hailandiere, Bishop of Vincennes; Rt. Rev. Dr. Miles, Bishop of Nashville; Rt. Rev. Dr. McClosky [*sic*], Coadjutor Bishop of New York and Rt. Rev. Dr Purcell of Cincinnati — being altogether nine Bishops, eight of whom had left their distant homes, moved by

[1] Martin J. Spalding (1810–1872) succeeded Flaget as Bishop of Louisville in 1850 and died as seventh Archbishop of Baltimore.

the Spirit of charity and kindness, to assist at the consecration. Sixty five clergymen, mostly from Ohio and Kentucky, took part in the services of the day, also the Seminarians of the diocese and Scholastics of the Society of Jesus; all of whom found room in the ample Sanctuary. Amongst them were the Provincials of the Dominican and Jesuit Orders in the West. The services of the Consecration were concluded about noon, having lasted nearly four hours, when the High Mass was celebrated by the Bishop of Mobile. The sermon was an appropriate and polished discourse, delivered with grace and emphasis by Bishop McClosky.[2] His text was from the eighty-third Psalm. "How lovely are thy tabernacles, O Lord of Hosts! my soul longeth and fainteth for the courts of the Lord. . . . For the sparrow hath found herself a house, and the turtle a nest for herself where she may lay her young ones: Thy altars O Lord of Hosts, my King and my God." In the evening the Rev. Mr. Hayden[3] addressed the audience in a very sound and beautiful discourse on Faith. During the ensuing day discourses were delivered by Rev. Mr. McGill[4] and Dr. Spalding of Kentucky, the reputation of both attracting large crowds who were pleased and instructed. Thus, after more than five years labor, the Catholics of Cincinnati have crowned their hopes by the erection and consecration of a Cathedral, which no one can behold without expressing their admiration of its beauty, proportions and durability.

86. Boniface Wimmer Outlines the Future of the Benedictine Order in the United States, November 8, 1845

THE origin of the work of the monks of St. Benedict in the United States was owed to Boniface Wimmer (1809–1887), one of the first five novices to be received at the Abbey of Metten after its restoration in 1830. This Bavarian-born religious began dreaming about an American foundation for the spiritual care of German immigrants as early as 1843. In 1845 Wimmer discussed the American situation with a fellow countryman, Peter Henry Lemcke (1796–1882), then pastor of a congregation at Carrolltown in western Pennsylvania, on the latter's visit to Munich. He likewise spoke with Canon Josef Salzbacher (1790–1867) of Vienna who had been in the United States three years before, and with the Vienna-born Frederick de

[2] John McCloskey (1810–1885) became second Archbishop of New York in 1864 and in 1875 the first cardinal of the United States.

[3] This priest was probably Thomas Heyden (1798–1870) who for years was pastor at Bedford, Pennsylvania, and a friend of Bishop Purcell.

[4] John McGill (1809–1872) became the third bishop of Richmond in 1850.

Held (1799–1881), provincial of the Belgian province, to which the Redemptorists' American missions were subject. It was a period when there was a great deal of criticism in German and Austrian Catholic circles about the money they gave through the Ludwig-Missionsverein and Leopoldinen Stiftung for their compatriots in the United States, being channeled off to non-German projects by Irish-American bishops. In answer to reports brought back by men like Salzbacher and de Held, Wimmer composed the document that follows and had it published anonymously. Fired by his zeal for the missions in the New World, and having secured the permission of his superiors, Wimmer set out in July, 1846, with four ecclesiastical students and fourteen young laymen who desired to embrace the Benedictine life in the United States. Accepting the offer of Michael O'Connor (1810–1872), first Bishop of Pittsburgh, to have his little community settle on some church lands in Westmoreland County, he invested his eighteen companions with the religious habit on October 24, 1846, and thus inaugurated his great work. Wimmer opened a college and a seminary in 1848 at St. Vincent's Priory and in August, 1855, Pope Pius IX granted his petition and raised his foundation to the rank of an abbey and at the same time made Wimmer president of the newly founded American congregation of Benedictines. During his forty years of unceasing labors he sent out missionaries from St. Vincent's who founded six future abbeys: St. John's in Minnesota (1856), St. Benedict's in Kansas (1857), Belmont in North Carolina (1876), St. Bernard's in Alabama (1876), St. Procopius in Illinois (1885), and Holy Cross in Colorado (1886), besides numerous smaller missions in parishes in twenty-five states which by 1885 were ministering to over 100,000 souls, especially among German, Irish, and Italian immigrants. By the time he died Wimmer had more than fulfilled the dream about which he had written over forty years before, in a document which is in many ways the charter of the American Benedictines since the aims and methods it embodied were consistently and successfully developed in the United States. Source: Augsburg *Postzeitung*, November 8, 1845. This document was printed as an appendix in Colman J. Barry, O.S.B., *Worship and Work. St. John's Abbey and University, 1856–1956* (Collegeville, 1956), pp. 345–351.

Every Catholic who cherishes his faith must take a deep interest in missionary labors; but religion as well as patriotism demands that every German Catholic should take a special interest in the missions of America. To us it cannot be a matter of indifference how our countrymen are situated in America. I, for my part, have not been able to read the various and generally sad reports on the desolate condition of Germans beyond the ocean without deep compassion and a desire to do something to alleviate their pitiable condition. Thus, I have given much thought to the question of how they might be practically assisted. It is not difficult to understand what should be done — more German-speaking priests should be found laboring for the spiritual welfare of our countrymen in America. The only question is how to get priests and what kind of priests will do the work most successfully. The answer to the second question will also give the solution for the first. I do not wish to offend anyone, but my opinion is that secular priests are not the best adapted for missionary labors. History shows that the Church has not availed herself of their services to any great extent in missionary undertakings. I do not mean to say that a secular priest cannot labor effectually within a limited territory in America, for there are many who labor successfully even at the present day. But they cannot satisfy themselves. They are in great danger of becoming careless and worldly-minded. I cannot agree with Dr. Salzbacher when he says that the spiritual needs of our countrymen can be provided by perambulating missionaries, who go about like the Wandering Jew from forest to forest, from hut to hut; for unless such a missionary be a *Saint* not much of the spiritual man would remain in him, and even then by such transient visits not much lasting good could be accomplished. The missionary, more than any other priest, stands in need of spiritual renewal from time to time, consolation and advice in trials and difficulties. He must, therefore, have some place where he can find such assistance: this may be given by his bishop but he will find it more securely in a religious community — in the midst of his confrères.

He should also have a home to receive him in his old age or when he is otherwise incapacitated for missionary labors; he should have no worldly cares, otherwise he might neglect or even forget his own and others' spiritual welfare. All this can be had only in a religious community. For this reason, therefore, religious are better adapted to missionary work than secular priests. In a community the experiences of the individual become common property; all have a common interest, stand together and have the same object in view. A vacancy caused by death or otherwise can be filled more readily and having fewer temporal cares, they can devote themselves more exclusively to the spiritual interests of themselves and others. Thus, all other things being equal, a religious priest in a community should be able to work more effectively on the missions than the secular priest who stands alone.

The next question is: What religious Order is most adapted for the American missions, not to convert the native Indians but to provide for the spiritual necessities of German immigrants?

As far as I know the only Religious in the strict sense of the word now found in America are the Jesuits and Redemptorists. The missionaries of the Middle Ages, the Benedictines, Dominicans and Franciscans are not yet represented in the New World, except by a few individuals who do not live in monasteries.[1] The Jesuits devote their energies principally to teaching in colleges; their students are mostly from the higher classes of society and many of them belong to Protestant families. Many Jesuits are also doing excellent work among the Indians, and others have charge of congregations in cities near their colleges. But while they accomplish so much in their sphere of labors, they can do little for Germans, because few of them speak their language. The Redemptorists are doing noble work for our countrymen in the States: in cities and thickly settled country districts they have large congregations, and also do what they can for others as travelling missionaries. Some secular priests likewise go about among the scattered Catholics doing good, but they naturally and necessarily concentrate in cities where there is a large Catholic population.

We see, therefore, that much is being done in America; very much, indeed, when we consider the small band of priests and the difficulties under which they labor. But as yet nothing has been done for the stability of the work, no provision has been made for an increase of German-speaking priests, to meet the growing demand for missionary laborers. It is not difficult to see that secular priests, whose labors extend over a district larger than a diocese, can do nothing to secure reinforcements to their own number. But why have the Redemptorists and Jesuits not accomplished more in this line? By his vows neither the Jesuit nor the Redemptorist is bound to any particular place, but he must always be prepared to leave his present position at the command of his superiors, and may also request, if not demand, his removal for weighty reasons. This has many advantages, but for America it seems to me also to have disadvantages. For the successor of the one who has been removed will require a long time to become acquainted with all the circumstances with which his predecessor was familiar, and even the uncertainty as to how long he will remain at any particular place will be an obstacle in his way. Moreover, the fact that Jesuits generally receive only the children of richer families, many of whom are Protestants, into their institutions, because they depend upon them for their sustenance, and that the Redemptorists are by their statutes required to devote themselves to missionary work, and can, therefore, not be expected to take charge of seminaries, gives us no reason to hope that the spiritual wants of Americans, particularly of German-

[1] Wimmer was unaware that Edward D. Fenwick, O.P. (1768–1832), first Bishop of Cincinnati, had opened St. Rose Priory near Springfield, Kentucky, as the first Dominican convent in the United States as early as December 1806.

Americans will be provided for by native German-speaking priests And in case the mission societies of Europe should unexpectedly be rendered incapable of supplying money or reinforcements in priests, the situation would become even more serious. But even supposing that everything remains as it is, we cannot hope to have an efficient supply of priests as long as we have no means of securing a native clergy for the United States of America. For the number of those who are educated at Alt-Oetting[2] or elsewhere in Germany is not in proportion to the continually increasing emigration to America, not to speak of the natural increase of Germans in America itself. Jesuits and Redemptorists are, therefore, doing noble work in America and their number should be increased as much as possible; but they will scarcely be able to remove the chief cause of the deficiency of German-speaking priests. We need not speak of the Dominicans and Franciscans; there are very few German Dominicans, and the present social condition of America seems not to call for Mendicant Friars.

We now come to the Benedictines, who are not as yet represented in the United States. In my opinion they are the most competent to relieve the great want of priests in America. In support of my opinion I will adduce some facts: but I must again state that I have not the remotest intention of belittling the efforts and successes of other religious Orders; on the contrary, I am desirous of seeing them labor in the same field, side by side with the Benedictines.

History abundantly proves:

1. That we owe the conversion of England, Germany, Denmark, Sweden, Norway, Hungary, and Poland almost exclusively to the Benedictines, and that in the remaining parts of Europe Christendom is deeply indebted to them.
2. That the conversion of these countries was not transient but lasting and permanent.
3. That this feature must be ascribed to the fact that the Benedictines are men of stability; they are not wandering monks; they acquire lands and bring them under cultivation and become thoroughly affiliated to the country and people to which they belong, and receive their recruits from the district in which they have established themselves.
4. That the Benedictine Order by its Rule is so constituted that

[2] Wimmer was doubtless referring here to the seminary for candidates to the diocesan priesthood at Altötting, permission for which he had received from King Ludwig I of Bavaria. Altötting was the site of a popular shrine to our Lady where Wimmer had served as an assistant priest for a short time.

> it can very readily adapt itself to all times and circumstances. The contemplative and practical are harmoniously blended; agriculture, manual labor, literature, missionary work, education, were drawn into the circle of activity which St. Benedict placed before his disciples. Hence they soon felt at home in all parts of Europe and the same could be done in America.

When we consider North America as it is today, we can see at a glance that there is no other country in the world which offers greater opportunities for the establishment and spread of the Benedictine Order, no country that is so much like our old Europe was. There are found immense forests, large uncultivated tracts of land in the interior, most fertile lands which command but a nominal price; often for miles and miles no village is to be seen, not to speak of cities. In country districts no schools, no churches are to be found. The German colonists are scattered, uncultured, ignorant, hundreds of miles away from the nearest German-speaking priest, for, practically, they can make their homes where they please. There are no good books, no Catholic papers, no holy pictures. The destitute and unfortunate have no one to offer them a hospitable roof, the orphans naturally become the victims of vice and irreligion — in a word, the conditions in America today are like those of Europe 1000 years ago, when the Benedictine Order attained its fullest development and effectiveness by its wonderful adaptability and stability.

Of course, the Benedictine Order would be required to adapt itself again to circumstances and begin anew. To acquire a considerable tract of land in the interior of the country, upon which to found a monastery, would not be very difficult; to bring under cultivation at least a portion of the land and to erect the most necessary buildings would give employment for a few years to the first Benedictine colony, which should consist of at least two or three priests and ten to fifteen brothers skilled in the most necessary trades.

Once the colony is self-supporting, which could be expected in about two years, it should begin to expand so that the increased number of laboring hands might also increase the products and revenues to be derived from the estate. A printing and lithographing establishment would also be very desirable.

Since the Holy Rule prescribes for all, not only manual labor and the chanting of the Divine Office, but also that the monks should devote several hours a day to study, this time could be used by the Fathers to instruct the Brothers thoroughly in arithmetic, German grammar, etc., thereby fitting them to teach school, to give catechetical instruction and in general to assist in teaching children as well as grown persons.

Such a monastery would from the very start be of great advantage to German settlers, at least to those who would live near it. They would have a place where they could depend upon hearing Mass on Sundays and hear a sermon in their own language; they would also have a place where they could always be sure to find a priest at home to hear their confessions, to bless their marriages, to baptize their children and to administer the last sacraments to the sick if called in time.

Occasionally the Superior might send out even the Brothers two by two to hunt up fallen-away Catholics, to instruct children for their first Communion etc. All subsequent monasteries that might be established from the mother house would naturally exercise the same influence.

So far, the services rendered by the Benedictines would not be extraordinary; any other priests or religious could do the same, except that they would not likely be able to support themselves without assistance from Europe; whereas a community of Benedictines, when once firmly established would soon become self-sustaining.

But such a monastery if judiciously located would not long remain isolated; all reports from America inform us that the German immigrants are concentrating themselves in places where churches have been erected or where a German-speaking priest has taken up his residence. This would also be found, and to a greater extent, if there were a monastery somewhere with a good school. In a short time a large German population would be found near the monastery, just as in the Middle Ages, villages, towns and cities sprang up near Benedictine abbeys. Then the monks could expect a large number of children for their school, and in the course of time, as the number of priests increases, a college with a good Latin course could be opened. They would not be dependent upon the tuition fee of the students for their support, which they could draw from the farm and the missions (though these would not be a source of much income in the beginning). Thus they could devote their energies to the education of the poorer classes of boys who could pay little or nothing, and since these boys would daily come in contact with the priests and other monks, it could scarcely be otherwise but that many of them would develop a desire of becoming priests or even religious. I am well aware that to many readers these hopes and expectations will appear too sanguine, since all efforts at securing a native American clergy have hitherto failed so signally. But we must remember that the annals of the missions as well as the oral reports of priests who have labored in America, inform us that these efforts were more theoretical than practical, that there was a desire of making such efforts, but they they were not really made, and that those which were really made were more or less restricted to the English-speaking clergy, and that in general there were neither sufficient means nor sufficient teachers to train a native German-speaking clergy. It is said that the young American is not inclined to devote himself to the sacred ministry because it is so easy for him to secure a wife and home; that the American has nothing in view but to heap up the riches of this world; that fathers need their sons on the farms or in the workshops and, therefore, do not care to see them study. But, let me ask, is it not the same here in Europe? Are the rich always pleased when their sons study for the priesthood? Are all Germans in America well-to-do or rich? Are they not as a rule the very poorest and to a certain extent the menials of the rest? Moreover, is the first thought of a boy directed to matrimony? Is it any wonder that he should show no inclination for the priesthood when he sees a priest scarcely once a year; when divine services are held in churches which resemble hovels rather than churches, without pomp and ceremony, when the priest has to divest himself of his priestly dignity, often travels on horse-back, in disguise, looking more like a drummer than a priest, when the boy sees nothing in the life of a priest but sacrifice, labor and fatigue?

But all this would become quite different if boys could come in daily contact with priests, if they received instructions from them, if the priest could appear to advantage, better dressed and better housed than the ordinary settler, if young men could learn from observation to realize and appreciate the advantages of a community life, if they could learn to understand that while the life of a priest requires self-denial and sacrifice, his hopes of a great reward are also well grounded. Yes, I do not doubt but that hundreds, especially of the lower classes, would prefer to spend their lives in well regulated monasteries in suitable and reasonable occupations, than to gain a meager livelihood by incessant hard labor in forest regions. Let us remember that here in Bavaria from the year 740 to the year 788 not less than 40 Benedictine monasteries were founded and the communities were composed almost entirely of natives from the free classes, who had enjoyed the advantages of freedom in the world and could have chosen the married state without any difficulty or hindrance. Why should we not reasonably expect the same results in the United States where the conditions are so similar?

But such a monastery in North America would not draw its recruits exclusively from the surrounding country, but also from the great number of boys, who either during the voyage or soon after their arrival in America lose their parents and thereby become helpless and forsaken. An institution, in which such unfortunate children could find a home, would undoubtedly be a great blessing for that country. And where could this be done more easily than in Benedictine monasteries as described above, in which young boys could not only attend school, but also do light work on the farm or in the workshops and according to their talents and vocation become priests or at least educated Christians and good citizens. Surely, many of these would gladly join the community as brothers or priests, and thus repay the monastery for the trouble of educating them.

In this way a numerous religious clergy could soon be secured, and then some of the Fathers might be sent out to visit those Catholics who scarcely ever see a priest; occasionally at least they might preach the word of God and bring the consolations of religion even to those who live at a great distance from the monastery; small congregations could be established, and the seminary could soon furnish a goodly number of the secular clergy.

But where could the Benedictines be found to establish such a monastery in North America, and where are the necessary means for such an undertaking? The writer is informed that there are several Fathers in the Benedictine Order here in Bavaria who would gladly go upon such a mission, and with regard to Brothers there would be no difficulty whatever; within a few years not less than 200 good men have applied for admission into one of our monasteries. It is a well known fact that of those who are studying for the priesthood many are joining the Redemptorist Order simply because it offers them the hope of becoming missionaries in America.

The necessary funds could easily be supplied by the Louis Mission Society.[3] Bavaria annually pays 100,000 florins into the treasury of this Society. Would it be unfair to devote one tenth of this sum to the establishment of monasteries in America, especially since just now hundreds of our own nationality are seeking homes in the United States, and consequently the money contributed would be used to

[3] The Ludwig-Missionsverein was founded in Munich in December, 1838, to assist German Catholic emigrants. Between 1842 and 1922 the society contributed $886,504.52 to the Catholic missions in the United States.

further the interests of Germans in general and our countrymen in particular? Could a better use of such contributions be made or could anything appeal more loudly to our national patriotism? Is it right that we should continually look after the interests of strangers and forget our own countrymen? Moreover, whatever would be done for the Germans would advance the well-being of the entire Church in America. We must not stifle our feelings of patriotism. The Germans, we hear it often enough, lose their national character in the second or third generation, they also lose their language, because like a little rivulet they disappear in the mighty stream of the Anglo-American population in the States. Is this not humiliating for us Germans? Would this sad condition of affairs continue if here and there a German center were established, to which the stream of emigration from our country could be systematically directed, if German instruction and sermons were given by priests going forth from these centers, if German books, papers and periodicals were distributed among the people, if German boys could receive a German education and training, which would make themselves felt in wider circles?

Let us, therefore, no longer build air castles for our countrymen in America. Let us provide for their religious interests, then their domestic affairs will take care of themselves. Benedictine monasteries of the old style are the best means of checking the downward tendencies of our countrymen in social, political and religious matters. Let Jesuits and Redemptorists labor side by side with the Benedictines; there is room enough for all and plenty of work. If every Religious Order develops a healthy activity within its sphere, the result will be doubly sure and great. North America will no longer depend upon Europe for its spiritual welfare, and the day may come when America will repay us just as England, converted by the Benedictines, repaid the continent of Europe.

87. The Inauguration of the First Conference of the Society of St. Vincent de Paul in the United States, November 20, 1845

ONE of the most important agencies of private charity in the United States is the Society of St. Vincent de Paul. Founded in Paris in 1833 by Frédéric Ozanam (1813–1853), a young professor of literature in the Sorbonne, it had an immediate appeal and rapidly spread throughout the Catholic world.

Through John Timon, C.M. (1797–1867), first Bishop of Buffalo, who witnessed its beneficent results on a visit to France, the idea was brought to St. Louis while Timon was still working in Missouri. Father Ambrose J. Heim (1807–1854), a French-born assistant pastor in the old cathedral parish, took it up and won the immediate support of a small group of zealous laymen who held their first meeting in the schoolroom of the old cathedral on November 20, 1845. A week later on November 27 a second meeting — the minutes of which are given below — worked out the details as to the procedure they would employ in relieving the city's Catholic poor. From these humble beginnings the society fanned out across the country until today it is a recognized feature of numerous parishes and embraces thousands of Catholic laymen in its membership. Source: Minute Book, St. Louis Old Cathedral Conference, St. Vincent de Paul Society, p. 26, quoted in Daniel T. McColgan, *A Century of Charity. The First One Hundred Years of the Society of St. Vincent de Paul in the United States* (Milwaukee: The Bruce Publishing Co., 1951), I, 79–80.

At a second meeting of the St. Vincent de Paul Society held at the Cathedral School Room on the Thursday evening of the 27th ultimo, the minutes of the preceding meeting were read by the Secretary and approved.

Dr. Linton[1] on the part of the committee appointed to wait upon the right Reverend Bishop[2] to apprize him of the organization and purposes of the Society read a letter received by the committee from him fully approving of the organization and objects of it, being designed to relieve and alleviate the suffering and wants of those in a poor and destitute condition during the inclement season of the year.

The Visitors selected at the previous meeting to ascertain the particular cases in the neighborhood of their respective Parishes requiring immediate attention and assistance on the part of the Society, made their reports, in which several cases of suffering and destitution were portrayed that appealed thoroughly to the liberal and charitable feelings of the meeting.

On motion it was resolved and carried that a collection be immediately taken up in furtherance of the objects had in view in the formation of the society, in order to place funds in the hands of the visitors whereby individual suffering for want of means may be relieved to the extent at least of the means placed by the Society at the disposal of the visiting committee.

The collection amounted to the sum of twenty dollars forty seven

[1] Moses L. Linton (1808–1872), first president of the society, was a convert to Catholicism and a professor of medicine in St. Louis University.

[2] Peter Richard Kenrick (1806–1896) was the second bishop and first Archbishop of St. Louis.

and a half cents which added to the sum collected at the previous meeting, made the total sum of thirty seven dollars seventeen and a half cents was placed in the hands of the Treasurer.

On motion it was resolved and carried unanimously that half the funds collected should be equally divided among the different Parishes, giving to each an equal proportion: and that one-fourth be applied to the immediate relief of the cases just mentioned to the meeting, and the remaining fourth be kept on hand for contingency.

A motion was made and carried that a committee of three be appointed to draft a letter of communication to the parent Society in Paris, whereupon the President appointed the following gentlemen as that Committee — Judge Mullanphy,[3] Judge Manning, Revd. Mr. Heim.

A motion was made and carried that the fourth of the funds for present distribution be numerically divided among the visitors present who were acquainted with the locality where the distress was to be found whereupon the President appointed the following gentlemen as distributors of this fund:

Mr. Everhart
Mr. O'Neil
Mr. O'Keefe
Mr. Ridener (Reidener?)

A motion was then put and carried that the several visitors appointed should severally report themselves to the Priests and distribute the funds entrusted to their care according to their sense of propriety, taking into consideration those most in need of their assistance, whereupon the President appointed as the Visiting Committee (one Visitor for each of the following) —

1) For the Parish of St. Vincent de Paul
2) For the Cathedral
3) For the Parish of Saint Francis Xavier
4) For the Parish of Saint Patrick

[3] Byran Mullanphy (1809–1851) was a judge of the Circuit Court who in 1847 became Mayor of St. Louis. He was the only son of the wealthy merchant and philanthropist, John Mullanphy (1758–1833), whose generosity brought about the first Catholic hospital in the United States at St. Louis in November, 1828, besides generous gifts to the Jesuits, the Religious of the Sacred Heart, and the Sisters of Loretto. Speaking of the elder Mullanphy's death in August, 1833, John E. Rothensteiner stated, "With him died the noblest Catholic layman St. Louis has ever known. . . ." (*History of the Archdiocese of St. Louis* [St. Louis, 1928], I, 450). At his death in 1851 the younger Mullanphy left one third of his estate, valued at about $200,000, as a trust fund to furnish relief to poor immigrants passing through St. Louis to settle in the West.

88. A Broadside on the Infant University of Notre Dame, January 1, 1847

AMONG American Catholic institutions of higher learning none has found a more secure place in the hearts of all Americans, and none has had a brighter record of achievement in education for Christian manhood, than the University of Notre Dame. Like most universities, its origins were humble and obscure. A generous gift of land from Father Stephen Badin to the Bishop of Vincennes, the latter's determination to have a college for boys, but above all the zeal and resourcefulness of Edward Sorin (1814–1893), American founder of the Congregation of Holy Cross, were the principal factors that brought it into being. Sorin came to Notre Dame in November, 1842, and the following year he and his little community of Holy Cross priests and brothers began classes with two students on a site hallowed by the missionary labors of priests like Badin and Louis Deseille. In January, 1844, the school received a university charter from the legislature of Indiana. Less than a week after his arrival at Notre Dame the founder had outlined the prospect he entertained for its future to Basile-Antoine Moreau, Superior-General of Holy Cross, and in his letter of December 5, 1842, he predicted, "This college will be one of the most powerful means of doing good in this country. . . ." (*Circular Letters of the Very Reverend Edward Sorin* [Notre Dame, 1885], I, 261). The ensuing century fully justified the prediction for the university that today enrolls some 5,500 students taught by a faculty of nearly 600 teachers. The following broadside — a way of attracting students used by all schools of the period — was printed when the college was three years old; it gives a picture of the conditions and rules of student life in the days of its infancy. Source: Archives of the University of Notre Dame.

UNIVERSITY OF NOTRE-DAME-DU-LAC,
St. Joseph County, Indiana.

UNDER THE DIRECTION OF THE PRIESTS OF THE HOLY CROSS.

This Institution commenced under the auspices of the Rt. Rev'd Bishop of Vincennes who presented to the priests of the Holy cross, the beautiful and elegant site upon which the buildings are erected, is now in full operation.

Notre-Dame-du-Lac is at a distance of 1 mile from South Bend, the County seat; 80 miles from Chicago, Illinois; 180 from Detroit, Mich. with which there is direct communication by railroad, and 80 from Fort Wayne, Ia.

The edifice is of brick, four and half story [*sic*] high and not inferior in point of style or structure to any of the colleges of the

United States, and is situated upon a commanding eminence on the verge of two picturesque and commodious Lakes, which, with the river St. Joseph and the surrounding country, present a most magnificent prospect. The rooms are spacious, well ventilated and furnished, with every thing conducive to regularity and comfort.

The Infirmary is intrusted to Sisters similar in their Institute to the Sisters of Charity; their well known kindness and skill are a sufficient guarantee, that the invalids will be attended to with all the diligence and care, which devotion and affection can suggest.

The disciplinary government is mild, yet sufficiently energetic, to preserve that good order, so essential to the well-being of the Institution. The morals and general deportment of the pupils are watched over with the greatest assiduity and solicitude; their personal comfort receives the most paternal attention, and no pains are spared to prepare them for fulfilling their respective duties in society. In their daily recreations, they are always accompanied by a member of the Institution; all books in their possession are subject to the inspection of the Prefect of Studies; and none are allowed circulation without his approval. Corporal punishments will never be inflicted, but more conciliatory and effective means of correction are judiciously used; should a pupil prove refractory, and incorrigible, he will be dismissed.

The faculty is formed of the priests of the Holy Cross: a member is annually sent to Europe to complete whatever contingent circumstances may require. In the reception of pupils no distinction of creed is made, and the parents of those, not professing the Catholic faith, may rest assured that there will be no interference with their religious tenets; they are required only to attend to the religious exercises with decorum, this being in conformity with the rules of all the catholic colleges in the United States.

TERMS,

Board, washing and medical attendance, with the English Course, embracing all the branches of a practical education;

Orthography, Reading, Writing, Arithmetic, Grammar and Composition, to which particular attention is paid; Geography, Ancient and Modern History; the most approved methods of Book-keeping, Surveying, Mensuration, Mathematics, Astronomy, the use of the Globes, Rhetoric, Vocal Music, &c. Free admittance to the Museum, lessons of natation and

Equestrian exercises &c. . . . . $100 per ann.
Half Boarders, ... 40 " "

Day scholars in the above course	20	"	"
The same in the preparatory School, ...	16	"	"
The classical course of Latin, and Greek an additional sum of	20	"	"
The French, German languages are taught at an extra charge of	12	"	"
Instrumental Music and Drawing	20	"	"
Piano	40	"	"

Class books, Stationary [*sic*], and Medicines furnished at the usual rates.

The payments must be made semi-annually in advance; from this rule there can be no deviation whatever, as the charges are based upon the lowest estimate, the object of the Institution being to increase the facilities of instruction, without any view to pecuniary reward.

The distribution of Premiums takes place on the 1st Tuesday of August, and the commencement of the scholastic year is irrevocably fixed on the 1st Friday of October.

The Institution being in possession of all the powers and privileges of a University: degrees will be conferred after the public examination.

No boarder will be received for a shorter term than half a year, and no deduction made for absence, except in case of sickness or dismission.

Examinations take place at the end of each Quarter, and reports are forwarded semi-annually to parents, informing them of the progress, health, &c., of their children. Public examinations, before the distribution of premiums, will take place in the last week of July in every year.

DIRECTIONS FOR PARENTS.

Each pupil must be provided with bed and bedding, (if furnished by the Institution, they form an extra charge,) six shirts, six pair of stockings, six pocket handkerchiefs, six towels (all of which must be marked,) a knife and fork, a table and tea spoon, a hat and cap, two suits of clothes, an over-coat, a pair of shoes and a pair of boots for winter; three suits of clothing and two pair of shoes for summer. No advances will be made by the Institution for clothing or other expenses.

The pupils will not be allowed to have money in their possession; their pocket money must be deposited in the Treasurer's hands, in order to guard against abuses, and to enable the Institution to apply the money as an incentive to virtue and industry. When parents wish to have their children sent home, they must give timely notice, settle all accounts, and supply means to defray their traveling expenses.

Visitors cannot be permitted to interrupt the pupils during the hours of study. The mid-day recreation commences at half past 12 and ends at half past one o'clock. This is the most appropriate time for the visits of parents and friends.

☞ All letters to pupils or members of the Institution must be post paid.

Rev. E. SORIN, President

Notre Dame du Lac, St. Joseph)
County, Indiana, January 1st, 1847.)
References to the Rt. Rev. Bishop of Vincennes and to the Rt. Rev. Bishop of Detroit Rev. Mr. Benoit, Fort-Wayne, Ia. [*sic*].

89. The Act of Foundation for the First Permanent Trappist Monastery in the United States, October 23, 1848

ONE of the most extraordinary developments in recent Catholicism has been the growth of the contemplative religious life among American men. As far back as 1802 a party of Trappists, hunted out of France by the anticlerical laws of the revolution and Napoleon I, had come to the United States under the leadership of Urban Guillet (1766–1817). But repeated attempts to establish a permanent foundation in various parts of the country — including the years 1805–1809 near the present site of the American mother abbey in Kentucky — ended in failure and in 1814 the monks returned to France. Thirty-four years later the superior of the Abbey of Our Lady of Melleray near Nantes, finding his house overcrowded and worried about the effects of the revolution of February, 1848, decided upon an American foundation. A party of forty-some monks arrived in Kentucky in December, 1848, and took up residence on a farm located about fifteen miles southeast of Bardstown, giving to their house the name of Our Lady of Gethsemani. Of its early years Thomas Merton has said, "The devil does not like monasteries, especially contemplative ones. He has spent a hundred years trying to interfere with Gethsemani — and in the early days the battle was not altogether to his disadvantage" (*The Waters of Siloe* [New York, 1949], p. 108). Gethsemani, however, endured and before the end of the century two other Trappist houses — founded from Ireland and Canada — had been established near Dubuque, Iowa, and Providence, Rhode Island. But it is our own day that has seen the amazing development of the contemplative life with the American Church now having eleven Trappist monasteries, eight of which have been founded since 1944, with a total of over 1,000 monks. Moreover, in 1951 the first house of Carthusians, the strictest order in the Church, was established at Sky Farm near Whitingham, Vermont. In the following document the Abbot of Melleray issued authorization for the new foundation in Kentucky and addressed his farewell words to the monks on the eve of their departure for the New World. Source: Archives of the Abbey of Our Lady of Gethsemani.

We, Brother Maxime,[1] Abbot of Our Lady of La Trappe of Melleray, of the Order of Citeaux, in the Diocese of Nantes, near Chateaubriand (Lower Loire), penetrated with the most lively gratitude toward God for the grace He has vouched to Us in calling Us to the religious state, and fully appreciating the wonderful merit there is in embracing a state of life wherein so many have so highly sanctified themselves; after having had recourse to God in prayer, and after having interceded long with Mary, the Most Blessed Virgin, and with St. Joseph, We have resolved for the greater glory of Our Lord, to make a foundation in Kentucky, in the neighborhood of Louisville, in the Diocese of Mgr. Flaget,[2] in a place called Gethsemani, which now, according to the custom of our Fathers of Citeaux, shall be called Our Lady of La Trappe of Gethsemani. For the establishment of this foundation We have sent out forty-four members under the jurisdiction of the Reverend Father Eutropius,[3] whom We have appointed Prior. Their names are FF. MM. Eutropius, Prior, Paulinus, Euthymius, Benezet, Robert, John Chrysostom, Emmanuel, Jerome, Timothy, Dorotheus, Edward, Ephrem, Michael and Adrian; to these choir religious we add the novices: Philemon, Augustine and Benedict. We send twenty-three lay brothers: i.e., Leo, Medard, James, Charles, Hilarion, Amedeus, Thomas, Augustine, Theodoret, David, Saturninus, Matthew, Isaac, Philibert, Antoninus, Julius, Eugene, Elias and Jerome, the novice Orsis, the oblate Lazarus, the postulants Ferdinand and Isidore; and finally three family-brothers: Julian, Bedoue, and Father Huig.

After furnishing them with all We judged necessary for the starting of such an enterprise. We have placed them in the hands of the good Providence, praying that He may cause this holy undertaking

---

[1] Maxim Maulouin (1801–1852) was elected abbot of the Abbey of Our Lady of Melleray in February, 1839.

[2] Benedict J. Flaget, S.S. (1763–1850), was the first Bishop of Bardstown. The see was transferred to Louisville in February, 1841.

[3] Eutropius Proust, O.C.S.O. (1809–1874), was made the first abbot of Our Lady of Gethsemani when the foundation was raised to the rank of an abbey on July 21, 1850.

to prosper and increase in numbers, that they may themselves one day be able to establish other houses, thereby facilitating the salvation of many souls.

Our dear Brethren will secure happy results if they persevere in the spirit of their holy vocation which will lead them to make a special study of the virtues of Charity, Obedience, Purity, Poverty, Mortification and Patience. Let Our Brethren never cease devoting themselves to the spirit of prayer; for then they shall be happily surprised to see the progress that they will make in virtue, provided only that they persevere in this holy exercise. Let perfect union reign in their midst. The world and the devil will be unable to achieve anything against them so long as they remain united. Let them remember: "every house divided against itself shall fall;" let them love their Superior reverently and with warm hearts. Let them console him in his solicitudes by union and obedience. Let them on no account adopt an attitude that might compel the Superior to tone down his orders to suit them. Considering their own misery, let them be humble of mind and heart. Do this, my dearly beloved Brethren, and you shall live. Amen. Amen.

Given at Our Abbey of Melleray, under Our seal and that of Our Secretary on this 23rd day of the month of October, in the year 1848 — the eve of their departure.

Fr. Maxime O.C. Abbot
Fr. Serapion, Secretary.

90. The Catholic Missions in the Far Northwest, January 12, 1849

WHILE missionaries in the Southwest were struggling against floods and rattlesnakes their counterparts in the far Northwest were contending with the bitterly cold winters as one of their chief handicaps. But in every section the Indian medicine men, epidemics, and general deprivation were their lot. Among the earliest Catholic missionaries in the Northwest were the Oblates of Mary Immaculate who arrived in September, 1847, with Bishop Magloire Blanchet when he came to take possession of his new Diocese of Walla Walla, erected on July 24, 1846, only a month after the treaty between the United States and Great Britain had settled the Oregon boundary dispute. In the party which had Pascal Richard, O.M.I., as superior were Eugene Casimir Chirouse and Jean F. Pandosy who were ordained on January 2, 1848, the first priests to be ordained in what would become Washington Territory in 1853. A year after his ordination Chirouse wrote a letter to Richard in which he described the hardships of his life in the Northwest,

but rigorous as it was he remained there until the Oblate missions were closed in 1878. The Archdiocese of Oregon City had been established in July, 1846, with Walla Walla as a suffragan see and in the tremendous area of both sees there were in 1850 only 10,000 Catholics who were served by about twenty priests. Source: *Annales de la Propagation de la Foi,* XXIII (1851), 75–80.

Holy Cross of Simkoné [*sic*], January 12, 1849.

My Reverend Father,

A few days after my return from Nesqually, I went to the camp of Kamayarken where I have built a small cabin with the aid of good Brother Verney and some savages. Saint Joseph is the patron whom the Bishop[1] wished to give to this poor, little house, and that great saint protected me until the winter. The cold commencing to make itself felt, the chief and all his Indians prepared to leave for their snow encampment on the Yakima River — a day's journey from St. Rose.[2] They begged me to go and spend the severe season with them. I acceded to their request only on condition that they build me a second cabin where I could be sheltered from the winds and snows. In less than a month the house was built from trunks of poplar trees. My new dwelling, thirty feet long by fifteen wide, gave me enough space to have two rooms — one for myself, and one for the assembly of the Indians for prayer. It is there, Reverend Father, that the troubles, the sorrows, and the crosses of everyone fall on me like hail upon a young plant which is commencing to bud. That is why I call my new residence by the name of the Holy Cross, a sweet name which always inspires me with the proper conduct in the trials of this life.

At this moment savages from nearly all the neighboring nations are assembled at Holy Cross. I count sixty cabins in my village, around one hundred families. There I have *Yellow-Serpent* [chief of the Yakima tribe] with his following as an opponent. He himself presides at all the abominations which are spoken or committed in his infernal den. An old trickster does his best to help him to embarrass me: irritated because my instructions are contrary to his maxims and diabolical acts, he has invented this strange calumny in order that I might be put to death: "The Blackrobe," he says, "catches rattlesnakes, and makes them vomit a black poison with which he poisons

---

[1] Augustin Magloire Blanchet (1797–1887) was first Bishop of Walla Walla.

[2] St. Rose, later called St. Rose of Simcoe, was located on the Yakima River about where it meets the Columbia.

the tobacco with the intention of killing everyone." That is the reason I no longer give tobacco to anyone. The result of that resolution has been a very happy one: I thus conserve my small supply of tobacco for myself, and all the men are furious against the old calumniator. I am afraid of only one thing, and that is that they will hang him at the first opportunity.

In spite of all the shafts of the enemy, I have only thanks to render to the Lord and to congratulate myself on the numerous blessings which he has bestowed on my feeble efforts. In the space of a month or two I have been able to baptize over thirty children and seven adults, well enough instructed in the principles of our holy Religion. Most of our new Christians of St. Rose have come to spend the winter at Holy Cross where they have edified more by their good example than I have by my preaching.

Up to the present I have been able to visit without fear the savages of my village and to instruct them publicly. Most of them now have the fever or the grippe. In each cabin there are some dead or dying. In less than fifteen days more than thirty people have died from this plague. Furthermore, the cold is so intense that several of our hunters have been frozen in the saddle; the animals succumb to these rigors united to the scarcity, because famine has added evils to such a degree that they overwhelm my poor neophytes. One has a treat when he has a horse, a dog, or a wolf to eat. The public calamity does not spare me, R. Father, and I consider myself very fortunate to still have in reserve a dog and two wolves for food. I hope that will last me until the end of the carnival and that at that time the good God, moved with compassion for us, will send us some venison or bears.

In the midst of this desolation I have rest neither day nor night. During the day I run from one cabin to another to baptize the children, to instruct the adults who wish to hear me, and to bury the new Christians whom death has taken from us. At night I baptize again, then I say my office if the first rays of the sun do not surprise me at the bedside of someone in agony. At this moment I have near me a little angel who sleeps the sleep of the just; I say a little angel because he is yet only six months old. Yesterday I purified him with baptismal water, and this morning at daybreak his beautiful soul went to heaven. This evening I shall accompany him to the cemetery. Five of my newly-baptized have refused the diabolical ministry of the deceiver; according to my advice, which they took eagerly, they have perspired and they now enjoy perfect health. The deceiver, furious because he is not able to cure any of the sick, in spite of his infernal contortions, does not cease to vomit forth against me a thousand maledictions. "You see," he has said in pointing out my cabin, "look at that wooden house, surmounted with a white cross; it is there whence comes our misery; it is there that death gets loose; it is the blackrobe who kills us by his prayer, by his words, and by his medicine water (baptism). Burn his cabin and cut off his head, after that I will heal all of you." The reprobates believe the speeches of the deceiver, and some have evil intentions against me. I do not deceive myself that I am not in danger; but what does it matter! I shall die with joy for the cause of Jesus Christ. With his grace I shall not cease to bring help to the unfortunate. No, I shall not allow all these poor children who expire every day to die without baptism. The good God will not abandon me.

According to the news that I receive, it seems that death has also extended itself among the neighboring tribes, especially near the mountains: among the *Nez-perces, the Cayuse,* and the *Flat-Heads* there are already over fifty victims. The horses and cattle are perishing, buried in the snow. I am told that there are seven to eight feet at *Conception.* Poor Father Pandosy and Brother Verney[3] can no longer leave, and are obliged to shiver night and day under a roof of a thousand windows. Fortunately, they have killed two oxen they had for a short time. I have sent them a pig of 190 pounds, four sacks of wheat and two sacks of potatoes; that is why I am reduced to eating a dog and a wolf. They will suffer, then, from cold, but not from hunger.

You ask me, R. Father, to tell you the most secure route by which to send the necessary supplies. It would be best for us to seek these articles at The Dalles, and from there we could take them to Vancouver. We are no longer able to cross the dangerous passes of the Nesqually Mountains where one is in danger of splitting his head open at each moment or of dying of hunger before he again sees the plains. As you urge me to mention my temporal needs, I will tell you that I no longer suffer from hunger since I have a dog and two wolves in my larder; but in the matter of utensils and vestments I am not so well supplied. Having only one tattered soutane, which does not protect me from the north wind, I have made one out of a rough, white wool blanket which I threw in some blueing-water; it turned violet and I thought I was a bishop: but the rains having come, my soutane returned to its original white, and all of a sudden I found myself the pope, but a pope so poor that having lost my only

[3] Jean F. Pandosy and Celestine Verney were among the first Oblate missionaries in the Northwest.

needle, I have not been able to find another in my Quirinal palace. Meanwhile it being necessary to sew up the holes in my old black soutane, what was I to do? I took off the head of a pin and made a needle out of it. This invention succeeded: the needle is coarse, but solid; it bends but never breaks. I had in all about a dozen nails for the construction of my house of the Holy Cross, and they have been stolen from me. Send me some trinkets which please the savages, I will use them to gain them to our holy religion. By the enticement of reward they assemble for work, and one profits by these gatherings to instruct them. Thanks to God, I make myself understood well enough, and the greater part of the adults are very attentive when I speak to them. There is really much to do at Saint Joseph of Simkoné; but poor little Chirouse will never be able to clear this field alone; at least two Fathers and two Brothers are needed here. I have been alone here for over four months; I am not able to speak familiarly with anyone except my cat and my dog; with the savages there is great reserve; familiarity would spoil everything. The great chief comes often to visit me; but what a pleasure to entertain oneself with naked princes who only know how to ask for a smoke or for food! ! ! . . . Think then of me, R. Father, and send me R. Father Sempfrit and Brother Sareau;[4] we will do wonders here.

I earnestly recommend myself to your fervent prayers and to those of all our Brothers and Fathers of Nesqually, and beg you to accept the homage of my respect.

C. Chirouse, O.M.I.

91. Conditions in the Diocese of Chicago, December 13, 1849

DURING the 1840's approximately 700,000 Catholic immigrants entered the United States. Although many of them settled in the eastern states, other thousands made the trek across the mountains into the rapidly developing states of the Middle West where they found work on the canals and railroads, in the rising towns, and on the rich farm lands. It proved practically impossible for the bishops to provide priests, churches, and schools fast enough to accommodate the increase, and since most of the immigrants were very poor the financial aid of the European missionary societies was all the more welcome. The See of Chicago had been erected on November 28, 1843, and embraced the entire state of Illinois (55,947 square miles). James O. Van de Velde, S.J. (1795–1855), the second Bishop of Chicago, was con-

[4] No identification of Father Sempfrit and Brother Sareau was found.

secrated on February 11, 1849, and ten months later he wrote the following letter to the Society for the Propagation of the Faith after he had completed his first visitation tour. At the time there were 80,000 Catholics in the diocese served by fifty-seven priests. It is difficult to imagine now that the Archdiocese of Chicago with its nearly two million Catholics was so impoverished as it was a little over a century ago. Yet the condition described was typical of most of the dioceses of the Middle West at the mid-century. Source: *Annales de la Propagation de la Foi,* XXII (1850), 313–314.

Since my consecration, I have visited almost a third of my new diocese. This episcopal journey, which corresponds to twelve hundred French leagues, has revealed to me all the misery of the flock entrusted to my care. You will judge it, Sirs, by this simple picture, whose distressing exactness I have verified with my eyes.

In general, the emigrants who arrive in this country, and who form almost all the Catholic population, are beyond the state of taking care of their particular needs. Poverty is so extensive that there is not one parish, even among the oldest, which has provided the most necessary things for the celebration of the holy liturgy. One priest sometimes has eight churches to take care of, and since for these different stations he possesses only one chalice, one missal, one chasuble, one alb, one altar-stone, he must carry all these things with him wherever he goes, no matter how tiring or how long the journey may be. As for ostensoria and ciboria, these types of articles are almost unknown in this diocese. Until the present time I have seen only three ostensoria and five ciboria in all the parishes which I have visited, over a space of 3,700 English miles. In lieu of these sacred vessels, the Most Holy Sacrament is kept either in a corporal, or in a tin box, or in a porcelein [*sic*] cup, etc., etc.

After these details, I believe it superfluous to give you a description of my episcopal residence. It is in harmony with the rest. I do not know if it is the most humble in the world, but at least it is certainly not the poorest in America.

92. The Advent of Bishop Lamy to the Southwest, June 29, 1851

ONE of the most attractive missionary bishops of the nineteenth century was John Baptist Lamy (1814–1888). He had come originally from France in 1839 to the Diocese of Cincinnati where his success recommended him to his superiors and on November 24, 1850, he was consecrated as first Vicar

Apostolic of New Mexico. It was Lamy's colorful career in the Southwest that inspired Willa Cather's charming novel, *Death Comes for the Archbishop* (New York, 1926). Following his consecration he left for New Mexico by way of New Orleans and Texas, and after being laid up some months in San Antonio as the result of an accident, he reached Santa Fe in the summer of 1851. New Mexico had formerly been part of the Diocese of Durango in Mexico and some of the Mexican clergy were not disposed to bow to Lamy's authority. He decided to settle the question of jurisdiction by a personal visit to Bishop José A. Laureano de Zubiria at Durango, traveling the more than 1,000 miles each way by mule pack. In the letter that follows Lamy described for Antoine Blanc, Archbishop of New Orleans, his experiences on his first trip to the Southwest. Source: *American Catholic Historical Researches,* XV (April, 1898), 136–137.

El Passo del Norte, Mexico, June 29, 1851.

Monseigneur:

After a journey of six weeks on the plains we arrived here. The country we saw has nothing very interesting — barren plains, barren mountains — with the exception of a few places. The last week there was a great scarcity of water and grass. Then we generally travelled at night. We had beautiful weather, some days rather too warm, but the nights were delightful; we generally preferred to sleep out than in our tent. We did not use it much except for Mass. We had the consolation to offer the Divine Sacrifice, at least one of us, almost every day. The first week I felt rather stiff from lying on a mere blanket, but I soon got use [*sic*] to it, and I never enjoyed my rest better.

There are three fine villages near El Passo on the Texas side. When the people heard of my arrival, they came several miles to meet us. In one place particularly, called Succoro, I had a grand reception with music, national guards, arks of triumph, etc. Circumstances obliged me the next morning to make *mon premier debut* in public *en la langua de Dios* to a crowded congregation. We are now at the house of the cura d'El Passon, who kindly offered us hospitality. This village of El Passo is truly a beautiful spot. They have here all kinds of fruits; they make good wine. It rains very seldom; it has not rained to any consequence these two years, but irrigation supplies the want of rain water. This is a place very much scattered. It contains at least eight thousand inhabitants. The people seem to be good and docile. Their houses are mud; they call it, I think, adobe, but very clean inside; it is so warm that many go half naked. The few churches that I have seen are of the same materials as the houses, but they might be kept in better order with very little trouble.

I have yet four hundred miles to go; but after I have traveled one-third of it. I will get in the pueblos of New Mexico, and see at least the half of my district before I reach Santa Fé. From what I have heard, and the little I have seen here, no doubt I may expect to meet with serious difficulties and obstacles, but my hope is in the God of power. Please, Monseigneur, to remember me in your prayers, and also to recommend me to the prayers of the Ursuline Sisters who have been so kind to me. I hope my little niece is well and doing well. I received news from her parents; they are all well. I expect to start this week for Santa Fé.

Your most obedient serv't and devoted friend,
✠ JOHN LAMY, Vic. Ap. of N. Mexico.

93. A Missionary Bishop on the Edge of the Great Plains, August 6, 1852

JOHN BAPTIST LAMY, who served the Church with distinction in the Southwest from 1851 to his death in 1888, was named first Archbishop of Santa Fe in February, 1875. He was one of only three American bishops to have been in attendance at all three of the plenary councils of Baltimore. He used his presence in the East and the Middle West for the council of May, 1852, to good advantage in recruiting personnel and supplies for the missions of New Mexico. But upon his return journey to his vicariate that summer he encountered more than the ordinary number of vicissitudes, and in the following letter to Archbishop Blanc of New Orleans he told of the losses he had sustained, indicating as well the hazards of travel in the trans-Mississippi West. Source: *American Catholic Historical Researches,* V (April, 1898), 137.

Blue River Camp [Mission], August 6, 1852.

Monseigneur:

I am writing to you from under a tree twenty miles west from Independence. The first time I went to New Mexico I met with some *contretemps;* but it seems that the Divine Providence has been pleased to send me this time more severe trials, disappointments and troubles than at my first start. A good priest from the diocese of Cleveland was coming with me to share the labor of our mission in New Mexico, but he died of the cholera at St. Louis on the 11th of July. His name was Rev. Mr. Pendesprat [*sic*].[1] From St. Louis to Independence the

[1] Father Peter Pandeprat had been a professor at St. Mary's Seminary, Cleveland.

Mother Superior of the Sisters of Loreto died also of the cholera, on board the steamboat *Kansas,* the 16th of July; the same day another Sister was taken sick and is yet very low. I have been obliged to leave for Independence to my great regret. Two more Sisters were also attacked by the same dreadful epidemic, but thank God, they got over it. My Mexican priest has been very sick, and now he is just able to travel in a carriage; besides, I have lost nine of my best animals. You know that we have to travel through the plains with caravans, and that everything has to be brought by wagons. Besides some animals I had here, I bought a few more, but I have lost a great number of them. I have been very much fatigued myself. but still God has given me the grace to bear all with patience, and my strong constitution has stood the labor and the care I had on my mind. I hope to take a fair start tomorrow for the plains; we are only two or three miles from the boundaries between the State of Missouri and the Indian Territory. I have twenty-five persons in my company, ten wagons or other conveyances. My expenses are very great; but still, with God's help, I hope to meet all in one or two years. Recommending myself to your prayers, I have the honor to be,

Your most grateful friend and ob't serv't.
✠ JOHN LAMY, Vic. Ap. of N. Mexico.

94. The Church in San Francisco in the Days of the Gold Rush, June 15, 1853

AT NO time in the nineteenth century were there enough native-born priests in the United States to care for the rapidly increasing Catholic population. No foreign country was more generous in supplying priests for the American Church than Ireland, and no institution of that land sent so many to the American missions as All Hallows College, Dublin, which had been established as a missionary seminary in 1842. Among the best known of the All Hallows men in the United States was Eugene O'Connell (1815–1891). He had come out to California for the first time in 1851 to collect funds but was induced by Bishop Alemany to remain and assist him with his infant seminary. O'Connell returned to the faculty of All Hallows in 1854 and remained there until 1861 when he was appointed the first Vicar Apostolic of Marysville, California. In 1868 he was made first Bishop of Grass Valley, a see that was the predecessor to the present Diocese of Sacramento. The following letter to Father David Moriarty, president of All Hallows, contains some picturesque details on the type of surroundings in which the Church operated in San Francisco in the years immediately after the gold rush. Source: *All Hallows Annual, 1953–1954* (Dublin: Browne and Nolan, Ltd., 1954), pp. 152–153.

San Francisco.
June 15th [1853].

My dear Father Moriarty, — Your welcome letter, after an unsuccessful search about the solitude of Santa Ynez,[1] reached me a few days ago in this noisy city. How then can I express to you my gratitude for your kind invitation to All Hallows after my wanderings in the Far West? I only await the arrival of one of the six missionaries whom Dr. Alemany[2] expects from All Hallows previous to my departure. You would really pity the poor Bishop were you to see the fluctuating soldiers he has to fight his battle; like Dr. Whelan[3] of Virginia, he was obliged to make the two seminarians he has swear to remain with him. Therefore, under these circumstances, I presume on your leave to remain. . . .

You must, I'm sure, have received letters from Dr. Alemany since March 5th which shew you the urgent need he has of Irish clergymen and the provision he is making to secure a constant supply from All Hallows now, in order to keep up an unbroken succession in this diocese of All Hallows missionaries. For the present, he can do no more for the institution than he has done, in consequence of being engaged in building St. Mary's Cathedral, which it is calculated will cost $100,000 — a work he is *bound* (*ut dicunt Americani*) to get through with, for many reasons, but principally to secure a fire-proof church in the neighborhood, that he himself and his clergymen may be without the daily and nightly apprehension of being *burnt out*. Owing to the scarcity of stone in this country and the dearness of brick-buildings, most of the houses here are constructed of wood and the six or seven fires that have already occurred haven't taught many to make an effort to build brick houses. Since the Bishop transferred me from Santa Ynez to this city about three or four months ago, there has been a fire almost every month and the value of thousands of dollars consumed. . . .

The temporal burnings of which I am speaking naturally remind me of the everlasting ones which they presage to thousands of the

---

1 The diocesan seminary, of which O'Connell was rector, was first established at Santa Inez and moved early in 1853 to Mission Dolores in San Francisco.

2 Joseph S. Alemany, O.P. (1814–1888), born in Spain, was named first Archbishop of San Francisco six weeks after O'Connell's letter was written.

3 Richard V. Whelan (1809–1874) was first Bishop of Wheeling.

citizens of San Francisco, unless they stop in their career of iniquity. The rage for duelling, the passion for gambling and barefaced depravity prevail to a frightful degree. . . . Venus has numerous temples erected to herself in this city but, thank God, the Catholic church is not deserted all the while. The two Catholic churches are crowded every Sunday and, notwithstanding the enlargement of one of them by Architect O'Connor (nephew of the Bishop), it is full to overflowing. William Hamill,[4] formerly of Maynooth, is the teacher of the Bishop's English school, *vice* Doctor Barry who was translated to the Dolores seminary with a salary of $50 a month. Mr. Hamill's salary is $60 a month in consideration of his acting as Sexton to the church — in fact $50 a month is the salary even of cooks in this country.

I don't know whether you are aware of some of our California liberties which beat the Gallican ones hollow. Take, for example, that of eating meat *toties quoties* on every Friday except the Fridays in Lent — and don't infer from this that the finest salmon in the world don't abound on our shores! There is again the universal custom of smoking cigars (*secluso scandalo ullo*), so that it is rather singular to be seen without a cigar save at Mass or at meals. The only scandal to my knowledge given by a smoking clergyman was owing to his having repeatedly put the *ignited end* into his mouth instead of the opposite extreme. Hence you perceive it is neither the simple fact of smoking *per se,* nor of drinking *per se,* but the unlucky combination of both by a clergyman which makes him confound both ends of a lighted cigar. Then, and not till then, do the ladies and gentlemen receive a slight shock!

Oh, my dear Father and brothers, please all pray for me and my speedy return to Alma Mater, where I hope to find rest for my soul.

Adieu, dear Father, until then.

Eugene O'Connell.

95. The Conversion to Catholicism of Eliza Allen Starr, February–December, 1854

THE number of converts to Catholicism in the United States in the years 1840–1860 was sufficiently notable to occasion the belief that the Oxford Movement might be duplicated in this country. Although the trend never

[4] William J. Hamill, born in County Antrim, Ireland, arrived in San Francisco in 1851; he later became the first editor of the *Monitor,* San Francisco's weekly Catholic newspaper. No identification of Barry could be found.

reached the proportions that it did in England, a considerable number of Americans of prominent Protestant families did enter the Church, including such Protestant clergymen as James Roosevelt Bayley, Thomas S. Preston, and Levi Silliman Ives. Among these mid-century converts was Eliza Allen Starr (1824–1901), a woman of Unitarian background whose ancestors on both sides stretched back to the earliest days of Massachusetts Bay Colony. Miss Starr was influenced in part by the conversion of her cousin, George Allen (1808–1876), professor of Greek and Latin in the University of Pennsylvania, who was received into the Church with his wife, the former Mary Hancock Withington, and their children by Bishop Francis P. Kenrick of Philadelphia in October, 1847. She later met Kenrick who exercised a strong influence on her views as likewise did Bishop Fitzpatrick of Boston. Miss Starr wrote poetry and popular essays and attained sufficient prominence through her lectures and writings on art to receive a medallion from Pope Leo XIII, the Laetare Medal of the University of Notre Dame in 1885, and a gold medal at the World's Columbian Exposition in Chicago in 1893. In the following letters to George and Mary Allen she recounted some of her ideas on religion and the circumstances of her reception into the Church. Source: James J. McGovern (Ed.), *The Life and Letters of Eliza Allen Starr* (Chicago: Lakeside Press, 1905), pp. 63–66, 67–68.

Baltimore, Feb. 17, 1854.

Dear Cousin Mary:

As a preparatory step to writing to you, I called on Monday to see our good friend, the Archbishop.[1] He always receives me with the most beautiful urbanity, exercises the greatest patience towards my weak head and unbelieving heart, and this time he was in unusual spirits; said he had received a visitor from Philadelphia, Mr. L., whom I immediately recognized as the object of your Christian solicitude fully five years ago. He added that Mr. L. had at length yielded himself to the Catholic rule, and gave me in a few words an account of all the persuadings which in the space between Saturday evening and Monday morning had finally made him one of the flock, and sent him back to Philadelphia thoroughly established and confirmed in the faith, concluding by saying with great glee that "this was better than some people had done." It would not, of course, be proper or at all consistent in me to congratulate him or you on such a termination to his long investigation, but I know, Cousin M., that you would feel so pleased that I could not help taking sides with you in the matter. I felt an involuntary sympathy with you. The good Archbishop tells me that Mr. L.'s parents were Unitarians, and that he was educated

---

[1] Francis Patrick Kenrick (1796–1863) was Coadjutor Bishop of Philadelphia, 1830–1842; Bishop of Philadelphia, 1842–1851; and Archbishop of Baltimore, 1851–1863.

one, and used to attend Mr. J.'s church.[2] It is strange from under what different stars and influences the converts of your faith have come out, but I will not trouble you with any of my speculations on the subject, as I feel that nothing I may say can ever strike you very favorably so long as I refuse allegiance. I am certain that to your ears one ejaculation of belief would sound sweeter than volumes of musical philosophy or practicing.

I am sorry I am not feeling better to-day, since I have commenced a letter to you, but I do not know how long I may wait if I put it off until body and mind are in tune. . . . My drawing furnishes me with the most salutary occupation whenever I can attend to it, and when I find my eyes actually tired of seeing my dull ears tired of even the little they hear, and my mind wearied with agitations, I take my knitting, turn by back to the light, and withdraw like an oyster into its shell. . . . My cousins here are all on the other side. What will you think when I tell you that I am in the midst of table-tippings, rappings, speaking and writing mediums, and such wonders as are enough to make one's hair stand on end or turn gray of a night? I have no doubt you will immediately conclude that I am up to the ears in this delusion, as I have so often manifested a *penchant* for such varieties. But for once I have escaped. The fear of leaving my wits has been a powerful motive, and then I could not shut my eyes to certain practices alluded to with terms of no measured reprehension in the Old Testament, such as the raising of spirits by the Witch of Endor, etc.[3] Hardly a night passes that the tables are not consulted in the house, but I have never yet been present during such manifestations. I resolved upon this course long ago, though with little expectation of ever being called to exercise my resolution. When, however, I found how the Baltimore current was turning, I consulted the Archbishop, and his opinion confirming me, I have been saved no little perplexity. . . . Will you tell your sister L. that I have read the first volume of the "Converted Christian." I remember what she said of this book last winter, and I believe she wanted me to read it.

[2] One turning point in Miss Starr's life came when she attended a sermon by Theodore Parker (1810–1860), the famous liberal Unitarian minister of Boston, in June, 1845, in the company of Richard Hildreth (1807–1865), the historian, and his wife who was an old girlhood friend from their days in Deerfield, Massachusetts. Miss Starr later said that as she listened to the sermon of Parker, "I found him demolishing every foundationstone of my religious faith, and even hope. . . . From the moment I left the music hall of old Boston on that bright June morning in 1845 this quest for an authorized faith was the quest of my life" (McGovern, *op. cit.*, pp. 34–35).

[3] 1 Kings 28:7 ff.

The second volume is upon ceremonies, so that I was not as sorry as I would otherwise have been when the Archbishop said it was missing. I presume it will be quite time for me to attend to the ceremonials when I shall have accepted the dogmas. I have not been to the cathedral at all. I do not like to go to hear the fine music, of which I hear so much, for the same reason that I go to a concert. To a Catholic I know it is something more, and until I can give myself up to it fully I do not wish to torture myself with balancing my emotions, and trying to make them consistent. . . .

Commending myself to your patience and love,

Your affectionate cousin,
Eliza.

Dec. 23, 1854.

My Dear Cousins:

I have something so joyful to tell that I cannot address myself to anyone of you. You will all bless God and the angels will rejoice with you, for now they can rejoice. This morning near 12 o'clock the Rt. Rev. Bishop Fitzpatrick[4] received me to your holy Mother Church in the sacrament of baptism, and on Christmas Day I am to make my first communion. I do not feel that I need say anything more, for what is already said covers everything else. I wrote to our saintly Archbishop Kenrick some three weeks ago, perhaps longer, but received a note saying that he had not returned yet from Rome. I then saw Miss Metcalf, hoping I could immediately see the Bishop, but he has been absent, and I did not see him until Thursday last, and it was not certain when I could be received until this morning. I was so desirous, however, to be received before Christmas that the Bishop gratified me. I have not yet seen your sister and Aunt Lydia. She does not know that I have had any idea of doing what I have done, or rather, what the good Lord has enabled me to do. I have reserved to myself the pleasure of telling her, and I shall write to her this afternoon. The weather has been too severe for her to come to me, and my intense occupation of mind to prepare for my reception, together with my daily and necessary avocations and the visit my dear father is making with us and little Mary, has made it impossible for me to go to her, and I would not allow any one to tell her but myself. I hope to

[4] John B. Fitzpatrick (1812–1866) was consecrated a bishop in March, 1844, and ruled the See of Boston from 1846 to his death.

be able to make my communion Christmas morning with her and Miss Metcalf at the Sisters' little chapel.

Do you think I can forget all the prayers you have all offered for me? I still need them for grace to keep my baptismal vows, and in your thanksgiving remember me. You will, I know, feel what I cannot write more now. I shall write to the Archbishop a line to meet him at his return. St. Agnes is my patron saint.

In the humble joy of a convert,

Your affectionate cousin,
Eliza.

You know better than I do who has been praying for me all these six years, in which God's patience for me has not faltered. Give to them, if you can, a word of gratitude from me. I have forgotten to tell you that my reception was as private as it could be. It is such a real thing that the little circumstances of it seem nothing.

96. Asiatic Cholera in the Diocese of Savannah, August 29, 1854

ALL through the nineteenth century the United States continued to be visited by periodic outbreaks of cholera and yellow fever. The third major epidemic of Asiatic cholera was brought in on immigrant ships entering New York harbor in 1854. Once more heroic efforts were put forth by bishops, priests, and religious to alleviate the suffering and distress of the populace, and as a consequence the loss of personnel to the Church was very heavy. In late August, Francis X. Gartland (1805–1854), first Bishop of Savannah, described conditions in his see city where he was being assisted by his friend, Edward Barron (1801–1854), former Vicar Apostolic of Upper Guinea, who had interrupted a holiday in the North and rushed to Georgia when he heard of the scourge there. Two weeks after Gartland had written the following letter Bishop Barron was stricken and died on September 12 in the midst of a hurricane which had hit Savannah and blown the roof off the cathedral and bishop's residence, and eight days later Gartland himself succumbed to the dread disease. Source: *American Catholic Historical Researches,* VII (January, 1890), 33.

Sav'h. Aug. 29th 1854

My Dear Friend: —

We are in a sad condition still — very sad — & God alone knows when a favorable turn will take place — Two of my priests are sick —

both convalescent however at present, do not know that either of them has the Yellow fever positively — but I believe one of them had it in its incipient stage. The place looks very desolated — at 8 o'cl. P.M. looks as deserted as at midnight at other season. Every night large fires are kindled in various parts of the city & great quantities of tar burnt. On approaching the city in the ev'g. as I did the other ev'g. from our Country, you see Clouds of dense black smoke rising up in all parts of the city, so that one w'd suppose that the city was on fire, or that our city was something like Pittsburgh is described to be. So far I keep well, though constantly on the go. Yet I know not whether I will pass through the scourge with safety to myself. I hope our Philadelphia friends are praying for us. I hope this letter will reach your city before the arrival of the steamer, as I wish you to inform my brother that Miss G. will leave in the steamer tomorrow for Philada. She is not at all well. Mr. Prendergast & his two sons, & a Mrs. Dillon & her son & two daughters will be with her. Great numbers of our people have left.

I write in great haste. My buggy is at the door for me to make my rounds.

Your most truly in Xst.
Fr's. Xav. Bp. &c.

To M. A. Frenaye, Philadelphia.[1]

97. A Plan for the Western Colonization of Catholic Immigrants, March 15, 1856

THE mounting Irish Catholic immigration of the 1850's, along with the antagonism aroused against Catholics and foreigners by the Know-Nothing movement, prompted men like Thomas D'Arcy McGee, editor of the *American Celt,* Patrick Donahoe of the Boston *Pilot,* and a number of western bishops and priests to urge the immigrants, crowded into the slums of the eastern cities, to seek new homes in the spacious rural areas of the West. As a consequence of their efforts an immigrant aid convention was held in Buffalo, New York, February 12–15, 1856, at which an organization was formed to implement the idea. Among the main supporters of the movement was Bishop Loras of Dubuque, and the following news item, under the heading, "Things in Dubuque," which appeared in the Boston *Pilot* of March 15, 1856, revealed how Loras and his followers sought to render effective the objectives of the Buffalo convention. The plan for moving Catholic immigrants from the East to the Middle West received wide

[1] Mark Anthony Frenaye (1783–1873) was a close personal friend and financial adviser to several bishops and priests in Philadelphia.

publicity, and nowhere more than in Donahoe's *Pilot,* but the opposition of certain eastern churchmen, the disinclination of the Irish themselves to separate from relatives and friends, and the difficulties of western travel all operated to prevent the movement from ever attaining the success which the Buffalo delegates had hoped. Source: Boston *Pilot,* March 15, 1856.

To the Editor of The Pilot:

Dear Sir: It has become my duty to communicate to you the following proceedings of a meeting held in the Cathedral, in this city, on Thursday evening last, to hear the report of the delegates from this place to the Buffalo Convention, and to organize a society for the purpose of aiding and encouraging Catholic settlements in Iowa. The Right Rev. Bishop Loras kindly tendered the use of the Cathedral for holding the meeting, and cheerfully volunteered his co-operation to further the object in view. After the meeting was called to order, Judge Corkery was chosen temporary chairman, and M. B. Mulkern, secretary. The chairman gave a very interesting account of the doings and proceedings of the Buffalo Convention. The feeling which pervaded the whole Convention was truly commendable; every delegate with whom he came in contact appeared to be actuated more by a desire to relieve his less fortunate neighbors from the social restrictions which they endure, than to acquire any personal advantage.

Men of capital in the Eastern States expressed their willingness to emigrate to the West, if some provision could be made for the masses, but not otherwise. He stated the plan of action proposed, and also that this meeting was in accordance with the course recommended by that convention. At the close of Judge Corkery's remarks, on motion of the Rev. J. Farvey [*sic*],[1] a committee of three, consisting of J. D. Jennings, Rev. P. McCabe,[2] and Dr. N. B. Matthews, were appointed to nominate permanent officers for the meeting, who would also continue officers of the contemplated organization. The committee made the following nominations: for President, Rt. Rev. Bishop Loras; Vice-Presidents, James Mullin and Dr. Matthews; Treasurer, Charles Corkery; Secretary, M. B. Mulkern; Agent, M. McLaughlin; Directors, Rev. P. McCabe, P. Quigley, F. Doyle, Dr. W. R. McMahon, and Owen Keenan. On motion of the Rev. J. F. Farvey, Dr. Matthews was appointed to conduct Bishop Loras to the chair. As for taking his place as president of the meeting, he said that he

---

[1] This was probably Father John Vahey, pastor of St. Andrew's Church, Bellevue, Iowa.

[2] Patrick A. McCabe was a pastor of St. Raphael's Cathedral, Dubuque.

felt very great pleasure in presiding over a meeting convened for so worthy an object, and composed of so many good and worthy citizens. He spoke of his own labors in this mission for the last nineteen years, and the affectionate manner in which he had been treated by the Irish Catholics with whom his spiritual labors brought him in contact. Of this kindness he was glad to have an opportunity to evince by appreciation, and he knew of no better way to do it than to co-operate with those who were laboring to rescue their Catholic brethren from oppression and persecution, and bring them to a country rich in resources and congenial to liberty-loving men. The Bishop's address was very touching, and his words were spoken with an earnestness that showed the fatherly solicitude with which he entered upon this great movement. On the motion of the Rev. J. F. Farvey, seconded by the Rev. P. McCabe, Judge Corkery, J. D. Jennings and Hugh V. Gildeo were appointed a committee to draft resolutions. While the committee were preparing their report, the Rev. Father Tracey [*sic*][3] addressed the meeting at considerable length.

He spoke of the proceedings of the Buffalo Convention with great satisfaction. Rarely, or never, had he seen a body of men possessed of higher talent, or animated with a nobler feeling. In their zeal for the general good, delegates carefully avoided introducing any question of a local character, hence, the action of the Convention was marked with the strictest unanimity of feelings and harmony. He was truly glad that the apathy of former years had given way to a spirit of active enterprise, and that a disposition was spreading on the part of Irishmen to submit no longer to a state of drudgery in the East. The movement, he was confident, would result in giving thousands of our poor countrymen a home — a home, though not blessed by the foot-prints of a St. Patrick, yet one in which they could enjoy the blessings of freedom in all things, temporal and spiritual.

Here Judge Corkery, on behalf of the committee on resolutions, reported the following:

Resolved — That we heartily approve of the action of the Catholic Convention recently held at Buffalo, N. Y., for the formation of Catholic settlements in the interior.

---

[3] At this time Jeremiah F. Trecy (c. 1823–1889) was pastor of St. Patrick's Church, Garryowen, Iowa, an Irish immigrant colony that had been fostered by Bishop Loras. Father Trecy was one of the most active promoters of Catholic colonization in the West, and a few weeks after the above report was written he led a party of Iowa settlers to Nebraska Territory where he established St. Patrick's Colony. On a trip to the East in March, 1857, to further the cause of western colonization Trecy encountered the personal opposition of Archbishop John Hughes of New York.

Resolved — That Catholic societies be formed throughout the State of Iowa for the promotion of the above object, subject to the directions of the Supreme Directory created by the Buffalo Convention.

Resolved — That the Catholics of Dubuque now form themselves into a Society of the character named above, and that all similar societies, that may hereafter be organized throughout the State, are recommended to recognize this, and co-operate with it, as the parent Society of the Diocese.

Resolved — That an initiation fee of $1.00, and a monthly subscription of twenty-five cents, be the full sum necessary to constitute a membership; but $3.00 a year, if paid in advance will be deemed an equivalent.

Resolved — That this society hold its regular meetings on the first Monday of every month, and at such other times as the Directors or majority of them may deem necessary; but applicants for membership may be enrolled as members by filing their applications with the Treasurer, and paying their initiation fees.

The above resolutions were unanimously adopted, after which the secretary proceeded to take the names of those present who desired to become members of the Society. The Bishop, as a further proof of his interest in the object for whose furtherance the Society was organized, enrolled himself as a member, and paid in twenty-five dollars. Father Tracey paid ten dollars, but the giving instances of generosity on the part of those present would occupy too much of your space. The meeting was large and enthusiastic, and afforded a cheering indication of the success that awaits the efforts that are now being put forth, East and West, North and South, on behalf of the poor Catholic immigrant.

It was moved, by Father Tracey, and seconded by Capt. M. M. Hoyden, that the secretary furnish an account of the proceedings of that meeting, to the "American Celt" and "Boston Pilot," for publication. This motion was unanimously adopted.

At the close of the business of the meeting, the venerable Chairman vacated the chair, and Judge Corkery was called thereto, when a vote of thanks was tendered to the Rt. Rev. Bishop, not only for the efficient and satisfactory manner in which he presided over the meeting, but for the deep interest he has manifested in this cause since it was first agitated. After going through some few other unimportant matters, the meeting adjourned to the first Monday in April, unless called together by the President.

You will pardon this intrusion upon your space, and believe me, to remain, very truly and respectfully yours,

M. B. MULKERN, *Secretary*

98. Father Kindekens Appeals for an American College at Louvain, November 5, 1856

THE first institution to be established abroad by the Catholic Church of the United States was the American College in Louvain, Belgium. When some of the American bishops were in Rome in December, 1854, for the definition of the dogma of the Immaculate Conception the idea of founding a college in the Eternal City was discussed, and among the chief promoters of the plan was Francis Patrick Kenrick, Archbishop of Baltimore. When, therefore, the Belgian-born Father Peter Kindekens (d. 1873), vicar-general of the Diocese of Detroit and pastor of Immaculate Conception Church, Adrian, was sent to Rome in the spring of 1856 on business for his ordinary, Peter P. Lefevere (1804–1869), Kenrick asked him to look for a location for a college. In the letter printed below Kindekens explained the reasons for his failure in Rome, but the brighter prospects which he had found in his native Belgium. Upon his return to the United States he sent out a circular to the American hierarchy, the substance of which is contained in his letter to Kenrick. But he met with very little success and the only two bishops who gave any practical response were Martin J. Spalding of Louisville and his own ordinary. It was due, therefore, to these two prelates that the college opened at Louvain on March 19, 1857, with Kindekens as rector, a post he held until 1860. By the time the institution celebrated its golden jubilee in 1907 it had furnished nearly 700 priests to the American Church. Most of these were European-born, but as the years went on there was an increasing number of Americans who were sent to the college by their bishops in order to avail themselves of the superior advantages of study offered by the famous Catholic University of Louvain. Source: Archives of the Archdiocese of Baltimore, Kindekens to Kenrick, Detroit, November 5, 1856.

My Lord: When, during the past summer, at Rome, I endeavored with the utmost diligence, by your special request to look for and secure a suitable location for the projected "American College" in that City, I found that not only is it impossible at present, but that it will probably remain impossible for some time to come, to establish such an institution in the Holy City. In point of fact, the Holy Father assured me that, under present circumstances (the occupation of Rome by the French, etc.) he could not say when it would be in his power to assign a suitable building for the purpose.

On my return, passing through Belgium, I learned that an earnest wish prevailed among persons of distinction to establish there a college for the foreign missions. I resolved at once to secure the fruits of these happy dispositions for the missions of the United States with the following success:

I obtained a promise from the Count Félix de Mérode[1] of the sum of between 50,000 and 60,000 francs towards founding a College for the Missions in the United States, in any city of Belgium of my choice.

His Eminence the Cardinal Archbishop of Malines,[2] and several other Prelates with whom I had the honor to speak on the subject, assured me of their warmest sympathies and promised their co-operation.

A subscription in aid of the foundation of the establishment will be opened in the columns of the Catholic journals of Belgium, as soon as I can assure them that the Right Rev. Bishops of the United States (or some of them) are earnestly engaged in promoting the good work.

The Rector of the University of Louvain[3] (the city selected for the College) has promised his aid, and is prepared to grant all we may reasonably require of the University, to secure the success and prosperity of the contemplated institution.

From the above, Your Lordship will easily perceive that the object of the Institution in Belgium would be, 1st, To serve as a nursery of properly educated and tried clergymen for our missions; and 2d. to provide the American Bishops with a college to which some at least of their students might be sent to acquire a superior ecclesiastical instruction and a solid clerical training, without much expense, as the College will require no other Professors than those for the English and German languages.

The basis of the government of the institution will be that of the "Propaganda" at Rome, and each Diocese of the United States will profit of its fruits in proportion to the amount it may have furnished towards the foundation, etc. For it could not be reasonably expected that the Catholics of the United States should have no share in the

[1] Félix de Mérode-Westerloo (1791–1857) belonged to one of the most distinguished families in Belgium. He held successively the portfolios of foreign affairs, war, and finance in the cabinets of King Leopold I. He was the father of Frédéric F.-X. de Mérode (1820–1874), Archbishop of Melitene, who figured prominently in the government of the Papal States under Pius IX. The elder de Mérode died before he learned that the project for which he had offered the money was to become a reality. This loss left Kindekens with only $2,000 to start the college, a sum which he had been given in equal shares by Bishops Spalding and Lefevere.

[2] Engelbert Sterckx (1792–1867) was made Archbishop of Malines in 1832 and a cardinal in 1838.

[3] Pierre F.-X. de Ram (1804–1865), a distinguished church historian, was the first rector of the Catholic University of Louvain when it was restored in 1834.

honor and merits of founding an institution designed exclusively for their benefit.

Will Your Lordship be kind enough to inform me, at your earliest convenience, whether you desire to take part in the work, and, if so, what amount your diocese may possibly furnish, by collection in the various congregations, or by any other way you may think proper, towards the proposed Institution.

Your Lordship is also requested to nominate the person whom you may wish to charge with the execution of the work and to become the Rector of the Institution, at least for the time being. An early reply is urged as necessary, as I must write to the Count de Mérode to inform him whether the design is entered upon by the Bishops of the United States in a manner worthy of success, or whether it may not be necessary to abandon the project and leave him free to apply his alms towards building a Church in Brussels as was his original intention. You will please also to offer any suggestions which you may judge proper on the subject.

99. Archbishop Hughes' Opposition to Western Colonization for Catholic Immigrants, March 26, 1857

THROUGHOUT the nineteenth century repeated efforts were made to bring about a large-scale colonization of Catholic immigrants on the cheap lands of the West. Although a number of these efforts met with success, they never materialized to the degree of making an appreciable dent in the massing of the immigrants in the large cities. One of the principal reasons was the opposition of John Hughes (1797–1864), first Archbishop of New York, who could never be won to the idea. Fifteen years after Hughes' death the Irish Catholic Colonization Association was organized at Chicago in the spring of 1879 and one of its chief founders was John Lancaster Spalding (1840–1916), Bishop of Peoria. Spalding expressed a view that has been commonly held when he said, "That Archbishop Hughes became the opponent of colonization is, I am persuaded, most unfortunate. No other man has ever had such influence over the Irish Catholics of the United States, and no other man could have done so much to make them realize that their interests for time and eternity required that they should make homes for themselves on the land" (*The Religious Mission of the Irish People and Catholic Colonization* [New York, 1880], p. 147). The fact that today there are in the United States 644 counties in the rural areas in which there are no Catholic priests, tends to emphasize how the policy of a century ago has effected the development of the Church in this country. A statement of Hughes' position is contained in the following document which he wrote out in rough draft but never published. Source: Archives of the Archdiocese of New York, edited and published in Henry J. Browne, "Archbishop Hughes and Western Colonization," *Catholic Historical Review,* XXXVI (October, 1950), 269–273.

There is no people in the world, whether at home or abroad, so overdosed with counsel and advice as the Irish. Their friends advise them, their enemies advise them, those who are indifferent about their welfare advise them in like manner.

The last gentle advice that has been rendered to them in this country emanates from what is called the Buffalo Convention.[1] The good intentions of those who composed that spontaneous and self-constituted assembly, it is unnecessary to question. There is one thing in its favor, that a considerable number of the Catholic clergy, whether of the United States or of Canada, were present and probably took part in the deliberations of the so-called Convention.

Without questioning the purity of motives of any one connected with this meeting, one may be allowed to say that it was a most superfluous, unnecessary and unprofitable assemblage. It has added no single new idea to the common stock of information by which individual emigrants might be guided in the selection of their future homes. It has repeated what was known before, that there is a great deal of waste land, fertile withal, in the Eastern and Western provinces of Canada and on the Western boundaries of the present United States. It has also proclaimed what was sufficiently known before, that in the Eastern large cities, whether of the seaboard or of the immediate neighborhood of the interior, there are great numbers of Irish emigrants who have to struggle against all the miseries incident to their condition. It has announced in substance what cannot be denied by any one, that the conditions of such persons could hardly be deteriorated physically, religiously, or morally by any transition from East to West. Having said thus much we have abridged the whole amount of new light which the discussion of the question in the Buffalo Convention has shed on this very important topic.

---

[1] On February 12–15, 1856, a group of Catholics interested in western colonization for immigrants had assembled in Dudley Hall, Buffalo, New York. The convention drew ninety-five delegates in all, fifty-two from the United States and forty-three from Canada, including the vicars-general of the Dioceses of Buffalo, Chicago, Pittsburgh, and Wheeling, and the Canadian Dioceses of Bytown, Kingston, and Toronto, as well as twenty-five priests who were serving on the rural missions,

Next however the convention volunteers its benevolent advice and thereby assumes the responsibility which should induce conscientious persons familiar with the whole subject to pause and hesitate before they offered it to the very few who may be imposed upon and deceived by their silly theories.

Our confidence in the wisdom of the advice thus offered to the Irish is considerably diminished by the fact that some at least of those who have taken a leading part in the movement have hardly proved themselves competent to manage their own affairs. If they would take a little advice from the experience and good sense of those whom they have the arrogance to instruct they would probably succeed better in the management of their own private and personal interests.[2] Still advice, like politeness, costs but little to those who administer it, though it should prove very dear to such as may be misled and deceived by its erroneousness. The writer of this is acquainted with the circumstances of Catholics both in the East and in the West, and nothing on earth could induce him to give such advice as has emanated from the Buffalo Convention in regard to Catholic emigrants in this country. It may happen that persons misled by that advice will commemorate it in the bitterness of disappointment by tears on their cheeks and maledictions on their lips.

Again if those members of the Buffalo Convention who are not anchored to their present domicile by bonds which cannot be sundered were in earnest, one might expect that they would offer themselves as leaders and pioneers to exhibit the practical reality of happiness which they have so gorgeously painted in the idea of owning land, more or less, in the Western country. This however is a test to which it does not appear that a single member of the convention was equal. Their language is in substance as addressed to their Catholic fellow countrymen, "Go you, we stay." It is difficult to

---

[2] This comment was probably directed at Thomas D'Arcy McGee (1825–1868), one of the organizers of the Buffalo meeting. McGee had figured in the Young Irelander movement, had been arrested and imprisoned, but succeeded in escaping to the United States in 1848 in disguise. In New York he started a paper which he called the *Nation* which incurred the ire of Archbishop Hughes. Speaking in October, 1914, of McGee's role, John Ireland (1838–1918), Archbishop of St. Paul, said, "It is today beyond a doubt that had the enlightened views of D'Arcy McGee and those who took part with him in the famous Buffalo colonization convention of 1856 been duly encouraged and pushed to a favorable issue, the Catholic Church would be immensely more prosperous in all the Western States than ever again she can hope to be. . . ." (James H. Moynihan, *The Life of Archbishop John Ireland* [New York, 1953], p. 21.)

perceive that if this advice is good for their neighbors it should not be good for themselves also.[3]

It must not be inferred that the writer is opposed to the diffusion of emigrants into those portions of the country in which land may be obtained and in which living is cheap and labor has its fair recompense. But there is a natural process by which this result is perpetually going on. Poor emigrants not finding employment in one place seek it in another. And then when they go westward especially, acquire a certain practical knowledge of the production of the soil or the mines in the neighborhoods in which they find themselves. With this necessary knowledge, as a far more important capital than the limited amount which they may have economized from their labors, they sometimes acquire a title to lands, or in other interests by which their temporal prosperity is increased. But the idea of disturbing the minds of those who may be already established, whether in the East or in the West by a gilded and exaggerated report of theoretical blessings, which are in reserve for them, provided they can acquire the nominal ownership of 60 or 100 acres of uncultivated land, not unfrequently teeming with fever and ague — remote from the church — remote from the school — remote [from] the Post Office — remote from the physician — remote from the neighbors — this idea is dangerous, just so far as any Catholic emigrant is liable to be misled and deceived thereby. Then besides, our convention have [*sic*] understood that capital, more or less will be necessary, for those who shall be found simple enough to follow their advice. This being the case, that advice is tendered to those who, wherever they are located whether in the East or in the West, have been already, to some extent, successful in their industrial efforts. One might suppose that if they are doing well, it would be unwise for them to give up the certainty which they have for the uncertainty which is proposed to them.

But passing from this class our attention is directed to another, the condition of which has exercised the deep reflection and roused the benevolence of the Buf. Convention. We mean the hundreds and thousands who in New York, Boston, Philadelphia, and New Orleans are living in the proverbial wretchedness usually associated with the idea of a residence in cellars and in garrets. Now this class could not but improve their condition by a change to the open fields of the

[3] The fact that the sessions in Buffalo were conducted in secrecy and that Hughes did not know the background of the persons in attendance may account for this rather ungenerous judgment concerning these men, a number of whom were veteran missionaries in the West.

rural districts. But then the convention has not been able to devise any practical system of ways and means by which this [*sic*] could be transported to better homes, even if they themselves were willing to go. A great majority of them are entirely unfit by any sudden transition to enter on the multifarious industry which a settlement on wild land pre-supposes. They know not how to use the axe, if the land is to be cleared of timber. They know not how to hew and shape the logs necessary for the construction of their first rude cabin. They know not how to guide the plough in the prairies. They are inexpert in almost every element necessary to carry out the impractical ideal of their Buffalo advisers. But even if this were not the case the Buffalo Convention has not suggested any adequate means, either for their transportation to the west, or for the means of living there until the combined fruitfulness of the earth and their own labor should furnish them with the sustenance of life. Suppose they were skilful in clearing the wild land of timber, the Buffalo Convention has not told us who shall provide them with an axe — who shall construct their first cabin — who shall provide them with a plough, and other necessary farming utensils.

They have indeed in the ungraciousness of benevolence, [ ] that there are here and there Catholics who by industry and enterprise have become wealthy — and they have modestly suggested that a portion of this wealth wh. is not theirs might be appropriate for the disbursement of expenses to be incurred by the General Committee in carrying out the project recommended by the Buf. Convention. They have also discovered that there are millions and millions of dollars owned by Catholics and emigrants deposited in the savings banks of large cities and have insinuated that if these funds were placed in the hands of the general committee for carrying out the philanthropic purposes of the convention, the project would not turn out to be so idle a speculation as we have supposed. There is only one mistake, and that is, that the convention in alluding to these resources undertook to dispose of property which they had not earned, which did not belong to them and of which, without special permission from its owners, they had no right either to dispose of, or to allude to as they have done.

100. Chief Justice Taney's Reflections on Slavery, August 19, 1857

ROGER BROOKE TANEY (1777–1864) was the descendant of two old families of the Maryland gentry that had become Catholics in the early eighteenth century. In politics Taney was at first a Federalist, but after the dissolution of that party he gave his allegiance to Andrew Jackson. In 1831 he was named Attorney General of the United States, two years later Secretary of the Treasury, and in 1836 he was nominated by Jackson to succeed John Marshall as Chief Justice of the United States. During the nearly thirty years that he served on the supreme bench he wrote and participated in many important decisions, but the most famous one was his Dred Scott decision which was handed down on March 6, 1857, two days after the inauguration of Buchanan as president. In it Taney ruled the Missouri Compromise of 1820 as unconstitutional by stating that Dred Scott, born a slave, was unable to sue in a federal court, nor was his status altered merely because he had escaped into the free territory of Minnesota. Taney's views on slavery were influenced by the southern rural environment in which he had been raised. Personally he had manumitted his own slaves years before, co-operated with the American Colonization Society in helping to settle free Negroes in Liberia, and even purchased slaves to put them at liberty. But he was strongly opposed to the abolitionist movement and he felt that the solution of the problem should be left to the people directly concerned. Moreover, it was Taney's belief that the courts should carefully guard against encroachments of the federal government on the sovereignty of the states. Taney was a faithful Catholic all through his life, in spite of the frequent embarrassments he had to suffer from those who disliked the Church such as the Know-Nothings. In his last years he told a cousin, "Most thankful I am that the reading, reflection, studies, and experience of a long life have strengthened and confirmed my faith in the Catholic Church, which has never ceased to teach her children how they should live and how they should die" (Samuel Tyler, *Memoir of Roger Brooke Taney* [Baltimore, 1872], p. 475). The Reverend Samuel Nott, a Congregationalist minister of Wareham, Massachusetts, sent Taney a copy of a pamphlet he had written on the slave controversy in which he had included an analysis of the Dred Scott decision. In reply the old chief justice elaborated on his philosophy of slavery in a letter which revealed his conservative views, his judicial temperament, and his clarity of mind. Source: *Proceedings of the Massachusetts Historical Society, 1871–1873* (Boston: Published by the Society, 1873), pp. 445–447.

Fauquier, White Sulphur Springs, Virginia
August 19th, 1857.

Sir, — I received some time ago your letter, and pamphlet on "Slavery, and the Remedy," which you have been kind enough to send me. They were received when I was much out of health, and about to leave home for the summer. And it was not in my power to give the pamphlet an attentive perusal until within a few days past. I have read it with great pleasure. The just, impartial, and fraternal spirit in which it is written entitles it to a respectful consideration, in the South as well as the North. And if any thing can allay the unhappy excitement which is daily producing so much evil to the African as well as the white race, it is the discussion of the subject in the temper in which you have treated it. For you have looked into it and considered it in all its bearings, in the spirit of a statesman as well as a philanthropist. I am glad to find that it has been so well received as to reach the fifth edition.

Every intelligent person whose life has been passed in a slave-holding State, and who has carefully observed the character and capacity of the African race, will see that a general and sudden emancipation would be absolute ruin to the negroes, as well as to the white population. In Maryland and Virginia every facility has been given to emancipation where the freed person was of an age and condition of health that would enable him to provide for himself by his own labor. And before the present excitement was gotten up, the freed negro was permitted to remain in the State, and to follow any occupation of honest labor and industry that he might himself prefer. And in this state of the law manumissions were frequent and numerous. They sprang from the kindness and sympathy of the master for the negro, or from scruples of conscience; and were often made without sufficiently considering his capacity and fitness for freedom. And in the greater number of cases that have come under my observation, freedom has been a serious misfortune to the manumitted slave; and he has most commonly brought upon himself privations and sufferings which he would not have been called on to endure in a state of slavery. In many cases, however, it has undoubtedly promoted his happiness. But all experience proves that the relative position of the two races, when placed in contact with each other, must necessarily become such as you describe. Nor is it felt as a painful degradation by the black race. On the contrary, upon referring to the last census, you will find that more free negroes remain in Maryland than in any one of the Northern States, notwithstanding the disabilities and stricter police to which they are subjected. And there is a still greater number in Virginia. I speak from memory, without having the census before me. But I think I am not mistaken in the fact.

It is difficult for any one who has not lived in a slaveholding State to comprehend the relations which practically exist between the slaves and their masters. They are in general kind on both sides, unless the slave is tampered with by ill-disposed persons; and his life is usually cheerful and contented, and free from any distressing wants or anxieties. He is well taken care of in infancy, in sickness, and in old age. There are indeed exceptions, — painful exceptions. But this will always be the case, where power combined with bad passions or a mercenary spirit is on one side, and weakness on the other. It frequently happens when both parties are of the same race, although the weaker and dependent one may not be legally a slave.

Unquestionably it is the duty of every master to watch over the religious and moral culture of his slaves, and to give them every comfort and privilege that is not incompatible with the continued existence of the relations between them. And so far as my knowledge extends, this duty is faithfully performed by the great body of hereditary slaveholders in Maryland and Virginia. I speak of these States only, because with respect to them I have personal knowledge of the subject. But I have no reason to suppose it is otherwise in States farther south. And I know it has been the desire of the statesmen of Maryland to secure to the slave by law every protection from maltreatment by the master than can with safety be given, and without impairing that degree of authority which is essential to the interest and well-being of both. But this question is a very delicate one, and must at all times be approached with the utmost caution. The safe and true line must always depend upon existing circumstances, and they must be thoroughly inquired into and understood before there can be any safe or useful legislation in a State.

The pains which have unhappily been taken for some years past to produce discontent and ill-feeling in the subject race, has rendered any movement in that direction still more difficult. For it has naturally made the master more sensitive and jealous of any new restriction upon the power he has heretofore exercised, and which he has been accustomed to think essential to the maintenance of his authority as master. And he also feels that any step in that direction at the present time might injuriously affect the minds of the slaves. They are for the most part weak, credulous, and easily misled by stronger minds. And if in the present state of things additional restrictions were placed on the authority of the master, or new privileges granted to them, they would probably be told that they were wrung from the master by their Northern friends; and be taught to regard them as the first step to a speedy and universal emancipation, placing them on a perfect equality with the white race. It is easy to foresee what would be the sad result of such an impression upon the minds of this weak and credulous race.

Your review of the decision in the case of Dred Scott is a fair one, and states truly the opinion of the Court. It will, I hope, correct some of the misrepresentations which have so industriously been made; and made too, I fear, by many who must have known better. But I do not mean to publish any vindication of the opinion; or of my own consistency, or the consistency of the Court. For it would not become the Supreme Court, or any member of it, to go outside of the appropriate sphere of judicial proceedings; and engage in a controversy with any one who may choose from any motive to misrepresent its opinion. The opinion must be left to speak for itself. And it is for that reason that I hope you will pardon me for requesting that you will not permit this letter to be published in the newspapers or otherwise. Not that I am not perfectly ready on all proper occasions to say publicly every thing I have said in this letter. But in the judicial position I have the honor to occupy, I ought not to appear as a volunteer in any political discussion; and still less would it become me out of Court and off the bench to discuss a question which has been there determined. And I have written to you (although a stranger) thus freely from the personal respect with which the perusal of your pamphlet has inspired me. I am not a slaveholder. More than thirty years ago I manumitted every slave I ever owned, except two, who were too old, when they became my property, to provide for themselves. These two I supported in comfort as long as they lived. And I am glad to say that none of those whom I manumitted disappointed my expectations, but have shown by their conduct that they were worthy of freedom; and know how to use it.

With great respect, I am, sir,

Your ob't serv't,

R. B. Taney.

The Rev[d] Samuel Nott,
Wareham, Mass.

101. Bishop Elder on the Apostolate to the Negro Slaves in Mississippi, 1858

ONE of the most difficult missionary problems for the Church in the nineteenth century was the spiritual care of the Negro slaves in the southern states. In no other area of the county was the Church poorer in numbers and resources, so that it was often impossible to provide proper facilities for even the few and scattered white Catholics. Three years before the outbreak of the Civil War the third Bishop of Natchez, William Henry Elder (1819–1904), outlined in a detailed way for the Society for the Propagation of the Faith the difficulties of the Negro apostolate in Mississippi. The following letter gives a picture which *mutatis mutandis* was descriptive of conditions in every southern diocese during the last years of slavery. Source: Archives of the Diocese of Natchez, photostat copy.

Gentlemen

The business of my Diocese has made it necessary for me to spend much time in travelling. I have now been absent from home nearly two months continually, & in the spring likewise I was nearly two months away. Hence it has been impossible for me to write to you earlier as I had intended; & even now I cannot give you the full & interesting account of our missions which I had hoped to prepare, both from want of time on my own part, & because I have not got reports from the Pastors on the various points on which I would desire to inform you. Moreover, being obliged even now to write at various times & in various places, without the facilities which I should have at home for rendering my letter into French, you must pardon [me] for simply writing to you in English.

I beg of you to send me a number of copies of the sheet you have printed containing the heads on which you desire information. I have only found one by accident, & not in time to ask of the Pastors information on those points. I shall follow them however & give you the best information at present in my possession.

The Diocese of Natchez comprises the State of Mississippi, & has an area of 47,000 square miles or about 5,400 square leagues.

The *Number* of *Catholics* was stated in the Almanac several years ago, to be about *ten thousand*. I have not been able to learn how that estimate was made, nor how much reliance can be placed upon it. I believe that if all the Catholics could be counted, who are scattered through the interior of the country, the number would be much greater. I hope that next year we shall know more about it.

The whole Population of the State according to the Census taken in 1850 was 606,526. Speaking generally we may say that all of them profess to be Christians. A great many however do not belong to any particular Denomination, & even among those who do, a considerable number have never been baptized. The Baptists expressly reject the practice of baptizing infants, & very few Protestants look upon it as necessary for salvation.

The most prevalent sects are the Methodists and Baptists. Presbyterians are likewise numerous; the Episcopalians or Anglicans are but few, so far as I have learned.

But it is necessary for you to understand that more than half our population consists of *negro slaves,* who number 309,878; besides free negroes to the number of 930.

These poor negroes form in some respects my chief anxiety. I believe they are generally well cared for, so far as health & the necessaries of life are concerned. But for learning & practising religion, they have at present very little opportunity indeed. Commonly their Masters are well disposed to allow them religious instruction, & sometimes they pay Ministers to come & preach on the plantation. They do not like to let the negroes go to a public church, because there is danger of their misbehaving when they are away from home, & out of sight of the Overseer; & because various inconveniences result from the servants of one plantation mingling with those of another. Each master has something particular in his regulations & his method of management, & if the servants have free intercourse together, they are apt to make each other jealous & dissatisfied.

Some masters indeed object to having a Minister come to preach to their slaves, & they rather encourage some one of the blacks themselves to become a preacher for the rest. You may imagine what kind of religious instruction the poor creatures get.

Catholic masters of course are taught that it is their duty to furnish their slaves with opportunities for being well instructed, & for practising their religion. And here is my anxiety, that I cannot enable those masters to do their duty because there are not Priests enough. The negroes must be attended in a great measure on the plantation, both for the reasons given above, & because in our case there are so few churches; & even where there is a church, the negroes of four or five plantations would fill it up, & leave no room for the white, nor for the other negroes of the neighborhood. The Priest then must go to the plantations, & these are scattered at great distances through the country. All the Priests that I have are residing in congregations from which they cannot be absent long. We need a band of travelling Missionaries who should attend to these plantations, & at the same time hunt out the Catholics scattered through the country. In both of these ways an immensity of good can be done. The poor negroes very often have at first a fear of a Catholic Priest, or imagine they can never understand him; but they are not ill disposed towards religion. Indeed they often have a craving for its ministrations. Having few comforts & no expectations in this world, their thoughts & desires are the more easily drawn to the good things of the world to come. I say often because often again they are so entirely animal in their inclinations, so engrossed with the senses, that they have no regard for any thing above the gratifications of the body. But even among such as these, the missionary often finds a good soil for the seed of religion, because their sensuality arises not so much from malice, as from the want of religious instruction — the want of knowing that there is anything better than this world within their reach. It is true, when from this ignorance they have formed habits of sin, they are not always ready to abandon them when better instructed; but patient & persevering instruction & exhortation, together with the use of the Sacraments, will commonly succeed at last in bringing them to a better life.

For the negro is naturally inclined to be dependent on others; therefore he is disposed to listen & believe what he is told by his superiors. When he resists the teachings of religion, it is not so much from stubbornness as from weakness of mind & will. This weakness of mind makes it hard for him to understand an argument; his weakness of will makes it hard to resist temptation, & still harder to break bad habits. It makes him also liable to great fickleness. This is one of the hard trials of a missionary among them. It is not uncommon for a negro to attend religious instruction for a considerable time with great fidelity & a lively interest, & yet drop off before receiving the Sacraments. Sometimes there is no apparent cause, but just fickleness of character, or perhaps secret temptation. But more generally it may be traced to some irregularity in the instruction, or some little neglect which begets an indifference on their part. They are very much creatures of feeling. If they are attended to regularly & if their instructor takes great interest in them, & gets them to realize the value of their souls, he can do a great deal with them for the glory of God. And he may have the unspeakable consolation of finding among them vocations to a high degree of sanctity. The humility of their condition & the docility of their character take away many of the ordinary obstacles to the workings of grace; & where other circumstances are favourable, these lowly ones in the eyes of the world sometimes rise very high in the favour of God. I have known a case of a servant girl's being really revered as a saint by the family in which she had been reared, & where she was working with all simplicity & fidelity in the lowest offices.

Oh! what a harvest of souls among these 310,000 negroes: every one of them immortal, made to the image & likeness of God, redeemed by the Precious Blood of the Son of God! Oh! what a frightful havoc

Satan is making among them! What numbers of children die without baptism! how many grown persons live & die in ignorance of God, and still worse, buried in miserable sins & habits of sins, which they neither know nor care to free themselves from. Oh! for a band of Apostles like Fr. Claver,[1] to devote themselves to the service of the negro. Not such service indeed as he rendered to them with so much heroism; for our blacks are not often in that bodily wretchedness which called forth so much of his charity. They need services less repugnant to flesh & blood, & yet not less fruitful in the saving of souls & promoting the glory of God. They need instructions & the Sacraments. The Masters provide for their bodies & even in a great measure for their exterior conduct. Are there not Priests of God — at least in the generous Apostolic land of France — are there not still some there, who are ready to put the sickle into this abundant field? It will cost pains & patience, but the consolations will be very great, as they gather those rich sheaves of more than golden fruit into the granary of heaven. *Euntes ibant & flebant mittentes semina sua: venientes autem venient cum exaltatione portantes manipulos suos. . . .*

102. Archbishop Hughes Interprets American Liberty and Its Abuses to the Holy See, March 23, 1858

THE spirit and intent of American liberty often proved puzzling to the Holy See and they were not infrequently misinterpreted at Rome. That this should have been true was not surprising in the light of the shameful treatment accorded Pius IX's representative, Archbishop Gaetano Bedini (1806–1864) on his tour of this country, June, 1853–February, 1854. The most commanding figure in the American Church at the mid-century was John Hughes (1797–1864), first Archbishop of New York. Hughes was a bold defender of the Church's rights against the nativists, the press, and other critics, and as a consequence he was in the thick of most of the controversies of the day. Realizing the effect that false information from the United States might have on the officials of the Roman Curia, Hughes prepared an elaborate report in 1858 on conditions in his archdiocese in which he included an analysis of the true concept of liberty among Americans and the abuses to which freedom in this country had been subjected by revolutionary elements from abroad who were hostile to the best interests of Church and State. The following excerpt furnishes a vivid picture of an aspect of American Catholic life in these years that is seldom emphasized.

[1] St. Peter Claver (1581–1654), a Spanish Jesuit, who performed heroic missionary labors among the Negroes at Cartagena in present-day Colombia from 1610 to his death.

Source: Henry J. Browne (Ed.), "The Archdiocese of New York A Century Ago. A Memoir of Archbishop Hughes, 1838–1858," *Historical Records and Studies,* XXXIX–XL (1952), 168–174.

We come now to the Revolutions in Europe. During the period last under consideration [immediately above Hughes had been deploring the excessive immigration of the previous twenty years] their rebound on New York was most perilous to the faith and morals of the people committed to my charge. I cannot help regarding it as a singular protection of Almighty God and a singular evidence of the interposition of the Blessed Virgin Mary, under whose patronage this Diocese had been especially placed from its origin, under the title of the "Assumption," now, under that of the "Immaculate Conception," that we have escaped the ordeal with so little injury to the principles of our Religion. In this Country, "Liberty" is the watch word, the boast, the pride of all men. The general tone of the Country would seem to require that every man should touch his hat whenever the word "Liberty" is pronounced in his presence. This, you can easily imagine, applies especially to all aspirants for public office, and to the very numerous and ubiquitous class of professional politicians. Sensible men though imbued in heart with the same feeling, yet oftentimes ridicule this extravagant display of it among the classes to which I have referred.

Liberty, in this Country, has a very clear and specific meaning. It is not understood in Europe, as it is here. Here, it means the vindication of personal rights; the fair support of public laws; the maintenance, at all hazards, of public order, according to those laws; the right to change them when they are found to be absurd or oppressive. Such, in brief, is the meaning of the word liberty, as understood by the people of the United States. Of course, you will think of the excesses that have been committed from time to time by mobs, "lynch laws" &c, as marring the correctness of the foregoing statement. But I can assure you that these excesses are regarded, here, as outrages and violations of liberty, the same as they would be in Europe. But in Continental Europe Liberty is understood to mean the overthrow of all existing governments, recognizing the principle of Monarchy. It is the genius of destruction and bloodshed: — ferociously bent on pulling down whatever exists, without the fore-sight or capacity to substitute any thing as good or better.

This distinction did not strike the American people at the outbreak of the late revolutions in Europe, as it does now Their national pride, as a republic, was much flattered by the anticipation that their example was about to be imitated by all the civilized nations of the earth. There were to be no more kings, or Emperors, or Pope, or Princes; but in their stead, *"the people" "the people" "the people."* Experience, however, has taught them their mistake; and they have become quite satisfied that the specimens of patriotism, from the different nations of Western Europe, who by flight or expulsion have reached these shores, are to be ranked among the veriest wretches that ever disgraced humanity, or disturbed the well-being of Society.[1]

This was not the case, however, fifteen years ago. About that time, there was established in this City a paper called the *"Echo d'Italia."*[2] This Journal was supported, not by Italians, but by the enemies of the Catholic Church; who employed it, to feed *their own papers* with the scandals and calumnies against Italy and its inhabitants, which might tend to damage the estimation of our holy religion throughout the world. Around this bad centre were congregated, as time went on, every renegade both to creed and country that Italy would not allow to live in her bosom. Among these, I am sorry to say, that even some bad priests distinguished themselves by their atrocious assaults upon the Catholic Creed and its ministers. The *"Echo d'Italia,"* was supported as I have remarked, as a *feeder* to the Anti-Catholic press. The tyranny of the church, the wicked lives of the prelates, the dreadful bondage of the noble Italian people, in their beautiful and classic land, — were themes inexhaustible under the pens of native writers for that Journal. Hence, the hypocritical homage manifested in this Country, by the bitterest protestants, in favor of Our Illustrious Holy Father on his accession to the Papal Throne.[3]

You will not be surprised if the Catholics were carried away in the enthusiasm of the Country at large — that they too were immensely flattered, at having lived to see the Holy Father regarded with such universal admiration. Under such circumstances, *they* became also the blind idolators of what both Americans and Europeans designated as "Liberty" — the "progress of human freedom" &c &c &c. I saw the impeding danger of association, on this principle, which it was intended to bring about between the Catholics of New York and the "Red

[1] Due to the failure of the liberal revolutions of 1848–1849 in the German and Italian States, the Austrian Empire, Ireland, and other countries, numerous political refugees found their way to the United States in these years.

[2] *Echo d'Italia* was a weekly paper that began publication in New York in 1850.

[3] The election of the liberal-minded Giovanni Mastai-Ferretti as Pope Pius IX on June 16, 1846, brought a wave of enthusiasm among liberals in the United States as well as in Europe.

Republicans" of Europe. I began early to put my flock upon their guard — not by a direct assault upon liberty, but against its abuse, indirectly and to a measured extent, whenever an opportunity presented itself. I had most to apprehend from the spurious patriotism of the "Young Irelanders."[4] You know how fond is the attachment which Irishmen cherish for their native land, and this attachment seems to grow stronger the farther they are removed from its shores and the longer they have been absent. They had been wrought to a high pitch of expectation, and hope for their country's freedom, by the bombastic rhetoric of the Dublin Nation and other journals of the same type. When these hopes were suddenly dashed in this Country by the result of Mr. Smith O'Brien's[5] campaign, they were broken down and almost ashamed of the soil of their nativity. This feeling was taken advantage of and turned into bitterness by some of the Irish Refugees, who, on reaching these shores, pretended to give a full account of the recent efforts in which they had been engaged. They charged the failure on the "Catholic Clergy," as enemies to the Irish people — denounced the hierchy [*sic*] and priesthood of Ireland, proclaimed that if any of them should show his face on this side of the Atlantic he should be met with "hisses," instead of the ordinary signs of reverence and respect.

Our poor people were not in a frame of mind to discriminate, and to detect the malice of these cowardly and unjust accusations whilst the Refugee Patriots from France, Germany, & Italy did not hesitate to proclaim, openly, that there was no hope of freedom for the down trodden people of Europe until the Catholic Church and its clergy, from the Pope downwards, should be overthrown, and if necessary, annihilated.

The first event which opened the eyes of the Catholics was the shout of joy which rang throughout the Country when it was announced that the Holy Father had been driven away from Rome.[6] The jubilee of our enemies made the Catholics sad. They could not foresee the

[4] The Young Irelanders grew restive with the conciliatory policies of Daniel O'Connell to win the freedom of Ireland, broke from his leadership in 1840, established the *Nation* as their organ in 1842, and espoused the policy of violence to win their goal.

[5] William Smith O'Brien (1803–1864) was one of the principal leaders of the Young Irelanders. A series of agrarian crimes, suspension for Ireland of the habeas corpus act, and the news of the revolutions on the continent prompted an uprising in Tipperary in July–August, 1848, which the British troops quickly crushed. The leaders were transported to Van Diemen's Land, but a number of them succeeded in escaping and reaching the United States where they carried on their agitation for Irish freedom.

[6] When the Mazzinian republicans seized Rome Pius IX fled on November 25, 1848, to Gaeta in the Kingdom of the Two Sicilies.

final result of the measures which the usurpers in the Eternal City had put into execution. The future looked dark, and they were downhearted. With a view to cheer them, and at the same time, to give their thoughts a better direction, as well as to withdraw them from association with the Red Republicans who were among us, and the abettors of their principles here, I preached what might be called a political sermon in my Cathedral, on the Sunday next following the receipt of the news, that the Holy Father had been obliged to quit Rome. This became a *turning point* in the thoughts of my own people, with the exception of a very few who were incurable, but who ceased from that time to have any influence. I send you a copy of the discourse which was taken down by a Reporter of one of the secular parents [*sic*], and published the next day.[7]

You can easily understand that from the period of its publication I became offensive to all those wild and unprincipled Republicans. They did not spare me; but neither did they convert me: and the words which I uttered from time to time, and on various occasions, were published not only here in New York but throughout the Country — in some papers out of enmity, in others, to let their readers know what I thought in regard to passing events. I have reason to know that these publications had a great influence in keeping the Catholics *steady,* and little by little, bringing "Red Republicanism" into utter contempt among protestants as well as Catholics.

The enthusiasm and admiration in which Kossuth was held by the American people were almost boundless.[8] When released from prison by the Sultan, this Government sent a vessel of war to receive him and bring him to the United States. When he reached Southampton, in England, he took occasion to make a grand speech, and in it, to

[7] Hughes preached his sermon on "The Present Position of Pius IX" in St. Patrick's Cathedral on January 3, 1849. For the text cf. Lawrence Kehoe (Ed.), *Complete Works of the Most Rev. John Hughes* (New York, 1865), I, 11–21.

[8] After the defeat of the Hungarian revolt Louis Kossuth (1802–1894) fled to Turkey in August, 1849. On December 5, 1851, he arrived in New York where he was given a tumultuous welcome. But after it became clear that Kossuth had come to the United States to seek money and support for his revolutionary cause the isolationist sentiments of Americans brought a change of attitude toward him and when he departed in July, 1852, there was not a single person at hand to bid him farewell. That Kossuth was a rallying point for the anti-Catholic nativists in this country there is no doubt, and it has been remarked of his first days in the United States that his enthusiastic reception "was due in part to the fact that he was a symbol of Protestantism as well as of liberty" (Ray Allen Billington, *The Protestant Crusade* [New York, 1938], p. 331). Hughes' stand against the Hungarian revolutionist unquestionably hurt the latter's cause with American Catholics, but the archbishop's account exaggerated the extent of his influence in this regard.

compliment England for its protestant feeling whilst he denounced at the same time the Pope and the Jesuits as the sworn enemies of human liberty. A report of this speech appeared in our newspapers before Kossuth's arrival in this City — and in a public meeting of Catholics convened for the purpose of receiving the Rev. Dr. Donnelly and the Rev. Dr. Devlin, who had just arrived as Collectors for the "Irish University,"[9] I took occasion as it were incidentally, in the course of my address, to criticise Kossuth and to denounce his principles. I dreaded the influence which his reception here might exercise on the Catholics, and wished them to be fore-warned.[10] Next day, I was assailed in the newspapers for my denunciation of Kossuth; I had to reply and justify myself; and thus my opinions of Kossuth were spread all over the Country, and his mission became a comparative failure precisely for the reason that the Catholics kept aloof wherever he passed. Even in New York the grand oration that had been arranged for him turned out to be a failure because the Catholics would have nothing to do with him. This was noted down by the politicians as a hint that their attentions to Kossuth might be remembered much to their disadvantage; and wherever the Hero of Hungary passed he was allowed to place himself in the hands of protestant Clergyman and Anti-Catholic bigots. He felt this deeply, and complained of it bitterly. He took occasion afterwards to make some remarks complimentary to the Catholics — but it was too late — and he fell so rapidly in public estimation that he was obliged within six months to leave the country clandestinely under the name of *"Alexander Smith."*

I should not give you an idea of the excitement which prevailed during the period now under consideration if I did not mention that so strong became the force of public opinion in favor of what was called the "European liberty," that it shook the firmness of not a few of the Catholic Clergy, and that from one Reverend pen, at least, I was called to an account in the secular journals for having misrepresented the sentiments of the Church on the subject of "political liberty."

In short, during the paroxysm about "European freedom," and the overthrow of "Kingly Governments" in Europe, it was as much as one

---

[9] The Catholic University of Ireland with John Henry Newman as rector opened for classes in Dublin on November 3, 1854. The identity of Donnelly and Devlin was not established, but the most recent scholarly history of the Irish university notes the fact that American Catholics contributed to the fund in 1851 the sum of £4,735 (Fergal McGrath, S.J., *Newman's University. Idea and Reality* [London, 1951], p. 102).

[10] Hughes' speech against Kossuth was delivered at Stuyvesant Institute, New York, on November 18, 1851.

could do to stand erect without bowing or bending to the force of popular sentiment, as portrayed in the newspapers. Details would be endless; and so I shall pass to the next division of my subject, which is a half opened *new* book in the history of the Catholic Church in America. . . . [Hughes then continues with a lengthy section on Know-Nothingism.]

103. An Appeal for the North American College at Rome, November 13, 1858

FOR obvious reasons the Catholic hierarchy of most countries has at one time or other given thought to the establishment of a national college at Rome where candidates for its priesthood may receive the special advantages of study in the Eternal City. From the late sixteenth and early seventeenth centuries colleges of this type were maintained for English, Irish, and Scotch seminarians. The question of such an institution for the Church of the United States was first seriously discussed when a delegation of American bishops visited the Holy See in December, 1854, for the definition of the dogma of the Immaculate Conception. At that time there were 590 seminarians enrolled in about thirty seminaries in the United States, and a total of 1604 priests, both diocesan and religious, a large number of whom had been born and educated abroad. The prelates most interested in this project were Archbishops Kenrick of Baltimore and Hughes of New York and Bishop O'Connor of Pittsburgh (1810–1872). In 1857 O'Connor acted as a delegate to Rome in the matter and returned to inform his fellow bishops of the high hopes of Pope Pius IX for the undertaking and the pontiff's practical support in the form of a building purchased at his own expense to house the college. At the outset some of the bishops demurred, but the initial difficulties were finally overcome and on December 7, 1859, the North American College opened with twelve students in an old Visitandine convent in the Via dell' Umiltà. Since 1859 the college has enrolled around 2100 students of whom about 1900 are numbered among its priest alumni. The needs of the greatly expanded Church in the United States ultimately proved too great for the old building in the Via dell' Umiltà and in October, 1953, a new college on the Janiculum Hill was dedicated with accommodations for approximately 300 students. In the following pastoral letter Bishop O'Connor sketched for his priests and people the advantages of an institution of this kind for the American Church, a subject on which he could speak with conviction by reason of his years in Rome as a student at the Urban College of Propaganda Fide. Source: *Pittsburgh Catholic*, November 13, 1858.

MICHAEL O'CONNOR, by the grace of God and the favor of the Apostolic See

Bishop of Pittsburgh.

To the Clergy and Faithful of the Diocese of Pittsburgh.

Grace unto you, and peace from God our Father, and from the Lord Jesus Christ.

The Archbishop of Baltimore having appointed the Sunday within the Octave of the Feast of the Immaculate Conception, December 12th, as the day on which will be made, in the Archdiocess [*sic*], the first collection for the American College at Rome, it is our wish that the same day a collection be taken up, for this object, in all the Churches of our Diocess [*sic*].

You are aware that the Prelates of the United States have felt deeply interested in the establishment of a National College at the centre of Catholic unity. The wishes of the Bishops in this matter, have been fully shared by their flocks ever since it became generally understood that such a measure was in contemplation. The Catholic Press has advocated the undertaking with zeal and perseverance, and some Catholic gentlemen of means, in the hope of insuring its speedy consummation, have pledged themselves to contribute liberally to its support. The late circular of his Eminence, the Cardinal Prefect of the Propaganda, which you have read in the public prints, gives the pleasing assurance that this most desirable institution may soon be established on a footing in every way worthy of the country it is destined to represent in the Eternal City. By this letter of his Eminence Cardinal Barnabo, we are informed that our present illustrious Pontiff has purchased, and placed at the disposal of the Bishops of the United States, a large and suitable building, to be used by them for the purpose of an American College.

The situation of this edifice is as desirable as any other in Rome. It is at once central and healthy, and in the immediate neighborhood of the schools which the students will frequent. Still, the house is, of course, wanting in all the appointments indispensable to a College. As it is presumed the institution will open with a very considerable number of students, it will be necessary, from the very first, to furnish it on an extensive scale, besides providing it with a suitable library. The fact, too, that the building was not originally intended for a college, will necessitate alterations in it, involving a large outlay. It is to defray these unavoidable expenses, and to create a fund for the maintenance of the establishment, your charity will be appealed to on the approaching 12th of December. Your liberality on that occasion will, we feel assured, be worthy of the object in behalf of which it will be invoked, and fitly correspond to the noble generosity of the Sovereign Pontiff, whose first offering to the good work has been so munificent.

The advantages of an ecclesiastical training in Rome, especially in a National establishment where this discipline will be specially suited to the character of our youth, and prepare them for the field in which they are to labor, can hardly be overrated. In that city the clerical student is surrounded by every thing that can elevate the taste, enlarge the mind, and strengthen the faith. Her galleries and churches spread out before him all that is excellent in Pagan and Christian art. Her libraries, the best in the world, place within his reach all the standard works of positive and abstract science, together with many other sources of knowledge, not found elsewhere. Her museums, rich in monuments of the past, whilst they greatly facilitate [*sic*], give a most lively interest to his historical and archaeological studies. His laudable ambition of distinction is here stimulated by the noble impulse of patriotism; for, at Rome, he must measure his intellectual strength with competitors from all nations. Her numerous colleges, monasteries, and academies, afford him frequent opportunities of listening to disputations on theology and philosophy, and to the lectures of distinguished scholars, on literature, history and science. He is made acquainted with the organization, and usages of the different courts of appeal, to which are referred difficulties and disputes on matters of doctrine, and discipline, all over the Church. His professors are always men of profound learning, and, not infrequently, of world-wide reputation. His course of studies is long and rigorous, and eminently calculated to beget habits of deep thought, and close criticism. And, since, at this centre of gospel light, all minds seem to be illumined, and illumined [*sic*], his constant, familiar intercourse with members of the Roman clergy, accustoms him to regulate his views on ordinary topics, by high principles of Catholic truth.

And, at Rome, what does he not see to excite his devotion, and glory in the cross? Her numerous charities, that reach every want and infirmity of the poor and the sick; the piety of her people; her many festivals; the splendor of her churches; the grandeur of her ceremonies, give him a lasting sense of the duties and the dignity of his religion. His piety is enkindled at the shrines of her saints; and he is filled with Christian fortitude at the tombs of her martyrs and apostles. Her ruins show him the strength of Christian faith, and the colossal proportions of that power, which labored for centuries to destroy it: whilst the mute, but eloquent witnesses that have arisen, and arise, from her catacombs, tell him what men may suffer for the Kingdom of Heaven. In Rome, too, as nowhere else, he is made to realize the fact, that the Church is the only organization that does, or can supply redemption, through Christ, to a fallen world. The thousands, from all nations, that visit her sanctuaries; the missionaries that leave her to carry the Gospel to distant lands, or return to give an account of their labors; the voice of the Supreme Pontiff, speaking authoritatively to the churches of Christendom; the Bishops that come, at stated times, to pay their homage to the Chair of Peter, give him the most exalted idea of the Church's unity and Catholicity.

But these advantages, venerable and beloved Brethren, for the most part, peculiar to a Roman ecclesiastical training, though valuable, on account of their [*sic*] learning and knowledge they directly foster, are chiefly so, because of their effects in those, amongst whom their recipients are afterwards called to labor. They who have drawn deeply at the source of Apostolic truth, will be likely to carry that truth pure, and in plenty, to others. They who have learned to love Rome, not only from principle, but also from the tenderest, holiest local attachments, will be likely to bind the faith and affections of others to this sacred, immovable centre of evangelical truth.

Rome is the capital of the Christian world; the new Jerusalem of the people of God. Sacrifice is now offered up: "from the rising of the sun, to the going down of the same." But the Arc [*sic*] of the Covenant, and the Holy of Holies are at Rome. Of Rome, too, we may say with the Prophet: "The law shall come forth from Sion, and the word of the Lord from Jerusalem." It is the mission of the Church of Rome to instruct all other churches in sound doctrine; to enlighten their doubt; to lead them, in difficulty and danger. For, in the person of the Roman Pontiff, Peter feeds the entire flock of Christ, both pastors and people. With that Church, all the other churches have lived, and must live, in the unity of faith; and, in this unity, find their safety and their prosperity. Severed from Rome, the most flourishing churches have fallen into heresy, and even into barbarism.

The national pride that would lead men, or nations, to suspect union in faith, with Rome, or to disregard whatever tends to promote, or preserve it, is a proper feeling, carried to unwise excess. There is but one sun to illuminate all lands; there is but one truth to enlighten all minds. The Church of Christ is necessarily one, and of all nations. Her government, then, must be one, and of universal jurisdiction. To the seat of that government, wherever established, is due the homage of true believers all over the world.

That an American College in Rome is necessary to impart a sound ecclesiastical education to our clergy, or to maintain our union with the Holy See, no one will pretend. That, whilst contributing much to secure these results, it will greatly promote the higher ecclesiastical studies among them, and add a new grace to our National Church, few, we think can deny. The clergy and people of the United States, yield to no others, in their loving attachment to Rome; and are second to none, in their zeal for the promotion of ecclesiastical, and secular learning. Indeed, it is these very dispositions, that have led us to ask of the Holy Father, a favor already enjoyed by so many nations of Europe and the East; and which is soon to be granted to the Catholics of the South American Continent. A National College at Rome will, it must be presumed, very much augment the number of the learned among our clergy, and prove a powerful means, under God, of perpetuating the orthodoxy of our young Church, which no taint of heresy has, thus far, touched.

Pray, then, Brethren, that God move the hearts of all to aid this good work, according to each one's ability. It has the blessing of the Supreme Pontiff upon it, and it must succeed.

The grace of our Lord Jesus Christ be with you all. May the Blessed and Immaculate Patroness of the American Church keep you ever under her powerful protection.

Given at Pittsburgh, this 10th day of November, in the year of our Lord, 1858.

Michael
Bishop of Pittsburgh.

J. Keogh, Secretary.

104. Father Hecker Sketches His Plans and Hopes for the Paulists, July 24, 1859

ONE of the most important figures in nineteenth-century American Catholicism was Isaac Thomas Hecker (1819–1888). Hecker became a Catholic in August, 1844, after a lengthy search for truth that had led him in 1843 to Brook Farm and Fruitlands. During this time he became very well acquainted with Orestes Brownson, Bronson Alcott, Henry Thoreau, and other New England religious thinkers. After a novitiate in Belgium he became a member of the Congregation of the Most Holy Redeemer in 1846, returning to the United States in 1851 where for some years he was engaged in giving missions with several other convert Redemptorists. Since the order's principal concern was for the German Catholic immigrants, Hecker and his missionary companions were convinced that it would benefit the missions if the Redemptorists would open an English-speaking house which would be a center for the English missions. With this in mind, and with the encouragement of Bishop Bayley of Newark and Archbishop Hughes of New York, Hecker went to Rome in August, 1857, as the spokesman for his associates, to lay the proposition before the Redemptorist rector major. Three days after his arrival, he was expelled without a hearing for having made the journey without the necessary permission. Hecker found a defender in Alessandro Cardinal Barnabò, Prefect of the Congregation de Propaganda Fide, who took his case to Pius IX. It was thus that the Paulist Fathers came into existence in July, 1858, and from that time until his death thirty years later Hecker remained the superior general. He was an intensely active man who wrote several books, e.g., *Questions of the Soul* (New York, 1852) and *Aspirations of Nature* (New York, 1857), founded the *Catholic World* in 1865, organized the Catholic Publication Society the following year, acted as theologian for Archbishop Spalding of Baltimore at the Vatican Council — in all of which he kept uppermost in his mind the dominant motive of his priestly life, the winning of American Protestants to the Catholic faith. Three years after his death one of his confreres, Walter Elliott, C.S.P., published *The Life of Father Hecker* (New York, 1891) which appeared in a French translation in 1897 and became the center of a theological controversy on both sides of the Atlantic under the name of the so-called heresy of Americanism. The following letter, written a year after the establishment of the Paulists, to Father Adrien-Emmanuel Rouquette (1813–1887), poet, writer, and Indian missionary of Louisiana, gives an excellent picture of Hecker's plans and aspirations for the future of his new congregation. Source: Archives of the Paulist Fathers, photostat of original in the archives of the Archdiocese of New Orleans.

New York, July 24, 1859

Rev. Dear Friend.

Six months and more have elapsed since the reception of your last letter so full of kindred sympathy and hope.[1] In it you say: "I will write to you soon my end, my means, & the degree of success which I have already attained." And also that "you would write to me more at length and intimately" & you throw out the suggestion that "one day we might meet in the same vocation." Your letter has been lying on my table ever since, & I had but to glance at it to awaken my sympathies and enkindle my enthusiasm. I will not disguise to you that your last suggestion has more than once also occurred to my thoughts. For I cannot refuse to recognize the same aims, thoughts, & sentiments which occupy your mind also occupy mine. Apparently our ways differ, but as you remark, they are not so different in reality.

---

[1] Correspondence between Fathers Hecker and Rouquette had begun in November, 1858, as a result of "some cheering words" written by Rouquette in the New York *Freeman's Journal.*

Your attrait [*sic*] for solitude, silence, prayer, contemplation is no greater than my own. There was a time when my Superiors hesitated whether it were not better for me to change my state, & enter a contemplative order. During my years of study the greater part of my time was given to such a life, & one year of this period was wholly given to it and the care of the sick. Not as a matter of choice but of inability to apply myself to scientific studies. Among the so many pressing occupations at present,[2] I cherish the same attrait, & act always with reluctance & from a sense of duty. But when unable to study & my attention absorbed in contemplation I was at the time aware that the grace of God was preparing me only for a more intensive & extensive action than all studies could have done. While most helpless and by others regarded as a fool, it was my most intimate conviction that God's Providence was preparing me for a great work, the conversion of our countrymen. And when compelled under obedience at the time to give in writing an explanation of my state, I did not hesitate to express this conviction.[3] The same conviction prompted subsequently *Questions of the Soul* and *Aspirations of Nature*. The position in which I am at present placed I cannot regard in any other light than in view of this conviction, & as a special providence of God.

The conversion of the American people to the Catholic faith has ripened into a conviction with me which lies beyond the reign of doubt. My life, my labours, and my death is [*sic*] consecrated to it. No other aim as an end outside of my own salvation and perfection can occupy my attention a moment. But all other things in view of this, — art, science, literature, etc. etc. enter in as a part of the means, and command my interest, & demand all the encouragement within my reach. In the union of Catholic faith and American civilization a new birth awaits them all, and a future for the Church brighter than any past. That is briefly my "Credo."

Individually the faith has been identified with American life. Our effort is to identify Catholicity with American life in a religious association. I feel confident of its practicability. I entertain the hope of our

[2] Hecker refers here to the organization of the Paulist Fathers, raising money for a new church and convent, and the fulfillment of a heavy mission schedule.

[3] Hecker wrote this statement on May 30, 1848, while still a Redemptorist student at Wittem, Holland. In it he stated: "I believe that Providence calls me to an active life; further, that he calls me to America to convert a certain class of persons amongst whom I found myself before my conversion; I believe that I shall be the vile instrument which he will make use of for the conversion of a multitude of those unhappy souls who aspire after truth without having the means to arrive at and possess it" (Archives of the Paulist Fathers, Hecker Papers).

opening a door to our young men who aim at consecrating their lives to God & Religion, and of our Institution becoming in the hands of Divine Providence a means of spreading the Faith among our people.

Thus far God's blessing have accompanied our labors, never were they more successful. The location secured for our community could not be more suitable, its value has increased doubly since its purchase.[4] Our house is large and now almost ready for its roof; & in October we expect to occupy it. A few applications by priests to join us have been made; and several by young men, but these we are *not yet prepared* to receive. A few days ago I received from Cardinal Barnabò the permission to increase our numbers.

Our institution is based on the voluntary principle, with the idea of practicing all the religious virtues in the same degree of perfection as those under the vows. These are our practical measures.

You will perceive My Dear Friend, that I have taken up your offer "to write to me more at length & intimately" & fulfilled it in respect to yourself, which I trust will suggest a reciprocal confidence.

With great esteem

Your devoted friend & Servant in Xt.

I. T. HECKER

105. James A. McMaster's Criticism of the Lincoln Administration, June 8, 1861

THE American Catholic press of the mid and later nineteenth century was a far livelier enterprise than the official Catholic newspapers of our day. In an era when famous New York editors like James Gordon Bennett of the *Herald,* Horace Greeley of the *Tribune,* Henry J. Raymond of the *Times,* and Charles A. Dana of the *Sun* were making newspaper history in this country the convert-editor of the New York *Freeman's Journal,* James A. McMaster (1820–1886) exchanged editorial blows with the best of them. The weekly *Freeman's* had been founded in 1840 and McMaster became the editor in 1848. For the first few years he confined himself mainly to fighting the Church's battles and remained relatively clear of politics. But gradually he became involved in the slavery controversy and in July, 1856, Archbishop Hughes, who differed with him, withdrew his approbation from the *Freeman's* as a diocesan organ and in July, 1859, started his own *Metropolitan Record.* Pained though he was at this rebuff, McMaster's independent mind and strong views would not permit him to quit and he bravely carried on until his sharp and persistent criticisms of the Lincoln

[4] This property was located on 60th Street, west of 9th Avenue, and was bought for $63,000.

administration brought suspension of his paper in August, 1861, while the editor himself was arrested and imprisoned in Fort Lafayette for nearly six weeks. He had seen what was coming, but he was defiant to the end and sought in his last issue to rally renewed support for the *Freeman's.* "We know not what enterprise we may yet be impelled to undertake," he said. "But you who *feel* that we are right — *help* us to continue, and even to do *more*" (*Freeman's Journal,* August 24, 1861). McMaster was by no means a lone voice in his attacks on the government, for as Frank Luther Mott has said, "Never was there a war in which arm-chair generalship from newspaper offices was more vociferous, in which more editors became military strategists over night" (*American Journalism* [New York, 1941], p. 339). The following editorial was only one of a series in which McMaster castigated Lincoln and his conduct of the war. Source: Editorial, "The Ship on the Breakers," New York *Freeman's Journal,* June 8, 1861.

Abraham Lincoln, county court lawyer of the village of Springfield, Illinois, elected President according to the letter of the Constitution — and whom we are ready to sustain in the place he so unworthily fills, *according to the Constitution* — has been playing some infamous tricks, of late. He has been creating new regular armies, and establishing an additional navy, without any act of Congress. By a certain stretch of executive authority he has the *right,* in the present exigency, under the act of 1795, to call out the *militia of such States as may be necessary,* but the legal limit of that authority expires *"thirty days after the next assembling of Congress."* Abraham Lincoln made demure protestations, in his inaugural, that it was his devotion to the Constitution of the United States, and the laws made in pursuance thereof, that would *compel* him to act in a manner disagreeable to millions of his "dissatisfied countrymen." Why, then, in view of the crisis, did he not call Congress together at an *earlier* day? Why did he not limit his proclamation, calling for seventy-five thousand militia men, to the term for which *alone* he had Constitutional power to call them — the expiration of thirty days after the next meeting of Congress? Why, in his subsequent proclamation, calling for a much larger force, did he not, in the same way, confine himself to his legal and Constitutional power, of calling on *the militia of States,* for the term for which alone he had power to call them — ending *thirty days after the meeting of Congress?* Why has he undertaken, without act of Congress, to increase the regular army and the navy of the United States? Why has he assumed the peculiar and restrictive prerogative of Congress — the *law-making* power — in *creating* military offices and commissions, in order that he may fill those assumed offices with officers selected by him? Congress, which *alone* has the power, has recognized but *one* Major-General of the United States regular army — Gen. Winfield Scott.[1] Mr. Abe Lincoln, who has no more authority to do so than Mr. Dogberry Kennedy of the New York Police, has *named* Major George B. McClellan,[2] a very meritorious Captain of the United States Cavalry; Benjamin F. Butler,[3] an unusually clever Brigadier of the Massachusetts State Militia; and some others, to be Major-Generals of the United States Army — that is, to fill offices that *do not exist* by the law-making power — Congress — which can *alone* create them, according to the Constitution of the United States.

The Constitution of the United States confers no such power on Mr. President Lincoln. The contemporaneous writings of the framers of that Constitution say *why* they did not. They say that they withheld such powers, because history showed them that a people, *"in proportion as they are free,* will disarm the Executive of the influence to exercise a war-making propensity."

In the light of the Constitution of the United States, and of the authoritative expositors and commentators of that instrument, there can be but one judgment — that Lincoln has sought to absorb and confound in his own action the legislative and the executive functions, which the Constitution of the United States, with such pre-eminent care, has distinguished and placed in separate hands.

It appears, also, that Mr. Abe Lincoln, as chief Executive of the United States, has directed various military Commandants, at their discretion, or in case of certain emergencies, to suspend the Writ of *Habeas Corpus.*[4] It is difficult, in a country so blessed as ours has been for three quarters of a century, to attract popular attention to the fundamental guarantees of the public security. Perhaps *Habeas Corpus* seems like an abstraction, or a pettifogger's trick. But it is the symbol of our rights as freemen. It is not simply a guarantee for personal liberty, demanded and gained from Charles II., but, in essence and in virtue, it is the characteristic of our free and superior civilization. In substance it was recognized in the *Magna Charta,* and had its origin far back of that, in the old *Frank law.* We call attention to the docu-

[1] Winfield Scott (1786–1866), although Virginia-born, remained loyal to the Union and as commander of the United States Army made the preparations for defending Washington.

[2] George B. McClellan (1826–1885), an officer of the Ohio Volunteers, was appointed a major general of the regular army on May 13, 1861, and placed in command of the Department of the Ohio.

[3] Benjamin F. Butler (1818–1893) was nominated a major general on May 16, 1861, after having been chosen to occupy Baltimore which he had done peacefully with 900 troops three days before.

[4] On July 2, 1861, Lincoln empowered General Scott to suspend the privilege of habeas corpus.

ments we furnish in another column on this subject. From them it will appear, so far as has been ascertained, that Lincoln — having been *constitutionally* elected by a minority vote to the executive office of President — has at one and the same time thought he could absorb the law-making power, and set at defiance — as he did even in his inaugural — the judicial branch of the Government. The *Constitution* divides our Government into three distinct and co-ordinate branches — the Legislative, the Judicial, and the Executive. The latter assumes to *dispense* with the other two, and to exert autocratic power, as completely as any Asiatic or Turkish despot could do, over a nation of slaves.

We have no *party* quarrel to wage against any one. Alas, we have, now, no *party* to sustain. Our wish, above all things, is that Lincoln's Administration *could,* and then *would,* adopt a course which, as loyal American freemen, we can sustain. The present course of the Executive is unconstitutional, outrageous, and *an open rebellion* against the United States Government as established and recognized. We cannot sustain it in this course, and we will not. We declare and protest, on the contrary, with the Chief Justice of the United States,[5] that it subverts all law as recognized by freemen, and attempts to place our persons, our property, liberty, and life, at the will of one or another army officer.

We have often adverted to the fact that, under anti-slavery as a cry, the anti-Democratic coalition known as "Republicans," have been seeking the substitution of a *centralized despotism* in place of the Constitutional Government of the United States. The very ridiculousness of the controlling elements of this coalition is an occasion of danger. If we cite the Red-Republican ravings of the *Tribune*[6] and *Post,*[7] it is replied: "Who regards such bran-bread socialists and poetasters!" If we cite the *Daily Times,*[8] we are told that the writers are "ninnies — nobody heeds them." If we hunt up a copy of the *Courier and Enquirer,* it raises a laugh. But, be it remembered, it was the influence of these papers, and others no whit more respectable, that brought into executive office Abraham Lincoln and his

---

[5] Roger Brooke Taney (1777–1864) was Chief Justice of the United States Supreme Court from March, 1836, to his death.

[6] Horace Greeley (1811–1872) was editor of the New York *Tribune* at the time.

[7] William Cullen Bryant (1794–1878) was editor of the New York *Evening Post.*

[8] Henry J. Raymond (1820–1869), editor of the New York *Times,* was the most steadfast of all the New York editors in their support of Lincoln.

coterie of incapables. The mistake is made of supposing that the dangers of the country come from *able* or from *great* men. Its dangers and its ruin are to be found in *weak* and *little* men — where great men ought to be. Despotism is a *petty* thing, and petty fellows are they who exercise it.

The *Daily Times,* one day last week, elaborates an article to show that we must, hereafter, keep up a large standing army — even when peace is restored. A large standing army, in time of peace — that is, a hundred thousand men or so, standing idle, with muskets in their hands, at the beck of the Government that pays them — would be the death-knell of political liberty. This is too plain — has been too often insisted on by our greatest statesmen — to render it necessary to argue it. It seems that the *minority,* who have climbed to power, through licentious presses and desecrated pulpits, playing on the ignorance and fanaticism of the country — recognizes that the American people, if left free, will take good care that they never attain a second, nor another, term of administration. It seems that the deliberate purpose has been formed of *subverting, from top to bottom,* the American system of government, and of trying to rule this people by an armed despotism. We do not say that the accursed project may not be accomplished, but we do say that the cowardly and incapable clique who inaugurate the system, will inevitably pay the forfeit of their crime, like Robespierre and Danton, in their own blood.

We have said that our chief danger is from the incapacity, the mental and moral weakness, of the faction now attempting to rule us — not from their strength. This will be our apology for quoting the following from a bombastic article of Webb,[9] in his *Courier and Enquirer,* published a few days before he was appointed Minister to Brazil. It is *his* offering of incense to the attempted military despotism, which he will help by keeping his Brigadier Generalship out of harm's way, while playing courtier at a South American court. He says:

> The war may soon pass away — we may have a quick and vital battle-field, and the North prove its prowess, as certainly it will; but the truth of *national unity* and *power* that these events have given, endures — combined — condensed — *concentrated in army and navy.*
>
> . . . We snall ask the question — *Why all these State lines? Why all this needless, cumbersome, intricate entanglement of different powers to make law and to decree judgment? We can afford now to efface the old*

[9] James W. Webb (1802–1884) was editor of the New York *Courier and Enquirer* from the time he merged the two papers in 1829 to his retirement in 1861. He was named Minister to Brazil on May 31, 1861.

Colonial Geography. It is the admitted powers of States within the nation that has been the source of all our trouble. Nor will the removal of State power, and the creation of a nationality, be a task so formidable.

"Nonsense!" Certainly it is; but we beg thoughtful and intelligent men who turn from it contemptuously, to remember that the miseries the country is now enduring have been brought on it by nonsense as palpable. Webb, who put this in his *Courier,* was, a few days after, named Minister to Brazil, by Lincoln's Administration. It is fair to conclude that he uttered the sentiments that are governing Lincoln's Administration. He says that the *national unity* is to *endure "concentrated in army and navy."*

He says that "State forms," recognized in the Constitution of the country as fundamental and essential, are to be blotted out. Nay, he asks, "why all this *needless, cumbersome, intricate* entanglement of *different* powers to *make law* and to *decree judgment."* It is true, it seems out of place for us to occupy our columns with language worthy only of a negro, or a John Chinaman; but consider the relations of the *Courier* and its editor to Lincoln's Administration, and a reason appears.

Nay, what is Lincoln doing, but *simplifying* the "cumbersome intricate entanglement of *different* powers," as prescribed in the Constitution of the United States, which three months ago, at the hands of Chief Justice Taney, he swore to observe inviolate?

The county court lawyer may not understand what he is doing. His Cabinet may not understand what they are doing. But ideas will rule. Causes will produce results. Men must reap the same that they sow.

Let those heed it who, one year ago, scoffed when we said that the election of Lincoln would cause civil war! We say, now, that if there be not conservatism enough in the country to stop and to rebuke the course of Lincoln and his Cabinet, we will have a bloody revolution and anarchy, resulting in a military despotism, with a different man from Lincoln at its head. We speak what we see and know. Our conscience forces us to speak, whether it please or offend.

106. Bishop Lynch Presents the South's Case for Secession, August 4, 1861

UNLIKE some of the Protestant churches, the organizational unity of the Catholic Church in the United States remained intact during the slavery controversy and the Civil War. But that did not mean that there were not deep sectional differences of opinion among the Catholics of the North and the South on the issues at stake. These differences were high-lighted for the general public when the New York *Metropolitan Record* of September 7, 1861, published an exchange of correspondence between Patrick N. Lynch (1817–1882), Bishop of Charleston, and Archbishop John Hughes of New York on responsibility for the war. Lynch had outlined his views for Hughes in a letter on August 4, and the latter took the somewhat unusual step of replying through his own newspaper on the grounds that, by reason of the disruption of the mails, it was his only chance of acknowledging Lynch's communication. He decided, therefore, to print his reply of August 23 and, as he told the Bishop of Charleston, "without special permission publish your letter at the same time. In this way it may happen that during the war, or afterwards, my answer will come under your inspection" (Lawrence Kehoe [Ed.], *Complete Works of the Most Rev. John Hughes, Archbishop of New York* [New York, 1865], II, 513). Lynch may have learned of Hughes' action because shortly thereafter he published the full text of his letter to the archbishop in his own diocesan paper. The exchange between the prelates attracted widespread attention and complete texts of the letters, together with accompanying editorials, were carried by the New York *Herald, Times,* and *Tribune.* In its issue of September 4, 1861, James Gordon Bennett's *Herald* stated that the "statesmanlike views and admirable temper" of the correspondence "will obtain for it a widespread and attentive consideration both here and abroad." The *Herald's* editorial took occasion to read a lecture to some of the Protestant clergy whose extreme statements were in striking contrast to the calm and tempered opinions of Lynch and Hughes, recommending the bishops' letters to "all the abolitionist and secessionist parsons throughout the country." Source: Charleston *Catholic Miscellany,* September 14, 1861.

Most Reverend Dear Sir: — The mails are so completely paralyzed that it is hard to get a letter from outside the Confederacy. Papers are scarcely ever seen. That, however, Jefferson would think a blessing, on the ground that "he who is simply ignorant is wiser than the one that believes error." A paragraph which has gone the rounds of the Southern papers, states that your Grace has spoken strongly against the war policy of the Government of the United States, fraught with much present suffering, and not calculated to attain any real advantage. What a change has come over these States since I wrote you a long letter last November, and even since I have had the pleasure of seeing you last March. All that I anticipated in that letter has come to pass, and more than I looked for. All the hopes cherished last spring of a peaceful solution have vanished before the dreadful realities of war. What is before us, who can say? Missouri, Maryland and Kentucky are nearer secession now than Virginia, North Carolina and Tennessee were four months ago. Missouri is a battlefield. I think that President Davis, after the victory of Stone Bridge, will probably throw a column into Maryland. Kentucky will, ere long, be drawn into the struggle, and the United States will, in less than ten months, be divided in two not unequal parts, marshalling hundreds of thousands of men against each other.

This war is generally dated from the bombardment of Fort Sumter. There we fired the first gun, and the responsibility is charged on us. But, in reality that responsibility falls on those who rendered the conflict unavoidable — The South, years ago, and a hundred times, declared that the triumph of the abolition or anti-slavery policy, would break up the Union. They were in earnest. When that party, appealing to the people on the Chicago platform, elected their candidate by every free State vote (excepting New Jersey, which was divided,) South Carolina seceded, and other States were preparing to do so. They were in earnest. Yet, as the people disbelieved it, or heeded it not at the ballot, so Congress heeded it not at Washington, and stood doggedly on the Chicago platform endorsed by the people. — This consummated success. The Confederate Government was formed. The dogged obstinacy of the Black Republicans at Washington last winter made all the South secessionists. Still there was peace. The new Administration professed an intention to preserve it. Peace gave time, and time can work wonders. The Confederate Government did not put much faith in those professions. The same hallucination as to their power, which rendered the Black Republicans arrogant and impracticable in Congress, would, it was apprehended, lead them to attempt to crush out secession by force. — And nothing was left undone to be prepared for this event should it occur.

Meanwhile Commissioners were at Washington to arrange a peaceful separation. Favorable intimations were privately given them, and they had hopes of success.

Nine Governors, however, it is said, put the screws on the Cabinet, which resolved on a war policy, and, as silently as they could, made warlike naval preparations. Then, after a month, the Commissioners were refused admission or dismissed, and it was plainly announced that here would be no negotiation. At this time other facts were coming to light here, in Charleston, where our batteries had, for a month or more silently looked on Fort Sumter. During the time of peaceful professions two special messengers (Fox[1] and Lamon[2]) from Presi-

[1] Gustavus V. Fox (1821–1883) was named Assistant Secretary of the Navy by Lincoln's government in August, 1861.

[2] Ward H. Lamon (1828–1893), a former law partner of Lincoln in Illinois, had been sent to Charleston as the president's personal agent in March, 1861,

dent Lincoln visited Fort Sumter. Before being allowed to go thither they gave their word of honor to our Governor that their object was really peaceful. The hotel conversation of the latter was very frank, it is said. Gentlemen here supposed that President Lincoln before ordering the evacuation wished, by these personal friends, to see, as it were, personally, and not simply to learn through official channels, how matters stood at Fort Sumter. When time rolled by without such an order, and it was rumored that the Cabinet had succumbed to the pressure of the Governors, the mails were stopped to and from Fort Sumter. Among the letters seized was one from Major Anderson[3] to President Lincoln, discussing the details of the plan of reinforcement, forwarded to him from Washington by these messengers. Our authorities were thus made aware of the breach of faith towards them, and of the details of the plan itself.

Then came the special messenger of the President, announcing that he intended revictualing the fort, quietly, if permitted, forcibly, if resisted; then the account of the sailing of the fleet from New York. The fort was at once attacked and taken without waiting their arrival. The attack was not made until the offer of negotiation and peaceful arrangement had been rejected, and until the United States Government was in the act of sending an armed force. But it is of little use now to inquire on whom the responsibility rests; we have the war on us, with all its loss of life and long train of evils of every kind. It is the latest, perhaps the strangest instance history gives us, *quam parva sapientia regitur mundus*. Here was a country, vast, populous, prosperous and blessed in all material interest, if any country was. The south producing Cotton, tobacco, sugar, rice and naval stores for the supply, as far as needed, of the North and Northwest, to the value of, perhaps, $50,000,000 a year, and exporting to foreign countries over $220,000,000; the Northwest producing chiefly grain, and supplying the North and the South, and when the European crops failed, having, as last winter, a large European market; the North manufacturing and supplying the South and the Northwest, and struggling to compete with foreign goods abroad, and doing the trading and commerce of the South and the Northwest.

Could the material interests of all the sections be more harmoniously and advantageously combined than in this Union, where each was free to develop to the fullest extent those branches of industry in which it could excel, and could draw from the others those products which it needed, but could not produce as well or as cheaply as they

[3] Robert Anderson (1805–1871) was the Union Commander at Fort Sumter.

could? Even a child could see the vast benefits to all from this mutual co-operation. No wonder that in all material interests the country was prospering to an extent that intoxicated us and astonished the world. We claimed to be pre-eminently sagacious in money matters. The Yankees, I believe, ranked next after the Chinese, in their keenness in business; yet they especially, with an inconceivable blindness, have originated, fostered and propagated a fanatical party spirit which has brought about a result foretold from the beginning, both North and South, as the inevitable consequence of its success.

Taking up anti-slavery, making it a religious dogma, and carrying it into politics, they have broken up the Union. While it was merely an intellectual opinion they might discuss it as they pleased; they might embrace it as they did any other ism. Even their virulent use and misrepresentation we scarcely heeded, provided they did not obtrude them upon us at home. We, as Catholics, might everywhere smile at this additional attempt to "reform" the teachings of our Savior. And the Protestants, South, could have churches and associations of their own. But when they carried it into politics, gaining one State Government after another, and defining their especial policy by unconstitutional laws and every mode of annoying and hostile action, and finally, with increased enthusiasm and increased bitterness, carrying the Presidential election in triumph, and grasping the power of the Federal Government, what could the South do but consult its own safety by withdrawing from the Union? What other protection had they? The Senate, which had still a Democratic majority? They had seen the House of Representatives pass into the hands of their enemies, and each session saw an increasing majority there. The Executive had gone for four years. Their own majority in the Senate was dwindling fast, while on the Territorial question not a few of the Northern Democrats were unsound. To the Supreme Court? That had spoken in the Dred Scott decision. The North would not sustain it, and the Black Republicans scouted it; and moreover, in a few years President Lincoln would have the privilege of placing on the bench new judges from the ranks of his party. To the sober second thought of the people? But this was no new issue on which they were taken by surprise. For years and years it had been discussed; North and South it had been denounced as fraught with disunion and ruin; and yet the Northern people had gradually come to accept it. But the South had spoken so often and so strongly of disunion, without doing anything, that the Northern people had no real belief that any evil consequences would ensue; they did not understand the full bearing of their action. At least, let them understand something of this before all hope of appeal to them is abandoned. Well, South Carolina seceded — other States were preparing to follow her. The matter was taken up in Congress. Many Southerners hoped that then, when the seriousness of the questions could no longer be doubted, something might be done. How vainly they hoped, the Committees of Congress showed. The alternative was thus forced on the South either of tame submission or of resistance. They did not hesitate. They desired to withdraw in peace. This war has been forced upon them.

It was necessary in the beginning. It brings ruin to thousands in its prosecution. It will be fruitless of any good. At its conclusion the parties will stand apart exhausted and embittered by it; for every battle, however, won or lost, will have served but to widen the chasm between the North and South, and to render more difficult, if not impossible, any future reconstruction. Will it be a long war, or a short and mighty one? The Cabinet and the Northern press has pronounced for the last. Yet this is little more than an idle dream. What could 400,000 men do?

I do not think there is a General on either side able to fight 50,000 men. And the North would need eight or ten such Generals. Certainly the 40,000 under McDowell,[4] after five hours' fighting, fought on mechanically without any generalship. The higher officers had completely lost the guiding reins. On our side the Southern troops ought to have been in Washington within forty-eight hours. But the 40,000 on the Confederate side was, I apprehend too unwieldy a body for our Generals. Did not Bonaparte say that not one of his Marshals could general fifty thousand men in battle?

Soult[5] could bring them to the field, and place them properly, but could go no further.

But without Generals, what could 400,000 men do against the South? By force of numbers, and a great loss, they might take city after city. But unless they left large permanent garrisons, their authority would die out with the sound of their drums. Such an army marching through a country covered with forests and thickets and occupied by a population hostile to a man, and where even school-boys can "bark a squirrel," would be decimated every hundred miles of its progress by a guerrilla warfare, against which it could find no protection. This

---

[4] General Irvin McDowell (1818–1885) and his Union army were routed by the Confederate forces at Manasses Junction, Virginia, on July 21, 1861.

[5] Marshal Nicolas-Jean-de-Dieu Soult (1769–1851) was one of the most prominent of Napoleon's generals.

mode of attacking the South can effect nothing beyond the loss of life it will entail, and the temporary devastation that will mark the track of the armies.

But it is probable that circumstances would again, as they have done, overrule the designs of the Washington Cabinet, and make the war slow, long and expensive — one to be decided, less by battles than by the resources and endurance of the combatants.

That portion of the former United States will suffer most in such a contest and must finally succumb, which is least able to dispense with the support it received from the other two sections. How the North can do without our Southern trade, I presume it can judge after three or four months' trial. But it would seem that the failure to sell to the South one hundred and twenty millions of their manufactures each year the stoppage of so much of their shipping interest as was engaged in the two hundred and twenty millions of our foreign exports and the return importations, and in our internal coasting trade, together with the loss of the profits and commissions on so vast a business, must have a very serious effect, too, that I see no way of escaping. Truly the North has to pay dearly for its whistle of Black Republicanism. The Northwest depended partially on the South for a market for its productions, and so far will suffer from the loss of it. It must also be incidentally affected by commercial embarrassments at the North. They will assuredly have enough to eat and to wear, but the "fancy" prices of real estate and stocks, by which they computed their rapidly increasing wealth, must fall in a way to astonish Wall-street. Should their own crops fail, as they sometimes do, or should the European crops be abundant, their commerce will fall. Yet, as the mass of the poor will have all that they ever get anywhere — food and raiment, and that without stint — the Northwest will suffer comparatively little.

How long will it fare with the South should the war be long and so powerfully waged as to require the Southern Confederation to keep say 100,000 men-in-arms, and if the ports are strictly blockaded? This is an important question, and one that can be answered only from a practical knowledge of the habits, resources and disposition of the Southern people. Our needs will be provisions, clothing, money for the government and war expenses, and for the purchase from abroad of what we absolutely require, and are not already supplied with.

As for provisions, I am satisfied that this season we are gathering enough for two years' abundant supply. Every one is raising corn, wheat and stock. On this point the South need not envy the Northwest. Again, manufactures are springing up on all sides. In this State we are providing for our wants — from lucifer matches and steam engines to powder and rifled cannon. Clothing, too, though of a ruder texture and sometimes inferior quality, is abundantly made and easily procured. The supply of tea and coffee will, I presume, in time run out. This will put us to some trouble, but otherwise, neither for provisions nor for clothes, will the South be seriously inconvenienced.

The blacks (by-the-bye more quiet and orderly now, if possible, than before) will remain devoted to agriculture, while the rapidly increasing demand for home productions of every kind gives ready employment to the poorer classes of the whites.

What amount of gold and silver there is within the Confederate States I can only guess at — I suppose about $25,000,000. But as the greater part of our expenses are at home, any currency we are satisfied to use will do, whether Bank bills, Confederate bonds or Treasury notes. When we go abroad, it must be with gold or with Cotton. This last is the spinal column of our financial system. The following is the proposed mode of operating with it: Two millions, or two and a half of bales will be conveyed to the Confederate Government, to be paid for in bonds or Treasury notes. This Cotton will be worth, at ordinary prices, one hundred millions of dollars. If it can be exported at once, it is so much gold. If it is retained, it will form the security for any loan that may be required abroad. The other third of the Cotton will be sold by the planters as best they can on their own account.

The chief difficulty is the blockade, which may prevent the export and sale abroad of the Cotton. A loan on it as security, while it is still unshipped, and scattered in numberless small warehouses, could not easily be affected.

Up to the present time, and for six months more, the blockade, so far from doing any serious injury, has, on the contrary, benefitted, and will continue to benefit the South, forcing us to be active, and to do for ourselves much that we preferred formerly to pay others to do for us. I presume that next January, with a crop of three and a half or four millions of bales on hand, the South would become very restive under a strict blockade. *Should it continue twelve months longer property at the South would go down as they say it has in New York.*

But, before that time comes, another very serious complication arises — how England and France will stand the cutting off their supply of an article on which depend two-thirds of the manufacturing interests of the one and one-third of those of the other? They cannot, try they ever so much, supply the deficiency. As far as the feelings of England are concerned, and, I presume, those of France, too, both nations are decidedly and bitterly anti-slavery; but neither will be guilty of the mistake of the North, and utterly sacrifice vast interests for the sake of a speculative idea. If they find that they cannot do without Southern Cotton, they will interfere, first probably to make peace, and if that effort fails, then in such other manner as will secure for them what will be a necessity. Mr. Seward's[6] letter to Dayton,[7] and its reception in Europe, the transportation of troops to Canada, and Admiral Milne's declaration as to the inefficiency of the blockade, are straws already showing the possible course of future events. Is the Federal Government strong enough for a war with England and France in addition to that with the South?

One other warlike course remains — to capture and hold all the Southern ports, and thus seek to control commerce, independent of secession, leaving the interior of the South to fret and fume as it pleases. This is the problem of belling the cat. The Northern forces would have to capture Norfolk, Charleston, Savannah, Wilmington, N. C., Pensacola, Mobile, New Orleans and Galveston, besides some fifteen other smaller points. At each of them they would find a Stone Bridge; and even if they succeeded, they could only hold military possession and be forever in arms against the attacks of the State authorities. Peace would never be established by any such course. It would not be successful, and even if successful, it would only hamper the South, it would never subjugate it.

The separation of the Southern States is *un fait accompli.* The Federal Government has no power to reverse it. Sooner or later it must be recognized. Why preface the recognition by a war equally needless and bloody? Men at the North may regret the rupture; as men at the South may do. The Black Republicans overcame the first at the polls, and would not listen to the second in Congress, when the evil might have been repaired. They are responsible. If there is to be fighting, let those who voted the Black Republican ticket shoulder their musket and bear the responsibility. Let them not send Irishmen to fight in their stead, and then stand looking on at the conflict, when, in their heart of hearts, they care little which of the combatants destroy the other.

---

[6] William H. Seward (1801–1872) was Lincoln's Secretary of State.

[7] William L. Dayton (1807–1864) had been appointed American Minister to France in 1861.

Most Reverend dear Sir, I am surprised and somewhat ashamed of the length to which my pen has run. But the night is hot — too hot for sleep. I arose from my couch, and have spent a couple of hours speaking to you as frankly and unreservedly as you have ever kindly allowed me to do. A trip to New York would be agreeable for more reasons than one. But that is impossible. Next to that I would like to see a file of the Record.[8] That, too, is impossible. Nothing seems now to span the chasm but that bridge of Catholic union and charity, of which your grace spoke so eloquently last St. Patrick's Day.

I must thank you, too, for your article in my defence against Tracy. He was a poor man with a growing family whom, at Rev. Mr. O'Connell's[9] instance, Bishop Reynolds[10] allowed to live on a place in Newberry District, belonging to him, rent free, and as an act of charity I did not trouble him. He says I saw him there once, years ago. Perhaps so, I do not remember. The first time I remember seeing him, was here in Charleston, after his expulsion. He was driven off, because he was suspected for years, and charged by the neighbors with stealing, and buying stolen goods habitually — was once tried and convicted — and afterwards, they were satisfied, continued the practice.

Commending myself to your holy sacrifices, I have the honor to remain, most Reverend dear Sir, your Grace's sincere and respectful son in Christ.

✠ P. N. LYNCH, D.D., S.C.[11]

---

[8] Hughes had started the *Metropolitan Record* in July, 1859, after falling out with McMaster of the *Freeman's Journal*.

[9] There were two priests of that name in the Diocese of Charleston at that time, Jeremiah J. and Lawrence P. O'Connell.

[10] Ignatius Reynolds (1798–1855) ruled the See of Charleston as its second bishop from 1844 to 1855.

[11] Patrick N. Lynch was consecrated as third Bishop of Charleston on March 14, 1858. In the spring of 1864 he received an official commission from President Jefferson Davis to go to Rome with the hope that he could win recognition for the Confederacy from the government of Pope Pius IX. The mission ended in failure, however, and it was not until late in 1865 that Lynch was able to return to his diocese after a presidential pardon had been won for him through the efforts of Archbishop Martin J. Spalding of Baltimore.

Hughes concluded his lengthy letter to Lynch by stating that there remained nothing for him to add except "that the Catholic faith and Catholic charity which unites us in the spiritual order, shall remain unbroken by the booming of cannon along the lines that unfortunately separate a great and once prosperous community into two hostile portions, each arrayed in military strife against the other" (Kehoe, *op. cit.*, II, 520).

107. Wisconsin Catholicism at the Outbreak of the Civil War, August 30, 1861

IN THE year that the Civil War broke out the Diocese of Milwaukee—founded only eighteen years before with about 15,000 Catholics—had approximately 190,000 Catholic people. In Wisconsin the Germans were the dominant Catholic group, and the following report, written by Michael Heiss (1818–1890), at the time rector of St. Francis Seminary, to the directors of the Ludwig-Missionsverein at Munich, shows among other things the emphasis which the Germans placed upon parochial schools. Since the diocese still embraced all of Wisconsin, Heiss reported on the smaller towns and rural areas of practically every section. The phenomenal growth of the Church soon proved too much of a burden for one bishop and on March 3, 1868, the Holy See erected the Dioceses of Green Bay and La Crosse to take care of the northeastern and northwestern portions of the state. Source: *Salesianum,* XL (October, 1945), 169–180, translated by Augustine C. Breig and edited by Peter Leo Johnson.

Milwaukee, August 30, 1861.

Prompted by sentiments of deep gratitude the Most Rev. Bishop John Martin Henni[1] has instructed the writer to submit a report to the governing board concerning the diocese of Milwaukee. The diocese, for the upbuilding of which the Ludwig-missionsverein has done so much, comprises the entire state of Wisconsin, nearly as much territory as at its erection in the year 1844. At that time the bishop of Milwaukee had only six priests of his own, and in the vast territory hardly more than 9–10,000 Catholics, who possessed only four inexpensive and unfinished churches. Now we count in the same territory 215 well finished churches and chapels, and besides, 23 others under construction, with a total of 117 priests and a Catholic population of approximately 190,000 souls. The largest part of the population consists of Germans and Irish who are about equal in number. Besides these we have some Canadian, Dutch, Belgian, and also a few Polish and Bohemian parishes, and two missicns among the Indians. It is not difficult to understand what incessant zeal, untiring solicitude, and keen prudence are required to govern a new, quickly developing and extensive diocese in order to preserve peace and harmony among the different elements and to foster and promote Catholic life. Eternal thanks and praise to the Lord, that even if at times difficulties arose

[1] John Martin Henni (1805–1881) was first Bishop of Milwaukee; he was promoted to become first Archbishop of Milwaukee when the see was raised to metropolitan rank on February 12, 1875.

and scandals appeared, everything went well again and never backward but ever forward. In the city of Milwaukee, the episcopal see, the Catholics have five churches, besides the cathedral, one for the Irish and three for the Germans, but soon a new church will be necessary for each of these nationalities.

Alongside the cathedral stands a roomy and well built orphanage which houses more than ninety orphan girls of the Irish parishes. St. Gall's church under the pastoral care of the Fathers of the Society of Jesus, also has a school. But the Germans in Milwaukee, as everywhere, manifest a special zeal for the Christian education of their children. The schools of the three German parishes are in excellent condition. They are mainly under the care of the School Sisters [Notre Dame] from Bavaria.[2] A second orphan asylum with fifty-six orphan boys is located near the seminary. A third one is under construction near St. Mary's hospital, which itself was built some two years ago, and both are under the care of the Daughters of Charity.

The motherhouse of the Bavarian School Sisters is a particular credit for Milwaukee. It is in a flourishing condition and sends its teachers to Catholic parishes throughout the Union. For the past several years from thirty to forty candidates have taken the veil annually and as many novices made their profession each year. The sisters are now about to enlarge their convent considerably.

Belonging to Milwaukee, the episcopal see, the diocesan seminary must now be mentioned. It is located about five miles from the city on the south point of the Milwaukee bay. After its patron, St. Francis de Sales, it is known as the Salesianum. As related in a former report, the establishment of the seminary was decided in the year 1853 at the consecration of the cathedral. In 1854 the preparatory work was done for the erection of a magnificent seminary building, and on July 15, 1855, the cornerstone was laid. The work was so speedily pressed that the entire building, excepting the chapel, was under roof before winter. By the end of January 1856, one section was also interiorly finished, so that on January 29, the feast of St. Francis de Sales, we were able to open the seminary with an enrollment of thirty-three students. Since then we have been busy improving the temporal and spiritual condition of the seminary. Of the students who had made

[2] The first group of six School Sisters of Notre Dame arrived in the United States from Bavaria in July, 1847. They established their mother house in Baltimore and the first foundation made from the mother house was at Milwaukee in December, 1850.

their classical studies elsewhere, and could therefore start with the study of philosophy and theology, eighteen have already been ordained priests. At present all of them, including fourteen with over a year's service, are working zealously in the vineyard of the Lord to the satisfaction of their bishops. For the next school year, which begins September 2, sixty-six students have registered. Sixteen belong to other dioceses, to-wit: St. Louis, Dubuque, Chicago, Detroit and Buffalo. The remaining fifty belong to Milwaukee. According to nationality there are twenty-one Irish, one Yankee (an American from New England), two Hollanders and the rest German. There are at present six professors but a seventh is expected by October. Five of them are priests. Since the beginning the seminary has been in charge of the writer as rector and of the Rev. Salzmann[3] from the Diocese of Linz, as procurator. On June 30 of this year we celebrated the completion of the seminary. On this date, the sixth Sunday after Pentecost, the seminary chapel was solemnly consecrated by the Most Rev. Bishop. The chapel is 115 ft. long, 32 ft. wide and about 50 ft. high inside and is built in a simple Byzantine style. The chapel was ready for the consecration some time ago but we wished to wait until the rest of the interior of the seminary was finished. Surrounded by about twenty priests, mostly graduates of our seminary, and the students, the Most Rev. Bishop performed the sacred function. In the meanwhile the Rev. Weninger,[4] a truly apostolic missionary of the Germans in America, blessed a 14 ft. gilt cross in front of the main entrance of this seminary. This was to be placed on the towering cupola in memory of the completion of the seminary. In an inspiring and touching sermon he explained to the large crowd the importance of this ecclesiastical seminary of our holy faith. It was really an important and truly epoch-making day for the history of the Milwaukee diocese. Since its completion the seminary building, with a frontage of 160 ft., with four stories and located on an elevation on the shore of the vast Lake Michigan, announces now by means of the far-shining cross on its cupola, that a good foundation has been laid with the help of God for the future of our holy faith in the state of Wisconsin. It is evident

[3] Joseph Salzmann was an Austrian-born priest who had come to Milwaukee in 1847. He served for a time as pastor of St. Mary's Church in the see city, founded the *Seebote,* a paper to counteract the anti-Catholic attacks of the *Flugblätter,* and was extremely active in winning financial support for St. Francis Seminary.

[4] Francis X. Weninger, S.J. (1805–1888), was Austrian-born and from the time of his arrival in the United States in 1848 until his death forty years later he was one of the most noted missionaries among the German Catholic immigrants.

that much labor had to be spent to raise the necessary funds for such a building and for the support of the students. Besides the charitable help from the Ludwig-missionsverein which we enjoyed during the first three years of our undertaking and the contribution of $21,000 from the Most Rev. Bishop Henni, which he had made in spite of the many other needs of the diocese and the episcopal see, everything had to be collected by the indefatigable and untiring procurator who literally begged from house to house. He collected not only among the Catholics, especially the Germans, in the diocese, but also outside of it. Indeed, we may say that the generosity of the Germans of Cincinnati gave us the means whereby we could dare construct such a spacious building and the Germans of St. Louis by their liberality built our beautiful chapel. Though the seminary has been erected, our task is not ended, because we are obliged to pay off the debts which encumber it. While these do not endanger the sacred undertaking, they hamper its efficient working, because the yearly diocesan collection is not sufficient to support students, the majority of whom are needy, and also pay the interest. Besides we are obliged this summer to undertake the building of a convent for a community of Sisters of the Third Order of St. Francis. Before the seminary was built a small convent of these sisters existed near the seminary land. First they took care of the children of the orphan asylum located as already mentioned near the seminary. Then when the seminary was started, they took charge of the kitchen, laundry and bakery, and thus rendered it invaluable services. But because the small convent became too limited and also beyond repair, we had to decide to build one which will cost about $3000 for the community whose services the seminary cannot dispense with. For this reason we believe that we may dare respectfully to ask the governing board for kind assistance to complete an undertaking which at its beginning enjoyed your special consideration. So this much will suffice in reference to the episcopal see and the seminary.

Now a few remarks will be made about the other parts of the diocese. I start with something I have observed recently. Eight days after the consecration of the seminary chapel the Rev. Father Weninger, S.J., conducted a week's retreat in German, and in the week following the Rev. Father Smarius, S.J.,[5] in English, for the diocesan clergy. The first retreat was attended by forty-eight and the second

[5] Cornelius Smarius, S.J. (1823–1870), was a Dutch-born Jesuit who attained fame as a preacher and an apologist; his best known work was *Points of Controversy* which first appeared in 1866.

by forty-four. Though such exercises when made with a group have usually a beneficial influence, I thought because I am at all times in the seminary, that it would be more beneficial for me to make a retreat alone somewhere else. So with the approval of the Most Rev. Bishop I went to the Capuchin monastery at Mt. Calvary.[6] The railroad runs north and is twelve miles distant from the monastery. To the right and left there is one Catholic parish after another, as for example, in Granville, Germantown, Richmond [Richfield], Schlesingerville, Horicon, and so on. How things have changed if I recall my first years in Wisconsin. On Tuesday after Pentecost 1844, I started out from Milwaukee on horseback for this same territory in order to visit German settlements. Near the Milwaukee River on the first day I found a congregation of about twenty families. Farther north in a very dense woods on the following day at sunset I found five or six families newly arrived from the vicinity of Trier. Here I was told that I could not go farther because there was no path open. For this reason I turned back and took a more westerly course. I discovered Germans but they were Protestants and only at sunset did I find another Catholic home. Here I was informed that beyond a nearby marsh there was a large settlement of German Catholics. Early the next morning I started out, but since I had to ride around the marsh, another day was spent before I finally reached this settlement. Here there were about forty families who dwelt rather far from each other. Fifteen miles north of here there were three more families. Here the road stopped and I was told that it was so far to the next house that I could not get there in a day and also would be obliged to spend the night under the open sky. As there was no question of a church or even a log chapel anywhere, I had to hold divine services in the poorest cabins which the newcomers had hastily built. This was the condition at that time. At present in the same territory one congregation follows another like St. Martin's, St. Michael's, St. Catherine's, St. Anthony's, St. James', St. Xavier's, St. Boniface, St. Hubertus', St. Joseph's, St. Mathias', St. Augustine's, St. Lawrence's, and so on. Everywhere there is a church and now there are more priests in this district than the whole diocese had then.

On this trip however I did not stop at any of these congregations but sped through them on the iron horse until I left the train at Fond du Lac, which is about sixty miles from Milwaukee. The former is a city of about 4 or 5000 inhabitants of whom Catholics are the

[6] Holy Cross Monastery at Mount Calvary, Wisconsin, was established by two priests from Switzerland in 1857.

larger number, but unfortunately they are of different nationalities, the most numerous being the Irish, but there are also many Germans and Canadians [French]. All attend the same church and are cared for by one pastor, a Frenchman, who speaks English well but German poorly. A spacious foundation has been laid for a new church, the construction of which will be finished next year. Although only a small part of the entire Catholic congregation, the Germans alone possess a school building and maintain therein a good Catholic school for their children.

From Fond du Lac I went on to the Capuchin monastery with a farmer who had hauled grain into the city. I had seen this section of the country once before but solely by night and then no monastery existed on the hilltop. For this reason I was pleasantly surprised to see at sunset on a little hill to the right the convent of the School Sisters and the Capuchin monastery to the left on a higher and steeper hill. Cordially received, I spent eight days there. At present the monastery houses three priests, two clerical and four lay brothers. Alongside of the monastery stands the old parish church, but piles of stone and timber are already on the grounds for the erection of a new church which will be started this year. I was very much edified by the strict observance of the rules of the Order in the monastery. May the Lord grant that the Order will gain a firm footing in the diocese. In an area of from five to ten miles about the monastery the people are nearly all Catholic. Five miles from the monastery is St. John's, a large parish with a fine church, and six miles in another direction is St. Mary's and several neighboring mission stations. Both places have a resident priest.

From Calvary I had to return to Fond du Lac in order to get to Green Bay, the destination of my journey. My first railroad stop was Oshkosh, a newly founded city, which has already about 10,000 inhabitants. Here there are two Catholic churches, one for the Irish and the other for the Germans, but both are under the administration of one priest, who, though Irish, speaks German pretty well. Here too the Germans have a Catholic school. I arrived at six o'clock in the morning, said holy Mass and at 8 A.M. continued my trip on the railroad thirty miles north to Appleton, where the railroad ends. We passed by the two newly founded cities of Menasha and Neenah. Both have Catholic churches which are tended from Appleton. Appleton is now the residence of the pastor. Here the church is well furnished, having both an organ and a bell. I met the priest, a Belgian, who was busy building a parish house. Appleton is also the home of a university controlled by the Methodists.[7] It was founded through the liberal bequest of an eastern capitalist. The building is imposing. The university is coeducational because it is attended by young people of both sexes, who, however, are separated in the classrooms by a thin partition so arranged that both groups can see the professor. The location of Appleton is very beautiful.

The Neenah [Fox] river, often mentioned in Jesuit mission reports of the 17th and 18th centuries, winds about the city through a deep valley. On this river I continued my trip to Green Bay on a steamboat about the size of those that ply the Rhine and Danube. It was on the same river in April of the year 1670 that for the first time a messenger of the Gospel travelled in a frail canoe, hewed from a tree trunk, whose occupants frequently were obliged to portage on account of the rocky bed and the many rapids of the river. This was Father Claude Allouez who may be called the apostle of the West as described justly by a historian. Soon other Jesuits followed him, including James Marquette. In 1673 the latter ascended this river [Fox] in order to reach the Mississippi, the great stream about which the Indians had spoken. Those were holy men and their missions ceased partly through the suppression of the Society of Jesus and partly through local conditions. But should one not believe that the special divine blessing which the diocese of Milwaukee has enjoyed to the present time may be attributed to the heroic sacrifices of the first missionaries to this region?

After we had passed Little Chute, Kakalin, other small places and through many locks, at least twenty, we arrived at De Pere, so called because Father Allouez settled here in 1669 on the feast of St. Francis Xavier and founded the mission of St. Francis Xavier. A few years ago a silver monstrance was unearthed here which I saw in Green Bay. Along both sides of the Neenah river valley also are Catholic parishes, mostly Dutch and French. There are resident priests at Little Chute, Freedom and Franciscus Busche. De Pere has a church which is taken care of from Green Bay. Near De Pere is the last lock and soon we had covered the remaining five miles. At half past five we arrived in Green Bay which at first sight made a pleasing impression on me. It is the oldest settlement in Wisconsin. By the year 1745 Canadians had settled here. But the settlement made such slight progress that in the year 1783 it had only fifty-six and in 1812 about 250 inhabitants. The wooded hills between which the

[7] Lawrence Institute was opened at Appleton in 1849.

Neenah river flows from Appleton gradually become smaller towards Green Bay, so much so, that only on one side of the wide stream a slight elevation appears on which [one page of the original, or of the photostat, is lacking].

Saturday evening I returned to Mt. Calvary. Here the Capuchin Fathers begged me to conduct a retreat for them and the brothers. It appeared to me preposterous that a secular priest should preach to monks, but because they insisted and I did not know of anybody who could take my place, I consented. We closed the retreat on the feast of the Assumption of the Blessed Virgin and then I preached in the parish church. The next day I spent examining several boxes of books which a priest had left at the monastery because he could not take them along with him to his new charge. I could hardly look over a third of them. There are excellent volumes on Church history, liturgy and canon law, including Mabillon, Hardouin, Lapus, the Bollandists, and so on. Saturday I drove to Fond du Lac and then arrived in Milwaukee about 3 o'clock by train.

Now I shall give a short notice of other parts of the diocese. To the south nearest to the seminary on Howell road is the parish of New Coeln, so called because most of the people hail from the vicinity of Cologne. To it belong the adjoining parishes on Kilbourn Road and in Caledonia. Then there is the Oak Creek parish which is taken care of from the seminary. Ten miles south is Racine with three churches of which one is German. The latest one built [St. Patrick's] will be blessed by the Most Rev. Bishop next Sunday. Again ten miles farther south, situated like Racine on Lake Michigan, is Kenosha with two churches and two priests. West from here are Brighton and Paris with two churches and one priest. About twelve miles from there is Waterford with its priest and church. Then comes Burlington where the Rev. Wisbauer[8] of the Linz diocese has been active for the last fourteen years and two years ago he built one of the finest churches in the diocese. Six miles south is Wheatland with a priest and church, which is located on a beautiful hill in the midst of a prairie and not far from the boundary line between Wisconsin and Illinois. To the West from here on a beautiful lake is Geneva which is near several missions. Farther westward is Beloit with two priests and then follow Janesville and Monroe. In the latter place a new church was blessed a few weeks ago. In the same westerly direction are Shullsburg and Sinsinawa Mound where the Dominican Fathers

[8] Michael Wisbauer was pastor of St. Sebastian's Church in Burlington.

have a college on a splendid site. From the hill at the foot of which the college lies one can view for a distance of five or six miles the Mississippi valley which forms the western boundary of the diocese. In the intervening region are the rich lead mines of Wisconsin with headquarters at Potosi and Mineral Point. In this territory there are a number of parishes of which however I know little. In Benton the Rev. Mazzuchelli,[9] a Dominican, built a very beautiful church and also established a convent of the Sisters of the Third Order of St. Dominic. In Potosi there are now two resident priests who are obliged to tend many missions. In Mineral Point there is a priest and church. Farther north in Highland there are two priests of whom the German one has to care for several missions. Where the Wisconsin river empties into the Mississippi Prairie du Chien is located, which after Green Bay is the oldest Canadian settlement in Wisconsin. But like Green Bay it has lagged behind other cities. There in the year 1843 quite a spacious church was built in the hope that Prairie du Chien instead of Milwaukee would become the see of the prospective bishopric of Wisconsin. But whilst Milwaukee has now 50,000 inhabitants Prairie du Chien has hardly 3000. La Crosse, which is hardly ten years old, grew much larger and has already 7000 inhabitants, so that it has been considered as the see of a new diocese for northwestern Wisconsin. At present there are two priests in La Crosse. Farther north up the Mississippi I know of only one priest, resident in Eau de Claire, who however has many missions. In Hudson and Chippewa Falls there were priests formerly but I do not know if any are there now. Next week the Most Rev. Bishop will come into this distant section, a new field of the diocese, in order to visit all these parishes in the northwest and to administer the sacrament of confirmation in most of them. Thence by railroad from La Crosse he will travel to Portage City and then going north again he will proceed to Stevens Point and Marathon City on the Wisconsin river. Here there are extensive pine forests and so for a long time numerous saw mills have existed which ship large quantities of lumber to St. Louis and New Orleans. Between La Crosse and Portage City there are several parishes, but of such recent origin that I am unable to give their names.

There are also several new settlements west of Portage toward

[9] Samuel Charles Mazzuchelli, O.P. (1806–1864), was born in Milan Italy, and came to the United States in 1828. He was one of the most famous missionaries of the Middle West in the mid-century; highly successful in winning converts among the Indians of Michigan and Wisconsin, and founding parishes in Iowa, Illinois, and Wisconsin. He died while pastor of St. Patrick's Church, Benton, Wisconsin, after being exposed to a blizzard in making a sick call to a parishioner.

Nordport on the Wolf river and then at Beaver Dam and Ripon. In these places are three or four priests who could talk a great deal about the present pathless wilderness there. Northward up the Wolf river is the mission of the Menominee Indians of whom about 800 are Catholics. Only about six weeks ago the son of the principal chief Oshkosh allowed himself to be baptized and for this reason we hope that all the Menominees of about 1200 souls will be converted. On the northern borders of Wisconsin on Lake Superior there is another mission among the Chippewas. The Most Rev. Bishop has placed this mission temporarily under the jurisdiction of the Most Rev. Bishop Baraga[10] of Sault Ste. Marie, because it can be taken care of more conveniently from there.

A railroad connects both La Crosse and Prairie du Chien with Milwaukee. Travelling from the latter place we pass several parishes until we come to Mazomanie, where a priest is stationed, if I am not mistaken. About twelve miles northwards on the Wisconsin river Sauk City is located, where there is a priest and church, and in nearby Roxbury there is also a priest. Somewhat south of Mazomanie there are two priests in the township of Cross Plains. Fourteen miles from here by railroad you arrive at Madison, the state capital, which is well located on a rather high hill in the midst of four lakes. There are two churches with resident pastors here. On a prominent site near the capital a magnificent church of cut stone was started some years ago and its walls were finished up to a bit above the windows, but it is still unfinished due to lack of money.

From Madison toward Milwaukee on the railroad is Whitewater with its priest and church and also Eagle Center with a church which is in charge of priests from East Troy and Waukesha. In Elm Grove nine miles from Milwaukee the School Sisters of Notre Dame have built an orphanage with a beautiful chapel through the generosity of his Majesty King Ludwig of Bavaria. At Whitewater the railroad running west is crossed by one coming from the south out of Chicago, and on this line northwards, Jefferson is soon reached which is about fifty miles from Milwaukee. I had visited the former place in 1844, and found only ten families. At that time the ague was raging in the vicinity so that among these families on one occasion I brought Holy Communion at Eastertime to ten of the stricken who were living

---

[10] Frederic Baraga (1797–1868) born in Slovenia in the Austrian Empire, became one of the most accomplished students of the Indian languages of any Catholic missionary in the United States. He was first Vicar Apostolic of Upper Michigan, 1853–1857, and first Bishop of Sault Sainte-Marie and Marquette from 1857 to his death.

in widely separated cabins. Now they have two churches, one in the 'ittle city of Jefferson, and the other a couple of miles outside of it on a beautiful hill. Here some day the Most Rev. Bishop intends to establish a convent. Eight days ago here and also in Whitewater, Ottawa and Golden Lake the sacrament of confirmation was administered. The two last places are taken care of by a priest of Watertown, a city of about 8 or 9000 inhabitants, which has two churches and two priests. For a long time there were three priests there on account of other missions nearby. Near Watertown there are also parishes at Fox Lake, Elba, Monches and others toward Milwaukee. Nearer to Milwaukee must be mentioned the parishes on the Beloit Road, in Franklin (with two priests), Greenfield and Menominee (Falls).

Of the many parishes I did not mention I wish in conclusion to speak of one about eighteen miles north of Madison, East Bristol. For some time this parish was very unfortunate because it rebelled against the bishop on account of the church property. Because their priest was recalled until such time as they would submit, they themselves installed a suspended priest from some Bavarian diocese who had fled here. They persisted for two or three years in open schism. At last their eyes were opened and the people realized their wrongdoing and now their parish is one of the best in the diocese. At present they intend to build a large church for which in a few weeks they have subscribed $5000.

From this, though not quite complete but true report, it is evident that the development of the diocese during the seventeen years since its erection has been an extraordinary one. The little mustard seed has grown into a very promising tree. No doubt this will be certainly consoling to the pious benefactors of the mission society, and especially to its governing board which helped to accomplish all this. At the same time and for the same reason we entertain the hope that the diocese of Milwaukee may also in the future enjoy the lively interest of our benefactors. Though much has been accomplished, still more has to be done, because everything makes such rapid progress in this country that one need quickly follows another. A church is hardly built when another is needed. This is also the case in other matters. In my opinion a special effort should be made to educate an efficient clergy in our own seminaries and thus with the mighty effort of such a clergy, provision would be made for an adequate number of Catholic parochial schools. Should this happen, the future of the Catholic Church in America is assured.

Asking your kind indulgence because of defects and errors in this report . . .

108. The Nursing Sisters in the Military Hospitals of Virginia, January, 1862–April, 1865

ONE of the most inspiring — and little known — chapters of the Civil War was written by the nearly 500 members of twenty or more congregations of religious women who nursed the wounded in the military hospitals of both the North and South. Among the most prominent of these congregations were the Daughters of Charity of St. Vincent de Paul whose mother house at Emmitsburg, Maryland, was only a few miles distant from the battlefield at Gettysburg. Speaking of that memorable encounter in July, 1863, Sister Camilla O'Keefe (1815–1887), a contemporary, stated, "They fought until the evening of the 3rd, advancing by their movements more and more towards our peaceful Vale, so that our buildings and the very earth trembled from their cannons" (Archives of St. Joseph's Central House, Emmitsburg, "Notes, 1863," p. 22). There is record of at least 232 of the Daughters of Charity who engaged in nursing the troops during the war. On September 20, 1924, a monument to the "Nuns of the Battlefield" was unveiled in Washington across the street from St. Matthew's Cathedral to commemorate the deeds of these heroic women of the many congregations who gave their services to the wounded soldiers. The following document of Sister Angela Heath (1830–1912), who saw service from January, 1862, to April 13, 1865, four days after the surrender of Lee at Appomattox, gives a good idea of the difficulties encountered by the sisters as they moved from one hospital to another during the campaigns of the Old Dominion. Source: Archives of St. Joseph's Central House, Emmitsburg, Maryland, "Annals of the Civil War, 1861–1865," pp. 95–98.

Left Richmond for Manasses on the 9th. of January 1862, at the solicitation of Dr. Williams[1] Medical Director of the Army of the Potomac. We were five in number, & found, on taking possession, 500 patients, sick & wounded of both armies. Mortality was very great, as the sick poor had been very much neglected. The wards were in a most deplorable condition, & strongly resisted all efforts of the broom to which they had long been strangers, & the aid of a shovel was found necessary. At best, they were but poor protection against the inclemency of the season & being scattered, we were often obliged to go through snow over a foot deep, to wait on the sick. For our own accommodation we had one small room, which served for dormitory, chapel, &c, &c. & when we were fortunate enough to get a chaplain, the holy sacrifice was daily offered in a little corner of our humble domicile. The kitchen, to which what we called our refectory, was

[1] An effort to identify Williams further was unsuccessful.

attached, was, I do not think I exaggerate when I say a quarter of a mile from our room, & often it was found more prudent to be satisfied with two meals than to trudge through the snow for a third, which at best, was not very inviting, for the culinary department was not under our control, but under that of negroes, who had a decided aversion for cleanliness. On an average, ten died every day, & of this number, I think I may safely say, four were baptized, either by Fathers Smoulders [*sic*][2] & Feeling [*sic*][3] or by our Sisters. It happened several times that men, who had been until then totally ignorant of our faith, & I may say even of God, sent to us in the middle of the night, when they found that they were dying, & begged for baptism which astonished as well as consoled & edified us. On the 13th of March we received orders from Gen. Johnson [*sic*],[4] to pack up quietly & be ready to leave on six hours' notice, as it was found necessary to retreat from that quarter. Oh the horrors of war! We had scarcely left our post than the whole camp was one mass of flame, & the bodies of those who died that day, were consumed. Our next field of labor was the military hospital at Gordonsville. We were but three in number & found 200 patients verk sick — pneumonia and typhoid fever prevailing. Here again privations were not wanting. The sick were very poorly provided for, although the mortality was not as great as at Manasses. . . . Father S. who was our chaplain at that time received about twenty-five into the communion of the Church some of whom died shortly after. One morning as Sister Ann Estelle[5] was visiting her patients before Mass, one called from the lower end of the ward, "Oh! Sister, Sister, do come & save me, let me die in the church that you Sisters belong to. I believe all that you believe." Father S. who was vesting for mass, was at first unwilling to wait on him until after, but as Sister insisted that no time was to be lost, he went and baptized him, & as we knelt at the "Et verbum caro factum est," he expired. The approach of the Federals compelled us to leave Gordonsville on Easter Sunday, & we retreated "in good order" to Danville. . . . Here we found 400 sick much better provided for than in M. or . . . . Most of our patients were Catholic, at least in name, for many had almost forgotten their duties

[2] Egidius (Giles) Smulders, C.SS.R. (1815–1900), was a Dutch-born priest, chaplain of the Eighth Louisiana Infantry, who served throughout the entire war.

[3] Henry Fehlings (1822–1888), a German-born priest, who was dispensed from his vows as a Redemptorist in May, 1861, and died as pastor of St. Mary's Church, Utica, New York.

[4] Joseph E. Johnston (1807–1891) was in command of the Confederate troops in northern Virginia at this time.

[5] An effort to identify this religious was not successful.

as such, but it was our consolation to see them entering upon them again with the simplicity of children. The zeal of good Father S. led many to a knowledge of our holy religion & about 50 were baptized. In Nov. the Medical Director removed our hospital to Lynchburg as there was no means of heating that in Danville. Our number had increased to five as the hospital was larger & contained 1000 patients, whom we found in a most pitiful condition. The persons who were in charge, had a very good will, but not the means of carrying it out, & although the fund was ample, the poor patients were half starved owing entirely to mismanagement. As we passed through the ward the first time, accompanied by the Dr., a man from the lower end called out, "Lady, oh lady — for God's sake gave me a piece of bread." To give you an idea of the care the sick had received, it will be sufficient to say that though the whole establishment had been cleaned for our reception, some of the Sisters swept up the vermin in the dust pan. The doctors soon placed everything under our control, & with a little economy the patients were well provided for, & order began to prevail. Father Gache,[6] a zealous & holy Jesuit, effected much good & removed many prejudices from the minds of those whom a faulty education had made enemies — bitter enemies of our holy faith. During the three years that we remained in L. he baptized 100. . . . The approach of the Federals placed our hospital in imminent danger & it was decided to move the sick & hospital stores to Richmond. The Surgeon General of the Confederate Army[7] begged that we would take charge of the Stuart hospital in that city which we did on the 13th. of Feb. 1865. We were then 10 in number, & as usual, we found plenty to do to place the sick in a comfortable situation, which we had just accomplished when the city was evacuated, & on the 13th. of April, the hospital being dispensed with, we left R. for our sweet valley home.

109. The Efforts of Archbishop Hughes to Keep France Neutral During the Civil War, January 29, 1862

THE personal friendship between Archbishop Hughes and William H. Seward (1801–1872) that had developed during the latter's time as Governor

[6] Hippolite Gache, S.J. (1817–1907), was a chaplain who entered the service from Louisiana.

[7] Samuel Preston Moore (1813–1889) was Surgeon General of the Confederate Army.

of New York continued when he became Lincoln's Secretary of State. In the early months of the Civil War the two were in close correspondence, and President Lincoln thanked Hughes for his "kind and judicious" letters which Seward "regularly allows me both the pleasure and the profit of perusing" (Archives of the Archdiocese of New York, Lincoln to Hughes, Washington, October 21, 1861). In October, 1861, Seward asked Hughes to go abroad in the hope that he could help to keep France neutral. It was a critical moment for the Union cause as Great Britain, France, and Spain had signed the Treaty of London on October 31, 1861, for the protection of their interests in Mexico and it was well known that they were friendly to the Confederacy. During his time in Europe Hughes visited England, France, Rome, and Ireland, and was given many opportunities to exert influence in behalf of the Washington government. High praise for his efforts was expressed by Alexander W. Randall (1819–1872) when the latter presented his credentials to Pius IX on June 6, 1862, as American Minister to the Papal States. Randall told the Pope, "It is a source of regret to thousands of good men that the Government of the United States cannot, in any appropriate way, testify its appreciation of such services" (Leo Francis Stock [Ed.], *United States Ministers to the Papal States. Instructions and despatches, 1848–1868* [Washington, 1933], pp. 251–252). The following letter from Hughes to Seward was written some weeks after his audience with the Emperor Napoleon III and the Empress Eugénie. Source: *Mission Abroad, 1861–1862: A Selection of Letters from Archbishop Hughes, Bishop McIlwaine, W. H. Seward and Thurlow Weed* (Rochester: University of Rochester Press, c. 1954), microfilm.

Paris, Jany 29, 1862

My Dear Governor.

I congratulate the President and his Cabinet, as well as the whole country, on the admirable tact, ability and success which have hitherto attended the President's administration under the most trying circumstances known to our history.

The Emperor's Speech,[1] at opening what in England they would call the Parliament, — what we would call the President's Message to Congress, has been all that, under present circumstances, we could have hoped for. Knowing, as I do, the condition of this Country, I look upon it as all we could reasonably expect. I regard it as a proclamation of peace on the part of France, from which England may take a lesson of wisdom; and if she will not let her look out for the consequences of a war with America.

[1] In a speech on January 27, 1862, to the legislative assembly Napoleon III had deplored the injurious effect of the Civil War on French commercial interests, but he added, "However, so long as the rights of neutrals are respected, we must confine ourselves to expressing wishes that these dissensions may soon be terminated" (Geraldine McGuire, "The Mission of Archbishop Hughes to Europe, 1861–62," unpublished master's thesis, Columbia University [1946], pp. 24–25).

My mind has been relieved of very great solicitude by the speech of the Emperor. It was not in my power to determine before hand, either directly or indirectly, the tone of that important document. But I have done all I could to bring about the result. I knew this people before I left home. I knew there could be no general hostility to the U. States amongst them. But at present the Sovereign is France — and if the Sovereign had adopted another style in his opening speech, France would have stood by him, and England would be rejoiced at his determination. As it is, England is compelled to pause before she enters into a contest with the United States. Still, it will be most important for us not to give any pretext for intervention by either France or England — or both united — for hostilities from this side of the Atlantic.

In the wise, prudent and, so far as I know, perfectly just policy of the Government in disposing of the late affair of the "Trent,"[2] Europe has been caught in its own trap. Let Europe be held strictly to what, nolens volens, it has been obliged to recognize — viz — the old principles of the American Government as to maritime and neutral rights.

Permit me to state my course, as a loyal citizen, since I came to France. I had no encouragement from our officials.[3] But, independent of their patronage, I have had, as you may suppose, the entrée to the best Society in Paris — as an American Bishop. At dinners & soirées it has come up invariably that the company, either before, or during, or after dinner referred to me for an explanation of the Civil War that is now existing between two sections of our once United States. I did explain as well as I could, perfectly satisfied that whatever I said would reach the ears of one or other of the Ministers within twenty four hours after its utterance. Besides, during my interview[4] with the Emperor, I felt no hesitation in stating what none of his Ministers would venture to say. I might almost add that on the same occasion I had the effrontery even to give advice. It is generally thought that certain men are above being influenced. This is a mistake. If there

[2] On November 8, 1861, the Confederate commissioners to Great Britain and France were removed from the British mail packet *Trent* by the American warship *San Jacinto* thus precipitating a crisis between the Washington and London governments.

[3] Hughes alluded several times in his correspondence with Seward to the generally cool reception he had received from American officials in France. At the time William L. Dayton (1807–1864) was the American minister.

[4] The archbishop was received in audience by Emperor Napoleon III and Empress Eugénie on December 24, 1861. Hughes' memorandum of the meeting may be read in John R. G. Hassard, *Life of the Most Reverend John Hughes, First Archbishop of New York* (New York, 1866), pp. 465–468.

ever was a man of such a type it would be General Jackson. And yet whilst General Jackson would disregard, under certain circumstances, the opinion of his whole Cabinet, General Jackson might take up and reflect upon a phrase uttered by the barber who shaved him. At all events, I think we might have fared worse in France than we have done.

Several of the Bishops from the districts that are suffering, owing to the interruption of trade with America, called upon me as they successively arrived in Paris.[5] To them also I had an opportunity of relating the state of the case. For the most part they came to see the Emperor on the following day — and to expose to him the state of destitution in which their poor people were suffering. Whether they made known to the Emperor the views which I communicated, or not, I have no means of ascertaining. But at all events I thought it no harm to make them acquainted with the substance of the Despatch, a copy of which you were kind enough to confide to me for private use.

I have just received your kind letter of the 9th inst. I am glad that the President does not deem it useful or necessary for me to execute the purpose which I had conceived only on the hypothesis that it might be useful to the Country.[6] By the by, in speaking of the President, I may be allowed to say that in this country at least, he is winning golden opinions for his calm, unostentatious, mild, but firm, and energetic administrative talents.

I intend to leave next Monday for a short visit to Rome. After that I shall have to visit Ireland, in consequence of invitations from that country — and for reasons of my own. From Ireland I shall sail for home, as soon as the severe winter months are over.

I remain, My Dear Governor, as ever, Your devoted Fd. & servt

✠ John Abp of New York

---

[5] A blockade of the southern ports was declared by the Union government in April, 1861, and it had brought acute suffering to the French textile industries which were so largely dependent upon southern cotton.

[6] Hughes was in all likelihood referring here to a projected visit to Madrid to try to influence the government of Isabella II (1830–1904). The necessity of the trip to Spain was obviated by his later conferences in Rome with the Spanish ambassador and the two new Spanish cardinals, Miguel García-Cuesta (1803–1873), Archbishop of Compostella, and Ferdinando de la Puente (1808–1867), Archbishop of Burgos.

110. American Diplomatic Relations With the Papal States, September 27, 1862

IN JUNE, 1797, the United States inaugurated consular relations with the Papal States. A half century later President Polk suggested the establishment of diplomatic relations between the two countries in his message to Congress of December 7, 1847, and in spite of bitter opposition from the American nativists the proposal was carried. During the crisis of the Civil War and the tension in Italy over the *Risorgimento* the American legation at Rome took on new interest as is reflected in the instruction (given below) of September 27, 1862, from Secretary of State William H. Seward to Richard M. Blatchford (1798–1875) who had recently been appointed minister. Five years later, on the pretext of an entirely false rumor that the church of the American Protestants in Rome had been ordered outside the city walls by the papal government, Congress refused to make the necessary appropriation and the mission was brought to an end with the resignation of Rufus King as minister on January 1, 1868, without even a formal notification to the pope's government. Source: Leo Francis Stock (Ed.), *United States Ministers to the Papal States. Instructions and Despatches, 1848–1868* (Washington: The Catholic University of America Press, 1933), pp. 258–260.

Department of State, Washington, 27th September, 1862.

Sir:

This Government has not now, it seldom has had, any special transaction, either commercial or political, to engage the attention of a Minister at Rome. Indeed, till a very late period the United States were without any representation at that ancient and interesting capital. The first colonists in this country were chiefly Protestants, who not merely recognised no ecclesiastical authority of the Pope, but were very jealous lest he might exert some ecclesiastical influence here which would be followed by an assumption of political power unfavorable to freedom and self-government on this continent. It was not seen that the political power of the Catholic Church was a purely foreign affair, constituting an important part of the political system of the European continent. The opening of our country as an asylum to men of all religions, as well as of all races, and an extension of the trade of the Union, in a short time brought with them large masses of the faithful members of that Church, of various birth and derivation, and these masses are continually augmenting. Our country has not been slow to learn that while religion is with these masses, as it is with others, a matter of conscience, and while the spiritual authority of the head of their church is a cardinal article of their faith, which must be tolerated on the soundest principles of civil liberty, yet that this faith in no degree necessarily interferes with the equal rights of the citizen, or affects unfavorably his loyalty to the republic. It is believed that ever since the tide of emigration set in upon this continent the head of the Roman Church and States has freely recognized and favored the development of the principle of political freedom on the part of the Catholics in this country, while he has never lost an opportunity to express his satisfaction with the growth, prosperity and progress of the American people. It was under these circumstances that this Government, in 1848, wisely determined that while it maintained representatives in the capitals of every other civilized State, and even at the capitals of many semi-civilized States which reject the whole Christian religion, it was neither wise nor necessary to exclude Rome from the circle of our diplomatic intercourse. Thus far the new relation then established has proved pleasant and beneficial.

Just now Rome is the seat of profound ecclesiastical and political anxieties, which, more or less, affect all the nations of Europe. The Holy Father claims immunity for the temporal power he exercises as a right incident to an ecclesiastical authority which is generally respected by the European States.

On the other hand, some of those States, with large masses in other States, assert that this temporal power is without any religious sanction, is unnecessary and pernicious. I have stated the question merely for the purpose of enabling myself to give you the President's view of what will be your duty with regard to it. That duty is to forbear altogether from taking any part in the controversy. The reasons for this forbearance are three: First, that so far as spiritual or ecclesiastical matters enter into the question they are beyond your province, for you are a political representative only. Second, so far as it is a question affecting the Roman States it is a domestic one and we are a foreign nation. Third, so far as it is a political question merely, it is at the same time purely an European one, and you are an American Minister, bound to avoid all entangling connexion with the politics of that continent.

This line of conduct will nevertheless allow you to express, and you are therefore instructed to express to His Holiness the assurances of the best wishes of the Government and of the people of the United States for his health and happiness, and for the safety and prosperity and happiness of the Roman people. And you will farther assure him that the United States constantly preserve a lively remembrance of the many generous and liberal manifestations they have received of his goodwill and friendship, and that he may confidently rely upon them for the practice of all the duties which grow out of the relations of the two countries as independent members of the family of nations.

You will find Rome a resort and temporary residence of intellectual persons from all parts of the world. Among them are many who, in various degrees, exercise an influence upon the opinions, and, perhaps in some cases upon the policies of nations. It will be a pleasing duty for you at this moment, when our unhappy domestic conflict is a subject of universal discussion, to vindicate the justice, the wisdom and the moderation of the Government and loyal people of the United States against those who, from interest, prejudice or passion, are directing their efforts to the overthrow of a republic which we must continue to think still holds in its keeping the best hopes of the human race.

111. A Catholic Chaplain With the Union Armies, October 2, 1862

EVER since Canadian-born Father Louis E. Lotbinière (1715–1786) was commissioned by the Continental Congress in January, 1776, to serve as chaplain to Colonel James Livingston's regiment of Canadian volunteers, Catholic priests in one capacity or another have been rendering spiritual aid to the American armed forces. Early in the Civil War President Lincoln informed Archbishop Hughes of New York that he had appointed three Protestant ministers as hospital chaplains, and he added, "If you perceive no objection, I will thank you to give me the name, or names, of one or more suitable persons of the Catholic Church, to whom I may, with propriety, tender the same service" (Archives of the Archdiocese of New York, Lincoln to Hughes, Washington, October 21, 1861). Eventually sixty-seven priests were enrolled as chaplains in the field with the Union and Confederate armies, together with a number of hospital and volunteer chaplains and nearly 500 sisters from over twenty congregations who cared for the wounded in hospitals. Among the Union chaplains Father Peter P. Cooney, C.S.C. (1822–1905), was one of the most prominent. He was attached to the 35th Regiment, Indiana Volunteers, from October, 1861, to June, 1865, and saw service in Kentucky, Tennessee, and Georgia during which time he conceived a deep admiration for the piety of General William S. Rosecrans (1819–1898), a convert to Catholicism from his days at West Point, and it was Cooney who received General David S. Stanley (1828–1902) into the Church early in 1864. The following letter depicted for his brother experiences which have been met by all chaplains who have seen active fighting with the American armies. Source: Thomas T. McAvoy, C.S.C. (Ed.), "The War Letters of Father Peter Paul Cooney of the Congregation of Holy Cross," *Records of the American Catholic Historical Society of Philadelphia,* XLIV (March, 1933), 67–69.

Louisville, Kentucky
October 2, 1862

My dear Brother:

After a long silence I am happy to have an opportunity to write you a few lines. Since I last wrote my health has never been better. It seems as if my health grows better as my hardships and fatigues increase; for all that I had to undergo since I entered on this new field of duty could not equal what I had to endure last month.

We started from McMinnville, Tennessee on the last day of August and we have been marching nearly ever since. We arrived here a few days ago, having traveled, without stopping but [for] the necessary rests, over three hundred miles and nearly the whole time in a dense cloud of dust, so that we looked like so many millers. There [were] between sixty and eighty thousand soldiers with us, making a fearful army. When we arrived here Munfordsville, Kentucky, we prepared for a battle, as the Southern troops were nearly as many as we were at this place and they have the benefit of a strong fortification. We stopped a day and a night to prepare for the battle between two large armies. I heard confessions all that night — no sleep. I sat eight hours without getting off my seat. It was a very cool night; for the nights, as a general thing, are colder in the South than in Michigan or Indiana but the days are warmer. About twelve o'clock, my legs were perfectly benumbed, until one of the poor soldiers brought me a blanket to roll around my thighs; for they think more of an inconvenience to me than I do myself. You might hear them whispering to one another words of sympathy for me. They little knew the joy that was in my breast, midst all these trials, when I considered how much God was doing with the hands of his unworthy son.

If [you] were to see my confessional that night you would laugh. In the evening one of the soldiers came to me and said: "Father, will you be hearing tonight?" "Indeed I will, my dear, with God's help," I answered and I jocosely asked him in presence of the others, "Did you not know I was hearing all day?" "No Father," said he, very innocently, and he noticed the joke only when the next commenced to laugh. I find it an advantage sometimes in camp to crack a joke with them; it cheers them up and enlivens the monotony of camp life. "What will you do Father," said one, "for a place to hear confessions in?" (For we were in the open field). "Never mind," I answered, "come this way four or five of you." They came and we made three stacks of guns, four guns in each, in this shape V, [and] the bayonets were locked into each other. Then we got three blankets, two covering two sides hanging on the bayonets; the other covered the top, leaving the front open. And in this I sat all night. This is a piece of architecture that you will not find in Monroe. Here the poor fellows came, impressed with the idea that perhaps this would be the last confession of their lives. Some of the officers gave me their wills and then went to confession. But it would take volumes to tell all.

Here, dear Brother, in such places life is valued as it ought — as worth nothing. That night I baptized a non-commissioned officer who was to that time an Episcopalian. But we came to Munfordsville the next day and the rebels had run away. We caught only the hind ones who could not keep up. All the march we were up at two o'clock in the morning; and generally it was ten or eleven o'clock before we could get to bed, without tents, but the broad canopy of heaven. I alone had a tent along but some nights it would be five miles behind in the wagon train. So you see we have "high living" when you come to add to this, that the men had to march some times eight hours without anything to eat.

The whole army started yesterday from here towards Bardstown forty miles from here to meet the enemy. I follow them tomorrow morning. I shall take a trip home to rest about the end of the month. I think the drafting system is given up, so you need not be troubled about it. Pray, pray, dear Brother, for me and for yourselves and heaven shall be our reward.

Your Brother,

P. P. Cooney, *Chaplain*
35th Reg. Ind. Vol.

Write immediately and let me know how my mother and all the folks are. Give my love to all. Direct your letter to me Chaplain 35th Reg. Ind. Vol., Louisville, Kentucky.

112. Father Purcell's Stand in Behalf of Emancipation of the Slaves, April 8, 1863

THE oldest continuous Catholic newspaper in the United States is the *Catholic Telegraph* of Cincinnati which began publication on October 22, 1831. Like its Catholic contemporaries, the *Telegraph* commented freely on political affairs and as the Civil War came on its editor, Father Edward Purcell (1808–1881), brother of John B. Purcell (1800–1883), first Archbishop of Cincinnati, became more outspoken in his opposition to slavery. It was not an easy policy to pursue in a border state like Ohio, and as a consequence Purcell had to pay dearly in loss of support from southern-minded Catholics in the area and in abuse from fellow Catholic editors like Courtney Jenkins of the Baltimore *Catholic Mirror,* McMaster of the *Freeman's Journal,* and John Mullaly of the New York *Metropolitan Record,* who charged him with being an abolitionist. But he did not retreat and, in fact, the *Telegraph* was the first Catholic paper in the country to come out clearly for emancipation of the slaves, a policy which Archbishop Purcell had publicly espoused as early as August, 1862. Lincoln's proclamation was formally issued on January 1, 1863, and caused widespread disagreement in the North. Two months after he published the uncompromising editorial which follows, Purcell announced that reaction had shown that many Catholics in all sections of the country had been brooding over "the multitudinous wrongs and anti-Christian proclivities of the 'peculiar institution.'" His mail proved that there were Catholics in every part of the United States who wished, as he said, "to express their satisfaction that there was a Catholic-Church-paper which was not afraid to raise its voice in favor of the most oppressed people on earth" (*Catholic Telegraph,* June 10, 1863). Source: Editorial, "The Church and Slavery," *Catholic Telegraph,* April 8, 1863.

In some remarks lately made on the emancipation of the serfs in Russia, we observed that the Church and slavery could never get along well together. The New York *Freeman's Journal* condemns our remarks, quotes St. Paul and Church Councils, and says that we are ignorant of ecclesiastical history. The writer in the *Freeman* also observes that he does not wish for a controversy with us. As the *Freeman,* on this occasion, is mild and uses no very offensive language, we reply to his comments at some length.

We assure our cotemporary [*sic*] that we, too, have no desire to enter into a controversy. It would be useless now, because the subject of slavery is dead. The first canon fired at Sumter sounded its knell. It would be much easier to take Richmond or open the Mississippi, than restore slavery in the United States. The thing is gone forever.

But our cotemporary suggests that we are not acquainted with ecclesiastical history and that slavery and the Church have got along well together, and quotes St. Paul and certain Councils. Our cotemporary has a right to entertain any opinion he pleases about our ignorance. His opinion is his own. But without acrimony we can write on this subject of slavery. It must be discussed; there is no help for it — and whilst we accord to those who are its advocates all liberty of speech, we hope that some license will be extended to us when we give our reasons on the other side. It is not in a factious spirit or a fanatical spirit that we write, but under the strong conviction that a great change is at hand in the political welfare of the country, and that it is of some consequence to Catholics to decide wisely what part to take. This cannot be done by crying out "ignorance," "abolition," but by friendly discussion. Whether we like it or not, slavery is extinguished in the United States, and all that we have to do is to decide how we shall accommodate ourselves "to coming events."

We have said and we now repeat it, that slavery and the Catholic Church could never get along well together. The Church never tries to correct evils by revolutionary means. When she has not the legislative power in her hands she is patient, long-suffering, gentle. What she could not suppress she tolerated. But she found slavery little disposed to imitate her meekness. When the slave power predominates, religion is nominal. There is no life in it. It is the hard-working laboring man who builds the church, the schoolhouse and the orphan asylum, not the slaveholder, as a general rule. Religion flourishes in a slave State only in proportion to its intimacy with a free State, or as it is adjacent to it. There are more Catholics in the Cathedral congregation of this city than in North and South Carolina and Georgia! There are more Catholics in one of our second-rate congregations than in the whole State of Alabama! Louisiana ought to be a Catholic State, but it has never sent a Senator or Representative to Congress who identified himself with the Catholic cause, so far as we know. The slave-owners are not the zealous men of the Church in that State.

What help is Cuba, with all its riches, to the Catholic cause? The poorest Irish or German congregation in the free States does more for religion than Havana, if we can rely upon the representations of those who ought to know and whose character forbids deception. It appears to us, therefore, that slavery is not friendly to the propagation of the Catholic Faith — or to its charity and fervor when it happens to be professed. If for telling these plain truths any subscriber wishes to withdraw his patronage, we hope he will do so at once. And if for telling these truths the ladies of a community in a slave State choose to burn our Paper again, they have our liberty, if that be of any consequence, to prove their amiability and piety by doing so. The time is near at hand when they will wish that they had been more tolerant to the expression of an opinion.

But to our knowledge of ecclesiastical history: "No one now ventures to doubt," says Balmes, "that the Church exercised a powerful influence on the abolition of slavery: this is a truth too clear and evident to be questioned. . . . It did all that was possible in favor of human liberty; if it did not advance more rapidly in the work, it was because it could not do so without compromising the undertaking — without creating serious obstacles to the desired emancipation. Such is the result at which we arrive when we have thoroughly examined the charges made against some proceedings of the Church. . . . That slavery endured for a long time in presence of the Church is true; but it was always declining, and only lasted as long as was necessary to realize the benefit without violence — without a shock — without compromitting [*sic*] its universality and its continuation."[1] These few words from the fifteenth chapter of Balmes' incomparable work, show the exact position occupied by the Church in reference to slavery. To say that she ever favored the system is a calumny. She proclaimed men's fraternity with each other, and their equality before God, and therefore could not be the advocate of slavery.

With respect to the words of St. Paul, so often quoted, we find a full justification of our position. He writes to Philemon, commending his faith and charity, and he says — "wherefore, though I might have much confidence in Christ Jesus *to command thee that which is to the purpose,* for charity's sake I rather beseech, *thou being such a one,* as Paul the aged and now also a prisoner of Jesus Christ, I beseech thee for my son Onesimus, whom I have begotten in my chains — whom I have sent back to thee. And do thou receive him as my own bowels. . . . Not now as a servant, but instead of a servant a most dear brother, especially to me; but how much more to thee, both in the flesh and in the good?"[2]

Any one who can find anything in this in favor of slavery, must have piercing optics. Would St. Paul have sent him back to a Heathen master — or one who would have the power and the will to despise him — to sell his wife and children into slavery? The thought is not to be entertained of the blessed apostle?

If a fugitive slave in this country was to be sent back to some master in Mississippi or Texas by a Catholic Bishop of our days, bearing such an epistle as the above, how would the master mock and the world laugh at the Bishop? What a joke it would be considered in the South?

But what did the Popes think of slavery? This will probably throw some light on ecclesiastical history. Paul III. in 1537, and Urban VIII. in 1639, condemned in the strongest terms the crime of reducing men to slavery, separating them from their wives and children, or in any manner depriving them of their liberty, or upon any pretext to preach

---

[1] James Balmes, *Protestantism and Catholicity Compared in Their Effects on the Civilization of Europe* (Baltimore, 1851), pp. 91–94.

[2] Philemon 1:8–16.

or teach that it is lawful. Pius II. in 1462, also denounces the system in the strongest terms. Gregory XVI., who, in his Apostolic Letter of the 3d of December, 1839, refers to the foregoing, uses this vehement language on the same subject — "Wherefore, we, desiring to turn away so great a reproach as this from all the boundaries of Christians, and the whole matter being maturely weighed, certain Cardinals of the Holy Roman Church, our venerable brethren being also called into Council, treading in the footsteps of our predecessors with Apostolic authority, do vehemently admonish and adjure in the Lord, all believers in Christ, that no one hereafter may dare unjustly to molest Indians, negroes or other men of this sort, or to spoil them of their goods or reduce them to slavery. We, therefore, with Apostolic authority do reprobate all the aforesaid actions as utterly unworthy of the Christian name; and by the same Apostolic authority do strictly prohibit and interdict that any ecclesiastic or lay person shall presume to defend that very trade in negroes *as lawful under any pretext or studied excuse,* or otherwise to preach, or in any manner, publicly or privately, to teach contrary to those things which we have charged in this, our Apostolic Letter."[3]

This is tolerably showy language. Its import, we think, is clear enough to any one who has a human mind. There can be "no pretext or studied excuse," says the good and great Pontiff. Are Catholics afraid or unwilling to read the admonition of the Vicar of Jesus Christ?

But it will be said that Gregory XVI. alluded to the foreign slave trade! This, however, is a pretext, and has not even the dignity of a "studied excuse." We have a word to say on the point.

Shortly before the appearance of this Apostolic letter, a religious order in the United States, by their close communication with Rome, received information of its existence and approaching publication. With more wit than piety the Superiors of that order collected together a large number of their slaves and sold them all to a Southern *gentleman,* we will call him so, who hurried them into Louisiana, and they were scattered over the South without reference to their relationship one to another. The whole Catholic community was shocked at the occurrence. Pope Gregory's letter appeared soon after, and it did not moderate the feeling of indignation. When the fact was known in Rome, such was the emotion felt by His Holiness, that the Superiors, on whom the responsibility rested, were ordered forthwith to proceed

---

[3] For the text of Gregory XVI's apostolic letter, *In supremo apostolatus,* cf. Antonius Maria Bernasconi (Ed.), *Acta Gregorii Papae XVI* (Rome, 1901), II, 387–388.

to the Eternal City and they did not return for years. Why they were detained it is unnecessary to discuss.[4]

This shows that slavery in every shape, is condemned and reprobated by the Church. In the meantime she did nothing violently. She only spoke the solemn words of admonition. Events have hurried on — what the Church would not or could not do the politicians have done. The door is now made open without any agency of Catholics, and those who wish to despise the venerable Pontiffs and be the jailors of their fellowmen, may endeavor to close and lock and bolt it. We take no part in any such proceeding.

113. Brownson Defines the World Mission of the American Republic, 1865

ONE of the most remarkable converts to the Catholic Church of the United States was the nationally known editor and publicist, Orestes A. Brownson (1803–1876). After a long search for spiritual peace that led him through many curious religious experiences he was received into the Church on October 20, 1844, by John B. Fitzpatrick, Coadjutor Bishop of Boston. In his immense literary output — amounting to twenty large volumes — the most famous single work was *The American Republic* which appeared as the nation was emerging from the Civil War. Brownson had written a great deal on government, but in the preface to this book he said: "This work is not only my latest, but will be taken as the authentic, and the only authentic statement of my political views and convictions, and whatever in any of my previous writings conflicts with the principles defended in its pages, must be regarded as retracted, and rejected" (p. viii). Of late years the original contribution and keen insights of *The American Republic* have found a deepening appreciation among political scientists. For example, two recent writers on Brownson's classic have declared it a work "accepted as an influential element in our intellectual development and heritage," and have stated that it "has found its way even into textbook discussions of American political ideas" (Thomas I. Cook and Arnaud B. Leavelle, "Orestes A. Brownson's *The American Republic*," *Review of Politics*, IV [January, 1942], 77). The excerpt which follows outlines Brownson's idea of the mis-

[4] Purcell was referring here to the sale in 1838 of forty-nine slaves for $25,000 by Thomas F. Mulledy, S.J. (1794–1860), then provincial of the Maryland province, to Henry Johnson (1783–1864) who had been Governor of Louisiana, 1824–1828, and was at the time serving his second term in the United States Senate. Cf. Mulledy to John P. Roothaan, S.J., General of the Jesuits, August 9, 1838, in Thomas Hughes, S.J., *History of the Society of Jesus in North America. Documents* (New York, 1910), I, 1122. The lasting effects of this episode on the Negroes of southern Maryland was commented upon by John LaFarge, S.J., *The Manner Is Ordinary* (New York, 1954), p. 184.

sion which the United States has to the world by reason of its unique form of government. Source: Orestes A. Brownson, *The American Republic. Its Constitution, Tendencies, and Destiny* (New York: P. O'Shea, 1865), pp. 3–7.

Every living nation has an idea given it by Providence to realize, and whose realization is its special work, mission, or destiny. Every nation is, in some sense, a chosen people of God. . . .

The United States, or the American Republic, has a mission, and is chosen of God for the realization of a great idea. It has been chosen not only to continue the work assigned to Greece and Rome, but to accomplish a greater work than was assigned to either. In art, it will prove false to its mission if it do not rival Greece; and in science and philosophy, if it do not surpass it. In the state, in law, in jurisprudence, it must continue and surpass Rome. Its idea is liberty, indeed, but liberty with law, and law with liberty. Yet its mission is not so much the realization of liberty as the realization of the true idea of the state, which secures at once the authority of the public and the freedom of the individual — the sovereignty of the people without social despotism, and individual freedom without anarchy. In other words, its mission is to bring out in its life the dialectic union of authority and liberty, of the natural rights of man and those of society. The Greek and Roman republics asserted the state to the detriment of individual freedom; modern republics either do the same, or assert individual freedom to the detriment of the state. The American republic has been instituted by Providence to realize the freedom of each with advantage to the other.

The real mission of the United States is to introduce and establish a political constitution, which, while it retains all the advantages of the constitutions of the states thus far known, is unlike any of them, and secures advantages which none of them did or could possess. The American constitution has no prototype in any prior constitution. The American form of government can be classed throughout with none of the forms of government described by Aristotle, or even by later authorities. Aristotle knew only four forms of government: Monarchy, Aristocracy, Democracy, and Mixed Governments. The American form is none of these, nor any combination of them. It is original, a new contribution to political science, and seeks to attain the end of all wise and just government by means unknown or forbidden to the ancients, and which have been but imperfectly comprehended even by American political writers themselves. The originality of the American constitution has been overlooked by the great majority even of our own statesmen, who seek to explain it by analogies borrowed from the constitutions of other states rather than by a profound study of its own principles. They have taken too low a view of it, and have rarely, if ever, appreciated its distinctive and peculiar merits.

As the United States have vindicated their national unity and integrity, and are preparing to take a new start in history, nothing is more important than that they should take that new start with a clear and definite view of their national constitution, and with a distinct understanding of their political mission in the future of the world. The citizen who can help his countrymen to do this will render them an important service and deserve well of his country, though he may have been unable to serve in her armies and defend her on the battlefield. The work now to be done by American statesmen is even more difficult and more delicate than that which has been accomplished by our own brave armies. As yet the people are hardly better prepared for the political work to be done than they were at the outbreak of the civil war for the military work they have so nobly achieved. But, with time, patience, and good-will, the difficulties may be overçome, the errors of the past corrected, and the Government placed on the right track for the future.

Index

Abbelen, Peter M.
  and German Catholic immigrants, 438n, 439n, 476n
  and neglect of the immigrant, 480
Acadians, in Massachusetts, 120-124
"An Act Concerning Religion," 112-114
Adams, Henry, influence of LaFarge, noted, 39n
Adams, John, impressions of a Catholic service, 132-133
Adams, John Quincy, and Bishop England's speech (1826), 229-231
Alexander VI, Pope, *Inter caetera* (bull), 1-3
Allen, George, and conversion of Eliza Starr, noted, 306
Allouez, Claude, S.J., and Sault Ste. Marie ceremony, 60-63
Altham, John, S.J., English missionary in Maryland, 100-108
American College
  in Louvain, appeal by Kindekens for, 315-317
  in Rome, O'Connor's appeal for, 335-339
Americanism
  controversy, 494-498
  Paulist Fathers' association with, 660
  Testem benevolentiae on, 537-547
American Protective Association
  and the Catholic Church, 499
  growth and activities, 483-485
  oath of, 483-485
  on Satolli's appointment as apostolic delegate, 513
American Protestant Association, constitution, 263-265
American Review of History and Politics, prospectus for, 190-197
Annual Letter
  on Catholicism in Maryland (1638), 108-110
  persecution of Catholics in Maryland (1656), 115-116
Anti-Catholicism, *see* Nativism; Persecution, religious
"Antillon," 128
Antonelli, Lorenzo, Cardinal, Carroll named superior of American missions, 142-144
Apostolic Delegation, established, 505n
Architecture, church, 19th century, 412-415
Arizona, missions, 24-27
Articles of Confederation, and religious freedom, 140
"The Ascension" (painting), John LaFarge, 441-444
Authorities, civil, Carroll's prayer for, 174-175
Ayguacen (archdiocese), suppressed, 5n-6n

Badin, Stephen Theodore, description of Catholicism in Kentucky, 179-184
Baltimore (archdiocese)
  Catholicism in, 19th century, 202-220
  Eccleston on state of (1838), 246-251
  erected, 163-167
Baraga, Frederic, Bp., Slovenian missionary in United States, 366n
Barron, Edward, Bp., and Savannah cholera epidemic (1854), 310
Bayunen (Bayuna) (see), suppressed, 5n-6n
Becker, Thomas A., Bp., and Catholic University of America, 464
Bedini, Gaetano, Abp., tour of United States (1853-1854), noted, 329
Benavides, Alonso de, Fray, description of New Mexico missions, 15-17
Benedictines
  and the German Catholic Brotherhood, 265
  need of, in United States, stressed by Wimmer, 279-288
Bennett, James Gordon, on Bishop Lynch and slavery issue, 348
Bergier, Jean, report on Illinois missions, 81-83
Bernardin, Joseph L., pastoral letter on war and peace, 696-702
Bigotry
  in Smith presidential campaign (1928), 616-621
  in Kennedy campaign (1960), 652-654
Bishop(s)
  appointment of first American, 163-167
  need for colonies, 125-128
  number in United States (1939), 629
The Bishops and the Catholic Press, 387-389
Bishops' Program of Social Reconstruction, 589-607
Bladensburg, Maryland, defeat of Americans at, mentioned, 239n
Blaine, James G., and school issue (1875), 395-397
Blaine Amendment, *see* Blaine, James G.
Blatchford, Richard M., American diplomatic relations with Papal States, 386-388
Bonaparte, Charles J., and Church-State relations, 470-473
Bosque, Fernando del, account of the first high Mass in Texas (1675), 23-24
Boston *Pilot*, editorial on western Catholic colonization (1856), 311-314
Bougainville, Louis Antoine de, founder of Falkland Island colony, noted, 123n
Bouquillon, Thomas

Index

Education: To Whom Does It Belong? noted, 475n
educational controversy, noted, 525n
Bowers, Henry F., founder of American Protective Association, 483
Brébeuf, Jean de, S.J., "Instructions for the Fathers of Our Society who shall be sent to the Hurons," 49-51
Brooks, Van Wyck, on Louise Guiney, 568
Brothers of the Sacred Heart, arrival in United States, noted, 515n
Browne, Robert (Augustinian), mentioned regarding trusteeism, 216n
Brownson, Orestes A., on mission of United States, 383-385
Buffalo Convention
Hughes' position on, 317-321
plan for western Catholic colonization (1856), 311-314
Burke, John J., C.S.P., National Catholic War Council, 607

Calderón, Gabriel Diaz Vara, Bp., report on Florida missions, 18-23
California missions, 31-47
Pious Fund and, 398-404
California (diocese), erected, 398
Calvert, Cecilius
and Baltimore charter, 95-98
instructions to colonists, 98-100
Calvert, George, conversion to Catholicism mentioned, 95
Canada, Quebec Act, 130-132
Capuchins, in Louisiana, 84-86
Carey, Henry C., political economist, noted, 237
Carey, Mathew, *Olive Branch*, 236-242
Carroll, Charles, defense of his religion, 128-130
Carroll, Daniel, ratification of Constitution urged, 157-159
Carroll, John, Abp.
appointment of, as first bishop of United States, 163-167
attack of Wharton on Catholic faith, 145-147
and coming of Sulpicians to Baltimore, 175-176
consecration as bishop, 172
defender of Am. principles governing Church-State relations, 683
prayer for the civil authorities, 174-175
report on Catholicism in United States (1785), 147-150
and selection of bishop for Louisiana, 185-188
sermon on taking possession of his see, 172-173
as superior of American missions, 142-144
Carthusians, in United States, noted, 295
Castañeda, Carlos E., quoted on first high Mass in Texas, 23
Castañeda, Pedro de, on death of Juan de Padilla, 9-10
Cathedral of St. Peter's in Chains (Cincinnati), consecration of, 278-279
Catholic Church
education
Catholic colleges for men (1842), 261, 263
Catholic University of America, 464-466
higher, 291-294, 530-531
necessity of, 405-408
state schools, 473-479
and Pious Fund, 398-404
in public affairs, 19th century, 499-511
and slavery, 378-383
and Spain in New World, 5-7
in Texas (1841), 253-258
in United States (1902), Leo XIII on, 547-549
in United States (1939), Pius XII on, 629-641
Catholic Church Extension Society, 560-565
Catholic Foreign Mission Society of America, 576-580
Catholic Press, 387-389
Catholic Publication Society, 389
Catholicism
and intellectual leadership, 415-417, 641-646
in Maryland (1638), 108-110
19th century, 202-220
Leclerc on, 495-498
in rural areas, 560
in United States (1785), 147-150
in Wisconsin
(1845), 274-277
(1861), 357-367
Catholics
and religious freedom (1776-1791), 137-140
disfranchisement of, in Maryland (1654), 114-115
number in
(1840), 263
(1910), 576
Wisconsin (1850), 274
persecution of, in Virginia, 110-111
Catholic Summer School of America, opening noted, 526n
Catholic University of America
and Bishop Spalding, 415
cornerstone laying, 464-466
enrollment (1956), 464
Keane's rectorship, 437
Catholic University of Ireland, opening noted, 334n
Catholic Worker, 625-629

Index

Challoner, Richard, Bp., on ecclesiastical jurisdiction in British colonies, 124-125
Chaplains, in Civil War, 376-378
Chardin, Pierre Teilhard de, 666
Charity
  Catholic, 625-629
  Society of St. Vincent de Paul in United States, 288-290
Charlevoix, Pierre François Xavier, S.J., on Catharine Tegahkouita's life, 63-71
Charter of Liberties and Privileges (New York), 116-118
Chicago (diocese), conditions in (1849), 300-301
Chirouse, Eugene Casimir, O.M.I., letter describing mission life, 296-300
Cholera, epidemic
  Mobile (1832), 231-233
  Savannah (1854), 310-311
Church of the Immaculate Conception (Mobile), first canonical French parish in the West, 82
Church of Rome in her Primitive Purity compared to the Church of Rome at the Present Day, The, 251
Church and State
  Charles Bonaparte on, 470-473
  in French colonies, 17th century, 60-63
  in United States, 19th century, 461-463, 494-498
  see religious freedom
Cincinnati, St. Peter's Cathedral, editorial on, 278-279
Civil War, *see* United States, Civil War
Claiborne, William, disfranchising of Maryland Catholics, 114-115
Clergy
  American, sesquicentennial of, 629-641
  anti-priest laws passed in Massachusetts Bay, 111-112
Cleveland, St. Elizabeth's Church, first Magyar parish in United States, 558n
Clorivière, Joseph Pierre Picot de Limoëlan de, and schism in Charleston, 218n
"Closed" Church, 660, 665
College of Notre Dame of Maryland, charter, 530-531
Colleges and universities, Catholic, number and enrollment (1956), 530-531
Colonies
  British, ecclesiastical jurisdiction in, 124-128
  English, 95-162
  French, 49-93
  Spanish, 1-47
Colorado, missionary activity in (1876), 409-412
Commager, Henry Steele, quoted on Finley Dunne, 531
Company of the Indies, 84-86
Company of the West, *see* Company of the Indies
Compulsory Education Act (1922), 613-616
Conception de la Vega, Haiti (diocese), erected, 6n
Congregation de Propaganda Fide, and necessity of Catholic education (1875), 405-408
Congregation of Missionaries of St. Charles Borromeo, founding noted, 468n, 483n
"Consecration of St. Peter's Cathedral" (Cincinnati), editorial, 278-279
Constitution, *see* United States, Constitution
Contemplative life, in the United States, 294-296
Continental Congress, reaction to Quebec Act, 134-136
Converts to Catholicism (1840-1860), 306-307
Cooney, Peter P., C.S.C., chaplain with Union Army, 376-378
Coote, Richard, Earl of Bellomont, and anti-priest laws, mentioned, 118
Copley, Thomas, S.J., Jesuit in Maryland, mentioned, 108
Corrigan, Michael A., Abp., and McGlynn, 458
Cox, Harvey, author, *Secular City*, 659
Coxey's Army, march noted, 509n
Czvitkovicz, Alexander, C.SS.R., on colonization project in Pennsylvania, 265-269

Dablon, Claude, S.J., the Sault Ste. Marie ceremony, 60-63
Danish West Indies, Maurice Egan and purchase of, 586-588
Daru, Napoléon, Comte, and papal infallibility, 391n
Darwin, Charles, author, *Origin of Species*, 669, 670, 672
Daughters of Charity of St. Vincent de Paul, and Civil War, 368-370
Daudin, Henri, Abbé, and Acadians in Massachusetts, 120
Day, Dorothy, and the Catholic Worker Movement, 625-629
Declaration on Religious Freedom of Vatican Council II, 683-696
Delegation, Apostolic, established, 505
Demarcation, line of, 1, 3-5
Democracy, and Catholicism (1835), 233-236
Democrats, and school issue (1875), 395
DeSmet, Pierre Jean, S.J., aid to Indian missions described, 259-260
Deutsch, Alcuin, O.S.B., and the liturgical movement, 622

Index

Disfranchisement, of Catholics, in Maryland, 114-115
Divino Afflante Spiritu (encyclical), *see* Pius XII
Divorce, Edward Douglass White on, 565-567
Dominicans
  and California missions, 398
  in Florida, 11-12
  and Franciscan concordat concerning California missions, 31-33
Dongan, Thomas, furthers religious toleration, 116-118
Dooley, Mr.
  The Church Fair, 534-535
  1924 (Democratic National Convention), 535-537
  The Philippine Peace, 531-534
Doyle, John T., and Pious Fund, 403n
Draft, Edward Douglass White on 1918 draft law, 565, 567-568
Dred Scott Decision, noted regarding slavery, 322
Drexel, Mother Katharine, founder, Sisters of the Blessed Sacrament for Indians and Colored People, 574-576
Drexel and Company, noted, 574
Dubois, Jean, Bp., mentioned as missionary in Maryland, 182n
Dubuque (Iowa), editorial on Buffalo convention, 311-314
Dulany, Daniel, debate with Carroll, 128-130
Dunne, Finley Peter, excerpts from Mr. Dooley, 531-537

Early, James M., and papal infallibility, 390-395
Eccleston, Samuel, S.S., and Society for the Propagation of the Faith, 246-251
Echo d'Italia, noted regarding American liberty and the Holy See, 331n
Education, Catholic, *see* Catholic Church, education
Education, freedom of choice in, 655-658
Education, religious, *see* Religious education
Education: To Whom Does It Belong?, noted, 475n
Egan, Maurice Francis, and purchase of Danish West Indies, 586-588
Elder, William Henry, Bp., on the apostolate to the Negro slaves, 325-329
Elliott, Walter, C.S.P., *The Life of Father Hecker*, and Americanism, 339, 537
Ellis, John Tracy, *American Catholics and the Intellectual Life*, 641-646
England, John, Bp.
  account of speech before Congress (1826), 228-231
  United States Catholic Miscellany, 227-228
England, literary trends in (1811), 190-197
England, Louise Imogen Guiney on, 568-574
Equitable Life Assurance Society, and Thomas Fortune Ryan, 580-586
Evolution
  ancestral, 671
  biological, 673, 674
  cosmic, 674, 675
  fossil witness for, 668, 669, 673
  historical fact of, 667, 668, 670, 672, 676, 677, 683
  philosophy of, 676-678
  process of, 670
  scientific, 666, 667, 675, 676
Ex hac apostolicae (brief), 163-167
Extension Magazine, 560

Faith, Congregation of the Propagation of the, *see* Congregatio de Propaganda Fide
Farmer, Ferdinand, S.J., on the missionaries' reasons for not wanting a bishop, 125-128
Fenwick, Edward D., O.P., death noted, 231
Figaro, Le, newspaper, noted, 462n
Filicchi, Filippo, friend of Mother Seton, 188n
Finance, Thomas Fortune Ryan and the Equitable Life Assurance Company, 580-586
"First Citizen," 128
FitzSimons, Thomas, and ratification of the Constitution, 154-156
Flaget, Benedict Joseph, S.S., impressions of his Middle West bishopric, 187-199
Florida
  conquest of, by Spain, 12-14
  Dominican missions in, 11-12
  missions, report of Bishop Calderón, 18-23
  withdrawal of Jesuits from, 14-15
France, neutrality of, during Civil War, 370-373
Francis Borgia, St., withdrawal of Jesuits from Florida, 14-15
Franciscans
  and California missions, 398
  and Dominican concordat concerning California missions, 31-33
  missions, 9-10
  in New Mexico, 15-17
Franciscans, French, *see* Récollets
Freeman's Journal (New York), editor noted, 342
Freemasons, condemnation noted, 418

Gallagher, Simon Felix, mentioned regarding trusteeism, 211n

Index

Galvéz, Don José de, noted as helper to Serra, 35n
Gartland, Francis X., Bp., description of cholera epidemic in Savannah (1854), 310-311
Gaston, William
  first student in Georgetown Academy, 168
  plea for religious freedom, 242-246
George, Henry, and opposition of condemnation by Gibbons, 457-460
Georgetown Academy, first Catholic college, 167-169, 530
German Catholic Brotherhood, colonization project, 265-269
Gervase, Thomas, S.J., English missionary in Maryland, 100-108
Gibault, Pierre, and the American cause, 141-142
Gibbons, James, Cardinal
  on Americanism, 538
  Church and State in United States, 460-463
  and condemnation of Henry George, 457-460
  defense of Knights of Labor, 444-457
  and friendship with Keane, 437-441
  and Ireland's stand on school controversy, 473-480
  and N.C.W.C., noted, 611n
Godefroy, Maximilien, architect, noted, 408
Grant, Ulysses S., and school issue (1875), 395-397
Guilday, Peter, on Shea, 422
Guiney, Louise Imogen, on living in England, 568-574
Guiney, Patrick Robert, noted, 568
Guy Fawkes Day, banned by Washington, 136

Haddock v. Haddock, 585-587
Hallinan, Paul J., Abp., pastoral letter on war and peace, 696-702
Healy, George P. A., American portrait painter, 485-488
Heath, Sister Angela, nursing sisters in Civil War, 368-370
Hecker, Isaac Thomas, C.S.P.
  Catholic University of America, 464
  founder of Catholic Publication Society, 389
  plans for the Paulists, 339-342
Heim, Ambrose J., and Society of St. Vincent de Paul, 289
Heiss, Michael, report on Wisconsin Catholicism (1861), 357-367
Helbron, John Charles (Capuchin), pastor of Holy Trinity Church (Philadelphia), 160
Hennepin, Louis (Récollet), work with Indians, 75-81
Henni, John Martin, Bp., report to Ludwig-Missionsverein on Catholicism in Wisconsin, 274-277
Hérésie fantôme, l'Américanisme, Une, 550
Hierarchy, *see* Clergy
History of the Catholic Clergy in the United States, 422-432
Holy See, *see* Vatican
Holy Trinity Church (Philadelphia), first national parish in United States, 160-162
Homestead Strike (1892), noted, 489
Hopkins, John Henry, *The Church of Rome in her Primitive Purity Compared to the Church of Rome at the Present Day*, 251
Hospitality, houses of, 625-629
"How Father Jogues was Taken by the Hiroquois and What He Suffered on His First Entrance into Their Country," 52-60
Hughes, John, Abp.
  on American liberty and the Holy See, 329, 335
  and Civil War, 347-356
  and French neutrality during Civil War, 370-373
  and North American College at Rome, 335
  opposition to Western Catholic colonization, 317-321
  pastoral letter on the Catholic Press, 387
Humani Generis (encyclical), *see* Pius XII
Hungarians
  in United States, parish life, 555-560
  population (1910), 555
Huret, Jules, interview with Archbishop Ireland, 489-494
Hutchinson, Thomas, on Acadians, 121-124

Illinois
  Catholic Church on frontier of, 141-142
  missions in, 81-84
Immigrants
  Catholic
    neglect of, protested, 480-483
    number entering United States (1840's), 300
    plan for Western colonization (1856), 311-314, 317-321
  German
    aided by Ludwig-Missionsverein, 274-288
    number of Catholics in Pennsylvania (1757), 160
    and trusteeism, 160-162
  Hungarians, parish life in United States, 555-560

Index

Italians, Leo XIII's plea for (1888), 466-469
number
in Kentucky (1790), 170
nineteenth century, 480, 481n
Indian and Negro missions, and Mother Katharine Drexel, 574-576
Indians, American
aid given by DeSmet, 259-260
evangelization of, 9-11, 34-47, 49-62, 72-84, 100-108
Hennepin's work with, 75-81
in Texas, 253-258
Indies, Company of the, 84-86
Infallibility, papal, *see* popes, infallibility
"Instructions for the Fathers of Our Society Who Shall be sent to the Hurons," 49-51
Intellectual life, American Catholics and, 641-646
Inter caetera (bull), 1-3
International Workers of the World, beginning noted, 628n
Intolerance, religious, *see* Toleration, religious; Religious liberty
Ireland, John, Abp.
on McGee and Buffalo convention, 319n
school controversy, 473-480
on socialism, 489-494
Irish Catholic Colonization Association, organization mentioned, 317
Isaac Jogues, St., 52-60

Jackson, Andrew, quoted on the *Olive Branch*, 237
Jackson, J. H., and the American Protective Association, 484n
Jefferson, Thomas, reassurance on future, given to Ursulines, 184-185
Jenkins, Courtney, and slavery, 379
Jesuits
and anti-priest laws in Massachusetts, 118-120
banished from Louisiana, 86-93
in Maryland, 100-107
missions, 49-51
opposition to bishop for the colonies, 125-128
and the Pious Fund, 398-404
withdrawal from Florida missions, 14-17
John II, of Portugal, and line of demarcation, 3-4
John XXIII, Pope, *Peace on Earth*, 698, 699
John Gilmary Shea Prize, instituted, 422
Journalism, American Catholic, beginning of, 227-228
Journalists, Finley Peter Dunne, 531-537
Juan de la Cruz, O.F.M., missionary to Indians, 9-10
Juan de Padilla, O.F.M., *see* Padilla, Juan de, O.F.M.
Julius II, Pope, *Universalis ecclesiae* (bull), 4-6
"Jus," writer for New York *Freeman's Journal*, 392n

Keane, John J., Bp.
advice to Gibbons, 437-441
on civil legislation in a democracy, 511-513
dismissal from Catholic University of America, noted, 514
Keely, Patrick Charles, and nineteenth century church architecture, 412-415
Kelley, Francis Clement, Bp., Catholic Church Extension Society, 560-565
Kennedy, John F., religion in presidential campaign, 652-654
Kenrick, Francis Patrick, Abp.
and American College in Louvain, 315-317
and North American College at Rome, 335
on papacy's relation to temporal affairs, 251-253
Kentucky, Catholic Church in, Badin's description of, 179-184
Kindekens, Peter, appeal for American College in Louvain, 315-317
King, Rufus, resignation as minister noted, 374
Kino, Eusebius, S.J.
missionary in colonial America, noted, 400n
report on missions of Pimería Alta (Arizona), 24-27
Klein, Félix, Abbé, impressions of Bishop McQuaid, 550-555
Knights of Labor
and Archbishop Ireland, 489
defended by Gibbons, 444-457
Knights of Labor (Canada), condemnation noted, 438n, 444
Kossuth, Louis, trip to United States, 333n, 334n
Ku Klux Klan, and religious bigotry of 1928 campaign, 616-621

Labor, John A. Ryan on, 589-607
Laetare Medal (1884), 412-415, 413n
LaFarge, John, and painting of "the Ascension," 441-444
Laffont, Jean Baptiste, attack on Vincennes, 141-142
Lai, Cajetan de, Cardinal, and the National Catholic Welfare Council, 608
Lalemant, Jerome, S.J., "How Father Jogues was Taken by the Hiroquois and What He Suffered on His First Entrance into Their Country," 52-60
Lamberville, Jacques de, S.J., conversion of Catharine Tegahkouita, 63

Index

Lamy, John Baptist, Abp.
 account of trip across the plains, 303-304
 impressions of the Southwest, 301-303
Lancaster, John, prominent Catholic in Kentucky, mentioned, 182n
Laval, François de Montmorency, first Bishop of Quebec, 82
Leakage, from Catholic Church noted, 481n
Leclerc, Maximilien on American Catholicism, 494-498
LeClercq, Maxim (Récollet), death noted, 72
Legislation, civil, in a democracy, Keane's views on, 511-513
Leo XIII, Pope
 on the Church in the United States, 547-549
 Longinqua oceani, on American society, 499-511
 plea for Italian immigrants in the United States, 466-470
 Testem benevolentiae, on Americanism, 537-547
Leopoldinen-Stiftung of Vienna, aid to German Catholic missions noted, 275n
Letter to the Roman Catholics of the City of Worcester, 145
Liberty, American, and the Holy See, Hughes on (1858), 329-335
Life of Father Hecker, The, 537
Lincoln, Abraham, criticism of administration by McMaster, 342-347
Linton, William S., and the American Protective Association, 484
Linnaeus, 669
Literary and Religious Magazine, beginning of, noted, 249n
Liturgical Movement, in United States, 621-624
Liturgical Press of St. John's Abbey, 621
Longinqua oceani (encyclical), on American society, 499-511
Loras, Mathias, Bp.
 and Buffalo convention (1856), 311-314
 description of cholera epidemic (1832), 231-233, 233n
Lotbinière, Louis E., Canadian chaplain, 376
Louisiana
 ecclesiastical jurisdiction of (1722), 84-86
 ecclesiastical state of (1806), 185-188
 religious conditions in (1795), 177-179
Ludwig-Missionsverein
 founding noted, 287n
 report on Catholicism in Wisconsin, 274-277
Lynch, Dominik, leading Catholic layman, mentioned, 171n
Lynch, Patrick N., Bp., and Civil War, 347-356

McClellan, George B., noted as commander of the Department of the Ohio, 344n
McDonnell, Charles E., Bp., and the National Catholic Welfare Council, 607
McGee, Thomas D'Arcy, noted as an organizer of Buffalo convention, 319n
McGlynn, Edward
 and advocacy of Henry George's theories, 457
 excommunication, 432, 436
McMahon Hall, Catholic University of America, dedication noted, 503n
McMaster, James A.
 criticism of the Lincoln administration, 342-347
 and slavery, 379
McQuaid, Bernard J., Bp.
 Abbé Klein's impressions of, 550-555
 and papal infallibility, 389-395
Madison, James, Secretary of State, on a bishop for Louisiana, 185-188
Magnien, Alphonse L., S.S., noted as Director of Society for the Propagation of the Faith, 561n
Maguen (Magua) (see), suppressed, 5n-6n
Magyars, first parish in United States, 558n
Man, brotherhood of, 7-9
Maréchal, Ambrose, S.S., Abp.
 report on American Catholicism (1818), 202-220
 report on trusteeism, 220-227
Martinelli, Sebastiano, O.S.A., appointed apostolic delegate, 513
Maryknoll, *see* Catholic Foreign Mission Society of America
Maryland
 Act of Religious Toleration, 112-114
 Catholicism in (1638), 108-110
 charter (1632), 95-98
 colonists in, 98-100
 Declaration of Rights (1776) and religious freedom, 137
 missions, 100-108, 124-125
 persecution of Catholics (1656), 115-116
 ratification of Constitution urged in, 157-159
Mason, Stephen C., president of the N.A.M., on *Bishops' Program of Social Reconstruction*, 589
Masons (secret order), *see* Freemasons
Mass, high, first time celebrated in Texas (1675), 23-24
Massachusetts
 Acadians in, 120-124
 anti-priest laws in
  (1647), 111-112
  (1700), 118-120

Index

Constitution (1780) and religious freedom, 139-140
Mathew, Theobald (Capuchin), temperance work noted, 272
Maurin, Peter, and Catholic Worker Movement, noted, 626n
Mazzuchelli, Samuel Charles, O.P., 365n
on Catholic temperance societies, 272-274
Membré, Zénobe (Récollet), missioner in Illinois, 72-74
Menéndez de Avilés, Pedro, and conquest of Florida, 12-14
Merton, Thomas, quoted on contemplative monasteries, 294
Metropolitan Record, started by Hughes, 342
Mexico, and Pious Fund, 398-404
Meyer v. Nebraska, 615n
Michel, Virgil, O.S.B., and the liturgical movement, 621-624
Michigan Essay or Impartial Observer, 202
Middle West, Flaget's impressions of, 197-199
Military training, Edward Douglass White on draft law, 565, 567-568
Missionary Sisters of the Sacred Heart of St. Francesca Cabrini, founding noted, 469n, 516n
Missions
Indian, 49-51
Oblate, 296-300
Mississippi Valley, Catholic Church in, 81-84
Mobile, Church of the Immaculate Conception, first French parish in the West, 82
Mott, Frank Luther, quoted on attacks on government (1861), 343
Moylan, Stephen, patriotism noted, 169
Mulkern, M. B., resolutions of Buffalo convention, 311-314
Mullaly, John, and slavery, 379
Mullanphy, Bryan, mentioned as Mayor of St. Louis (1847), 290n
Mullanphy, John, St. Louis philanthropist, noted, 290n
Mulledy, Thomas F., S.J., and slavery issue, 383n
Murray, John Courtney, principal author of Declaration on Religious Freedom of Vatican Council II, 683

Nagot, François Charles, S.S., first superior of Sulpicians in United States, 176n
Napoleon III (France), on effect of Civil War and French commercial interests, 371n
National Catholic War Council
Bishops' Program of Social Reconstruction, 589-607
see also National Catholic Welfare Conference
National Catholic Welfare Conference founding, 607-613
National Liturgical Week, noted, 622
National Municipal League, founder noted, 470
National War Labor Board, appointment noted, 597n
Nativism, American, beginning of, 263-265
Neale, Francis, S.J., president of Georgetown College, mentioned, 183n
Negroes
and John Boyle O'Reilly's campaign for, 432-436
Bishops on discrimination against, 646-652
see also Sisters of the Blessed Sacrament for Indian and Colored People; Slavery; Xavier University
New Mexico
impressions of Lamy (1851), 301-303
missions, 15-17
New Orleans, Satolli's visit, 513-530
New Theology of the Era of Vatican Council II, 666-683
New York
Constitution (1777) and religious freedom, 138-139
grant of religious toleration (1683), 116-118
lay trusteeism in (1786), 150-154
New York Committee of State Senate, on *Bishops' Program of Social Reconstruction*, 589
New York *Freeman's Journal*, editor noted, 342
Nogar, Raymond J., author of *Wisdom of Evolution*, book condensation appears on 666-683
North American College at Rome, appeal for, 335-339
North Carolina, Gaston's plea for religious freedom in, 242-246
Notre Dame, University of, broadside on, 291-294
Nuclear warfare, 696
Nugent, Andrew (Capuchin), and lay trusteeism, 151-154
Nursing, sisterhoods in Civil War, 368-370

Oblates of Mary Immaculate, Northwest mission life described, 296-300
O'Brien, William Smith, a leader of Young Irelanders, 332n
O'Brien, William V., O.P., and lay trusteeism, 151
O'Callaghan, Edmund B., noted, 422
O'Callaghan, Eugene M., *see* "Jus"
O'Connell, Eugene, on the Church in San Francisco (1853), 304-306

Index

O'Connor, James, on school issue (1875), 395
O'Connor, Michael, Bp., appeal for North American College at Rome (1858), 335-339
Odin, Jean Marie, Bp., on missions in Texas, 253-258
O'Keefe, Sister Camilla, 368
Olive Branch, writing of, 236-242
Ollivier, Emile, and papal infallibility, 407n
Open Church, 660, 662, 665
The Open Parish, 658-666
Orate Fratres, 621
Orban, Alexis, S.S., and Satolli, 513-530
Oregon and right of private schools, 613-616
O'Reilly, John Boyle
  and campaign against racism, 432-436
  and Dr. McGlynn, 432, 436
Origin of Species, *see* Charles Darwin
Our Lady of Gethsemani Abbey (Kentucky), founding, 294-296
Ozanam, Frédéric and Society of St. Vincent de Paul, 288

Padilla, Juan de, O.F.M., murder of, 9-10
Painters
  Healy, George P.A., 485-488
  LaFarge, John, 441-444
Papacy
  relation to temporal affairs explained by Kenrick, 251-253
  see also Popes
Papal infallibility, *see* Popes, infallibility
Papal States
  and United States diplomatic relations, 374-376
  see also Vatican
Parish
  "closed," 660, 661, 663, 665
  inner city, 659, 663
  "open," 663, 664, 665, 666
  territorial, 665
  traditional, 658
  urban, 661, 663, 664
Parish life, in United States, 575-579
Paul III, Pope, *Sublimis Deus* (bull), 7-8
Paul VI, Pope, at the U.N., 697, 702
Paulist Fathers, Hecker's plans for, 339-342
Peace on Earth, *see* John XXIII
Pelikan, Jaroslav, 658-659
Peñaalver y Cardenas, Luis Ignacio Maria de, on religious conditions in Louisiana (1795), 177-179
Pennsylvania
  Declaration of Rights (1776) and regious freedom, 137
  missions, 125-128
  St. Mary's colonization project, 265-269
Persecution, religious
  in Maryland (1654), 114-115
  in Maryland (1656), 115-116
  in Massachusetts (1647), 111-112
  in Massachusetts (1700), 118-120
  in Virginia, 110-111
Philadelphia, Holy Trinity Church, first national parish in United States, 160-162
Philip II (Spain), and conquest of Florida, 12-14
Pierce v. Society of Sisters, 613-616
Pilot (Boston), editorial on western Catholic colonization (1856), 311-314
Pious Fund (1875), 398-404
Pius VI, Pope, *Ex Hac apostolicae* (brief), 163-167
Pius IX, Pope, portrait of, by Healy, 485-488
Pius X, Pope
  and liturgical movement noted, 624n
  Sapienti consilio, missionary status of United States, 576
Pius XII, Pope
  Divino Afflante Spiritu, beginning of improvement in Catholic biblical scholarship, 681
  Humani Generis, repudiated philosophies of evolutionism, 676; upheld Council of Trent's teaching on monogenism, 682
  Sertum laetitiae, on sesquicentennial of the American hierarchy, 629-641
Plenary Council, Baltimore, 1st and 2nd, and necessity of Catholic education, 405, 407n, 408n
Plenary Council, Baltimore, 3d, and forbidden societies, 418-421
Plessis, Joseph Octave, Bp., impressions of Richard, 200-202
Politics, and religion, 616-621
Polk, James Knox, U.S. diplomatic relations with Papal States, 578
Popes, infallibility, 389-395
Portuguese, right of patronage in India, noted, 222n
Poughkeepsie Plan, 479n
Powderly, Terence V., Knights of Labor, noted, 447n
Price, Thomas Frederick, M.M., Catholic Foreign Mission Society of America, 576-580
Propagation of the Faith, *see* Congregatio de Propaganda Fide
Protestant revivalism, impressions of Spalding on, 269-272
Pugin, Augustus Welby, architect, noted, 413
Pullman Company, strike (1894), noted, 489
Purcell, Edward, stand on slavery, 378-383

Index

Purcell, John B., Abp.
and papal infallibility, 393n
and slavery issue, 378

Quebec Act, 130-132
and Continental Congress, 133-136

Racism, American bishops on, 646-652
Randall, Alexander W., and Abp. Hughes, 371
Raymbault, Charles, S.J., missioner to Indians, 52
Raymond, Henry J., editor, noted as supporter of Lincoln, 345n
Récollets, French, in Illinois (1680), 72-74
Redemptorists, and the German Catholic Brotherhood, 265-269, 277n
Religion and State, *See* Religious Freedom
Religious education
need for North American College at Rome, 335-339
and public funds (1875), 395-397
and Supreme Court decision (1925), 612-616
Religious Freedom
a civil right, 685, 688, 694, 695
essential for proper worship, 684, 690-691
foundation in the dignity of the individual, 685, 691, 693
in religious education, 687, 688
necessary in and for religious communities, 687, 688, 689
obliges man to fulfill his civic responsibilities, 690
of the family, 687
personal responsibility for, 690
proper regulation of, 689
right of the individual, 685, 689, 690
supported by the Church, 693
Religious liberty, 137-140
in Canada, 130-132
Gaston's plea for, 242-246
in Maryland, 137-138
in Massachusetts, 139-140
in New York, 138-139
in Pennsylvania, 137
see also Persecution, religious; Toleration, religious
Religious of the Sacred Heart, arrival in Louisiana, noted, 524n
Republicans and school issue (1875), 395
Ribourde, Gabriel de la (Récollet), missioner in Illinois, 72-74
Richard, Gabriel, S.S., 200-202
death noted, 231
Michigan Essay or Impartial Observer, 227
Ridder, Herman, newspaper manager, noted, 429n
Rochdale Pioneers, co-operative enterprise, noted, 600n
Rosecrans, William S., noted, 376
Ryan, John A., *Bishops' Program of Social Reconstruction*, 589-607
Ryan, Thomas Fortune, and the Equitable Life Assurance Society, 580-586

St. Anthony Falls (Minneapolis), discovery mentioned, 75
St. Bernard's Seminary, Rochester, New York, description, 550-555
St. Charles College, Ellicott City, opening noted, 251n
St. Elizabeth's Church, Cleveland, first Magyar parish in United States, 558n
St. Mary's Seminary, Baltimore, opened, 175-176
St. Mary's Seminary, Perryville, Missouri, establishment noted, 253n
St. Raphaelsverein, and neglect of the immigrant Catholics, 480-483
St. Rose Priory (Kentucky), opening noted, 282n
St. Vincent's Priory (Pennsylvania), founding noted, 280
Salzbacher, Josef (Canon), report on American Catholic Colleges for men (1842), 261-263
Salzmann, Joseph, founder of *Seebote*, 359n
San Carlos de Monterey Mission, report of Serra on, 34-47
San Domingo, Diocese of (Haiti), erected, 5n
San Francisco, Catholic Church in (1853), 304-306
San Juan, Diocese of (Puerto Rico), erected, 5n
Santa Maria Institute (Cincinnati), noted, 409
Sapienti consilio, 576
Satolli, Francesco, Cardinal, visit to New Orleans (1896), 513-530
Sault Ste. Marie, and France's new colonial policy, 60-63
Schlesinger, Arthur Meier, quoted on American Protective Association, 483
Schneider, Theodore, S.J., 160
School Sisters of Notre Dame, arrival in United States, 362n
Schools
private, in Oregon, 613-616
public
and Catholic children's attendance, 405-408
and parochial, Ireland on, 473-479
religious, federal aid to, 650-654
see also Catholic Church, education; Religious education; Names of individual schools

Schrembs, Joseph, Bp., and the National Catholic Welfare Council, 608
Scott, Winfield, loyalty to the Union noted, 344n
Secession, and the South (1861), 347-356
Second Plenary Council of Baltimore, 387
Secret societies, *see* Societies, secret
Sedella, Antonio de (Capuchin), and Louisiana bishopric, 185
Segale, Sister Blandina, and Colorado missionary activities, 409-412
Selective Draft Law (1918), Edward Douglass White on, 565, 567-568
Semmes, Thomas J., American Bar Association president, noted, 518n
Serra, Junipero, O.F.M.
  departure for California missions, 27-31
  report on San Carlos de Monterey mission, 34-47
Sertum laetitiae (encyclical), on sesquicentennial of American hierarchy, 629-641
Seton, Elizabeth, Blessed, letter planning her religious community, 188-190
Seward, William H.
  American diplomatic relations with Papal States, 374-376
  and French neutrality during Civil War, 370-373
Shea, John Gilmary
  History of the Catholic Church in the United States, 422, 432
  Laetare Medal recipient, noted, 413n
  Prize instituted, 422
Simmons, William J. and the Ku Klux Klan, 616
Sisterhoods, contributions in United States, 409-412
Sisters of the Blessed Sacrament for Indians and Colored People, constitution, 574-576
Sisters of the Good Shepherd (New Orleans), arrival in United States, 519n
Sisters of the Holy Family, founding noted, 528n
Sisters of the Holy Names of Jesus and Mary, and Oregon school law, 613-616
Slavery
  and the Catholic Church, 325-329, 378-383
  controversy (1861), 347-356
  in Mississippi (1858), 325-329
  Taney's views on, 322-325
Smarius, Cornelius, S.J., *Points of Controversy*, 360n
Smith, Alfred E., and religious bigotry of the 1928 campaign, 616-621
Socialism, Abp. Ireland on, 489-494
Social justice, John A. Ryan on, 589-607
Social reform, programs in United States (1919), 589-607
Societies, secret
  and Knights of Labor, 444-457
  and Third Plenary Council of Baltimore, 418-421
  see also American Protective Association; Freemasons
Society, American, *Longinqua oceani*, 499-511
Society of Jesus, *see* Jesuits
Society of St. Vincent de Paul, first conference in the United States, minutes, 288-290
Sorin, Edward, C.S.C., broadside on University of Notre Dame, 291-294
South, and secession (1861), 347-356
Spain
  and Catholic Church in New World, 4-6
  colonization of Florida, 11-12
  and conquest of Florida, 12-14
  territorial claims (1493), 1-3
Spalding, John Lancaster, Bp.
  and Catholic intellectual leadership, 415-417
  and Catholic University of America, 464-466
  noted as one of the founders of Irish Catholic Colonization Association, 317
Spalding, Martin John, Abp.
  and American College, Louvain, 315-317
  impressions of Protestant revivalism, 269-272
Sparks, Jared, noted, 426
Stanley, David S., conversion noted, 376
Starr, Eliza Allen, conversion to Catholicism, 306-310
Starr, Ellen Gates, and liturgical movement noted, 624n
Students, college life (1847), 291-294
Sublimis Deus (bull), 7-8
Suffolk Resolves, 133-136
Sulpicians, in United States, nineteenth century, 175-176, 202-220

Tablet, The (London), *The Vatican: A Weekly Record of the Council*, 408n
Taney, Roger Brooke
  as Chief Justice, noted, 565
  letter on slavery (1857), 322-325
Tax, single, Henry George on, 457-460
Tegahkouita, Catharine, 63-71
Temperance
  in America, Mazzuchelli on, 272-274
  societies in United States (1844), 272-274
Testem benevolentiae (encyclical), on Americanism, 537-547
Texas, Catholic Church in (1841), 253-258
"Things in Dubuque," editorial, 311-314

Index

Thornton, Sir Edward, and Pious Fund, 398
Timon, John, C.M., and Society of St. Vincent de Paul, 289
Tocqueville, Alexis de, on American Catholicism and democracy, 233-236
Toleration, religious
  in 1842, 263-265
  in 1843, 265-269
  in Maryland, 95-98, 112-114
  in New York (1683), 116-118
Tordesillas, Treaty of, 3-4
Trappists, in United States, 294-296
Treaty of Ryswick, mentioned, 118
Treaty of Tordesillas, 3-4
Tracy, Jeremiah F., promoter of western Catholic colonization, 313n
Trent, Council of, upheld position of monogenism, 682
Trusteeism, 220-227
  in first national parish in United States, 160-162
  in New York (1786), 150-154

Ubeda, Luis de, O.F.M., missionary to Indians, 9-10
United States
  and papal diplomatic relations, 374-376
  world mission of, Brownson on, 383-385
United States, Civil War
  and neutrality of France, 370-373
  nursing sisters and, 368-370
  and slavery, 347-356
United States, Constitution
  ratification of
    urged by Carroll, 157-159
    urged by FitzSimons, 154-156
  religious freedom and, 140
United States history, national period, 163-654
United States, Supreme Court and private religious schools (1925), 613-616
United States Catholic Historical Society of New York, founding noted, 428n
United States Catholic Miscellany, prospectus, 227-228
Universal brotherhood, 698
Universalis ecclesiae (bull), 4-6
University of Notre Dame, *see* Notre Dame, University of
Ursulines, Jefferson's reassurance on their future in United States, 184-185

Van de Velde, James, S.J., on conditions in Diocese of Chicago (1849), 300-301
Van Dyke, Henry, quoted on Maurice Egan, 586
Vassar College, charter of, noted, 549
Vatican, American liberty and, Hughes on, 329-335
Vatican: A Weekly Record of the Council, The, 392n
Vatican Council (1870) and papal infallibility, 389-395
Vatican Council II
  Declaration on Religious Freedom, 683-696
  on world peace, 698
Vay, Peter, Hungarian parish life (1905), 556-560
Velasco, Lúis de, and Florida missions, 11-12
Vietnam, 697, 700
Villeneuve, Alphonse, on Catholic leakage, 481n
Vincennes, Gibault's part in attack on, 141-142
Virginia
  laws against Catholics (1642), 110-111
  trusteeism in, 220-227

Waldeck-Rousseau, René, and the French Church, 547
Wallace, Alfred R., co-founder of the principle of natural selection, 672
Walmesley, Charles, O.S.B., consecreation of Carroll as bishop, 172
Walsh, James Anthony, Bp., Catholic Foreign Mission Society of America, 576, 580
Walsh, Robert
  on literary trends in England (1811), 190-197
  prospectus for *American Review of History and Politics*, 190-197
Wappeler, William, S.J., 160
War and Peace: A Pastoral Letter to the Archdiocese of Atlanta, 696-702
Washington, George
  bans Guy Fawkes Day, 136
  Catholics' congratulations to (1790), 169-172
Watrin, François Philibert, S.J., on banishment of Jesuits from Louisiana, 86-93
Webb, James W., noted as editor of New York *Courier and Enquirer*, 346n
"Webster Replying to Hayne," painting by Healy, 485
Weninger, Francis X., S.J., missionary among German Catholics, 359n
Wharton, Charles H., attack on Catholic faith, 145-147
Whelan, Charles (Capuchin), and lay trusteeism, 151-154
White, Andrew, S.J., on the missions of Maryland, 100-108
White, Edward Douglass
  decision regarding divorce, 565-567
  decision on selective draft law (1918), 565, 567-568
Whitty, Sister Eulalia, 409n

Index

Williams v. North Carolina, 565
Wilson, James, participation in drafting Constitution, mentioned, 159n
Wimmer, Boniface, O.S.B., on future of Benedictine Order in the United States, 279-288
Winsor, Justin, noted, 422
Wisconsin
  Catholicism in (1845), 274-277
  Catholicism in (1861), 357-367
Wisdom of Evolution (book condensation), 666-683
Wolcott, Oliver, probable author of *Olive Branch*, 242n
Worcester, Letter to the Roman Catholics of the City of, 145
World peace, pursuit of, 697
Worship, 622
Wright, John, Jr., Bishop, on intellectual life and Catholics, 642-646

Xavier University, New Orleans, founded, 574

Youmans, Henry M., and the American Protective Association, 484
Young Irelanders, American Liberty and the Holy See, 332n